THE CULTURAL LIVES OF CAUSE LAWYERS

This book seeks to illuminate what we call the cultura examining their representation in various popular media (i marketed nonfiction, television, and journalism), the work t products, and the way those representations and products by various audiences. By attending to media representations and the culture work done by cause lawyers, we can see what material is available for citizens and others to use in fashioning understandings of those lawyers. This book also provides a vehicle for determining whether, how, and to what extent cause lawyering is embedded in the discourses and symbolic practices around which ordinary citizens organize their understanding of social, political, and legal life.

This book brings together research on the legal profession and work that takes up the analysis of popular culture. Contributors include scholars of popular culture who turn their attention to cause lawyers and experts on cause lawyering who in turn focus their attention on popular culture. This is a joining of perspectives that is both long overdue and fruitful for both kinds of scholarship.

Austin Sarat is William Nelson Cromwell Professor of Jurisprudence Political Science at Amherst College and Five College Fortieth Anniversary Professor. He received his PhD from University of Wisconsin and JD from Yale Law School. He is former president of the Law and Society Association and of the Association for the Study of the Law, Culture and the Humanities and of the Consortium of Undergraduate Law and Justice Programs. He is author or editor of more than sixty books, including *Mercy on Trial: What It Means to Stop an Execution*; *When the State Kills: Capital Punishment and the American Condition*; *Something to Believe in: Politics, Professionalism, and Cause Lawyers* (with Stuart Scheingold); and *The Blackwell Companion to Law and Society*.

Sarat is editor of the journal *Law, Culture and the Humanities* and of *Studies in Law, Politics and Society*. His public writing has appeared in such places as the *Los Angeles Times* and the *American Prospect*, and he has been a guest on National Public Radio, *The News Hour*, *Odyssey*, *The Abrams Report* on MSNBC, *World News Tonight* on ABC, and *The O'Reilly Factor*. His teaching has been featured in the *New York Times* and on *The Today Show*.

In 1997, Sarat received the Harry Kalven Award given by the Law Society Association for distinguished research on law and society. In 2004, he was co-recipient of the 2004 Reginald Heber Smith Award, given biennially to honor the best scholarship on the subject of equal access to justice. In 2006, the Association for the Study of Law, Culture and the Humanities awarded him the James Boyd White Prize for distinguished scholarly achievement in recognition of his "innovative and outstanding" work in the humanistic study of law.

Stuart Scheingold, Professor Emeritus of Political Science, University of Washington, has written widely on rights, the politics of crime and punishment, cause lawyering, and, early in his career, on law and politics in the European Union. He is co-director (with Austin Sarat) of the International Cause Lawyering Project. Among his books are the *Politics of Rights*, *The Politics of Law and Order*, *The Politics of Street Crime*, and *Europe's Would-Be Polity* (with Leon Lindberg).

The Cultural Lives of Cause Lawyers

Edited by

Austin Sarat

Amherst College

Stuart Scheingold

University of Washington

CAMBRIDGE UNIVERSITY PRESS
Cambridge, New York, Melbourne, Madrid, Cape Town, Singapore, São Paulo, Delhi

Cambridge University Press
32 Avenue of the Americas, New York, NY 10013-2473, USA

www.cambridge.org
Information on this title: www.cambridge.org/9780521884488

First published 2008

Printed in the United States of America

A catalog record for this publication is available from the British Library.

Library of Congress Cataloging in Publication Data

The cultural lives of cause lawyers / edited by Austin Sarat, Stuart A. Scheingold.
p. cm.
Includes bibliographical references and index.
ISBN 978-0-521-88448-8 (hardback) – ISBN 978-0-521-71135-7 (pbk.)
1. Cause lawyers – United States. 2. Cause lawyers – United States – Public opinion.
3. Public interest law – United States. 4. Culture and law. I. Sarat, Austin. II. Title
KF299.P8C85 2008
344.73 – dc22 2007037904

ISBN 978-0-521-88448-8 hardback
ISBN 978-0-521-71135-7 paperback

To my son Ben,

in celebration of his many gifts and the joy he brings to my life (A.S.)

Contents

Acknowledgments

We are grateful to the scholars whose work is collected in this book and with whom we have collaborated. Some are veterans of the cause lawyering project; others are newcomers to it. Yet, each of them made important contributions to the conceptualization of the project as well as to its execution. We are also grateful to Greg Coy, the Dean of the Faculty of Amherst College, for his generous financial support and interest in our work. Almost a decade ago, Amherst College provided a congenial setting for our first cause lawyering conference. We were delighted to have the chance to return. Finally, we owe a debt of gratitude to whatever twist of fate brought the two of us to think about cause lawyering. Our joint work, as organizers, editors, and authors, has been, and remains, for both of us, a treasure.

Contributors

Kevin R. den Dulk, Political Science, Grand Valley State University. Den Dulk is co-author of *Religion and Politics in America*, as well as numerous journal articles, book chapters, and reviews. His primary area of research is religion and public life, with an emphasis on religious uses of law and courts.

Aaron Fichtelberg, Department of Sociology and Criminal Justice, University of Delaware. Fichtelberg's research is on international criminal law and legal theory. He is the author, most recently, of *Crime Without Borders: An Introduction to International Criminal Justice* (Prentice-Hall, 2007).

Benjamin Fleury-Steiner, Criminal Justice, University of Delaware. Steiner's recent research focuses on cause lawyers and activists who work on behalf of HIV-positive prisoners. This study documents the struggles of such actors in both institutional and broader sociopolitical contexts in the United States. His latest book, *Dying Inside: HIV/AIDS in the Penal Health Care Crisis from Limestone Prison*, will be published by the University of Michigan Press in 2008.

William Haltom, Political Science, University of Puget Sound. Haltom is a professor of political science and is co-author of *Distorting the Law*.

Laura J. Hatcher, Political Science, Southern Illinois University. Hatcher's research has centered on the production of legal ideology, specifically beliefs about property and land ownership as they relate to processes of social change and the structure of environmental regulation. Her current work includes a book project entitled *Drawing Lines in the Sand: Takings* *and the Mobilization of Libertarian Legal Activism*, as well as several journal articles.

Thomas M. Hilbink, Legal Studies, University of Massachusetts-Amherst. Hilbink's research, focusing on the historical development of cause lawyering in the United States after 1945, has appeared in *Law & Social Inquiry*, *Studies in Law, Politics & Society*, and *Cause Lawyers and Social Movements*.

Tim Howard, Law & Policy, Northeastern University. Howard is a former Visiting Health Law Scholar and Instructor in Constitutional Law, Judicial Process, and Media & Politics, Boston University Law School in the Department of Public Health and Department of Political Science. He is a practicing consumer interest cause lawyer and the former Florida Assistant Attorney General and Senior Health Care Attorney.

Valerie Karno, English, University of Rhode Island. Karno teaches courses in Law and Literature and contemporary American culture. Her work can be found in such journals as *Postmodern Culture*, *American Quarterly*, *Critical Matrix*, and *Studies in Law, Politics, & Society*. She is currently researching a book on small claims court television shows.

William P. MacNeil, Griffith Law School, Griffith University. MacNeil has published widely in Australia, the United Kingdom, the United States, and Hong Kong on critical and cultural legal studies and has been a guest speaker at a variety of international conferences and symposia. His most recent book is entitled *Lex Populi: The Jurisprudence of Popular Culture*.

Richard J. Maiman, Political Science, University of Southern Maine. Maiman is a Fellow at the Human Rights Centre of the University of Essex. His current research is on litigation activity based on human rights legislation in the United Kingdom.

Michael McCann, Political Science, Law, Societies and Justice, University of Washington. McCann is the author of *Taking Reform Seriously: Perspectives on Public Interest Liberalism*, *Rights at Work: Pay Equity Reform and the Politics of Legal Mobilization*, and *Distorting the Law: Politics, Media, and the Litigation Crisis*. He is co-editor, with David Engel, of a forthcoming book tentatively titled *Fault Lines: Tort Law as Cultural Practice*.

Stephen Meili, Consumer Law Litigation Clinic, University of Wisconsin Law School. Meili's past publications have focused on a variety of areas that include transnational comparative analyses of the legal profession, complex litigation, and clinical legal education. His current research is on attitudes of members in consumer class actions toward the U.S. justice system. He is also analyzing novel regulatory approaches to payday lending, subprime mortgages, and other forms of predatory lending that focus on the disparate racial impact of such products.

Leslie J. Moran, School of Law, Birkbeck College. Moran has published extensively on law and visual culture. His current research project focuses on the cultural lives of the judiciary. This work examines not only representations of judges in film and television but also includes a multi-jurisdictional study of judicial portraiture.

Austin Sarat, Law, Jurisprudence and Social Thought and Political Science, Amherst College. Sarat is the author or editor of more than sixty books. He co-authored, with Stuart Scheingold, *Something to Believe in: Politics, Professionalism, and Cause Lawyers*. He has also written in the area of capital punishment and is currently at work on a book entitled *Hollywood's Law: Film, Fatherhood, and the Legal Imagination*.

Stuart Scheingold, Emeritus, Political Science, University of Washington. Scheingold is co-director (with Austin Sarat) of the International Cause Lawyering Project. Among his books are the *Politics of Rights*, *The Politics of Law and Order*, *The Politics of Street Crime*, and *Europe's Would-Be Polity* (with Leon Lindberg).

Corey S. Shdaimah, Social Work, University of Maryland, Baltimore. Shdaimah teaches social policy with a particular interest in street-level policy and the role of academics in policy debates. She is currently looking at how judges, lawyers, and social workers use discretion in child welfare decisions around housing-related concerns. Her forthcoming book is entitled *Public Interest Lawyering: The Practice and Pursuit of Social Justice* (New York University Press).

Bringing Cultural Analysis to the Study of Cause Lawyers: An Introduction

Austin Sarat and Stuart Scheingold

I. Introduction

This book seeks to illuminate what we call the cultural lives of cause lawyers by examining their representation in various popular media (including film, fiction, mass-marketed nonfiction, television, and journalism), the work they do as creators of cultural products, and the way those representations and products are received and consumed by various audiences. Attending to media representations and the culture work done by cause lawyers, we can see what material is available for citizens and others to use in fashioning understandings of those lawyers. It also provides a vehicle for determining whether, how, and to what extent cause lawyering is embedded in the discourses and symbolic practices around which ordinary citizens organize their understanding of social, political, and legal life.

This fifth edited volume of the Cause Lawyering Project adds an important new dimension to the body of research that has been growing steadily in the decade since the publication in 1998 of our first volume, *Cause Lawyering: Political Commitments and Professional Responsibilities*. As we detail below, all of the previous volumes have, in one way or another, focused on the place of cause lawyering in the legal profession and on its political aspirations, activities, and achievements. In contrast to the actions and institutions that were the subject of that research, here we turn to the broader context of cultural "sensibilities" and "mentalities." This book is but a first step into an area of research rather than the culmination of a research enterprise. It offers glimpses of cause lawyers in a few political and legal contexts in the United States, United Kingdom, and Latin America rather than a systematic survey. It is the start of an effort to make sense of the resonance of, and receptivity to, cause lawyering in different time periods in the United States and elsewhere.

The importance of beginning to try to understand that resonance and receptivity stems directly from the guiding premise of our previous inquiries into cause lawyering. From the start, we have argued that cause lawyers serve both to subvert and legitimate mainstream conceptions of the legal profession. As a consequence legal professions everywhere are both threatened by, and yet need, cause lawyering.

Cause lawyering, we have argued, is everywhere a deviant strain within the legal profession.[1] The cause lawyer is a "moral activist . . . [who] shares and aims to share with her client responsibility for the ends she is promoting in her representation."[2] In so doing, cause lawyers threaten the profession by destabilizing the dominant understanding of lawyering as properly wedded to moral neutrality and technical competence. In rejecting nonaccountability, cause lawyers establish a point from which to criticize the dominant understanding from within the profession. They also denaturalize and politicize that understanding.[3] As a consequence, cause lawyers challenge ongoing professional projects and put at risk the political immunity of the legal profession and the legal process.

However, that same moral activism also serves the legal profession. Because cause lawyers commit themselves and their legal skills to furthering a vision of the good society, they provide an appealing alternative to the value-neutral, "hired gun" imagery that often dogs the legal profession. In thus enhancing the civic stature of the bar, cause lawyering makes a significant contribution to a profession that is frequently on the defensive. It is in this sense that cause lawyers are needed, by the legal profession.

Cause lawyering will, however, be deemed a need, not just a threat, only so long as its activities are viewed as consonant with, not in conflict with or subversive of, prevailing political and social values. Whether cause lawyers are viewed in this way will be substantially dependent on how their

[1] Madelaine Petrara, "Dangerous Identifications: Confusing Lawyers with Their Clients," 19 *Journal of the Legal Profession* (1994), 179.

[2] David Luban, *Lawyers and Justice: An Ethical Study* (Princeton: Princeton University Press, 1988), xxii.

[3] See William Simon, "Visions of Practice in Legal Thought," 36 *Stanford Law Review* (1984) 469.

activities are represented to, and received by, multiple audiences: peers, participants in the movements they serve, and the broader populace. In addition, previous research has established that, to achieve their objectives, cause lawyers often combine political with legal mobilization, and the success of these mobilizing strategies depends in a large part on how cause lawyers are perceived by relevant publics. Whereas the views of peers and activists may be shaped by direct contact with cause lawyers, the general public is dependent on mediated images and cultural products, though the ways those images and products are consumed are highly contingent and deeply contextual.

II. The Cultural Problematic

Invoking the term "culture" at the start of the twenty-first century means venturing into a field where there are almost as many definitions of the term as there are discussions of it, and where inside as well as outside the academy arguments rage. As Renato Rosaldo puts it, "These days questions of culture seem to touch a nerve..."[4] Where once the analysis of culture could neatly be assigned to the respective disciplines of anthropology or literature, today the study of culture refuses disciplinary cabining, and forges new interdisciplinary connections.

Traditionally the study of culture was the study of "that complex whole which includes knowledge, belief, art, morals, law, custom, and any other capabilities and habits acquired by man as a member of society."[5] This definition, in addition to being hopelessly vague and inclusive, treats culture as a thing existing outside of ongoing local practices and social relations. In addition, by treating culture as "capabilities and habits acquired..." culture was made into a set of timeless resources to be internalized in the "civilizing" process through which persons were made social. Finally culture was identified as containing a kind of inclusive integrity, of parts combining into a "whole." This conception of culture still has its defenders and may even be on the rise as a political knowledge.

[4] Renato Rosaldo, *Culture & Truth: The Remaking of Social Analysis* (Boston: Beacon Press, 1989), ix.

[5] Edward Taylor cited in Stephen Greenblatt, "Culture," in *Critical Terms for Literary Study*, ed. Frank Lentricchia and Thomas McLaughlin (Chicago: University of Chicago Press, 1990), 225.

Today, however, within the academy critiques of the traditional, unified, reified, civilizing idea of culture abound.[6] As Luhrmann observed, the concept of culture is "more unsettled than it has been for forty years."[7] In this unsettled moment in the life of the concept of culture, efforts are underway to rehabilitate and reform it. In this effort, contemporary cultural studies have played an especially important role. Cultural studies have had a bracing impact in giving new energy and life to the study of culture, freeing it from its homogenizing and reifying tendencies. It has done so by radically extending what counts in the analysis of culture beyond the realm of "high culture," inviting study of the quotidian world. Film, advertising, pop art, and contemporary music – these and other products of "popular culture" have been legitimized as objects of study.

The Cultural Lives of Cause Lawyers takes up that invitation, extending the domain of cultural study to new terrain, namely the work of politically engaged, cause lawyers. The research reported in this book is premised on the growing scholarly recognition that legal meaning is found and invented in the variety of locations and practices that comprise culture and that those locations and practices are themselves encapsulated, though always incompletely, in legal forms, regulations, and legal symbols. Thus the interpretive task for cultural analysts is endlessly challenging as they seek to read everyday cultural forms.

This book brings together research on the legal profession with work that takes up the analysis of popular culture. Our contributors include scholars of popular culture who turn their attention to cause lawyers and experts on cause lawyering who turn their attention to popular culture. This is a joining of perspectives that is both long overdue and fruitful for both kinds of scholarship.

We confront the challenge of this joining of perspectives by analyzing a variety of cultural forms. In so doing we address the following questions:

- First, how does popular culture define and understand cause lawyers? What sense does it make of this category of lawyering? How does it turn an analytic category into a folk concept?

[6] For one example see Robert Brightman, "Forget Culture: Replacement, Transcendence, Reflexification," 10 *Cultural Anthropology* (1995) 509.

[7] T. M. Luhrmann, "Review of Hermes' Dilemma and Hamlet's Desire: On the Epistemology of Interpretation," 95 *American Anthropologist* (1993), 1058.

- Second, how are relations between lawyers and causes treated in popular culture? And when and how do cause lawyers become active producers of culture?
- Third, what perspectives does popular culture make available from which to criticize and analyze what cause lawyers do, as well as the impact and significance of their work? And how are those perspectives received by various audiences?

III. Relation to Previous Books

In four previous edited collections we have explored the complex relations between cause lawyers and the organized legal profession and the way cause lawyering is shaped by, and shapes, processes of political change associated with globalization and democratization. The first edited volume, *Cause Lawyering: Political Commitments and Professional Responsibilities*, originally asserted and presented evidence in support of, our foundational claim: that legal professions everywhere both need and, at the same time, are threatened by cause lawyering. As we indicated above, by reconnecting lawyering with morality, cause lawyers make tangible the idea that lawyering is a "public profession" and that its contribution to society goes beyond the aggregation, assembling, and deployment of technical skills. On the other hand, in many countries lawyers are, to varying degrees, bound by an ethical code that requires that they vigorously represent their clients "regardless of their own personal beliefs." Cause lawyering thus threatens the ethical premises of the legal profession by demonstrating that these principles are contingent, and constructed, and, in so doing, raises the political question of whose interests are served by the dominant understanding of legal professionalism.

Our second edited collection, *Cause Lawyering and the State in a Global Era*, spoke to a distinctive gap in the scholarly literature on the legal profession. Rarely had that literature taken the connection of lawyers to the formation and transformation of states as its subject. Although state transformation and globalization clearly influence, and are influenced by, law and lawyers, with a few notable exceptions, available research tends to ignore these interdependencies. Instead, as Terrence Halliday puts it, most research on lawyers focuses "on the internal organization and behavior of legal professions, overwhelmingly attends to single countries and, within national studies; it is the economic organization and behavior of professions, especially the market for legal services, that has captured most scholarly attention."[8] Similarly, the literatures on state transformation and globalization, again with a few important exceptions, ignore law and lawyers almost entirely and tend to treat the rule of law as something of a taken-for-granted black box. The result is that not only are lawyers neglected but so too is the wealth of research that decenters law and documents its pervasive presence and constitutive power as social practice throughout civil society, culture, politics, and the economy. *Cause Lawyering and the State in a Global Era* responded to the situation by connecting research on one kind of lawyering, cause lawyering, to the analysis of the state and state transformation in a global era.

Our third book, *The Worlds That Cause Lawyers Make*, turned from the large, macro-sociological questions that we took up in our two previous edited collections to examine what cause lawyers do in regard to social movements, how they make their practices, and what they do in marshaling social capital and making strategic decisions. It examines the dynamic interactions of cause lawyers and the political and professional contexts in which they operate. It does so by taking a constructivist view of cause lawyering. Instead of an essentialist approach to this phenomenon that assigns certain fixed traits to cause lawyers, we examined what cause lawyers do, how they do it, and what difference it makes. We analyzed the way in which cause lawyers "fabricate" (in an Arendtian sense) the political and professional contexts in which they operate. *The Worlds Cause Lawyers Make* documents the various ways in which cause lawyers both innovate within, and are constrained by, those contexts. Another way of making this point is to note that cause lawyering takes place within a framework of opportunities and constraints. The research compiled in this book examines the strategies that cause lawyers use to navigate within this framework.

Our fourth edited book, *Cause Lawyers and Social Movements*, took up one of the themes explored in *The Worlds That Cause Lawyers Make*,

8 Terrence Halliday, "Lawyers as Institution Builders: Constructing Markets, States, Civil Society, and Community," in *Crossing Boundaries: Traditions and Transformations in Law and Society Research*, ed. Austin Sarat et al. (Evanston, Il: Northwestern University Press, 1998).

namely the way cause lawyers work with and for social movements. Doing so allows for a reorientation of previous scholarship, turning the theoretical lens away from studies of the legal profession and toward the scholarly literature on movements. Our analytic interest was the same in this collection as it was for each of the previous books, namely to explore tensions and challenges that cause lawyers confront. Yet here we began with the world of politics, locating tensions between professional identity and political work from the perspective of movements and their agendas.

Can lawyers, we asked, maintain their professional identities and, at the same time, work as movement activists? If they seek to maintain a distance from the movement to protect their professional role, can they effectively serve movements? Does their usual preference for litigation as a tool for advancing movement goals facilitate the achievement of those goals or distort them? Do the social capital and prestige that lawyers bring to social movements lead to lawyer domination and threaten to undermine the internal solidarity necessary to social movement success?

By examining cause lawyers as both producers of culture and cause lawyering as represented in popular culture, *The Cultural Lives of Cause Lawyers* takes us closer than previous volumes to the core premise that cause lawyering both contributes to and threatens the legitimacy of the organized legal profession. Because legitimacy is dependent on public perceptions and understanding, it is necessary, in other words, to learn about the images of cause lawyering that are disseminated and made available to the public. Each of the chapters in this book is based on original research and written expressly for this volume by specialists in the fields of law and/or popular culture. Taken together, their work suggests that the representations of cause lawyers in popular culture are often hard to distinguish from representations of mainstream lawyers, that where those representations are distinctive they sometimes provoke and at other times allay anxiety about the political movements cause lawyers serve, and that the cultural lives of cause lawyers are politicized in ways that constitute cause lawyers as pushing the boundaries between law and politics.

The first section of this book – **The Cultural Work of Cause Lawyers** – contains three essays that examine cause lawyers' production and defense of cultural products. Although for some cause lawyers this activity is not integral to their work, it nonetheless helps associate them with causes they might wish to disclaim. For others cultural production is a self-conscious extension of cause lawyering work.

We begin with William MacNeil's subtle exploration of the ways lawyers live inside and outside cultural texts and how the content of those texts bleed outward, shaping the identities of lawyers. At the same, this essay raises questions about the ways we identify lawyers and their causes.

In MacNeil's study of a classic of American popular culture – Margaret Mitchell's *Gone With the Wind* and King Vidor's film version of that same text – he notes the distinct *absence* of cause lawyers in both the novel and the film, and the *overabundance* of lawyering committed to guarding the sanctity of the text itself. As MacNeil puts it, "*Gone With the Wind* is one of the most law-*full* – meaning lawyer regulated – fictions in history, a barristerial barricade having sprung up around it, like those around Atlanta in the last days of Sherman's final assault." He describes one aspect of the cultural work of cause lawyers, namely their work in policing cultural representation, and he asks whether any lawyer can avoid associating him- or herself with the substantive commitments the work seeks to advance. In so doing MacNeil problematizes the boundary between cause and conventional lawyering.

The absence of lawyers in *Gone With the Wind* stands in sharp contrast to the intense effort of lawyers to police its cultural standing. Since its publication the heirs of its author, trustees of her estate, and litigators have fought to protect it, even as they professed their indifference to the "cause" the novel ensconced, namely what MacNeil designates the "Cause of the Confederacy." Is it possible, MacNeil asks, to represent the text as cultural product without taking on the baggage of representing that cause? He suggests that at least in this case the answer is no.

The Stephens Mitchell Trust (which owns publishing rights to the book) for a long time has been represented by the Madison Avenue law firm, Frankfurt, Kurnit, Klein & Selz, whose lawyers hardly fit the usual profile of cause lawyers. Because of their professed indifference to the substance of the novel they sought to protect, MacNeil dubs them "causeless cause lawyers."

In 2001, Houghton Mifflin published a book, *The Wind Done Gone*, by African American writer Alice Randall. That novel is set in the same place and period as *Gone With the Wind*, and the protagonist in both novels is an attractive, independent young woman. The crucial difference is that

The Wind Done Gone's protagonist is a mulatto slave girl named Cynara. Though the story-line is actually quite different from *Gone With the Wind*, it is obvious to all who read it that *The Wind Done Gone* is "thoroughly embedded in the diegesis" of the other novel.

In a copyright infringement suit, Tom Selz, counsel for the Mitchell Trust, denounced the publication of *The Wind Done Gone* as "wholesale theft." And the U.S. District Court for Northern Georgia agreed, ruling that it qualified as a sequel to *Gone With the Wind* and thus was subject to the Mitchell Trust's copyright. In the court's view, Randall was free to write about the history of the South and its 'ideas' about civil war, slavery, etc., but the fiction that someone creates, a.k.a. their "expression," is legally protected under copyright law.

"But what if," MacNeil asks, "that 'fictional world,' in all of its imaginative expression – characters, plot, scenes – comes to stand for, perhaps even instantiate a place, and its past? Here, copyright's idea/expression dichotomy . . . begins to break down; the boundary between the two becoming blurred, their shared border crossed, their integrity violated – much like a war, and its skirmishes between two contiguous, inextricably linked (federated?) jurisdictions." Randall chooses to parody Mitchell's "expression" because *Gone With the Wind's* Scarlett O'Hara has come to represent the South by synecdoche and because the novel is so "thoroughly saturated by, so completely imbued with an 'idea' of history."

The Wind Done Gone serves as both an historical record and as a means of giving voice to those who are voiceless in the history of the South, including those who were voiceless in *Gone With the Wind*: mulattos. Thus MacNeil contends that the work of the Mitchell Trust lawyers is political, in its meaning if not its inspiration, and the lawyers who do that work serve as lawyers for a cause. In this case they are still attempting to keep mulattos out of the *Gone With the Wind* world by banning any mention of miscegenation in authorized sequels. As MacNeil says, "Scarlett anticipated [the lawyers] textually, carving out a place for them in the narrative by instantiating their very values; and Frankfurt, Kurnit, in turn, not only defend Scarlett and her story, they *enact* it, becoming an avatar of Scarlett in their aggressive prosecution on behalf of the Mitchell Trust, going to any and all lengths for their client." In this way, MacNeil argues, "the law firm becomes a Scarlett-like paradox, embodying the persona of both Yankee mercenaries and Confederate racists." Their lawyering, he believes, stands in for the cause and, in so doing, becomes a kind of cause lawyering. Here the cultural representation generates and transforms the lawyering that seeks to protect it.

The next chapter, Kevin den Dulk's study of evangelical cause lawyers, describes the identities of cause lawyers and the work they do as generators of cultural products as more explicit and self-conscious than that of the lawyers at Frankfurt, Kurnit. Drawing on the work of Murray Edelman on symbolic construction, den Dulk investigates how a cultural symbol, the idea of "culture war," plays out in the work of evangelical lawyers. For them, "culture war" suggests that two worldviews, progressive (urban dwellers, usually secular, generally open to alternative understandings of morality) and orthodox (suburban or rural dwellers, overwhelmingly religious, support tradition views of morality), are locked in conflict. "Many evangelical cause lawyers use the culture war trope," he notes, "as both a marker of their own identity and a rallying cry for legal mobilization."

Den Dulk's "goal is to examine the *symbolic* role the notion of a culture war plays in the mobilization of a small subset of often self-described 'warriors' in battle, namely evangelical cause lawyers" and how they have appropriated certain modes of cultural expression – from authoring nonfiction novels to producing radio programming and video documentaries – to define their place in the culture war. Through their work evangelical lawyers seek to control cultural consciousness, not merely influence certain areas of legal rights. As den Dulk writes, "The nature of evangelical subculture, with its arrays of media outlets, enables this kind of cultural engagement. In fact, in some instances the relationships across professions within the tradition have provided opportunities."

Evangelical law firms have become aware of the strength and popularity of cultural analysis, and some have started using that popularity to their advantage by creating what den Dulk calls "advocacy conglomerates." Each constituent of these conglomerates focuses on distinct portions of the public and benefits from each other's resources. Thus, legal, media, educational, and political evangelical groups can work together and provide the means for lawyers to participate on the broader plane of cultural criticism. Through this work, evangelical lawyers, like the lawyers for Mitchell's *Gone With the Wind*, found themselves taking on a paradoxical mix of elements and a distinctive, heroic role within the evangelical movement.

Tim Howard's chapter on the campaign against "Big Tobacco" in Florida provides another example of the cultural work of cause lawyers, an example in which they produced a narrative of the struggle that built on, and appealed, to prevailing public assumptions. These lawyers, Howard argues, tried to fashion a heroic persona in and through the mass media. Theirs, he says, were stories of "heroic, humble perseverance and resilience in a cause to redeem society." However, this heroic narrative ran up against prevailing public suspicion of tort lawyers. Hence in media portrayals they were often treated as ambulance chasers rather than key actors in an important struggle for justice.

Howard pays particular attention to what he calls Florida's "Cracker" culture, a culture derived from Celtic farmers who settled in the Florida backwoods and who value personal independence over material prosperity. Florida's courts and government were controlled by Cracker populist leadership for nearly 100 years, until 1988. "Progressive southern cause lawyers and progressive Northeastern intellectual realists," he notes, "allied with Florida Cracker governmental leaders and their press platform effectively interacted with the instruments, institutions, and ideologies to change that narrative frame of Florida tobacco liability litigation."

The new narrative framework "changed to a comparison of who is more appropriately liable between: (1) the wealthy tobacco companies that knew the harm and addiction their product would cause and made the profits from selling addiction and death, (2) the poor indigent Medicaid nicotine addict who cannot pay for their health care, (3) the innocent state taxpayer nobly paying for the health care costs of the indigent?"

Cause lawyers worked to align their narrative with Cracker ideology in the battle against Big Tobacco, because "[b]eing born in depression-era Florida, despite being in the conservative South, there is a deep undercurrent of populism, and the narrative of taking on a wealthy corporate giant that kills working people and sticks innocent taxpayers with the bill resonates with them as much as it did in the mock juries." Developing and marketing this narrative are other examples of the cultural work of cause lawyers, who, in the case of the Florida tobacco litigation, created a persuasive story that resonated with a broader public and mobilized the support of the majority.

The next section, **The Cultural Construction of Lawyers and Their Causes**, analyzes the way popular culture understands "causes" and the sorts of legal motivations that qualify people as "cause lawyers." It begins with a chapter on the representation of British human rights lawyers in the British press. This chapter, by Richard Maiman. is particularly interested in whether and to what extent these lawyers have been depicted by newspapers as having a "commitment to the achievement of the good."

British newspapers are distinctive in that they are very open about their political partisanship, both in their editorials and standard news stories. In the course of his analysis Maiman describes the political bents of six British newspapers. The "tabloids" are the (1) *Daily Mail*: anti-Labor Party, extremely conservative to the point of being called prejudiced; (2) *Daily Mirror*: most closely aligned with the labor movement, essentially centrist on most issues; and (3) *Sun*: strong supporters of Thatcher on domestic issues, critical of Blair for lack of control over illegal immigrants. The "quality newspapers" are the (4) *Guardian*: left-wing, anti-conservative; (5) *Daily Telegraph*: right of center without of being conservative; and (6) *Times*: moderately conservative.

Maiman studied the number of articles on human rights lawyers (HRL) in each paper and categorized them as to the nature of their coverage. He found that quality newspapers published more than twice as many HRL stories as the tabloids: "The *Guardian* carried almost three times as many HRL stories as the *Telegraph*, and more than twice as many as the *Times*, while the *Daily Mail* printed about one-third more HRL pieces than either the *Daily Mirror* or the *Sun*."

As to whether their articles were predominantly positive, negative, or neutral about HRL, Maiman notes, "Among the tabloid papers, the *Daily Mirror* had by far the most favorable coverage of human rights lawyers; HRL stories in the *Daily Mail* and the *Sun* were overwhelmingly negative. Among the tabloids as a whole, there were more than twice as many as [sic] negative stories as positive ones.... Among the broadsheets, the *Guardian's* coverage of human rights lawyers was highly favorable. The *Times*' slightly less so.... The *Daily Telegraph*'s HRL coverage was fairly negative, though not as negative as the right-wing tabloids.'"

Four narratives played a role in shaping the newspaper's coverage of the HRL stories:

1. New Labor: "The tone of the papers' HRL coverage – particularly the negative coverage – was shaped to a considerable degree by their attitudes toward the Blair government itself, toward what might be called the New Labor 'culture,' or more plainly, its 'style.'" Because many of the members of Blair's cabinet, including Blair himself, were

lawyers, the conservative papers wrote scathing, though nonspecific, references to "fashionable" Blairite lawyers. Eventually they began to accuse one particular group of lawyers – human rights lawyers – of being direct beneficiaries of Blair's new policies. The papers portrayed the Human Rights Act as a type of cronyism.

2. The Human Rights Act: The act itself also played a role in shaping newspaper's opinions. "Their views ranged from highly positive (*Guardian, Daily Mirror*) to cautiously hopeful (*Times*) to extremely negative (*Daily Telegraph, Daily Mail*, and *Sun*). Once those positions were set, they remained unchanged and helped shape the way the legal work triggered by the act was depicted."
3. Immigration and political asylum: In the late 1990s, a sudden spike in asylum applications caused a backlog of unresolved cases. Those who were rejected often immigrated illegally. They were often represented in legal proceedings by HRLs. The newspapers that supported stricter asylum and immigration policies were more negative regarding human rights lawyers, and vice versa.
4. The UK and Europe: The UK's controversial relationship with the European Union and the Council of Europe also influenced the tone of the stories. A highly negative view of European institutions often led to negative portrayals of human rights lawyers, and vice versa.

Although Maiman has no information about the impact of these stories, he suggests that they have important implications for the long-term success of human rights lawyering in the UK.

The next chapter takes up Maiman's interest in representations of cause lawyers by shifting media and cultural context. Valerie Karno examines representations of one infamous and successful reparations lawyer, Ed Fagan. Fagan, in Karno's view, was a prototypical cause lawyer. But Fagan was also involved in a number of unethical scandals, including stealing Holocaust reparations from two of his clients, hiring an underage prostitute, and several malpractice suits. The media went to great lengths to publicize those scandals. In doing so they remind us that cause lawyers are not simply altruistic or dedicated to a particular conception of the good. "Instead of mimicking identity politics – where the alignment of personal identity and coalitional identity often merge – media coverage of Ed Fagan shows us that cause lawyers represent much more than another day of identity politics. . . . The cause of Ed Fagan as we know him through the media might be a way that the law is loosening its grip on governing through identity categorization." In this way, cause lawyering may come to be understood as an identity born of "mutable [components] which the law might later take into account."

Karno's chapter challenges two key assumptions about cause lawyers: that they work for the "good" and that they mimetically reproduce their own belief system through their work. "The reason for challenging these rather fundamental presuppositions lies in opening the distinction between the representation of cause lawyers themselves, as people with fixed identities, and the *doing* of, or the performance of, cause lawyering." Karno uses the example of Ed Fagan to explore the discrepancy between working for the "good" and the reproduction of that "good" as an identificatory stance; in other words, the discrepancy between cause lawyers and cause lawyering. She suggests that focusing on the lawyering rather than the lawyers would complicate media representations while, at the same time, making it harder for newspapers or other media to call all cause lawyers to account for the failings of particular cause lawyers.

The next chapter, by Laura Hatcher, also describes media constructions of cause lawyers, cause lawyering, and their causes. Hatcher's chapter examines conservative cause lawyers, specifically property rights lawyers, and how they have been represented in press narratives. Her research shows that the journalists writing about property rights cases rarely focus on the larger political narratives surrounding those cases, and instead focus on individual client's stories.

Unlike Ed Fagan, property rights lawyers themselves hardly figure in those stories other than to bring in necessary legal information or clarify their clients' statements. This effectively erases their identities as activists within the larger conservative movement. "Rather, the narratives that are told by the press fit the commonly held beliefs about the way in which 'the little guy' can eventually come before the U.S. Supreme Court, and ultimately reinvent the 'myth of rights.'" Hatcher argues that the absence of lawyers from the media portrait of the broader conservative movement romanticizes the cause, treating property rights litigants as "the persons who tilt at windmills."

Hatcher's chapter is based on the analysis of newspaper coverage of a specific case, *Palazzolo v. Rhode Island*, as it made its way up to the

Supreme Court. In 1959, Anthony Palazzolo bought eighteen acres of land along the Rhode Island coast. Mr. Palazzolo was aware at the time that only two acres were dry enough for development. During the 1960s, Palazzolo's building permits were denied for various reasons and by various state agencies. "Finally, in the wake of the Supreme Court's decision in *Lucas v. South Carolina Coastal Commission*, in which a taking was found when an owner was unable to use his land, Mr. Palazzolo demanded that the state pay him $3 million for the property, alleging that the various regulations amounted to a regulatory taking, like the one in *Lucas*, of his property." The case eventually was brought to the U.S. Supreme Court with litigation sponsored by the Pacific Legal Foundation (PLF).

In newspaper coverage, Palazzolo was described as just a "regular guy," a poor man who nevertheless had amazing legal knowledge of property rights law, and who was fighting to build a beach on his land to support his family. Without the PLF's support, his case would have never made it to the Supreme Court, yet the newspapers hardly mentioned the Foundation or its broader political goals. While Howard, in Chapter 3, shows how lawyers crafted stories to romanticize themselves and their causes, in the property rights context Hatcher shows how newspapers *erased* the lawyers to romanticize the litigant.

Unlike Hatcher's analysis of the disappearance of cause lawyers in media accounts, Tom Hilbink's chapter is a study in the domestication of the image of radical cause lawyers in 1970s American television programs. With the Vietnam War, civil rights issues, environment rights issues, the 1960s and 70s saw a cause lawyering "explosion." "With this explosion came debates in many venues about the proper role of lawyers in social change, in democracy, and in society at large." One of the venues, television, brought the debate to the homes of millions of Americans with three dramatic, hour-long series premiering in 1970–71: *The Storefront Lawyers*, *The Young Lawyers*, and *The Bold Ones: The Lawyers*. These shows showed Americans that cause lawyers did not "pose a threat to the professional, political, social, cultural, or legal status quo."

Hilbink points to the importance of the 1968 Chicago conspiracy trial in setting the context for those shows. Based on that trial, the characterization of cause lawyers as radicals out to "undermine American democracy became a common trope on the right." This characterization aroused widespread public anxiety that radical lawyering might undermine public confidence in the law, thus threatening national stability.

Each of the three main networks at the time aired hour-long shows that spoke to these anxieties. While earlier lawyer programs had shown lawyers as traditional, middle-aged, Anglo-Saxon men in three-piece suits, these new lawyers were young men in blazers and tight pants, sometimes not even wearing a tie. Hair was worn longer, and women were present in small numbers wearing mini-skirts. Most significant, though, was the diverse racial, ethnic, and gender makeup of the young attorneys.

As Hilbink notes, these portrayals of lawyers "showed that while the attorneys might talk and dress differently from the three-piece suit and Brylcreemed lawyers of another generation, they were nonetheless constrained by conventional concepts of professionalism and legal precedent, guided by more conventional older attorneys and ultimately contemptuous of radical politics and its lawyering equivalent." These young lawyers were hardly rebelling against the rule of law. The shows emphasized the lawyers' praiseworthy "neutral, passive, dispassionate, yet zealous representation of a client."

"The prime-time lawyers of the 1970–71 season," Hilbink writes, "may still have been cause lawyers, but what I have called 'proceduralist' cause lawyers. They treated law and politics as separate and distinct, they believed the legal system to be essentially fair and just, and they tackled social ills at an individual level." The television programs of 1970–71 worked, Hilbink contends, to soothe anxieties in an era of social upheaval by showing that, even in the hands of young cause lawyers, the legal system was safe and stable.

McCann and Haltom's chapter changes the focus from the 1960s and 1970s to the present and the medium from television to film. Although contemporary film seems frequently to valorize cause lawyers, in McCann and Haltom's view it often actually reinforces the stereotypes that lawyers are corrupt, sleazy, and lazy. Focusing on *Erin Brockovich* and *North Country*, McCann and Haltom argue that cause lawyers are trivialized and lambasted in contemporary films in four ways: (1) the lawyer's motives: "The more recent movies . . . forfeit nuance by making cause lawyers appear to differ little from amoral, immoral, greedy, egotistic defense attorneys or from unscrupulous, voracious, imperious corporate clients whom they battle"; (2) the lawyer's responsiveness to the needs and preferences of the client over their own: "Cause lawyers in action almost every time tend to represent themselves first and foremost. When they do good by their clients, it is almost invariably due to the interventions of some person, persons, or events beyond the cause lawyer's initiative"; (3) the relationship between cause lawyers and the legal profession: "... The celluloid cause lawyer flails about in the same amoral or immoral swamp as do other professional lawyers"; and (4) an absence of a discussion of the effectiveness of legal tactics for advancing justice: "Most films do not ruminate on the intrinsic potential of litigation as a tactic ... but most make the victory of ordinary people a miracle for which the audience owes neither barristers nor adjudicators much thanks or credit."

Although McCann and Haltom cannot say with any certainty how these films about cause lawyers are received or interpreted by society, the pervasiveness of the four themes is striking. "On the one hand, to the extent that these films undermine a simplistic 'myth of rights' view that lawyers and litigation can successfully render corporate power accountable and beneficent, we applaud them." Moreover, McCann and Haltom continue, "If these films undermine faith in lawyers as unqualified moral heroes ... that is probably a good thing." "On the other hand," they write, film encourages "not only simplistic understandings but cynicism about the type of complex, collective political action necessary to narrow the huge gap between law and its elusive promises of justice."

Steve Meili takes up the theme of cynicism in relation to the work of cause lawyering by examining the representation of cause lawyers in Chilean film and television. Meili asks whether the historically cynical portrayal of Chilean lawyers in Chilean popular culture survived the social upheaval at the end of the Chilean authoritarian regime and compares a movie, *Death and the Maiden*, made just after the fall of the regime, with the television drama *Justicia Para Todos* ("Justice for All"), which was created after Chile had enacted a series of legal and civil reforms.

Death and the Maiden was released just after the fall of Pinochet but well before legal reforms were enacted. "*Death and the Maiden*," Meili writes, "is a stinging critique of cause lawyers, showing them as immobilized by the tension between law and social justice, as well as professionalism and public service." One specific criticism the film "levels at cause lawyers is that by adopting the professional mien of attorneys in service to the rule of law, they have abandoned the idealism that led them to pursue a cause lawyering career in the first place."

Although the legal and social terrain has changed since the release of that film, Meili questions whether pop culture's depiction of cause lawyers has changed as well. He analyzes the TV series that premiered fourteen years after the fall of the regime and roughly at the same time the government was implementing significant criminal procedure reforms. The show revolves around four attorneys working as both prosecutors and public defenders. Analyzing five episodes, Meili comes to several conclusions about the ways in which the public perception of cause lawyering has both evolved and stayed the same.

One of the similarities between the older film and the newer TV series is that in both "the cause lawyers who believe most ardently in the importance of the rule of law . . . are portrayed as honorable in an idealistic sort of way, but out of touch with what is really going on." Also, both posit that "law can bring about order, but not necessarily justice, and that sometimes disorder produces a deeper form of justice." Another difference marking the evolution of representations of cause lawyers is the amount of personal information included in the TV show that was irrelevant to the film. Thus, personal background becomes vital to individuals' identities as cause lawyers. Third, the legal system in both the program and the film is portrayed as flawed and anything but heroic. Therefore, even after the reforms, doubt and cynicism remained for the Chilean public. In addition, *Justicia* introduces distinctions among cause lawyers, both personal and professional, which, Meili suggests, implies a softening in the critique of cause lawyers since the end of the dictatorship. Finally, *Justicia* conveys the idea that the new system prevents many falsely accused criminals from being convicted, portraying a much more optimistic view than is found in *Death and the Maiden*. Yet despite these differences, Meili notes, the film and television program present a similarly cynical perception of cause lawyering, "at least to the extent that they seek to uphold the cause of the rule of law in post-authoritarian Chile."

The authors of the next chapter also take up *Death and the Maiden*. In contrast to Meili's article, they reimagine Paulina Escobar, the female lead character who was raped and tortured in prison during the authoritarian regime, doing the work of a cause lawyer without a lawyer's professional identity. Fleury-Steiner and Fichtelberg argue that, although the film is not a law film in the typical sense, it problematizes the roles of law and justice in times of social and political upheaval. Attending to the historical moment in this film, the authors say, is crucial for understanding Paulina as a radical cause lawyer.

"That Paulina has been raped by a representative of the fascist regime, that she is consumed with anger and grief, and capable of violence to achieve such ends – but as a committed veteran to the cause of human rights ultimately resists imposing the death sentence – incites the reader to reimagine her neither as passive victim nor as a vigilante pursuing purely personal revenge." Rather, she is a kind of an advocate because she uses the discourse and symbolism of law (including law's violence) to achieve her goals. The authors write, "Even in some of the most brutal imagery, Paulina's behavior is not mere violence or vengeance, but a powerful statement about law and justice after totalitarianism.... Like a rape victim recounting her violation before a jury, the terms that were used to subordinate the victim, descriptions of her body and dress are now used to empower the disempowered."

Death and the Maiden, in Fleury-Steiner and Fichtelberg's view, suggests that old and new regimes, totalitarian and liberal legal systems, often have more in common than one might hope. *Death and the Maiden*, they suggest, can be read not simply as a story about a human rights law animated by questions of the morality of punishment – although, it certainly can be read as such – but more generally as a "story constituted by a field of endless struggle for equal justice under law."

Like, Karno in Chapter 5, Fleury-Steiner and Fichtelberg problematize the definition of cause lawyers and cause lawyering as they make the point that cause lawyering is not as idealistic, moralistic, and one-sided as it may seem. Cause lawyers are complicated, and cause lawyering is often messy. Moreover, the causes the lawyers represent are often unrepresentable through traditional legal discourse. The film makes it "abundantly clear that societal change does not evolve in a clean, evolutionary process." It invites us to see cause lawyers as key participants in a "complex, living, breathing, historically situated legality...."

Our book concludes with Part III, **The Cultural Reception of Lawyers and Their Causes**. Its three chapters provide examples of research that investigate how the cultural work of cause lawyers and their representation in newspapers, television, and film are received and consumed.

In the first of these Les Moran explores the character of Rumpole of the Bailey as a morally committed, politically engaged lawyer. Rumpole, at first sight, "is hardly the stuff of which forensic champions of social justice are made. His credentials as a political animal and a moral activist, however, cannot," Moran argues, "be quickly dismissed."

Moran focuses on the Rumpole character found in the television programs rather than in the original novels because "through the television series.... Rumpole became an international popular cultural phenomenon. At its peak in the mid-1980s the program was attracting a UK audience of over 10 million viewers. The series was broadcast by more than 300 public television stations in the United States (representing 95 percent of PBS stations) as part of the *Mystery* series. It also had a long run in Australia, on the Australian Broadcasting Corporation's network."

Moran considers "a range of materials drawn from a number of sources, scholarly articles and reviews from law journals, Web sites, newspapers, obituaries and short stories" to analyze how the character Rumpole has "been read and used, particularly by people associated with the legal communities."

Initially, Rumpole, Moran notes, is portrayed as a cynical lawyer whose main professional interest is to make the most money in the shortest amount of time and with the least energy expended. But "far from being misanthropic, Rumpole's cynicism is a response generated in the context of his commitment to his clients and his struggle for social justice in their encounter with the legal system and in particular the criminal justice system... the audience is directed to read his cynicism in a particular way, to focus on the sense of irony and to take it as satire that works with some idea of an alternative and more specifically a leftist critique."

From this reading of the representational strategies of the TV series, Moran moves on to discuss how the Rumpole character has been received and used by lawyers and legal scholars in the United Kingdom and elsewhere. There is, he says, "ample evidence of the character of Rumpole being used as a cultural resource for lawyers in various parts of the common law world." Lawyers' treatment of Rumpole is, Moran notes, marked by "a process of selection and editing. Parts of the character may stand for the whole. His advocacy skills are most frequently identified as *the* character of Rumpole as a positive fictional lawyer."

For some lawyer viewers Rumpole is a stand-in for "'lawyerly virtues'. These are identified as a, '...love of language...ready wit...imaginativeness that lets him solve his mysteries...capacity for detachment...

independence of mind...'" Others use Rumpole "to make sense of the peculiarities of the English legal system and perhaps more importantly to thereby differentiate and distance the United States from other common law systems and the English legal system in particular." Still others "draw attention to the importance of the commitment of lawyers to moral and social justice." For them, Rumpole "is a character that exemplifies standing up for justice no matter how unpopular or odious the client or cause as 'lawyerly virtues.'"

The reception of Rumpole within the legal community exemplifies the fact that representation does not ensure any particular reception. Viewers, Moran contends, use popular culture strategically. Thus, Rumpole is "not a fixed character. In part this movement is demanded by the dictates of his move to the different cultural and economic environment of the world of commercial TV. In part it is a movement that takes place in various uses of Rumpole."

Stuart Scheingold takes the study of reception from television to print, focusing in particular of Jonathan Harr's *A Civil Action*, a book that Scheingold admires for its "subtle, complex, and compelling" portrait of cause lawyering by a plaintiff's lawyer – Jan Schlichtmann – in a class action suit brought by families of leukemia victims. Scheingold credits Harr with providing an unusual view of what he calls the "intrinsic contingencies" of "cause lawyering by personal injury lawyers." However, he is interested in more than celebrating Harr's achievement. His interest lies, instead, in tracing the process through which Harr's portrait of Schlichtmann is transformed as it is received and interpreted by book reviewers, film makers and film critics.

Scheingold argues that the novel weaves together the following elements that shed light on cause lawyering in personal injury practice. The resource imbalance between the corporate defendants and the plaintiff law firm, combined with the legal opportunities to delay, to obfuscate, and to manipulate legality – thus, enabling the defendants to bleed the plaintiffs dry. A judge predisposed to side with the defendants' attorneys who are members of a legal elite that includes the judge but not the plaintiffs' attorney, Schlichtmann, who is a parvenu practitioner from the lower hemisphere of a sharply stratified bar. Schlichtmann's grandiose expectations that lead him to reject big settlement offers in a vain attempt to win even larger sums for his firm and his clients while at the same time striking a blow for social and political justice.

Moreover, the book tells a cause lawyering story in tandem with what Scheingold calls "the structural parameters of the civil justice system."

Reviews of the book almost uniformly distort the book's complex argument. "What dominates media representations are the arbitrary vagaries of struggle between David and Goliath – leading inexorably to an indictment of the process of civil litigation. As for Schlichtmann, he is portrayed not as cause driven but as money-obsessed – and any inkling of his idealism that survives can only be seen as at best incidental and perhaps accidental." While reviewers for "mainstream" news outlets "are particularly prone to scapegoat Schlichtmann," reviewers for "opinion journals" read the book in ways that reflect "their own personal values and/or the values of their publications." Yet the net effect of the reception of *A Civil Action* in all review media was to "efface cause lawyering."

The film version of *A Civil Action* shares with the book a "compelling and complex portrait of Schlichtmann – emphasizing both his mixed motives and narcissistic grandiosity. More broadly the film effectively dramatizes the excruciating complexity, both legal and scientific, of the litigation; the victimization and isolation of the plaintiffs as well as the disproportionately heavy burdens borne by them and by Schlichtmann; how his dogged determination comes excruciatingly close to forcing his will on two major corporations." Yet Scheingold worries that the film plays up Schlichtmann as "money-driven, self-absorbed and unprincipled" and suggests that "obstruction and delay are the currency of civil litigation; that truth is nowhere to be found; and that virtue is a vice."

In the end Scheingold sees the reception of *A Civil Action* as a process of misrepresentation, a process in which "Harr's shrewd and fine-grained portrait of a personal injury lawyer's efforts to mobilize the law to empower victims of corporate misbehavior is transformed into a validation of the campaign of the so-called tort reform movement to discredit personal injury lawyers and regulatory interventions into corporate practices more generally." This rereading and reinterpretation damages an important segment of the cause lawyering bar and undermines one of its primary legal resources.

The final chapter, by Corey Shdaimah, treats clients of public defenders as consumers of popular culture's complex, contingent images of cause lawyers. Unlike Moran, who emphasizes the multiplicity and unpredictability of processes of reception, Shdaimah finds those clients to be uniformly skeptical and suspicious of public defenders.

Her chapter is based on interviews with a variety of low-income legal service clients of a large, urban legal service program that Shdaimah calls Northeast Legal Services (NELS). Shdaimah notes that few clients described their experiences with lawyers by making explicit references to popular culture. Yet, clients' images were based around "a remarkably consistent stock of ostensibly real-life cautionary tales that circulate among the people I interviewed originating in the experience of others, usually friends and relatives, with court-appointed attorneys in the criminal justice system." Their perceptions of their lawyers were also based on their own experiences with other government bureaucracies.

Despite their skepticism, clients believe that lawyers are necessary for three reasons. First, they have the professional knowledge and skills to navigate the legal system, a feat that clients believe from their experiences with other bureaucratic agencies is too difficult to do alone. However, this fact also makes it difficult for clients to assess their lawyer's performance, likely making clients more suspicious of their lawyers. Second, a lawyer's professional status, clients believe, is a prerequisite for being heard or listened to. Lawyers become for clients a step in the chain of command, a mediator between them and the higher power of justice. Third, although they have very little empirical evidence to back it up, clients believe lawyers have connections within the legal system, which are important to success in the legal system. This also contributes to client suspicions of lawyers because they believe the lawyers are "in cahoots" with the very bureaucratic branches of government the clients are fighting.

Shdaimah's study suggests that the very things that draw these clients to use lawyers contribute to a culture of suspicion and that negative images available in popular culture frame real-life experiences. The clients she studied do not recognize "a distinct or special breed of…'rebellious' lawyers but rather identify all lawyers with a more generalized notion of what lawyers do, how (well) they do it, and for whom." Here it seems that the cultural representations and cultural work of cause lawyers blur into a more generalized set of expectations and images of lawyers as a group. Just as Meili in Chapter 9 described how *Death and the Maiden* and *Justicia Para Todos* called into question the efficacy of cause lawyering when attempting to achieve justice within the rule of law, Shdaimah notes the same phenomenon when she writes, "While many legal services lawyers conceive of themselves as a special breed of oppositional outsiders…, they are nevertheless lawyers who must play by the rules…" As a result, clients who see themselves as generally disadvantaged by those rules see their lawyers less as champions than as complicit in the very system that disadvantages them.

That the cultural lives of cause lawyers are rich and complex is one of the clear lessons of the research reported in this book. Context matters – whether it is history, nation, or medium. Cause lawyering lives in and through the cultural work that cause lawyers do and in its mediated representations. Cause lawyers are hardly in control of the uses to which those products or representations are put or the ways they are consumed. Nonetheless, it is clear that the significance of cause lawyering is, in substantial part, fixed in worlds and relations far beyond the domain of the legal profession – namely, in the inchoate, ever-changing worlds of culture itself.

Acknowledgment

We thank Tovah Ackerman for her skilled research assistance.

THE CULTURAL WORK OF CAUSE LAWYERS

1

"No sacrifice is too great for the Cause!"

Cause(less) Lawyering and the Legal Trials and Tribulations of Gone With the Wind

William P. MacNeil[1]

I. Introduction: "...fighting on the field. Fighting for the Cause" (*GWTW*, DVD): *Gone with the Wind's* Adversarial Ashley Wilkeses and the Cause of the Confederacy

"Ashley's fighting on the field. Fighting for the cause. He may never come back. He may die. Scarlett, we owe him a well-born child."[2] So goes an extract of dialogue from one of the lesser known scenes from a very well-known, in fact overexposed American movie classic. The speaker is that filmic voice of oratorical conscience, Dr. Meade, a character played by Broadway stalwart, Harry Davenport. His auditor is Southern belle extraordinaire (and survivor par excellent), Scarlett O'Hara, aka Hamilton, aka Kennedy, aka Butler, a role taken by the British ingenue – at least for U.S. audiences at the time – Vivien Leigh. And the film? Naturally, King Vidor's 1939 adaptation of Margaret Mitchell's Pulitzer Prize winner, *Gone with the Wind*.[3] Now anyone familiar with the movie – and is there anyone out there who isn't? – knows (or should know) that Scarlett's acquiescence here owes more to promises previously rendered than to Dr. Meade's persuasive

[1] This article is dedicated, with much affection, to my favorite fellow Vivien Leigh fan and former Victoria College, University of Toronto classmate, one for whom, as well, tomorrow *is* another day: Jeannette Adams Strathy of Toronto, Ontario, Canada. Fiddlededee Miss Jeannette! – from your friend Bill who, as a Dalhousie Law School graduate, literally did "go to Halifax!" (GWTW, 620).

[2] All references to the film are to the following version: *Gone with the Wind* (DVD) directed by King Vidor (1939, Selznick International Picture; 2000, Time Warner Entertainment Company).

[3] All references to the novel are to the following edition: Margaret Mitchell, *Gone with the Wind* (London: Pan MacMillan, 1974).

powers. In an earlier scene – now recalled in hindsight ("I promised Ashley . . . something") – Scarlett had vowed to her thwarted love interest, Ashley Wilkes, that she would take care of his frail wife, the gentle and kindly Melanie.

For it is this *enceinte* Miss Melly (played by "swashbuckler" leading lady, Olivia de Havilland), off-camera, and sequestered in the movie-set backdrop of Aunt Pittypat's elegant Atlantan Peachtree Street home, who is the real source of Dr. Meade's considerable concern, and with whom Scarlett agrees to stay throughout what will soon turn out to be the most famous (and grueling) delivery in cinematic history. Indeed, so famous (and grueling) is it that its high drama all but obliterates the scene in question – excepting, of course, the (in)famous intervention, in her trademark falsetto, of Butterfly McQueen's stereotyped (though thoroughly upstaging) Prissy: "I knows . . . I knows . . . I knows how to do it. I seen it done lots and lots. Let me, doctor, let me. I can do everything" (*GWTW*, DVD). Between her and Aunt Pitty's *hysterically* funny hysteria ("It's like the end of the world. Uncle Peter, my smelling salts!", *GWTW*, DVD – smelling salts as a salve for Armageddon?!), the viewer is left with only the vaguest memory of Scarlett's muted surrender to Dr Meade's quietly impassioned plea.

Here, though, I want to "rewind" to Dr. Meade's dialogue and "pause," as it were, over a particular proper noun, so proper in fact that you can practically hear the capitalization in the doctor's voice; one uttered not only by him, but repeated throughout movie and book by characters, both minor (Dolly Merriwether, Mrs. Elsing) and major (Scarlett, Melanie, even Rhett!); one that attracts no qualifier, needs no modifier – aside from the definite article "the" – because in the world of *Gone with the Wind, the* Cause for which Ashley is fighting, for which "there isn't any sacrifice too great" (*GWTW*, 162) is "*the* Cause" of the Confederacy and its "peculiar" – to say the least – "laws"[4]: secession and slavery. Not that these so-called laws

[4] For an analysis of the strange legalism of the Confederacy (bereft as it was of *Recht*), see: James A. Gardner, "Southern Character, Confederate Nationalism, and the Interpretation of State Constitutions: A Case Study in Constitutional Argument," (1997–1998) 76 *Tex L Rev* 1220; Marshall DeRosa, "The Rule of Law v. The Misrule of Ideology: The Confederacy and Constitutional Interpretation" (book review), (1999) 77 *Tex L Rev* 789; Col H. Wayne Elliott, "A Government of Our Own" (book review) (1995) 148 *Military Law Review* 282.

and the very dubious "rights" they encode (to secede from the Union, to own another person), figure very much in *Gone with the Wind*, on screen or page. Unlike, say, in *The Birth of a Nation*,[5] *Gone with the Wind's* focus on the domestic sphere of the Civil War home front hives off the legal-political backdrop against which (un)constitutional secession took place. And, unlike, for example, other "plantation" fictions – either filmic or literary, complimentary or critical – *Gone with the Wind's* largely metropolitan mise-en-scène of Atlanta at war, then under siege, and, finally, during Reconstruction euphemizes, as an urban "service" culture (e.g., Mammy, Pork, Uncle Peter, Prissy, etc . . . , as town-based "house servants") the very real agrarian legal-economic base of Southern slavery.[6]

This sidelining of the "rights" of both secession's politics and slavery's economy not only evacuates the law from *Gone with the Wind*; it renders lawyers scarce on the ground, as if, like the white and black population of Atlanta – Aunt Pittypat, Uncle Peter, the Meades, the Merriweathers, the Elsings – they have "refugeed" elsewhere. This absence is made all the more strange by the fact that Margaret Mitchell herself was the daughter (of Eugene Mitchell) and sister (of Stephens Mitchell) of two prominent Georgia attorneys. Only one legal practitioner is featured in her novel, Scarlett's curmudgeonly in-law, Uncle Henry Hamilton,[7] and he is edited

[5] *The Birth of a Nation*, directed by D. W.Griffith (1915, Epoch Producing Corp).

[6] Indeed, the only two actual references to slavery are in connection with whites. First, in the scene set at the Atlanta bazaar during the early days of the war, when an irate Dolly Merriwether – played to dowager perfection by Jane Darwell – accusingly confronts Caroline Meade and Aunt Pittypat, and calls into question Dr. Meade's judgment in conducting what she calls, disdainfully, "this slave auction": that is, a fund-raising raffle of belles' dances (at which Rhett, of course, bids $200 for Scarlett, scandalizing polite society and "ruining" her reputation). Later, during Reconstruction and at a scene set at Scarlett's new sawmill, Ashley questions the morality of using convict labor. To which Scarlett retorts, with no small justification: "You didn't mind owning slaves?" "That was," Ashley assures her, "different," with the implication that white indenture trumps black slavery for cruelty; and, in any event, "he would have freed them (i.e., his slaves) when Father died, if the war hadn't freed them already." Aside, from these instances any explicit reference to slavery is heavily coded: for example, Pork refers to himself as a "house worker," Suellen calls them, "servants," and the opening credits describe the O'Hara slaves, like Big Sam, as "in the fields" or those like Mammy, as their "house servants."

[7] An "irascible" (*GWTW*, 152) though ultimately good-natured character who pops up a number of times throughout the novel, and, at least twice, in professional contexts: first, at the outset of Scarlett's relocation to Atlanta in 1862, when, as trustee of Charles's estate, he advises her of her extremely comfortable financial circumstances, including her "half-interest" in Aunt Pittypat's house (*GWTW*, 152); then second, on Scarlett's return to postwar Atlanta in January, 1866, amidst the devastation wrought by the Union occupation, where he is described as "battling

out of the movie.[8] But if lawyers (and the law) have gone, like Confederate troops, "missing in action" from what might be called the *enonce* – that is, the diegetic content or story-line – of *Gone with the Wind*, then this lack is more than compensated for, indeed overcompensated, by the pervasive presence of lawyering with regard to its *enunciation*: that is, its narrative form, its text *qua* text. For *Gone with the Wind* is one of the most law-*full* – meaning lawyer-regulated – fictions in history, a barristerial barricade having sprung up around it, like those around Atlanta in the last days of Sherman's final assault. Only, instead of Gov. Brown's Home Guard or Tara's Big Sam "dig(ging) for the South" (*GWTW*, DVD), the bulwarks here are manned by a surfeit of solicitors, be they heirs (like Mitchell's brother Stephens, mentioned above who, with his two sons, served as her legatees); trustees (like counsel for the Stephens Mitchell Trust); and, most importantly, a cohort of litigators who, like adversarial Ashley Wilkeses who is "fighting on the field" in Cobb's Legion, mount various courtroom sorties in defense of *Gone with the Wind*, protecting its legend, upholding *its* Cause. Even when, as far as the Cause of the Confederacy is concerned – of which *Gone with the Wind* is often read as emblematic – these lawyers are more likely than not to be publicly indifferent (and doubtless privately disapproving, even hostile) to the clarion call of its "Rebel yell" so as to be deemed "causeless."

It is with this curial contingent that I am concerned here. First, in this essay, I want to locate and identify *Gone with the Wind's* "causeless" cause lawyers, asking not only where they are situated and who they are but also what they are about; that is, what they are fighting for *or against*. To that end, I want to look at one of the more recent skirmishes that they have been drawn into by the book that trumpets, though is anything *but*, a "Lost

valiantly to save the house and the one piece of downtown prcoperty where the warehouses had been, so Scarlett and Wade would have something left from the wreckage" (GWTW, 543). But, far from debilitating him, this Reconstruction practice, defending "the widow and the orphan" from the Carpetbaggers, has made him, in Rhett's words, "young again" (*GWTW*, 752).

[8] Edited out as well is the profession of his nephew, Scarlett's first husband Charles, described as "a lawyer" (GWTW 879), and whose (legal?) studies included a stint at that bastion of Unionist, Abolitionist Yankeedom – Harvard (GWTW, 142). Gone too is the hapless Hugh Elsing, "all set to be a fine lawyer" (GWTW, 545), then reduced to wood peddling and wagon driving. Even Boyd Tarleton's academic aspirations to "read law in Judge Parmalee's office in Fayetteville" (GWTW, 7) are postponed, initially, by the outbreak of the War, and then, indefinitely, by his death – with the twins – at Gettysburg.

Cause": a 2001 courtroom raid for injunctive relief against, on the eve of its publication, a brilliant riposte to *Gone with the Wind* entitled, with a fitting chiastic irony, *The Wind Done Gone*[9] by African American writer, Alice Randall. Second, I want to turn to Randall's book, briefly reviewing its structure and style and then examining, in more detail, its complex textual interactions – characterological, dialogic, scenic – with *Gone with the Wind*. Third, I want to sketch the legal responses, on the part of lawyers and judges, to this sort of textual interaction – piracy or parody? – focusing on the case *against* Randall and her book. Here I want to contextualize that case in two ways: on the one hand, as evidencing a "Civil War" raging in U.S. copyright law with its "idea/expression" binary serving something like a stand-in for the Union/Confederate dichotomy; on the other hand, as instancing, in American courts, the ongoing curial "War Between the States" and its disputes over flags, license plates, etc. The Cause-committed lawyers of these cases are, I suggest, the unlikely professional colleagues of *Gone with the Wind's* "causeless" Cause lawyers, each in his or her own way still fighting for the "Stars and Bars." Fourth, I want to return in a broader, more sweeping vein to Randall's astonishing book, examining its motives, gauging its effects. Here I want to set off *The Wind Done Gone* against not only Mitchell's flawed yet powerful text (as well as, *en passant*, Vidor's definitive film translation) but also its pallid, authorized 1991 sequel: Alexandra Ripley's *Scarlett* (and its even more demystifying TV mini-series[10]). Fifth, and last, I want to return to what Randall herself called the 'repellently attractive'[11] character of Scarlett O'Hara – in all her ambiguous "glory": feminist forerunner and rape fantasist, familial defender and reactionary racist. By way of conclusion, I want to speculate about *her* loyalties and which cause – lawful or otherwise – she might support: a study in shifting alignments that, at the end of the day, might cast her lot, once more, with those "white trash," no account Carpetbagging, damn Yankees! In this case, the New York lawyers for the Mitchell Trust whose vigilant but "causeless" cause lawyering of her patented literary celebrity threatens – like Dr. Meade's overzealous medical treatments (e.g., sawing off gangrenous legs) – to kill the patient with the cure.

[9] Alice Randall, *The Wind Done Gone* (Boston: Houghton Mifflin, 2001).

[10] *Scarlett* (1994: RH1 Entertainment: Betta Entertainment, VHS).

[11] "Alice Randall document" at http://www.answers.com/topt/alice-randall

II. "Ah, Scarlett, how the thought of a dollar does make your eyes sparkle! Are you sure you haven't got some ... perhaps Jewish blood?" (*GWTW*, 751): Fiddledee-oi gevalt! Frankfurt, Kurnit, Klein & Selz and the New York Lawyer as the Last Confederate[12]

But who are these "causeless" cause lawyers for *Gone with the Wind*? At first blush, nothing could be more remote, physically *and* psychically, from *the Cause* and the world of the novel than the law firm representing the Stephens Mitchell Trust: those last, and, to say the least, *very odd* Confederates, Frankfurt, Kurnit, Klein & Selz[13] (hereafter Frankfurt, Kurnit). For with them, and their "boutique" practice in entertainment and intellectual property law, we find ourselves relocated to the "Big Apple" of the North – New York – rather than waylaid in the hub of the Deep South, Atlanta. And not just anywhere in New York City, but the center of midtown moxie and gridiron glitz, Madison Avenue – a far cry from Peachtree Street's shabby-chic gentility. Moreover, location is not all that has changed; identity itself has been transmogrified. Instead of the old Anglo-Celtic/Huguenot clans of Clayton County – O'Haras, Wilkeses, Tarletons, Fontaines, Calverts, Monroes, McRaes – and their citified cousins (Hamiltons, Burrs, Robillards), the names that roll off the partnership list here sound, preponderantly, immigrant Germanic, even Ashkenazic,[14] their putative "Jewish blood" (GWTW, 751) – as Rhett puts it – doubtless, a part of their appeal to the Mitchell Trust, and that organization's strategy to de-"Southernize" *their cause*. But fight for that cause, Frankfurt Kurnit does, in a struggle that would bring, surely, a real "sparkle" (GWTW, 751) to Scarlett's eyes. Indeed, Frankfurt, Kurnit's watchdog efforts in court, when joined with the "tenacious ... scrap(piness)"[15] of the Mitchell Trust's Atlanta-based instructing

[12] For a variation on this theme, see Alfred Uhry's acclaimed play about Southern Jews in 1939, *The Last Night of Ballyhoo*, and its principal character, LaLa Levy, nicknamed "Scarlett O'Goldberg." For a critical analysis, see: Gary Richards, "Scripting Scarlett O'Goldberg: The Production of Southern Jewishness in *"The Last Night of Ballyhoo," Southern Quarterly*, Summer 2001.

[13] For their Web site, see http://www.fgks.com.

[14] Of course, the firm includes, as partners and associates, a range of ethnicities and races: black, Asian, Italian, Irish, *and* Jewish – as befits its Northeast base. The real homogeneity of Frankfurt, Kurnit lies in education, their law schools being largely "Ivy" and their undergraduate training, often "little Ivy," like Amherst.

[15] As described by novelist Pat Conroy, who approached him to write a further sequel, presumably about Rhett Butler, after the publication of Ripley's *Scarlett*. See: "Declaration of Pat Conroy" at http://www. houghtonmifflinbooks.com

counsel, Paul Anderson and Hal Clarke, have become the stuff of legal legend, rivaling even those of the attorneys for the Hill family and their copyright of "Happy Birthday." For it is copyright law and the efforts of the litigators, Frankfurt, Kurnit, in their client's cause that have made Margaret Mitchell's heirs – nephews Eugene and Joseph – richer than any Scallywag's (even Scarlett's!) wildest dreams of avarice.

What's more, this client's cause is spreading, Frankfurt, Kurnit literally "looking away" and taking the fight, in the last few years, much farther afield than "Dixie-land" itself. Indeed, as far away as *another* South, the Southern Hemisphere and its Antipodes. There, the target is the Australian affiliate of the proto-"Creative Commons" U.S. organization, Project Gutenberg, a nonprofit and voluntary corporation committed to the free dissemination, in the digital public domain, of copyright-free books.[16] In line with this practical/political commitment, Project Gutenberg has posted *in Australia* the full – and fully accessible – text of *Gone with the Wind* on the Web. And that action is perfectly legal, too – at least, by the laws of Australia, where the novel's copyright expired in 1999, fifty years after Mitchell's death – as is (or was) usually the case in a number of common law countries (e.g., Canada, New Zealand, previously the United Kingdom). America, however, is a different story. There, the so-called Sonny Bono amendment[17] to the copyright laws extended protection for an additional twenty years, raising it anywhere from seventy years following the death of the author to, in some cases (e.g., "corporate authorship"), ninety-five years subsequent to the date of publication. All of which means that, at least from the point of view of Frankfurt, Kurnit, *Gone with the Wind* remains the intellectual property of the Mitchell Trust well into the twenty-first century (reckoned at 2031, on the calculation of the date of publication – 1936 – plus ninety-five years); and that Project Gutenberg, insofar as it has made the novel available to American readers, is in breach of that copyright and guilty of a theft for which it should and will be prosecuted. To that end, the firm launched a campaign of intimidation against Project Gutenberg, threatening legal action. The threat succeeded, and *Gone with the Wind* disappeared from its Australian Web site. The result: the Mitchell Trust and its lawyers have

[16] See, e.g., Victoria Shannon, "Leeching Off the Dead: 95 Year Copyright Stifles Creativity and Progress," *New York Times*, November 8, 2004.

[17] Sonny Bono Copyright Term Extension Act 1998.

become as much the *bete noire* of the "copyleft/-free" movement in 2007 as they were of the literary avant-garde in 2001.

It is with this latter date, however, that I am most concerned here, because 2001 is the year of publication for Randall's *The Wind Done Gone*, as well as the year of its widest and most wildly enthusiastic reception – at least after the preliminary injunction, sought by Frankfurt, Kurnit and awarded against it, was "vacated" by a subsequent court order.[18] With that court order in hand, Boston's Houghton-Mifflin proceeded with the book's publication. Success was fast coming. *The Wind Done Gone* was an almost instant, even "overnight" hit, both commercially and critically, climbing, easily, within weeks of its appearance, to a "top ten" spot on the *New York Times*' best seller list[19]; and attracting a round of largely good, and, in some cases, glowing responses from reviewers across America (and overseas) who felt the time was ripe, if not long overdue for a revisionist "take" on Mitchell's text.

In fact, no one missed, or failed to get Randall's point – and pointed critique here, and all the newspaper notices, like the Mitchell Trust and its lawyers before them, picked up on her subtext. After all, the book's title, *The Wind Done Gone*, recalls and invites comparison, even in its ebonic-like patois, with *Gone with the Wind*. That comparison is strengthened by the similitude of both novels' place and period: principally Atlanta and its environs, during the antebellum, Civil War, and Reconstruction eras. Similar, too, is the characterological focus of the two narratives: in each, on the life and loves, ups and downs of an attractive, headstrong young woman, making her way in the world of the nineteenth-century American South. Here, though, a key difference in character trait is introduced, indeed one so critical that it made *all the difference* (or at least should have) to these two characters and their respective stories. That difference is, of course, *race*. Whereas *Gone with the Wind* gives its readers, in the figure of Scarlett O'Hara, a heroine who is "whiteness" personified, *The Wind Done Gone* does, for its readers, the obverse: depicting, unabashedly, a heroine of color – albeit of mixed race: the mulatta, Cynara.

[18] *Suntrust Bank* v. *Houghton Mifflin Co*. 136 F. Supp. 2d 1957, 1364 (N. D.Ga 2001), *vacated* 252 F. 3d 1165 (11th Cir. 2001).

[19] Peaking at ninth, and remaining on the list for a six-week period.

III. "Othering" Scarlett: Cynara's Song of the South and the "Double Session" of *The Wind Done Gone*

Cynara (or "Cinnamon/Cindy" – as her white masters alternatively and reifyingly called her) is not only the subject but also the *source* of *The Wind Done Gone*, its narration. The book is a first-person account of her *peripatetic* life journey in all of its temporal-spatial flow, beginning with her birth on a North Georgia cotton plantation in 1845. Shuttling backward and forward in time (1873, 1845, 1855, 1858, etc.), changing from place to place ("Cotton Farm/Tata," Charleston, Atlanta, London, Washington, D.C., etc.), this narrative movement is captured, structurally, by the text's episodic form: an extended series of short *pensees*, meditative in tone, lyrical in style, and out of which emerges slowly, gingerly, and requiring much patient, readerly piecing together, the lineaments of a plot. This plot, in turn, is organized around a theme that, for all the text's formal experimentation with the conventions of storytelling, unfolds in a reasonably linear fashion, recalling any number of African American autobiographies of the period and their tales of "up from slavery."[20] For, like Booker T. Washington's book (and others, such as that of Frederick Douglass[21] and Harriet Tubman[22]), *The Wind Done Gone* tracks Cynara's travails from servitude to freedom. At the start of the story, she is an *object* of property whom we see sold (at least) twice[23]: first, privately, by her original owners, who see her sale as removing a potential source of white male sexual temptation; second, publicly, at a Charleston slave market, by her subsequent and impecunious, "quality" owners to the *demimondaine*: an Atlanta brothel owner. By the story's close, however, Cynara is property's subject: that is, a property *owner* in her own right – and the owner, no less, of the very plantation that was her birthplace.

20 Booker T. Washington, *Up from Slavery* (New York: Avon Books, 1965).

21 Frederick Douglass, *Narrative of the Life of Frederick Douglass, an American Slave* (New York: W.W. Norton, 1997).

22 Sarah Bradford, *Scenes in the Life of Harriet Tubman*, 1868.

23 The sequence of sale and resale is more involved than this, and condensed by Cynara herself with a well-rehearsed, and comically overblown (*Tristam Shandy*-esque?) stock response to whorehouse queries, by "blue-blooded gentleboy(s)," as to how she came to be there: "A strange series of deaths in rapid succession following an influenza epidemic left a trail of inheritances that led me to the flesh market with a stop of work with a family that couldn't afford to keep a second ladies' maid" (*TWDG*, 21).

While traveling along this path, and its circuitous route from "status to contract," Cynara meets (at the Atlanta brothel), consorts with (as his mistress), and, ultimately, *marries* (on the death of his first wife) a wealthy white man and former Confederate, with whom she travels extensively (a Grand Tour of Europe, which includes London, Paris, Venice, etc.), visiting, *inter alia*, Washington, D.C., in the postwar period. There, Cynara is launched in the heady whirl of Gilded Age "society," taking her place in the capital's burgeoning black bourgeoisie where she is introduced to, in addition to historical figures like Frederick Douglass, a black Congressman from Alabama, Adam Conyers.[24] The two have a brief (yet intense) love affair: but they part, Cynara, forever compromised by her past as a white Confederate's courtesan (and spouse), stepping aside so that Adam may marry the respectable – though barren – "gap-toothed" Corinne (*TWDG*, 108, 112, 206) and thereby preserve his high standing in the black community. In time, though, Cynara gives birth to the Congressman's son, Cyrus – or Mose, whom she gives to Corinne to rear as her own. There, Cynara's tale ends. A postscript to the narrative proper – now revealed as a long-lost manuscript – gives a summary account of Cynara's descendants and sketches the subsequent fate of other characters, ending with a line that summons up, but also separates the story from the closing of *Gone with the Wind*: "For all those we love for whom *tomorrow will not be another day* (italics mine), we send this sweet prayer of resting in peace" (*TWDG*, 208).

So from beginning (its title) to end (its last line), *The Wind Done Gone* is a refraction rather than a reflection, departing from *Gone with the Wind*, at the very moment it defines itself in (literary) terms of that book. Or so it *seems*. I italicize "seems" because Cynara's story would be a departure, indeed a radical one from Mitchell's (where, as a character, she is nowhere to be found) if only it wasn't obvious to all who read it – publishers, lawyers, courts, the public – that it is thoroughly embedded in the diegesis of an(O)ther novel. So Frankfurt, Kurnit and the Mitchell Trust *do* have a point because that "other," *Gone with the Wind*, is evoked, intentionally and skilfully, on every page of *The Wind Done Gone* – and not,

[24] A possible reference to John Conyers, prominent, modern-day Michigan Congressman and black community leader in Randall's native Detroit. Most certainly, though, a historical composite figure of the many black Congressmen elected to the Reconstruction House of Representatives, of whom Benjamin Turner, Jeremiah Haralson, and James T Rapier were from Alabama. The last, Rapier, is referenced directly in *The Wind Done Gone* (115).

I might add, solely by the character, "Other" (the book's code name for Scarlett). For Randall weaves a rich thread of allusions and references into the very fabric of her text, inviting (or challenging?) readers to lay these two books, in the manner of a Derridean "double session,"[25] side-by-side, tracing their patterned parallelism, drawing out their shared design. Not that *Gone with the Wind* is the sole source stitching up Randall's story.[26] On the contrary, *The Wind Done Gone* draws on a patchwork of literary (and other[27]) materials, quilting together – to name but a few – citations from, and to Dickens,[28] Harriet Beecher Stowe,[29] Shakespeare,[30] Du Maurier,[31] Hawthorne,[32] Austen,[33] Faulkner,[34] and Dowson.[35] The reference to Dowson, however, brings us back to *Gone with the Wind*, the title of which Mitchell took from his famous poem, itself a borrowing from Horace's *Non Sum Qualis Eram Bonae Sub Regno Cynarae* – and which, of course, functions as the epigraph to *The Wind Done Gone*.

This kind of complex cross-referencing is continued throughout the book. Consider how all the supporting characters in *The Wind Done Gone* are encrypted as alphabetic, punning, or generic ciphers, decoded all too easily, with very little stretch of the imagination, into the *dramatis personae*

[25] Jacques Derrida, *Dissemination*, trans. Barbara Johnson (Chicago: University of Chicago Press, 1981).

[26] Randall herself identifies a range of authors – such as Austen, Richardson, Defoe – as sources for her book. "A Conversation with Alice Randall" from *A Reader's Guide to The Wind Done Gone*, at Houghton-Mifflin (Readers Guide for The Wind Done Gone published by Houghton Mifflin Company).

[27] Randall references, as well, a number of historical figures, prominent in African American history, such as Jefferson's partner, Sally Hemmings (*TWDG*, 75), and the "Moses" of her people, Harriet Tubman (*TWDG*, 39). Reconstruction politicians, Robert B. Elliott and James Rapier , referred to earlier, are also mentioned (*TWDG*, 115). There may even be a very oblique nod to the contemporary critical race theorist, Columbia's Patricia Williams, in the text's highly suggestive metaphor, the "alchemy of slavery" – a possible allusion to Williams' now-classic *The Alchemy of Race and Rights: Confessions of a Mad Law Professor*.

[28] With Cynara analogizing herself to *Great Expectations*' Pip, *TWDG*, 19.

[29] "Uncle Tom sounded just like Jesus to me, in costume," *TWDG*, 7.

[30] Quoting an exclamatory Miranda from *The Tempest*, "O brave new world," (*TWDG*, 115).

[31] "Last night I dreamed of Cotton Farm" (*TWDG*, 10) – a conscious echo of *Rebecca's*, "Last night I went to Manderly."

[32] Whose novel, *The Marble Faun*, is alluded to by Cynara when "(i)n Rome I met a coloured woman . . . who lived there as a sculptor of . . . marble fauns" (*TWDG*, 23).

[33] Referencing a Said-inspired reading of *Mansfield Park* with "Fanny hated slavers" (*TWDG*, 157).

[34] Evoked in the elliptical citation, "Light in August" (*TWDG*, 72).

[35] Whose much-quoted lyric, "I have been faithful to thee, Cynara! In my own fashion," names Randall's heroine (*TWDG*, 7).

of *Gone with the Wind*. As noted above, Cynara's half-sister, "Other" – "the belle of five counties" (*TWDG*, 1) – is none other than Scarlett herself. Their shared father, "Planter," is the bluff Gerald O'Hara, and his wife, "Lady," the aristocratic Ellen. Their daughters, "China" and "Kareen," are stand-ins for the younger O'Hara girls, Suellen (her renomination, "China," being a geographic nod to "India" Wilkes) and Careen (destined in each book for a Roman Catholic convent). Their plantation, "Tata," is, but for one consonant, a mimesis of "Tara," on which live "Garlic" (Pork), major-domo, butler, and valet combined, and "Pallas" (Mammy), the head woman of the house servants, as well as mammy to the daughters of the family. A neighboring plantation, "Twelve Slaves Strong as Trees," bears more than a passing resemblance to that *echt*-planter paradise (and Frances Parkinson Keyes cliché), "Twelve Oaks"; its owner, "Dreamy Gentleman," is a thinly disguised Ashley Wilkes – who, in turn, is married to Other's sister-in-law, "Mealy Mouth" (Melanie). In Atlanta, one finds the spooneristic "Aunt Pattypit" (Aunt Pittypat), local bordello madam "Beauty" (Belle Watling), and the dashing, mysterious "R." – later known by the moniker, "Debt Chauffeur," husband of both Other and Cynara *seriatim*: namely, Rhett Butler.

This one-to-one characterological correspondence is not the only area of similitude between the two texts. Memorable passages, snatches of well-known dialogue, even whole scenes are replayed through the optic of Cynara's gaze. For example, consider this passage about Other from *The Wind Done Gone* – "She was not beautiful, but men seldom noticed this, caught up in the commotion and scent in which she moved" (*TWDG*, 1) – and its immediate evocation of the celebrated opening line of *Gone with the Wind*: "Scarlett O'Hara was not beautiful, but men seldom realized it when caught by her charm as the Tarleton twins were" (*TWDG*, 5). Or take another example, a line of Pallas's – "What's mah lamb gwanna wear" (*TWDG*, 5) – that is almost an exact copy, but for orthographic differences in rendering dialect, of dialogue that is unmistakeably Mammy's, both in Mitchell's novel and Howard's film script: "Whut mah lamb gwine wear?" (*GWTW*, 79). Significant scenes, as well, are restaged: like that of a disconsolate R., driven mad with grief and holed up with the corpse of his daughter, refusing her burial because she's "afraid of the dark" (*TWDG*, 17) recalling, in all its lachyrmose detail, Rhett's anguish over the death of little "Bonnie Blue" Butler (*GWTW*, 963–975), killed in a riding accident. Even minor narrative details from *Gone with the Wind* recur, with unerring accuracy, in *The Wind Done Gone*: that Lady married Planter on the rebound from a failed romance with her scapegrace cousin, "Fee-leepe" (*TWDG*, 47) (as did Ellen, after the untimely and violent death of her "wild" cousin, Philippe Robillard in a New Orleans brawl, *GWTW*, 55–56); that three little boys, all dead in infancy, were born to Lady and Planter (*TWDG*, 57, 63, 65) and are buried in the family plot at Tata (as, in fact, is the situation at Tara, all three gravestones bearing the name of "Gerald O'Hara Jr.," *GWTW*, 58); that Garlic was won by Planter in a card game, from a young rake of a planter from St. Simon's Island, Georgia (as was also the case with Pork whom, like Garlic, the St. Simon's gambler offered to buy back, *GWTW*, 46–47; *TWDG*, 51–52).

IV. Randall's Courtroom Cakewalks: Piracy, Parody, and the Legal Response(s) to *The Wind Done Gone*

The effect of this elaborate and sustained textual "borrowing" is to situate, at least for the *literary* sensibility, *The Wind Done Gone* squarely within at least one genre of postmodern metafiction: a kind of recontextualizing replication that might be called, simply, "rewriting." For, with its dense heteroglossia and resonant appropriations, Randall's work is a worthy intertextual successor to such earlier "rewritings" as Jean Rhys' *Wide Sargasso Sea*[36] (a retelling of *Jane Eyre* from the point of view of Rochester's wife, Bertha Mason, the "mad woman in the attic") or Peter Carey's *Jack Maggs*[37] (*Great Expectations*, as retold by Pip's transported convict benefactor, Magwitch).[38] Only that, unlike Jack Maggs or Antoinette Cosway, Cynara is, as noted above, wholly the invention of Randall, and *sui generis* to *The Wind Done Gone*. Not that this originality made much difference to the *legal* sensibility and its *rezeptionaesthetik*. "Wholesale theft"[39] was the ringing denunciation of Frankfurt, Kurnit's Tom Selz, counsel for the Mitchell Trust, in a condemnatory "rush to judgment" with which the court of first

[36] Jean Rhys, *Wide Sargasso Sea* (London: Deutsch, 1966).

[37] Peter Carey, *Jack Maggs* (St Lucia, Queensland: University of Queensland Press, 1997).

[38] This distinguished roster, however, includes less salubrious company. For example, a recent brouhaha has erupted, this time in France, and concerning a very inferior sequel to *Les Miserables – Cosette's Story*. Its publication is being challenged on the grounds that it violates Hugo's "moral rights," now held by his descendants.

[39] "Frankly My Dear They All Give A Damn," Associate Press at http//www.freedforum.org

instance, the U.S. District Court (Northern District of Georgia), not only agreed but also amplified in its censorial rhetoric.[40] For "unabated piracy" (14) was the finding of Mr. Justice Charles Pannell, one that, doubtless, would have delighted Rhett with his piratical Butler grandfather (*GWTW*, 665); and that prompted the court to *slap* a preliminary injunction on *The Wind Done Gone* even faster than the stinging swipe an incensed Scarlett takes at Prissy after her desperate, eleventh-hour confession: "I don't know nothin' 'bout birthin' babies" (*GWTW*, DVD).

In point of fact, though, Prissy may very well know more about "birthin' babies" than Judge Pannell knows about law-and-literature – which isn't saying much. For, despite textual evidence strongly to the contrary and a host of supporting, and *supportive* documentation – including declarations from literary luminaries such as Nobel Prize winner, Toni Morrison,[41] and Harvard-based cultural critic, Henry Louis "Skip" Gates[42] – Judge Pannell accepted the submissions of opposing counsel (Tom Selz, as well as Maura Wogan of Frankfurt, Kurnit), and held *The Wind Done Gone* was a "sequel" (27), to which the "right to write," as it were, is vested solely in the Mitchell Trust: "When the reader of *Gone with the Wind* turns over the last page, he may well wonder what becomes of Ms Mitchell's beloved characters and their romantic, tragic world. Ms. Randall has given us her vision of how to answer those . . . questions. . . . The right to answer those questions . . . however legally belongs to Ms. Mitchell's heirs, not Ms.Randall" (48). Just why this last right of reply to the text's many riddles (the key being: does Scarlett ever win back Rhett?) should lie, exclusively, with Ms. Mitchell's mute heirs is a function as much of the laws of copyright as of inheritance. For fictional characters, "beloved" or otherwise (Jonas Wilkerson? the Slatterys? the Union deserter?), as well as "settings," "themes," and "plots" (10) are, as Pannell states, "copyrightable" (10) – and are, *here*, copyrighted. Indeed, the Mitchell Trust's copyright in *Gone with the Wind* is the one issue not in dispute in this case. Nor, as it turns out here, is Randall's *violation* of that copyright. At least, that is the court's holding, here at first instance, when it found that *The Wind Done Gone*

[40] *Suntrust Bank, as Trustee of the Stephens Mitchell Trusts f/b/o Eugene Muse Mitchell and Joseph Reynolds Mitchell v. Houghton Mifflin Co.*, United States District Court, Northern District of Georgia, Atlanta Division.

[41] "Declaration of Toni Morrison (with curriculum vitae)" at http://www. houghtonmifflinbooks.com

[42] "Declaration of Henry Louis Gates, Jr. (with exhibit A (curriculum vitae) and B (sample passages from *Gone With the Wind*)" at http://www. houghtonmifflinbooks.com

pilfers "fifteen characters" (14) and countless "storylines" (11) and "quotes" (15) that Randall then "renames in some instances but otherwise adopts verbatim, in many instances, those contained in *Gone with the Wind*" (12).

Missing from the judicial analysis here is any sustained or systematic account of the very real points of divergence between *The Wind Done Gone* and *Gone with the Wind*. Of course, the court acknowledges the innovation of Cynara's character (34), and notes, with a significant reservation, the relegation of principal players to the margins of the story – like Other, or Scarlett, banished off-stage.[43] But "parodic transformation" (20)[44]? The court equivocates about and, ultimately, nullifies such a defense – "parody" being a form of constitutionally protected "fair use" – largely because it seems to find, on the whole, not much that is particularly parodic about *The Wind Done Gone*. One suspects that, quite simply, for Judge Pannell, like the plaintiffs (i.e., the Mitchell Trust) before him, the book isn't all that *funny* – a definition of parody that links it with the "slapstick" of Carol Burnett's classic spoof of Scarlett, "dressed to impress" in "Miss Ellen's po'teers" (GWTW, 531) *including* the curtain rod[45]; or that of the British comedy duo, French and Saunders' equally entertaining send-up, with Dawn French, a kerchiefed white Mammy, and Jennifer Saunders, a stuttering Scarlett, stumbling over "Fiddlediddlediddle . . . "[46] – and so on. Some "parodic elements" (31), however, are grudgingly conceded by the court; though, interestingly, this element of parody is found (31) in the depiction of Planter who, for all his Irish blarney, has become "culturally African" (31), the "marionette" (*TWDG*, 63) of his – covertly – much cleverer slave, Pork.[47] Apart from this, supposedly, ridiculous relationship – of a black slave, Figaro-like, besting his white master – the court is as blind as Iustitia herself to most of Randall's transformative parody of Mitchell's text, prompting me to ask my own "unanswered question": did Judge Pannell even read *The Wind Done Gone*? If so, how in the name of Peggy (Mitchell) Marsh could he possibly miss the following: Other's disfigurement from smallpox and her death from either alcoholic mishap and/or

[43] Indeed, that reservation turns this marginalization inside our, rendering Other even more significant to the story proper. Pannell writes: "Other's (relegation) . . . does not cause the reader to ignore her but, rather, demands that the reader pay attention to her . . . " (31).

[44] *Campbell v. Acuff Rose Music Inc*, 510 US 576, 114 S Ct 1164.

[45] "Went with the Wind," Episode 1.20 (1968) from *The Carol Burnett Show* (CBS, 1967–1978).

[46] Episode 5, Season 3 (1990) , *French and Saunders* (UK, 1987–2005).

[47] In addition to the (re)burial of Mammy *between* Planter and Lady, as she was in life – a wedge between them in death as much as in life.

suicidal intent; R.'s increasingly obvious senescence, his aged appearance displacing all memories of the romantic blockade-runner, leaving only an aging roue; Dreamy Gentleman's not-so-closeted homosexuality, thwarted and still pining for his long-dead great love, Miss Priss's brother; and Mealy Mouth's murderous psychosis, the jealous rage of which dispatched that very brother of Priss, as well as aiding and abetting in other criminal fatalities.

This sort of transformation – comic? parodic? critical?: call it what have you – is not confined to *Gone with the Wind's* four central characters; it extends to, indeed *intensifies* with the text's secondary characters and their traits or details. Consider the examples mentioned earlier as "minor": Tara's saintly mistress, Miss Ellen; collectively, the Gerald O'Hara Jr. infants; and Pork, Gerald's loyal and long-serving valet. All three in *The Wind Done Gone* are transmuted into something, as Rhett – quoting Shakespeare – might put it, "rich and strange" (*GWTW*, 759), leaving behind Mitchell's action-packed, though recognizably "real" world for a realm of Southern Gothic that rivals (and may outstrip) the Yoknapatawpha *grotesquerie* of Faulkner's *Absalom, Absalom!*[48] and others. For, in Randall's book, Pork – or Garlic – is exposed, as noted above, as the true mastermind behind "Tata," having engineered his *own* transfer of ownership by drugging the St. Simon's rake before the card game so that he would lose to the oafish, but much more malleable Planter (*TWDG*, 64). The plot grows more *grand guignol* with the O'Hara baby boys, here revealed[49] as the victims of a group infanticide perpetrated by Garlic/Pork and Pallas/Mammy to maintain their hegemony over a feminized (and, therefore, more pliable) household (*TWDG*, 63, 65) Finally, the story well and truly stumbles into Sutpen's Hundred territory when, like Thomas Sutpen's first (and renounced) wife, Lady is "outed" as the great-granddaughter of a Haitian "Negresse" (*TWDG*, 124), an ironic inversion of Ellen's high-born heritage as a French Creole, turning her haughty mother, Grandma Robillard (born Solange Prudhomme, to Haitian planter emigres, *GWTW*, 41) into an "octoroon" and her daughter, Scarlett, into "just a nigger" (*TWDG*, 133).[50]

48 William Faulkner, *Absalom, Absalom!* (New York: Modern Library, 1964).

49 By Miss Priss, who says, "Your Mama killed those boys soon as they were born.... Wha would we a done with a sober white man on this place?" (*TWDG*, 63).

50 And *her* daughter, Precious/Bonnie nothing but a "high yellow gal in a blue velvet riding habit" (*TWDG*, 133).

1. The Civil War in Copyright Law: The Johnny Reb of "Idea" and the "Billy Yank" of Expression (or vice versa)

So, to return to my initial question: how did the court miss all of this? The answer, I hazard, lies in the law itself and, in particular, in a doctrine that has clouded, if not entirely obscured justice's gaze, placing the scales, in this instance, over its eyes rather than in its hands. That doctrine is the axis on which copyright turns, and takes the form of two poles – "expression" and "idea," with the former subject to, and the latter outside the ambit of legal regulation. Not that much is made of this binary, at least here, at first instance, – in sharp contrast to the appellate level where it is reviewed, explicitly and at length.[51] But Pannell's judgment registers, implicitly, the significance of the idea/expression divide when, in response to the searching query of Toni Morrison's declaration ("Who controls how history is imagined?"[52]), he states: "(T)he question before the court is not who gets to write history, but rather whether Ms. Randall can permeate most of her critical work with copyrighted characters, plot and scenes from *Gone with the Wind* in order to correct the 'pain, humiliation and outrage' of the ahistorical representation of the . . . antebellum South" (33). So Randall is free (emancipated?), according to Pannell, to redress the historical record and its "ideas" of slavery, states' rights, and secession; but the realm of fiction, of imagination – that is, "expression" – is off-limits and the private property of the creator, no matter how altered it may subsequently become: "two works," he writes, may present opposing "viewpoints of the same fictional world, but that fails to mitigate the fact that it is the same fictional world" (14).

But what if that "fictional world," in all of its imaginative expression – characters, plot, scenes – comes to stand for, perhaps even instantiate, a place and its past? Here, copyright's idea/expression dichotomy, far from being an axial fixity, its poles, separate and distinct, begins to break down; the boundary between the two becoming blurred, their shared border crossed, their integrity violated – much like a war and its skirmishes between two contiguous, inextricably linked (federated?) jurisdictions. Indeed, there *is* war, a "civil war" going on in the copyright law, with the shattered union of "idea" and "expression" marauding in each others' terrain, carrying on

[51] *Suntrust Bank* v. *Houghton Mifflin Co*, *supra*, note 15 at 10–11.

[52] See "Declaration of Toni Morrison," *supra* note 38.

razzias as if they were "Johnny Reb" and "Billy Yank" – or vice versa. To see, though, how this highly metaphoric account of copyright law plays itself out in practice, take an example close at hand: Mitchell's Scarlett O'Hara and the way in which her very biography mimes the history of Atlanta – and the South writ large. After all, the two – city and character – had their start in 1845, the year of Scarlett's (as well as Other's *and* Cynara's) birth and Atlanta's founding – or so Gerald, never one to let the truth get in the way of a good story,[53] used to tell Scarlett as a child (*GWTW*, 139). Furthermore, Scarlett's breathless trajectory – from planter aristocrat (an "O'Hara of Tara," as put, rather manorially, by Gerald, *GWTW*, 686), to prosperous urban *rentier* (the "well-to-do" widow of Charles Hamilton, with her "town property" and "farmlands," *GWTW*, 152), finally becoming a capitalist mill owner (as the wife, successively, of modest retailer Frank Kennedy; then "riverboat gambler" turned "speculator"/robber baron, Rhett Butler, *GWTW*, 881) – encapsulates, in a single lifetime, Atlanta's steep upward curve from prewar market town to wartime *entrepot*, winding up, in its final incarnation, as a postwar industrial-commercial boomtown. And even though Atlanta's story is scaled on a macro-level, and Scarlett's, on a micro-level, both proclaim, in unison, "The South shall rise again!" One could go even a step further and say: Scarlett *is* the South – a prosopopoeia of it, or a synecdoche, the part standing for the whole. Which is precisely *why* Alice Randall chose this particular fiction, this unique "expression" to parody (and why, doubtless, Judge Pannell objected so strenuously to it): because it is so thoroughly saturated by, so completely imbued with an "idea" of history, both temporal and spatial, that it answers Toni Morrison's anything but rhetorical question, misquoted by the court as "who gets to write history?" The answer? The Confederacy, and its *cause*, that's who!

2. Whistlin' Dixie, *Neo*-Confederate Style: The Return of "the Cause" by and Through the Law

That "the Cause" of the Confederacy lost the historical (Civil) war, but won the ongoing, ideological battle is a truism borne out by more than just

[53] And corrected by the text's omniscient – Mitchell? – narrator who advises that Atlanta, previously Terminus, then Marthasville was "christened" as such in 1845, the year of Scarlett's birth *and* christening.

the persistent popularity of *Gone with the Wind*. Think of other "southern fried" Civil War fictions like the recent *Gods and Generals* (best seller[54] and movie[55]) or *Cold Mountain* (again best seller[56] and movie[57]) – as well as the '80s TV miniseries[58] (and book[59]) *North and South*, the '50s film epic[60] (and book[61]) *Raintree County*, the '30s Academy Award winner *Jezebel*,[62] to name just a few. Of late, though, the Confederate cause has looked beyond video, celluloid, and literary media, turning instead to the legal and law-making arenas of courts and legislature. This "going to law" has been, to a certain degree, *reactive*, and prompted in response to the strenuous lobbying efforts to resignify the Southern "imaginary"[63] – removing, for example, the Confederate battle flag, the "Southern Cross,"[64] from state legislatures and flags[65] – carried out by well-established organizations like the NAACP. Recognizing in the NAACP a formidable opponent and one well worth emulating in its tactics – lawsuits rather than lynchings, counterclaims rather than cross burnings – the Confederate cause has undergone what might be called an extreme makeover. Dropping the nostalgia, as Rhett might put it (GWTW, DVD), of the "moonlight 'n magnolias" kind (the stock-in-trade of "genealogical" organizations like the United Daughters of the Confederacy), as much as the redneck violence of "Cracker culture"

54 Jeff Shaara, *Gods and Generals* (New York: Ballantine Books, 1989) .
55 *Gods and Generals*, dir. R. F. Maxwell (2003, Antietam Filmworks).
56 Charles Frazer, *Cold Mountain*: A *Novel* (New York: Vintage, 1998).
57 *Cold Mountain*, dir. Anthony Minghella (2003, Miramax Films).
58 *North and South*, dir. Richard T Heffron (1985, Warner Bros Television).
59 John Jakes, *North and South Trilogy Series* (New York: Signet, 2000).
60 *Raintree County*, dir. Edward Dymtryk (1957, Metro-Goldwyn-Mayer).
61 Ross Lockridge Jr, *Raintree County* (Boston: Houghton-Mifflin, 1984).
62 *Jezebel*, dir. William Wyler (1938, Warner Bros).
63 Alexander Tsesis, "The Problem of Confederate Symbols: A Thirteenth Amendment Approach" (2002) 75 *Temple L. Rev*. 540.
64 The unofficial flag of the Confederacy, and adopted in battle – at the behest of Gen Beauregard – because the official "Stars 'n Bars" was too easily confused with the Union's "Stars and Stripes." A popular variant of the battle flag, if bumper stickers are anything to go by, is the "Navy Jack."
65 A campaign that started as far back as 1988 when the NAACP filed a suit against Alabama Governor Guy Hunt, protesting that the flying of the "Stars 'n Bars" atop the legislature buildings violated their constitutional rights, *NAACP v. Hunt*, 891 F.2nd 1555 (11th Cir. 1990). Other challenges followed: in Georgia (*Coleman v. Miller*, 912 F.Supp. 522 (N. D. Ga. 1996), aff'd 117 3d 527), South Carolina etc. The results were disappointing, and affirmed the flying of the flag. But change did arise, doubtless, because of these actions: in Georgia, the flag was altered; in South Carolina, it was moved to a less conspicuous spot. See Bennett Capers, "Flags" (2004) 48 *Howard Law Journal* 121 See also: James Forman Jr., "Driving Dixie Down: Removing the Confederate Flag from Southern State Capitols," (1991–1992) 101 *Yale Law Journal* 505, 504.

(associated with outfits like the Klan in its '50s and '60s incarnation), the Cause (re)emerged in the 1990s, slickly rebranded as "neo-confederate," mindful of its manners, appearance, and public image; but embracing a tough, hard-line ethic of "No surrender" coded as "heritage" and ready for a long, protracted *legal* war. Since then, a Cause-driven counterblast (to adapt an overworked meteorological metaphor) has been gusting through states south of the Mason-Dixon line, determined to blow away any challenge to all icons – monuments, street names, *and* flags – associated with "a civilization of Cavaliers and Cotton Fields" (*GWTW*, DVD) supposedly (but anything but) "gone with the wind."

To that end, actions were launched – and won – against certain Southern state governments (e.g., Maryland,[66] North Carolina,[67] Virginia[68]) for their refusal to customize (*a la* Dukes of Hazzard?) license plates with the battle flag for members of an organization known as the Sons of Confederate Veterans. This and other neo-confederate outfits, like the League of the South, have brought actions defending the high-profile display of the battle flag in a range of contexts: as school insignia, on the football field, and even woven into an evening dress.[69] This last case, only recently launched, argues for "the right" of Russell, Kentucky, honor student, May Jacqueline Duty, to wear a sequined gown of her own design, emblazoned with the battle flag, to her high-school prom[70] – apparel attesting to a neo-confederate fashion sense, more Ellie Mae Clampitt than Scarlett O'Hara! The case, however, is significant for more than its profiling of white trash couture:

[66] *Sons of the Confederate Veterans Inc v. Glendening*, 954 F. Supp. 1099 (D. Md 1997).

[67] *North Carolina Division of the Sons of the Confederacy v. Faulkner* 509 S.E.2d 207 (N.C. Ct. App. 1998).

[68] See Jack A Guggenheim and Jed M Silversmith, "Confederate License Plates ath the Constitutional Crossroads: Vanity Plates, Special Registration Organization Plates, Bumper Stickers, Viewpoints, Vulgarity and the First Amendment (2000) *University of Miami Law Review* 563; James C. Colling, "General Lee Speaking: Are License Plate Designs Out of the State's Control? A Cricial Analysis of the Fourth Circuit's Decision in *Sons of Confederate Veteran, Inc.* v. *Comm'r of the Va. Dept of Motor Vehicles*," (2003–2004) 12 *Geo. Mason L. Rev.* 442.

[69] For overviews of these developments, see: Michael J. Henry, "Student Display of the Confederate Flag in Public Schools" (2004) 33 *Journal of Law and Education* 4, 573; James M. Dedman, "At Daggers Drawn: The Confederate Flag and the School Classroom – A Case Study of a Broken First Amendment Formula" (2001) 53 *Baylor L. Rev.* 4, 877. Kathleen Riley, "The Long Shadow of the Confederacy in America's Schools: State Sponsored Use of Confederate Symbols in the Wake of *Brown v. Board of Education* (2001–2002) 10 *William & Mary Bill of Rights Journal* 2, 525; Ronald J. Rychlak, "Civil Rights, Confederate Flags, and Political Correctness: Free Speech and Race Relations on Campus" (1991–1992), 66 *Tul. L. Rev.* 1412.

[70] "Kentucky Division of the Sons of Confederate Veterans Support Jacqueline Duty Confederate Prom Dress Law Suit," Web site of the Southern Party of Georgia at http://spofga.org

its significance lies in the identity of Ms. Duty's lawyer, Earl Ray Neal, and the organization he works for, the Southern Law Resources Center (SLRC). For the SLRC is the very storm center of the neo-confederate movement, the brainchild of North Carolina-based attorney, Kirk Lyons,[71] long a stalwart of Southern "exceptionalism" and a familiar figure on the bizarre and murky landscape of the American Far Right (a former intimate of the Christian Identity leadership, and previously linked with various paramilitary militia groups, etc.).

Not, though, for Lyons and his group, the covert, vigilante, "Death Squad"-style initiatives (bombings, shootings) of his erstwhile fascist friends – or, for that matter, even the heavily "whitewashed" operations of *Gone with the Wind's* Klan that, for all the text's strained ("It isn't to be borne!", *GWTW*, 633[72]) and *strange* justifications (given Mitchell's cradle Catholicism and the Klan's vehement anti-Romanism), are *still* clandestine and violently criminal: "All of them, all the men she [i.e., Scarlett] knew [i.e., in the Klan], even the drowsy-eyed Ashley and fidgety old Frank, were like that underneath – murderous ... if the need arose" (*GWTW*, 633). The law rather than (hooded) criminality, however, is Lyons & Co.'s modus operandi; and, as such, SLRC members wear their legal credentials (JDs, bar admissions, professional memberships) ensleeved and parade their Cause publicly, both curially and legislatively – a kind of "gentrification" that not only returns the Cause to its *ancien regime* roots (as consisting of "gentlemen" rather than "rabble," *GWTW*, 111) but also updates itself, theoretically, in terms of the most current and *recherche* thinking of the Western Marxist Left. Consider "The New Dixie Manifesto" of the League of the South, the forerunner and fellow traveler of the SLRC, which states the Cause's case in language virtually (if inadvertently?) lifted, especially in its conceit of imperium, from Hardt and Negri[73]: "What has been a genuinely federal union has been turned into a multicultural, continental

[71] See, "In the Lyons Den" from the Intelligence Report of the Southern Poverty Law Center (previously Klanwatch) at www. splcentre.org

[72] Whitewashed, in the sense, that the reader does not actually see the Klan lynching their victims, but as to their overarching *animus* the text is quite clear. Mitchell uses the character of fugitive from Yankee justice, Joe Fontaine, wanted for killing both a black man (Mimosa's former foreman, Eustis, who was bold to his sister-in-law, Sally Monroe Fontaine) and a Carpetbagger (Jonas Wilkerson), here as the ventriloquizer: "'And if they give the Negroes the vote, it's the end of us. ... Soon we'll be having nigger judges, nigger legislators – black apes out of the jungle'" (*GWTW*, 630).

[73] Michael Hardt and Antonio Negri, *Empire* (Cambridge, MA: Harvard University Press, 2001).

Empire ruled from Washington by federal agencies and under the thumb of the federal judiciary."[74] Given this sort of rhetoric, no wonder that 'the jurisprudential' and 'the governmental' figure so prominently on the neo-confederate agenda – an agenda that ranges from the (delusional) heights of Southern secession (and the reconstitution of the Confederacy[75]) to the lows of orthographic triteness (and the readoption of Oxford spelling conventions[76]). But behind all the flummery here of secession and spelling, of states' rights and Southern pride, there lies one real – and completely malignant *cause*: that of the restoration (preservation?), by and through law, of *white* supremacy.

V. Killing Katie Scarlett: Alice Randall, Alexandra Ripley, and the Revenge of Melanie/Mealy Mouth

It is precisely against this cultural, political, and, especially, *legal* background – of Southern "whiteness" *redivivus* and the return of the repressed Cause – that Randall's book must be situated. Indeed, she does so herself; in her declaration to the District Court, Randall contextualizes *The Wind Done Gone* in terms of the legal "controversy surrounding the flying of the Confederate flag"[77] and the "image of the South"[78] this flag and other emblems – like *Gone with the Wind* – conveyed: "an image where blacks are buffoonish, lazy, drunk . . . physically disgusting."[79] But such a willful and wanton misrepresentation is not the only source of Randall's ire – or impetus in writing her book. Of course, in its conjuring up of a South that includes Frederick Douglass *and* Miss Priss, *The Wind Done Gone* corrects *Gone with the Wind's* slanted and ahistorical record; but, even more than that, Randall's book addresses the "not-said" of Southern history, occupying, in the astute words of Toni Morrison, the latter's "narrative . . . silences"[80]

74 Michael Hill and Thomas Fleming, "The New Dixie Manifesto: States Rights Will Rise Again," League of the South at http://leagueofthesouth.net

75 See the petition, "States Rights, Secession and Big Government" on the League of the South website at http://www.petitiononline.com

76 Embraced as more in sync with Southern sensibilities than the "Yankee" spelling of Noah Webster. The only item on the New Dixie agenda with which I – a product of a number of systems adhering to Anglo-Commonwealth spelling conventions (Canadian born, British educated, Australian based) – have some sympathy. See, e.g., http://fireater.org

77 "Declaration of Alice Randall" at http://www. houghtonmifflinbooks.com

78 *Id.*

79 *Ibid.*

80 "Declaration of Toni Morrison," *supra* note 28.

not only in the way it endows *Gone with the Wind's* slave and ex-slave characters with an interior life, but in how it engages the rich variety of what postcolonial theory has called "negritude" silenced, even suppressed by Mitchell's text. After all, "Where", asks Randall, are "the mulattos on Tara"[81] – a fair question, particularly, for someone who counts among her ancestors slave owners – specifically, antebellum planter and Confederate officer, General Edmund Pettus[82] – as much as slaves. But while the Old South's mixed race progeny are absent from the *dramatis personae* of *Gone with the Wind*, they do not go entirely unreferenced. Indeed, it is sharp-tongued Grandma Fontaine, "Ole Miss" and the matriarch of "Mimosa," one of Tara's neighboring plantations, who says to Scarlett of the slave girls who have run off with Union troopers, in the wake of Sherman's march, that "all they'll get will be yellow babies" (*GWTW*, 439), adding, "Don't pull such a shocked face. . . . God knows we've seen mulatto babies before this" (*GWTW*, 439). Or, at least, *heard* of – as here – if not actually *seen*.

But if mulattos are nowhere to be *seen* in *Gone with the Wind*, then they are not even *heard* of in its sequel, Alexandra Ripley's (justly) much maligned, *Scarlett*. This silence is hardly surprising. That is, if one is aware of the stringent requirements and strict regulations imposed on all potential follows-up to *Gone with the Wind*, and their prospective authors – as Pat Conroy,[83] as well as Emma Tennant[84] and Anne Edwards,[85] have found out to their dismayed chagrin. For all three had to comply with, as a condition precedent to their book contract, an *apartheid*-like ban, worthy of Kirk Lyons himself, and one that the Mitchell Trust lawyers, both in-house and instructed, have enforced with an officious punctilio and dogged determination rivaling that of Mammy on manners. Only here the negative bar is not some prohibition concerning lady-like deportment – not showing

81 "Declaration of Alice Randall," *supra*. Note 72; see also: "A Conversation with Alice Randall," *supra*, note 23.

82 "A Conversation with Alice Randall," *id*.

83 After Ripley's clunker, *Scarlett*, came out, and Tennant's manuscript was rejected (see below), author Pat Conroy was approached by the Mitchell Trust to write a further sequel – this time about Rhett. With the breakdown of negotiations there, St. Martin's Press, the London-based publishing house and the holder of sequelization rights, has one last chance to secure a writer before forfeiting their rights and sequelization reverting to the Trust. See "Declaration of Pat Conroy," *supra*. note 12.

84 Tennant's reasonably well-received sequel to *Pride and Prejudice*, *Pemberley*, commended her to the Mitchell Trust as a suitable candidate to write *Gone with the Wind's* follow-up. Her manuscript, *Tara*, was rejected as unsaleable by St. Martin's Press.

85 Engaged in the '70s by the Trust to write a sequel, following on from her successful biography of Vivien Leigh. Her manuscript was rejected.

"your buzzum before 3 o'clock" (*GWTW*, 39), not "gobbl(ing) lak a hog" (*GWTW*, 38), or not riding "astraddle" (*GWTW*, 964), but one that goes to the very crux of the South's – and indeed America's – complicated and contentious race relations: that is, *no* miscegenation.[86] This is a taboo that, thirty years after *Loving v. Virginia*,[87] is firmly, even fiercely, upheld by the lawyers of the Mitchell Trust, either expressly like its Atlanta-based counsel or, impliedly, by its New York litigators. And one to which Alexandra Ripley accedes by writing race out of her continuation's story-line, dispatching Scarlett, after some dalliances in Charleston (with Rhett's family) and Savannah (with the Robillards), to her father's homeland, Ireland. Though, as it turns out, Scarlett goes to an Ireland that Gerald O'Hara would never recognize: more "Finian's Rainbow" than Fenian, a "faith 'n begorrah" fantasy populated by Scarlett's close-knit kin, as well as quaint cottagers, colorful eccentrics, and elegant "Ascendancy" squires – all of them whiter than white, and with nary a black face to be seen.

This "deracialization" of *Gone with the Wind* – its "gating" in Ballyhara as a kind of *faux*-Celtic theme park (Ballykissangel?) – has been commented on by others: notably historian Jim Cullen.[88] I want to argue, *in tandem* with Cullen's acute analysis that, in decontextualizing Scarlett, Ripley not only deracializes the narrative but she also drains her eponym of its characterological core. Consider how, under Ripley's treatment, Scarlett undergoes a startling diminution that one *could* describe as a "maturation," but that smacks – at least for me – of a "Melly-ization." For Scarlett not only exhibits a sense of shame here[89]; she seems to grow a conscience,[90] and most telling of all, develops a desperate love for *her* love-child,[91] Cat, the product of a

86 *Id.* at 1, 3.

87 *Loving v. Virginia*, 388 U.S. 10, S.Ct. 1817; 18 L.Ed. 2d 1010.

88 Jim Cullen, *The Civil War in Popular Culture: A Reusable Past*, 105–106. See also: Tara McPherson, "Seeing in Black and White: Gender and Racial Visibility from *Gone With the Wind* to *Scarlett*." In Jenkins, H., McPherson, T., Shattuc, J. (eds.), *Hop on Pop: The Politics and Pleasures of Popular Culture* (Durham, NC: Duke, 2002).

89 During a dark night of the soul, Scarlett muses, "Have I ever in my life paid attention to what I was doing? Have I – even once – thought about the consequences? Despair and shame gripped Scarlett" (*Scarlett*, 481).

90 "All the impetuous, unconsidered errors of her life crowded around Scarlett.... Oh, God, forgive me, I never thought once about what I was doing to them, about what they were feeling. I hurt and hurt and hurt all of them, because I didn't stop to think" (*Scarlett*, 481)

91 "The baby opened her eyes. They stared directly into Scarlett's. And Scarlett felt love. Without conditions, without demands, without reasons, without questions, without bounds, without reserve, without self" (*Scarlett*, 535).

brief, and literally stormy "brief encounter" with Rhett – all pathetically "pathetic fallacy" and raised on the sly, *a la Tenant of Wildfell Hall*, in Ireland. Indeed, one could say that Ripley's Scarlett represents "the revenge of Melly," transforming one of the larger-than-life icons of popular culture into a kind of suburban "dixie chick" whose "good ol' gal" adventures in life and love are splashed over the screens and pages of other "Southern Comfort"-soaked fictions as *Sweet Home Alabama*,[92] *Divine Secrets of the Ya Ya Sisterhood*,[93] and *Steel Magnolias*.[94] No wonder *Scarlett* was such a flop as a sequel, but a success as a miniseries because with its palely imitative characters and its dumbed-down narrative – part bodice-ripper; part *Dynasty/Dallas* camp – it approximates that of a "fancy dress" sitcom, perfect for the "B list" casting of Joanne Whalley-Kilmer (Scarlett) and Timothy Dalton (Rhett), and proving the truth of the old Marxist adage about Napoleon III – and echoed by Rhett[95] – "first time as tragedy, second time as farce." And, to my mind, the effect of Ripley as *farceur* is, ultimately, *lethal*; her inadvertent satire, both as sequel and miniseries, does thoroughly – as if she was the psychopathic Mealy Mouth on a rampage – what Randall does only half-heartedly: she kills off Scarlett by laughing her to death.

So the *real* parody lies with Ripley's book and its translation *to* and *by* that most demystifying of experiences, television. Seen from this vantage then, *The Wind Done Gone* does not so much parodically bury as *praise* Scarlett who, after all, is described by Randall elsewhere and variously as "ambitious," "resilient," "hard working," and "hard loving"[96]: a figure of feminine strength, soliciting admiration, even awe. A feeling that, in turn, is displaced onto, and replaced by Cynara who can be seen as the dramatic vehicle allowing, ironically, Scarlett *to live again*. Admittedly, Cynara is much more literate than Scarlett and has far more insight into people than she does; but as *The Wind Done Gone* unfolds, her character assumes,

92 *Sweet Home Alabama*, dir. Andy Tenant (2002, Touchstone Pictures).

93 *Divine Secrets of the Ya Ya Sisterhood*, dir. Callie Khouri (Gaylord Films, 2002); Rebecca Wells, *Divine Secrets of the Ya Ya Sisterhood* (New York: Harper Paperbacks, 2004).

94 *Steel Magnolias*, dir. Herbert Ross (Rastar Films, 1989).

95 "That weak imitation of Napoleon," as Rhett refers to him, dismissing any chance that France might recognize the Confederacy – especially when it so thoroughly relishes the opportunity afforded by America's Civil War to build, contra the Monroe doctrine, its own client-state in Mexico (GWTW, 235).

96 "A Conversation with Alice Randall," *supra*., note 23.

more and more, the functions of Other, assimilating many of her features so that the two figures begin to bleed into each other, becoming indistinct, if not identical. Think of these equivalences: both Cynara and Scarlett suffer through failed and/or thwarted love affairs (Other, for Conyers; Scarlett, for Ashley); both marry men they do not love (Cynara, with R.; Scarlett, with Charles, followed by Frank, then Rhett); both have children they lose (Cynara, by fostering; Scarlett, by death – Bonnie – or neglect – Wade, Ella); and both inherit homes – Tata and Tara – at which neither of them ultimately live (Tata is left, jointly, to Miss Priss and Cynara's son by Conyers; Tara, to Suellen and her Cracker husband, Will Benteen). These analogues are not as strange as they may seem at first blush because Randall's announced intention in writing *The Wind Done Gone* was, not so much to supplant Scarlett and her story, as to "supplement" it: "As I got older . . . I come to realize that the world of the South was my world . . . and I realized that I came from a storytelling people. . . . And I wanted to write among them. . . . I feel this book bows to Faulkner, and Capote, and Lee and says 'Yes, and this too is true. There is more. Listen and I'll tell.'"[97]

This claim, I argue, complicates, if not confounds the appellate court's finding that *The Wind Done Gone* "shatters *Gone with the Wind's* window on life in the antebellum and Civil War South."[98] For Randall, a self-described "not-so-tragic mulatto,"[99] writes under the sign of "irony"[100] rather than critique: an irony intent on and in releasing a "doubleness" inscribed in Scarlett's story, and *authorized*, in the end, by Mitchell. After all, doesn't Randall's portrayal of Mealy Mouth's bloodthirstiness make more sense of the demure Melanie's perplexing and unqualified approval of the Union deserter's murder ("Scarlett, you killed him. I'm glad you killed him", *GWTW*, DVD) and, later in the novel, her sponsorship of ex-convict (and wife murderer), mountaineer Archie? And isn't Randall's "outing" of Dreamy Gentleman's same-sex desire a logical inference drawn from all the '30s innuendo about Ashley's masculinity, virility, etc.? Indeed, does not Mitchell's text, in these instances and elsewhere – Rhett's dissipation, Scarlett's incipient alcoholism – underwrite and endorse, on its own terms, Randall's alternative account? Even *The Wind Done Gone's*

[97] *Id.*
[98] *Suntrust Bank* v. *Houghton Mifflin Co*, *supra*, note 15.
[99] "A Conversation with Alice Randall," *supra*, note 23.
[100] "Alice Randall document," *supra*, note 11.

most fanciful flights have an air of likelihood, explaining the otherwise inexplicable – like the strange symmetry (*a la* Brady Bunch?) of the three dead O'Hara boys and their three surviving sisters; or the bizarre ban on Ellen and Philippe's relationship, and the agreement of the snobbish, blue-blooded Robillards to the suit of the entirely unsuitable Gerald O'Hara, "'a new man'" (*GWTW*, 53) with a "lack of family" (*GWTW*, 56). The alternative answers – "foul play" or "passing" – seem *quite* possible, even if not entirely probable. What most definitely *is* probable, though, is the representation of Tata/Tara as Garlic/Pork's creation, a fictional rendering of an indisputable fact: that slave labor, physical and psychic, built the Old South.

VI. "Law, law, law – this law talk is spoiling all the fun at every party": Scarlett's Choice and Driving (the Cause of) Old Dixie Down

In positing this kind of countertext, Randall highlights and teases out the fractured duality that lies at the center of *Gone with the Wind* and constitutes its *real* "War Between the States." Nowhere is that division more clearly in evidence than in the person of Scarlett herself, the most (in)famous split self – barring Tolkien's Gollum – in twentieth-century cult fiction. Even at the very opening of the novel, when Scarlett is at her most foolishly flounced, she is described as a character internally at war with herself, her surface "sweet, charming and giddy" while her core is "self willed, vain and obstinate" (*GWTW*, 61). That conflict is externalized, increasingly, throughout *Gone with the Wind*, with Scarlett attracting, initially, quiet disapproval (dancing at the Bazaar; abandoning mourning; shirking her duties at the hospital); then open censure (snagging her sister's beau; running a successful business; riding a buggy on her own); and finally ending up an "outlaw" (*GWTW*, 841), both literally (making good on her hunger-defying promise to "lie, steal, cheat or kill," *GWTW*, DVD) and figuratively (having "outraged" every tenet of her class's code: "(r)everence for the Confederacy, honor to the veterans, loyalty to the old forms, pride in poverty, open hands to friends and undying hatred to Yankees," *GWTW*, 823). Although this account of Scarlett's career suggests a gradual escalation of outlawry, the text makes it pretty clear, from its start, her enormous criminogenic potential, not the least of which is her utter contempt for the Cause: "Somehow . . . the white of devotion to the cause that was still shining on every face seemed – why it just seemed silly! . . . she knew that the Cause meant nothing to her . . . (and) (t)he war didn't seem to be a holy affair, but a nuisance" (*GWTW*, 169–70). In fact, during the filmic flight from Atlanta, Scarlett's contempt becomes open hostility, voicing anti-Confederate sentiments: "They make me sick," she says of the retreating army, "all of them getting us into this with their swaggering and boasting" (*GWTW*, DVD).

Thus, Scarlett O'Hara, *the* iconic figure of the Old South is, in fact, one of its most formidable adversaries, embodying all the values antagonistic to its Cause, and, doubtless, "ready to drive Old Dixie down" – *if*, of course, it redounded to her advantage. "Selfish and shrewd," says Rhett admiringly of Scarlett, "and able to look things in the eyes and call them by their names" (*GWTW*, DVD). Indeed, so much is made, by book and film, of Scarlett's ruthless pragmatism, relentless money-grubbing, showy vulgarity, and pushy social climbing that one might well wonder with Mrs Elsing, Mammy, et al., if she *is* Miss Ellen's daughter (*GWTW*, 841, 532). Or, for that matter, a Southerner; because throughout *Gone with the Wind*, she is described in terms that insistently "Yankee-ify" her as part of "a race of dollar lovers" (*GWTW* 169). All of which is to say that maybe Frankfurt, Kurnit are not very far removed from the spirit of *Gone with the Wind* as this essay suggested at its outset. Indeed, Scarlett anticipates them textually, carving out a place for them in the narrative by instantiating their very values; and Frankfurt, Kurnit, in turn, not only defend Scarlett and her story but they also *enact* it, becoming an avatar of Scarlett in their aggressive prosecution on behalf of the Mitchell Trust, going to any and all lengths for their client. So Frankfurt, Kurnit *is* Scarlett, and Scarlett *is* Frankfurt, Kurnit. That is to say, the law has become the outlaw and vice versa, rendering indeterminate any clear line between right and wrong. This in turn raises the distinct possibility that the very legal process itself – namely, litigating in *Gone with the Wind's* "cause" – may, itself, flip over and turn into something else: a criminal act that threatens to destroy what it purports to defend.

Not a bad thing as it turns out. For by chasing every last nickel, by challenging every supposed copyright infringement, and, especially, by enforcing all anachronistic conditions precedent on race and sexuality, Frankfurt, Kurnit (as well as Anderson and Clarke) will have achieved Scarlett's ontic status as a self-combusting paradox, becoming at once "Yankee" mercenaries *and* "Confederate" racists; and undoing, in this unholy alliance of the worst of both possible worlds – of both North and South – not only the Cause of the Confederacy but *their own* "causeless" cause lawyering. Here the latter's professional neutrality – fighting, as they would argue, selflessly, for the cause of their client – is now exposed as thoroughly mired in, and tainted by a racist and sexist quagmire; whereas the former's "gracious plenty" (*TWDG*, 4) – as Randall calls the Old South's *douceur de vivre* – is nothing more than another form of exploitative exchange. Both are judged and found wanting – and all to the good too. After all, isn't it about time that "whiteness" stopped, not only sentimentalizing the regime of "Master and Slave" (*GWTW*, DVD) but also *justifying* that delusion – as legally defensible and worthy of curial/jurisprudential protection? And isn't it time that firms defending the Mitchell Trust – like Frankfurt, Kurnit – acknowledged their complicity, however "inadvertent," with Kirk Lyons and *his* Cause of white supremacy, instead of hiding under the guise of intellectual property's putative causelessness? Finally, isn't it time for a profession that purports to be causeless – that is, the unbiased, detached, nonjudgmental profession of *law* – take a good hard look at the causes, lawful or otherwise, its very causelessness embraces? I close this series of (largely rhetorical) questions by leaving *le dernier cri*, "the last word" on causes (and causelessness) to *the* voice of skepticism in *Gone with the Wind*, and one that is, perhaps, the closest to Mitchell's own: that "rapscallion" (*GWTW*, 584), Rhett Butler, who says to Scarlett, as the grim news of Gettysburg pours in with its endless lists of Confederate dead and wounded, "The Cause, Scarlett, the Cause. The Cause of living in the past is dying before us in the present" (*GWTW*, DVD). So here's to living in the present, one that is, I caution, neither cause-ful *nor* causeless, but that is all too aware of the manifold and multiple ethical choices that confront lawyers, judges, and jurisprudes. Here's, then, not only to that present but also to a more ethically informed future, a more choice-responsible tomorrow because, after all, as Scarlett herself might put it, tomorrow *is* another day.

2

Purpose-Driven Lawyers: Evangelical Cause Lawyering and the Culture War

Cultural Lives of Cause Lawyers

Kevin R. den Dulk

I. Introduction

The trappings of a typical lawyer's office – legal texts on a shelf, files here and there, a diploma on the wall – were scarcely evident when I visited a prominent evangelical attorney in his office in 1999. He devoted less desk space to legal work than to bobble heads and plastic figurines from popular films and television. A large poster of Bob Dylan hung on the wall behind his chair. A mask of then-President Clinton sat on a bust on a nearby table, topped with a Rastafarian wig. His bookshelf was as likely to display Kerouac or Tolstoy as *Black's Law Dictionary*. Indeed, the office was doubly dissonant: not only did it flaunt lawyerly conventions but it also belied the stereotype of the evangelical as withdrawn from the broader culture. The entire scene appeared as a paean to mass culture, and in some respects our interview confirmed the impression. The attorney was clearly immersed in modern art, music, and literature.

Yet his exposure to these cultural expressions was not without a critical edge; I discovered very soon into our interview that the artifacts around him represented his own cultural ambivalence. On the one hand, he was fascinated intellectually by modern culture and enjoyed experiencing it. On the other hand, he envisioned that culture as reinforcing a perspective about the human condition that was both deeply flawed and dangerously influential. He saw culture as all-encompassing and directed toward a purpose, and that purpose is for better or worse; there is no escape from culture's grip and no gray area or indifference in its message. The problem, he surmised, is that American culture had taken a turn for the worse. His religious faith required a response.

This essay examines the evangelical cause lawyer as culture warrior. The language of culture war has often been a convenient rhetorical hook for scholars of the so-called Christian Right; books with such titles as *Onward Christian Soldiers*, *God's Warriors*, *Religion and the Culture Wars*, or *Marching to the Millenium* are standard fare.[1] But the culture war is also an important symbol for many evangelicals themselves – evangelicals who have a sense of alienation from mass culture and a desire to transform it. It is no coincidence, for example, that the man I visited was both a lawyer and a student of culture. He had wedded cultural critique to the politics of rights – or, more precisely, cultural critique enveloped his practice of the politics of rights. And he was not alone. Many evangelical lawyers use the culture war trope as both a marker of their own identity and a rallying cry for legal mobilization. In addition, these lawyers have been remarkably adept as cultural producers themselves. They have appropriated certain modes of cultural expression – from authoring nonfiction and novels to producing radio programming and video documentaries – to define their place in the culture war.

I begin with a discussion of the concept of culture war itself, but not with the intention of weighing in on the active debate about the reality of that "war" in mass politics. My primary purpose is to generate several propositions about how the concept frames the self-consciousness of evangelical attorneys and shapes their tactics. These propositions lead to an examination of the battle lines in the culture war – that is, how evangelicals use a populist rhetoric of conflict – and especially the identification of a "secularist" enemy – to connect the culture war to the politics of rights. I conclude by suggesting that the symbolic use of the culture war leads to some potential results that can undermine its populist appeal. More specifically, I explore what happens if evangelicals perceive that the war has fewer combatants than they initially thought. Some evangelical activists and attorneys have indeed reached that conclusion, which I suggest has led

[1] Clyde Wilcox, *God's Warriors: The Christian Right in Twentieth-Century America* (Baltimore: Johns Hopkins University Press, 1992); Clyde Wilcox, *Onward Christian Soldiers? The Religious Right in American Politics* (Boulder, CO: Westview, 2000); John C. Green, James L. Guth, Corwin E. Smidt, and Lyman A. Kellstedt, *Religion and the Culture Wars: Dispatches from the Front* (Lanham, MD: Rowman and Littlefield, 1996); John C. Green, Mark Rozell, and Clyde Wilcox, *The Christian Right in American Politics: Marching to the Millennium* (Washington, DC: Georgetown University Press, 2003).

to heightened interest in the minoritarian politics of rights and the emergence of a heroic self-image among cause lawyers within the evangelical subculture.

The cause lawyering literature, which has explored, among other things, the interplay of rights-advocacy with social movements,[2] underlies much of this analysis. But it is important to note at the outset that the idea of lawyer-as-culture-warrior complicates the concept of cause lawyering. As the title of this chapter suggests – and as I discuss more fully below – "purposive" lawyering may better describe the phenomenon of evangelical rights-advocacy, because evangelical attorneys often think of specific causes as derivative of weightier purposes. Moreover, like elite activists in the movement, evangelical lawyers see the tactic of rights-advocacy as only one means of serving these purposes, which has liberated these "warriors" to try their hand at cultural production that goes beyond the practice of law to such roles as novelist, documentarian, or musician. They do not engage in nonlegalistic tactics merely because they see those tactics as "realistic and actionable."[3] They perceive their cultural efforts as *obligatory*, and hence they have not ceded the use of those tactics to other movement activists.

II. Lawyering for a Purpose in the Culture War

"Culture war" is a powerful metaphor. The scholarly proponents of the culture war thesis tell an elegant story about a widespread dualism in American public life, a conflict over values with lines drawn between two fundamental worldviews. The most prominent academic proponent of the thesis, sociologist James Davidson Hunter, describes these worldviews as "progressive" versus "orthodox."[4] Progressivism is characterized by a modern and urbanist spirit; its adherents are often secular, and they are generally open to unconventional or "alternative" understandings of morality and

[2] Austin Sarat and Stuart Scheingold, *Cause Lawyers and Social Movements* (Palo Alto, CA: Stanford University Press, 2006).

[3] Michael McCann and Helena Silverstein, "Rethinking Law's 'Allurements': A Relational Analysis of Social Movement Lawyers in the United States," in *Cause Lawyering: Political Commitments and Professional Responsibilities*, eds. Austin Sarat and Stuart Scheingold (New York: Oxford, 1998), p. 281.

[4] James Davidson Hunter, *Culture Wars: The Struggle to Define America* (New York: Basic Books, 1992).

family life. In contrast, the orthodox are overwhelmingly religious, they live largely in rural and suburban areas, and they are vigorously supportive of traditionalist views of morality and family. The distinction between the progressive and orthodox worldview is perhaps best summarized in terms of the concept of moral *authority*, particularly whether one accepts a traditionalist system of morality based in the "external, definable, and transcendent."[5]

Hunter's categories have decidedly religious overtones, and for some observers the culture war was indeed inflamed by profound changes in American religion over the past half-century. Whereas in the 1950s Will Herberg, in the title of his seminal work on sociology of American religion, could speak succinctly (and in many respects accurately) of "Protestant, Catholic, Jew," thirty years later those divisions had less power in explaining the role of religion in public life.[6] Robert Wuthnow, in his own landmark study, suggests that by the 1980s American religion had been restructured, such that certain similarities of worldview cut across the older religious traditions, thereby creating new "symbolic boundaries" among religionists.[7] In short, religious tradition matters less today than religious tradition*alism*.[8] Hence traditionalist Catholics and evangelical Protestants are more likely to have common cause with each other than with modernists from within their own traditions – and they are mobilizing around these commonalities to fight the culture war.[9]

Recent events seem to have reinforced this scholarly analysis. The basic logic of the culture wars thesis, for example, became an underlying theme of media punditry in the wake of the 2000 and 2004 elections, when a bicolor map – America in "red and blue" – and compelling statistics – for example, 22 percent of the American public voted "moral values" in 2004, eleven states banned same-sex marriage through a popular vote – combined to

5 Hunter, *Culture Wars*, p. 44.

6 Will Herberg, *Protestant-Catholic-Jew: An Essay in American Religious Sociology* (Garden City, NY: Doubleday, 1960).

7 Robert Wuthnow, *The Restructuring of American Religion* (Princeton, NJ: Princeton University Press, 1988).

8 David E. Campbell, "A House Divided? What Social Science Has to Say About the Culture War," *William and Mary Bill of Rights Journal* 15 (2006): 16.

9 Green et al., *Religion and the Culture Wars*; Andrew Kohut, John C. Green, Scott Keeter, and Robert C. Toth, *The Diminishing Divide: Religion's Changing Role in American Politics* (Washington, DC: Brookings Press, 2000).

suggest an electorate that was hopelessly bifurcated along cultural lines. Those lines were defined by geography (rural/urban/suburban), ideology, income – and, most impressively, religion. Level of attendance at religious services was a powerful predictor of vote choice in the elections; other religious factors seemed to have similar effects.[10] There is, of course, considerable disagreement about the scope and persistence of the culture war,[11] as well as the kinds of experiences and identities that generate it. Although some, following Hunter's lead, see the war as real, consequential, and ongoing,[12] others insist that it is at least exaggerated or even nonexistent.[13] But most of these studies take the similar approach of examining a broad swath of the American citizenry to determine the extent to which the culture war thesis explains the role of mass behavior in recent electoral, partisan, and policy conflicts.

For my purposes in this essay, however, it is irrelevant whether or not we can actually find polarization in the survey data or whether the two sides really divide as neatly as the theory suggests. My goal is to examine the *symbolic* role that the culture war plays in the mobilization of a small subset of "warriors" in the battle, namely, evangelical cause lawyers. Nor do I take sides in the notoriously vexed question in sociology, anthropology, and cultural studies of how to define "culture" as an analytical concept. Rather, I treat the evangelical *perception* of culture as an empirical datum, as a symbolic construction of evangelical cause lawyers and the opinion-makers who influence them. Elites in democratic regimes frequently use symbols such as the culture war to play on collective anxieties and to ensure quiescence,[14] but those symbols can also shape elite identity itself. Indeed, recent sociolegal scholarship suggests that the symbols of law (e.g., the

[10] James L., Guth, Lyman A. Kellstedt, John C. Green, and Corwin E. Smidt, "America Fifty/Fifty," *First Things* 116 (2001):19.

[11] See Campbell, "A House Divided"; James Davidson Hunter and Alan Wolfe, *Is There a Culture War? A Dialogue on Values and American Public Life* (Washington, DC: Brookings, 2006); Geoffrey Layman and John C. Green, "Wars and Rumors of Wars: The Contexts of Cultural Conflict in American Political Behavior," *British Journal of Political Science* 36 (2006): 61.

[12] Stanley Greenberg, *The Two Americas* (New York: Thomas Dunne, 2005); Thomas Frank, *What's the Matter With Kansas? How Conservatives Won the Heart of America* (New York: Henry Holt, 2004).

[13] Morris Fiorina, *Culture War? The Myth of a Polarized America* (New York: Pearson, 2006); Alan Wolfe, *One Nation, After All* (New York: Viking, 1998).

[14] The seminal work is Murray Edelman, *The Symbolic Uses of Politics: Mass Arousal and Quiescence* (Chicago: University of Illinois Press, 1964).

"myth of rights") possess a "constitutive" quality that shapes the consciousness and tactics of cause lawyers.[15] Those symbols of law also intersect other aspects of a lawyer's experience, including religious faith, creating a dynamic interaction of religion, law, and vocation.

I have suggested elsewhere that evangelical intellectuals – many of whom were clergy-activists – were key participants in paving the way for the evangelical movement into rights-advocacy from the late 1970s to the present.[16] I argue in this essay that the martial symbolism of a "culture war" was particularly salient for these intellectual activists and the lawyers they counseled. Even if the culture war thesis does not explain empirically the breadth and depth of mass political attitudes and behavior in the past two decades, the *belief* – perhaps the myth – that there is a widespread and deep-seated cultural conflict has been powerful in motivating the rights-advocacy of evangelical cause lawyers. From the perspective of these lawyers and elite activists, five interrelated propositions about culture stand out: (1) culture determines the values (or morality) that society advances, so whoever controls culture ineluctably shapes society's values and virtues; (2) there is an active conflict between two distinct cultural understandings in the United States, hinging on different views of moral authority; (3) evangelicals have an obligation to take sides in the conflict through moral activism; (4) this cultural conflict encompasses more than politics (including the politics of rights); and (5) because cultural conflict encompasses more than politics, evangelicals (including evangelical lawyers) should be engaged beyond merely political means.

For evangelical cause lawyers, one implication of these propositions is to problematize the idea of lawyering for a *cause*. The language of "cause" that has now become conventional in the cause lawyering literature often suggests a discrete movement or area of policy that the lawyer chooses to pursue. Although many evangelicals do pursue such causes (e.g., religious freedom, opposition to abortion rights), their lawyering is motivated by something more fundamental than the cause itself. In fact, many insist

[15] See, e.g., Stuart Scheingold and Austin Sarat, *Something to Believe In: Politics, Professionalism, and Cause Lawyering* (Stanford, CA: Stanford University Press, 2004). For a discussion of sociolegal research and the "constitutive" understanding of political symbols, see Patricia Ewick and Austin Sarat, "Hidden in Plain View: Murray Edelman in the Law and Society Tradition," *Law and Social Inquiry* 29 (2004): 439

[16] Kevin R. den Dulk, "In Legal Culture, But Not of It: The Role of Cause Lawyers in Evangelical Legal Mobilization," in *Cause Lawyering and Social Movements*.

they have not chosen a cause to pursue at all, but rather that they have been *called* to a vocation.[17] That vocation defines for evangelical cause lawyers a purpose that gives substance to their identity as both religionists and legal professionals.

The rhetoric of "purpose" is familiar to the evangelical mind. It is summed up in the opening passage of Rick Warren's wildly successful *The Purpose-Driven Life*, which he wrote as an alternative to the popular self-help genre and as a warning to readers about the misplaced priorities of the broader culture. The book, presented in a devotional style, begins with the following assertions in reply to an elemental question, "What on earth am I here for?":

> It's not about you. The purpose of your life is far greater than your own personal fulfillment, your peace of mind, or even your happiness. It's far greater than your family, your career, or even your wildest dreams and ambitions. If you want to know why you were placed on this planet, you must begin with God. You were born *by* his purpose and *for* his purpose.[18]

There are assumptions of great philosophical import in this passage – assumptions that are central to the evangelical understanding of culture. Purpose is given, not chosen. Purpose is transcendent; it is larger than our own will and imagination, and certainly larger than a political cause (religious freedom) or tactic (lawyering). And purpose is all-encompassing; it does not belong to an elite, but to all of us – indeed, to the culture itself. Much of the rest of Warren's book, in fact, is a call to Christian relevance, partly through activism in the culture.

The notion of a purposive lawyer involved in cultural conflict suggests a mode of engagement that expands the location of the battle beyond the familiar venues of the politics of rights. The fight is not primarily in legal offices, courtrooms, or even mass protests in the streets; it is in the more amorphous realm of culture as they understand it, which comprises the various ways to express worldview. As is often the result of war, the ultimate goal is fundamental transformation; the point is nothing less than regeneration of cultural consciousness and a renewal of commitment to

[17] den Dulk, "In Legal Culture, But Not Of It."

[18] Rick Warren, *The Purpose-Driven Life: What On Earth Am I Here For?* (Grand Rapids, MI: Zondervan), 17.

moral traditionalism, not merely to "redeem" or transform this or that area of legal rights through the coercive power of the state. If the primary goal of the culture warrior is the transformation of errant worldviews – if lawyering and specific political causes are really secondary matters – then the cause lawyer might feel duty-bound to go wherever the battle is raging, which includes mass media and entertainment as much as courts and other political institutions.

The evangelical subculture provides a field for their multifaceted combat. The various media in this religious tradition – not only books, but innumerable niche magazines, television and radio programs, movies, documentaries, music of all sorts, church-based theater, and Web sites – are rarely noticed by the broader culture unless there is crossover appeal (e.g., Warren's book sold more than twenty million copies and remained on national best seller lists for three years). Ordinary evangelicals, however, often consume these media as their primary sources of information and entertainment, in part because many evangelicals trust their own cultural purveyors more than the "secular" alternatives. James Dobson is a good example. His weekly radio program is broadcast on more than 3,000 radio stations in North America and beyond, and his organization, Focus on the Family, uses media of all types to present traditionalist views of family life. Pat Robertson and, to a lesser extent, other clergy-activists such as D. James Kennedy and the late Jerry Falwell, have a similar media presence. The reach of evangelical mass culture is so wide that one recent survey suggests that in a given month an average American is more likely to use religious media than attend religious services.[19]

Although no evangelical cause lawyer approaches Dobson et al.'s media prominence, many regularly use various media on a smaller scale (and occasionally appear on Dobson et al.'s own outlets). These lawyers have been remarkably productive not only as legal advocates but also as social commentators, novelists, documentarians, magazine editors, musicians, and television talking heads. Indeed, many of the lead attorneys at key evangelical firms have melded their cultural avocations and professional

[19] Barna Research Group, "Christian Mass Media Reach More Adults With Christian Message Than Do Churches," *Barna Update*, July 22, 2002; http://www.barna.org (accessed June 10, 2007). On religious media generally, see Robert Booth Fowler, Allen D. Hertzke, Laura R. Olson, and Kevin R. den Dulk, *Religion and Politics in America: Faith, Culture, and Strategic Choices*, 3d ed. (Boulder, CO: Westview Press., 2004), Ch. 6.

lives in ways that undoubtedly affect (for better or worse) their ability to mobilize support and maintain their organizations. As we shall see, their cultural work, which draws from within and outside their tradition, both shapes and reflects distinctive understandings of how the culture war intersects the politics of rights.

III. An Enemy with a Human(Ist) Face

In 1980 the Moral Majority was in its infancy, and its founder, Jerry Falwell, issued a clarion call to the "silent majority" in the United States. American civilization was "sick" and "in trouble"[20]; its condition was "perilous,"[21] and collective decisions about its immediate future would be "fateful."[22] Yet the cause of its condition was not economic malaise or threat of an external power; it was deeply cultural, "the spiritual condition of [the American] people."[23] Society was on the verge of losing its moral bearings because traditionalist religion had not been sufficiently assertive. Having uncovered the general cause, Falwell went on to identify a particular causal mechanism. "We, the American people," he declared, "have allowed a vocal minority of ungodly men and women to bring America to the brink of death."[24] An enemy had been defined in the culture war.

From the moral traditionalist's point of view, there were several salient characteristics of this enemy. First, there is the matter of troop strength: the "ungodly" had not yet won the hearts and minds of the American majority. Hence that majority could proceed with some confidence, if only it could find its voice and mobilize for moral activism. This is a familiar cultural motif – the populist invocation – and it is especially prevalent in evangelical circles, from William Jennings Bryan of the early twentieth century to Pat Robertson and Jesse Jackson today.[25] The typical story plays on some kind of mass-based alienation from a small yet influential group of cultural elites whose machinations have resulted in moral decay, poverty, or some other social ill.

[20] Jerry Falwell, *Listen, America!* (New York: Bantam, 1981), 7.
[21] Falwell, *Listen, America!*, 243.
[22] Falwell, *Listen, America!*, 7.
[23] Falwell, *Listern, America!* 244.
[24] Falwell, *Listen, America!*, xi.
[25] Allen D. Hertzke, *Echoes of Discontent: Jesse Jackson, Pat Robertson, and the Resurgence of Populism* (Washington, DC: CQ Press, 1993).

This populism points to a second characteristic of the enemy: cultural elites are "ungodly." On this account, to be godless is synonymous with adherence to secular humanism, the belief that the only legitimate basis for meaning and morality is the human will, not divine authority. As a result, the combatants in the culture war are neatly divided into two camps, each under the banner of a discernible worldview. Falwell is succinct in his description of the two sides: "The rising tide of secularism threatens to obliterate the Judeo-Christian influence on American society."[26] D. James Kennedy echoes the sentiment and ties it explicitly to the culture war:

> God forbid that we who were born into the blessings of a Christian America should let our patrimony slip like sand through our fingers and leave to our children the bleached bones of a godless secular society. But whatever the outcome, one thing is certain: God has called us to engage the enemy in this culture war. That is our challenge today.[27]

The contrast of "Judeo-Christian" influence and godless secularism reveals competing visions of moral authority: the objective versus arbitrary, transcendent versus immanent, fixed versus mutable, divine versus human. These oppositions helped define evangelical understandings of the interplay of culture and "legality," what Ewick and Silbey describe as those "meanings, sources of authority, and cultural practices that are commonly recognized as legal."[28]

Falwell's claim about the "rising tide" of secularism reflects a third key characteristic of the enemy: its ubiquity. Despite the minority status of the secular humanists, they are nevertheless "vocal" and their cultural presence is pervasive. Falwell's and Kennedy's concern about this presence – critics would say their paranoia – provides some insight into battlefield tactics. On the one hand, evangelical opinion leaders over the past three decades have been relentless in linking secularism to political institutions, and they have established a range of political organizations to combat secularism within those institutions. Pat Robertson, for example, in explaining his creation of

[26] Ed Dobson and Ed Hinson, *The Fundamentalist Phenomenon: The Resurgence of Conservative Christianity* (Garden City, NY: Doubleday, 1981), 186.

[27] D. James Kennedy, *Character and Destiny: A Nation in Search of Its Soul* (Grand Rapids, MI: Zondervan, 1994), 191

[28] Patricia Ewick and Susan S. Silbey, *The Common Place of Law: Stories from Everyday Life*. (Chicago: University of Chicago Press, 1998), 22.

the American Center for Law and Justice (ACLJ), an evangelical law firm, claimed the group was formed to root out secularism's insidious influence within cherished institutions. "From the French Revolution on," he asserts, "the secularists have tried to destroy the Christian religion. They are still entrenched in the schools, the courts, and many parts of government."[29] Note the martial overtones of "destruction" and "entrenchment," leaving the impression that the ACLJ will indeed engage in a cultural war for our public institutions.

On the other hand, the battlefield in the culture war covers a lot of territory. As noted earlier, evangelicals tend to see institutional engagement as part of a broader cultural struggle, and perhaps not the most important priority in that struggle. Even while arguing for political mobilization at the inception of the Moral Majority, Jerry Falwell confessed that "America will [not] be turned around solely by working in the area of politics, economics, and defense, as important as these may be." "These are crucial issues that face us in the 1980s," he continued, "but America can only be turned around as her people make godly, moral choices.[30] Only the *total* culture war – marshalling resources to fight on every front – would be truly regenerative. At a conference in 1995, Kennedy suggests the breadth of the conflict:

> Our job is to reclaim America for Christ, whatever the cost. As the vice regents of God, we are to exercise godly dominion and influence over our neighborhoods, our schools, our government, our literature and arts, our sports arenas, our entertainment media, our news media, our scientific endeavors – in short, over every aspect and institution of human society.[31]

All of these features of evangelical elite opinion about the culture war – even the rhetoric and cadences of those elites – are picked up by cause lawyers in the tradition. Consider, for example, the claims that secular humanism is a rejection of transcendent moral authority and a widespread threat to society. Reflecting on his early years of rights-advocacy, John Whitehead, founder of The Rutherford Institute, an evangelical law firm,

[29] Pat Robertson, *The New Millennium* (Dallas: Word Publishing, 1990). 70

[30] Falwell, *Listen, America!*, p. 8.

[31] Quoted in Bob Moser, "The Crusaders," *Rolling Stone*, April 21, 2005, 41–42. The Reclaiming America for Christ conference is an annual event sponsored by Kennedy's Coral Ridge Ministries. In 2007, the conference was advertised as an opportunity to attend "power-packed training sessions by 'culture war' veterans."

describes the "pervasive" threat of a "secular monolith,"[32] as represented in the legalization of abortion rights, the proliferation of pornography, the decline of the traditional family, and the denial of religious freedoms across the country. Michael Farris, founder of the Home School Legal Defense Association (HSLDA) and an early leader among evangelical cause lawyers, notes a "profound cultural shift" toward humanism, which is "built on the foundation of evolution" and "denies that there are any moral absolutes and contends that man holds within himself the solution to all problems."[33]

Evangelical cause lawyers also shared with elites the skepticism that any specific form of political mobilization – including legal mobilization – could prove decisive in the culture war. Farris, for example, sees such skepticism as directly related to his conception of God:

> There are four groups in Washington and [each] revolves around a belief in [a different] god.... The way you figure out which group [a person is] in is to ask this question: "Here's a problem, who's going to solve it?" If the answer is, "we'll just let the ... free market solve it," you are most likely in the money-is-god crowd. If you say, "we just need more government programs or more efficient government programs," either way it's just different sides of the same coin, then you are in the government-is-god crowd. If you say just let everybody do what they want, that is the man-is-god crowd. And if you say that only God changing hearts is going to change society at large, then you believe God is God.[34]

Farris's self-understanding as a member of the last group does not mean that he sees no societal role for government. Far from it; his organization is an active participant in public life, though often by litigating rights claims and lobbying to prevent government from taking action against home-schooling families. The key issue is the nature and extent of the evangelical role in political contestation, which is only one means of cultural transformation – and perhaps, on Farris's account, not a terribly effective one. In fact, Farris calls his own agency into doubt, suggesting that divine intervention, not human activity, will "change hearts."

Still, the fear of the humanist threat cried out for response, in the legal arena and elsewhere. Many evangelical lawyers followed the lead of elite

[32] John Whitehead, *True Christianity* (Wheaton, IL: Crossway, 1989), 17.
[33] Michael Farris, *Where Do I Draw the Line?* (Grand Rapids, MI: Bethany House, 1992), 16
[34] Michael Farris, interview by author, Purcellville, Virginia, July 27, 1999.

activists – Robertson and Falwell, as well as Francis Schaeffer, James Dobson, and others – who made explicit connections between the culture war and law. For those attorneys, law is best understood as an "objective realm of disinterested action"[35] or, more precisely, a realm where the "interests" are divinely ordained. For some evangelical attorneys, the key jurisprudential touchstone is natural law theory, which rejects the human will as a basis for the moral validity of the law. For others, natural law theory was only half-right: it correctly envisioned morality as a precondition of law, but it erred in suggesting that morality is accessible to human reason. Harking to the Protestant tradition of *sola scriptura*, these advocates insisted that God's purposes were only identifiable through scriptural revelation.[36] But however they understood the source of valid law, they agreed that it was something more than a mere human – and therefore secular – construction.

Yet, it is notable that, from the beginning of the evangelical movement into the culture war in the late 1970s, evangelical cause lawyers did not fixate simply on the politics of rights in their own cultural production. To be sure, in books, articles, and other media they spoke of the need to confront the political elites – Supreme Court justices, elected officials, leaders in opposed groups such as the ACLU – who had replaced a "transcendental" perspective on law with a secular humanist one. The rhetoric and practice of rights-advocacy, however, were contextualized as part of a larger story – a story of cultural conflict that was cosmic in scope.

One gets a general sense of this pattern in the books produced by cause lawyers and other evangelical leaders from the 1970s to the present.[37] As one can see from the figures on publishing trends, evangelicals were actively writing on an array of rights-based cultural conflicts in the time period,

[35] Ewick and Silbey, *Common Place of the Law*, 28.

[36] John Whitehead, for example, argues that "without the reference point in the Bible, there is no basis to judge which laws of nature are applicable to government and man. Depending on the man or elitist group in power, many different things can be perpetrated . . . on the basis of natural law." Whitehead, *The Second American Revolution* (Elgin, IL: Cook Publishing, 1982), 185 For a more sympathetic view, see the collection in Michael Cromartie, *A Preserving Grace: Protestants, Catholics, and Natural Law* (Grand Rapids, MI: Eerdmans, 1997).

[37] These figures were derived by compiling a list of all books published by major evangelical presses and authored by either an identifiable evangelical cause lawyer (typically the general counsel or a prominent staff attorney at an evangelical firm) or an evangelical intellectual who is referenced in the work of at least two evangelical cause lawyers. I then sorted the books according to content. The total number of books from 1971 to 2005 equals 120.

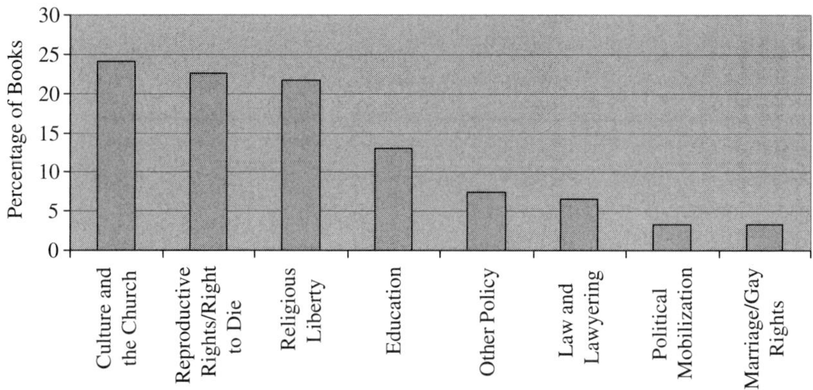

especially reproductive rights, the right to die, education, and marriage. But a prominent category of publication – indeed, the area that gets the highest percentage of attention – is broader cultural analysis, which often takes as its starting assumption the secularist threat to society and the regenerative power of the culture war. In contrast, lawyering and the practice of law receive far less attention, and to the extent they do evangelical writers focus largely on concerns with judicial "tyranny" or ways for Christians to keep disputes out of court (e.g., alternative dispute resolution as a biblically sound model).

John Whitehead's cultural work is illustrative. He is perhaps the most prolific writer among evangelical cause lawyers (by my count, he has authored more than twenty books), but his writings are often only tangentially related to a politics of rights. The tone of his works is that of a culture warrior – for example, the title of his memoir is *Slaying Dragons*[38] – and he continues to accept the general notion that secularism explains much of what ills the United States (though he challenges his fellow evangelicals nearly as much as the secularists who serve as his primary target). The evidence he marshals, however, subsumes the politics of rights into a broader cultural struggle. His books in the late 1980s and 1990s are as likely to use examples from the world of popular culture as from his legal advocacy work at the Rutherford Institute, and in at least two instances he has even used a favorite medium of popular culture itself – the visual documentary – as a companion to his written work. One of these documentaries is a seven-part

[38] John Whitehead, *Slaying Dragons: The Truth Behind the Man Who Defended Paula Jones* (Nashville: Thomas Nelson, 1999).

video series titled *Grasping for the Wind*,[39] a sweeping analysis of the spiritual emptiness of art, literature, film, and music in the modern era. In 1998, he also created a now-defunct magazine titled *Gadfly*, which offered eclectic commentary (including from *Village Voice* writer Nat Hentoff) on all aspects of popular culture and won accolades from secular outlets, such as the *Utne Reader* and the *Washington Post*.[40] "None of the disciplines – art, film, science, or politics – is isolated," Whitehead argues as justification for his manifold efforts. "They all seem to work together, sometimes almost in unison, giving birth to a new worldview and thus bringing about change. And it was clear that these disciplines had moved away from a Judeo-Christian worldview, even ridiculing it."[41]

Other key evangelical cause lawyers have made similar cultural forays into this clash of worldviews. In addition to books on parental rights, Michael Farris of the HSLDA has authored nonfiction "how-to's" on parenting girls and maintaining the "home-school marriage," as well as three novels in a legal thriller vein. He has also followed the lead of evangelical clergy-activists Oral Roberts, Pat Robertson, and Jerry Falwell in establishing the ultimate in cultural institutions, a college, which he named after Patrick Henry and formed to cater to home-schooled children whose parents wanted a "classical" education in a Christian liberal arts environment. Its motto: "For Christ and for freedom."

The nature of the evangelical subculture, with its array of media outlets and interpersonal networks, enables this kind of cultural engagement in myriad ways. In some instances the relationships across professions within the evangelical tradition have provided key opportunities. The use of the video medium in *Grasping for the Wind* in 1999, for example, was not Whitehead's own innovation. Francis Schaeffer, an evangelical intellectual who greatly influenced Whitehead and innumerable other evangelical lawyers, had used the documentary form two decades before Whitehead in *Whatever Happened to the Human Race?* (1979), a far-reaching portrayal of humanism in Western intellectual history.[42] Whitehead used Schaeffer's son, Franky, himself a Hollywood filmmaker, to produce *Grasping*

[39] John Whitehead, *Grasping for the Wind* (Worcester, PA: Vision Video, 1999).

[40] The *Utne Reader* awarded *Gadfly* its award for best "cultural coverage" at its 1999 Alternative Press Awards.

[41] Whitehead, *Slaying Dragons*, 255.

[42] Francis A. Schaeffer, *A Christian Manifesto* (Westchester, IL: Crossway Books, 1981): Francis A. Schaeffer and C. Everett Koop, *Whatever Happened to the Human Race?* (Old Tappan, NJ: Revell, 1979).

for the Wind (though the relationship between the two men eventually soured).

Evangelical firms themselves have become keenly aware of the popularity of cultural (in contrast to narrowly legal) analysis. For some, that means giving key attorneys the freedom to pursue their cultural concerns, as clearly the boards of directors at Rutherford and the HSLDA have done with Whitehead and Farris, respectively. For other groups, the use of various media for both cultural and legal commentary is an integral facet of organizational structure. This enables a complementarity of evangelical lawyers and activists in the movement, a synergy that is often lacking in other movements.[43]

Some rights-advocacy groups are part of what I call *advocacy conglomerates*. The constituent parts to these conglomerates cover various portions of the public square and benefit from each other's unique resources. Pat Robertson founded the clearest example of an advocacy conglomerate. His creation of the rights-advocacy group, the American Center for Law and Justice (ACLJ) in 1990, complemented his media (Christian Broadcasting Network), political (Christian Coalition), and educational organizations (Regent University, including Regent's College of Law). Not only did this arrangement provide a steady source of evangelical leaders for organizations like the ACLJ – Robertson, Herbert Titus, former dean of the Regent College of Law, and Ralph Reed, former executive director of the Christian Coalition, have all served on ACLJ's Board of Directors – but it also served as a platform for lawyers to cross over into the wider plain of cultural criticism. Jay Sekulow, ACLJ's media-savvy Chief Counsel, has been a frequent guest on the *700 Club*, Robertson's primary outlet for television commentary on all manner of political and social events. These appearances have given the ACLJ greater visibility in the evangelical community.[44]

These various cultural incursions reveal a breadth of purpose for evangelical cause lawyers. They believed that conflict could be regenerative, an opportunity for rebirth of traditional understandings of moral authority. The attorneys would have influence, however, only if their intended audiences were attentive and willing to enter the cultural fray. But were they? And if not, how does that affect their ability to fight the war?

[43] Sandra R. Levitsky, "To Lead With Law: Reassessing the Influence of Legal Advocacy Organizations in Social Movements," in *Cause Lawyers and Social Movements*.

[44] Sekulow's son, Logan, also has a television show billed as hip Christian comedy that ACLJ advertises on its Web site, www.aclj.org.

IV. A War Without Combatants

In February 1999, Paul Weyrich, head of the Free Congress Foundation and the man who had coined the phrase "Moral Majority" twenty years earlier, published an open letter to his fellow religious conservatives.[45] After two decades of evangelical societal engagement, his thesis was particularly jarring to his audience: American society had become a "culture of decadence," an "ever-widening sewer" that had forsaken its Judeo-Christian heritage and seemed impervious to the cleansing efforts of conservative Christians and their allies. Echoing the fight-or-flight tension within evangelicalism from earlier in the twentieth century, he urged like-minded readers to practice a cultural self-quarantine, insulating their families from the broader society by forming parallel networks of schools, businesses, media, and entertainment outlets. At roughly the same time, Cal Thomas and Ed Dobson published *Blinded by Might*,[46] a book that charged that religious conservatism had failed as a moral movement because it traded its Christian moorings for the trappings of political power. Like Weyrich, these authors are not easily dismissed. Thomas, a syndicated columnist, and Dobson, until recently a pastor of a large nondenominational evangelical church, both served as lieutenants to Falwell in the early days of the Moral Majority, and they remain sympathetic to socially conservative goals. Nevertheless, they argue that, despite the Christian Right's best efforts, "the moral landscape [in America] has become worse." For Dobson and Thomas, the best indicator of this moral decline is perhaps its greatest irony: Christian leaders themselves had become morally compromised and enslaved to the temptations of power.

Predictably, these claims by prominent conservatives did not sit well with other elites in the world of evangelicalism. The debate was taken up in the Christian press, with several periodicals inviting responses from Christian activists.[47] Jerry Falwell declared that he would "do it all again"; Ralph Reed, former executive director of the Christian Coalition, urged that "we can't stop now"; and Charles Colson, the head of Prison Ministries, ruminated on "what's right about the religious right." Speaking for many of

[45] Paul Weyrich, "The Moral Minority [Reprint]," *Christianity Today*, September 6, 1999, 43.

[46] Cal Thomas and Ed Dobson, *Blinded by Might: Can the Religious Right Save America?* (Grand Rapids, MI: Zondervan, 1999).

[47] Editors, "Blinded By Might?" *World Magazine*, May 15, 1999, 21–24; Editors, "Is the Religious Right Finished?" *Christianity Today*, September 6, 1999, 43–61; and Anonymous, "Why We Won't Quit." *Focus on the Family Citizen*, April 1999, 14–19.

the respondents, James Dobson of Focus on the Family provided a summary exhortation, arguing that "faith compels us... to fight on and do honor to [God's] cause whether we win or lose."

The challenge in this exchange among elite activists is that the "orthodox" side of the culture war had been co-opted by the very culture it was fighting. And, to some extent, scholarly treatments of the so-called Christian Right would seem to indicate a subtle appropriation of ideas – particularly ideas about rights – that evangelicals had once held as anathema. In the early 1980s, conservative evangelicals arrived on the political scene with great interest and force, ready to do battle against secularism under the leadership of organizations like the Moral Majority. But they failed to accomplish many of their objectives, partly as a result of their uncompromising and politically unsophisticated approach.[48] The Moral Majority folded in 1989, for example, and is widely viewed by scholars today as less influential than popular perception would suggest. Ironically, the intensity of their convictions seemed to be a barrier to their effectiveness.

Although activity waned in the late 1980s, it enjoyed a "second coming" in the early 1990s after the founding of the Christian Coalition and similar groups.[49] Some analysts suggest that these new groups, in seeking greater political success, adapted to the broader societal consensus, emphasizing a wider range of issues and regularly invoking values of choice, equality, and rights.[50] The transformation should be unsurprising to scholars of rights consciousness, which can be highly dynamic and adaptive.[51] Evangelicals were less likely to target homosexual "behavior," but rather demanded "no *special* rights" for gays and lesbians,[52] thereby framing the issue in

48 Steve Bruce, *The Rise and Fall of the New Christian Right* (Oxford: Claredon, 1988); Steve Bruce, "The Inevitable Failure of the New Christian Right," in *The Rapture of Politics*, ed. S. Bruce, P. Kivisto and W. Swatos, Jr. (New Brunswick, NJ: Transaction Publishers, 1995; Robert Booth Fowler, "The Failure of the Religious Right," in *The Religious New Right in American Politics*, ed. M. Cromartie (Washington, DC: Ethics and Public Policy Center, 1993).

49 Mark Rozell and Clyde Wilcox, *Second Coming: The New Christian Right in Virginia Politics* (Baltimore: Johns Hopkins, 1996).

50 Matthew Moen, *The Transformation of the Christian Right* (Tuscaloosa, AL: University of Alabama Press, 1992); Moen, "The Changing Nature of Christian Right Activism, 1970s–1990s," in *Sojourners in the Wilderness: The Christian Right in Comparative Perspective*, ed. Corwin Smidt and Jim Penning (Lanham, MD: Rowman and Littlefield, 1996).

51 Michael McCann, *Rights at Work: Pay Equity Reform and the Politics of Legal Mobilization* (Chicago: University of Chicago Press, 1994).

52 Evan Gerstmann, *The Constitutional Underclass: Gays, Lesbians, and the Failure of Class-Based Equal Protection* (Chicago: University of Chicago Press, 1999), 99–114; Hubert Morken,

the liberal language of equal treatment. School prayer was no longer a matter of (Christian) obligation, but a "voluntary" choice of individual schoolchildren. Tax breaks for parents who send their children to private schools gave way to support for the seemingly more egalitarian voucher system for all families, often described in terms of school *choice*. Changes in abortion rhetoric are perhaps most striking. Rather than articulating the issue in terms of the "sacredness" of life, with its religious connotations, many religious conservatives speak of the *right* to life or even the federalist language of the states' rights to impose restrictions on abortion access.[53]

For some evangelicals, this "second coming" of the Christian Right also failed. It was too adaptive and accommodating, and its organizations could not sustain themselves. The Moral Majority's successor, the Christian Coalition, certainly had some success in electoral politics in the mid-1990s, but by the end of the decade its financial base and membership had declined, leading it to scale back both its staff and agenda.[54] Other groups – the Family Research Council, the Concerned Women for America, Coral Ridge Ministries – were maintaining their presence, but recruitment was a chronic problem and sustained attack was difficult against an enemy that was widely perceived as increasingly powerful, perhaps to the point of achieving majority status. The apparent message was that supporters, including some activists, had become too war-weary to be of use. Hence leaders such as Weyrich, Ed Dobson, and Thomas concluded that the culture war was a losing – or at least very long-term – proposition.

A common response to this kind of self-consciousness is to gravitate toward the "minoritarian" politics of rights and to focus on a smaller cadre of elite warriors who are motivated for service: the cause lawyers. It has become a truism among scholars of social movements and the politics of rights that groups often move in that direction as the only resort under conditions of political disadvantage. There is some evidence that this is what happened in the 1990s, which saw a proliferation of evangelical rights-advocacy

"No Special Rights: The Thinking Behind Colorado's Amendment #2 Strategy," presented at American Political Science Association, New York, 1994.

53 Of course, this claim can be overstated. In fact, another form of pro-life rhetoric – the development of a "culture of life" – has also emerged in the past two decades, and it deliberately avoids the rights-talk of other approaches to the abortion issue.

54 Alan Cooperman and Thomas B. Edsall, "Christian Coalition Shrinks as Debt Grows," *Washington Post*, April 10, 2006, A1.

firms.[55] Perhaps evangelicals had fallen prey to a myth of rights, but, as Scheingold reminds us,[56] it is a powerful myth.

It is also a myth that works in a complex fashion. The response of some cause lawyers is illustrative. Lawyers associated with evangelical organizations began to reinforce an impression of their status of warrior-heroes. Such warriors exhibit a kind of heroic individuality, perhaps most familiar in the popular symbolism of military elites today.[57] It is also a common symbol in television and print representations of lawyers, and especially litigators. The warrior is drawn from the crowd but is also *above* it, where the warrior benefits from superior perspective. The warrior is also cunning and brave. In fact, I would argue that this perceived bravery reflects the problematic nature of the myth of rights itself for many evangelicals. Evangelicals perceive that their attorneys must be brave precisely because they see the politics of rights as a dangerous countermobilization against a secular "monolith." If the war is indeed regenerative, the warrior-hero is the self-sacrificial catalyst.

Evangelical cause lawyers have cultivated these images of the warrior-hero in various ways. Consider again attorney and cultural provocateur John Whitehead, whose Rutherford Institute took the controversial step of sponsoring Paula Jones's civil lawsuit against President Bill Clinton. In *Slaying Dragons*, Whitehead explains that this decision, among others in his life, had been intensely controversial within evangelical circles, and may have cost Whitehead some support. But he issued a dual response: (1) he defended Jones and other controversial people because of his abiding belief in the rule of law, including the bedrock principle that no one is above the law[58]; and (2) evangelical criticism was generally rooted in misplaced pietism and, fundamentally, fear. The underlying message of Whitehead's criticism was not unlike others who had developed misgivings about evangelical commitment to mass-based cultural combat. Evangelicals were

[55] Hans Hacker, *The Culture of Conservative Christian Litigation* (Lanham, MD: Rowman and Littlefield, 2005); Kevin den Dulk, *Prophets in Caesar's Courts: The Role of Ideas in Catholic and Evangelical Rights Advocacy* (Ph.D. diss., University of Wisconsin – Madison, 2001), Ch. 2.

[56] Stuart Scheingold, *The Politics of Rights: Lawyers, Public Policy, and Political Change* (Ann Arbor, MI: University of Michigan Press, 2004).

[57] Edward Tabor Linenthal, *Changing Images of the Warrior Hero in America: A History of Popular Symbolism* (Lewiston, NY: Edwin Mellen, 1982).

[58] Incidentally, Whitehead has not hesitated in his criticism of the Bush administration's policies, which also did not endear him to his evangelical brethren.

losing their stomach for conflict; in fact, they had often sold out to culture rather than engaged it. But Whitehead added another dimension to the message: there were a few determined individuals who remained in the fight. They were largely alone, slaying dragons on behalf of their fellow citizens, and often at great expense and without the gratitude of those they were serving. They were, in short, heroes for the faith.

Others presented the cause lawyer as warrior-hero as well, often with themselves as the exemplar. Favorite themes include the against-the-odds victor or the honorable, long-suffering loser (who will win in the end). Evangelical lawyers are fond of publicizing their number of appearances in court – the U.S. Supreme Court, of course, is the most envied prize – and in itself such self-promotion does not distinguish them from other cause lawyers. But their descriptions of these appearances leave the impression of the lawyer heroically entering a lair of secularism, which is a useful impression whether the lawyer wins ("I defeated the secular dragon!") or loses ("We are up against a powerful enemy!").

A similar theme is shot through the books published by evangelical cause lawyers, which usually rehearse a range of secularist attacks on religious freedom or traditionalist values, with the lawyer and his or her organization positioned as the last line of defense. The ACLU or gay rights groups are preferred antagonists; titles include *The Homosexual Agenda: Exposing the Principal Threat to Religious Freedom Today*, and *The ACLU vs. America*, by Alliance Defense Fund Chief Counsel Alan Sears,[59] or *From Intimidation to Victory*, by the ACLJ's Jay Sekulow.[60] The same premise even emerges in fiction. Farris's novels, with such titles as *Guilt by Association* and *Anonymous Tip*, generally follow the story of an intrepid Christian attorney as he faces down corrupt government bureaucracies (a favorite is Child Protective Services) that are bent on imposing a set of values that are clearly out of step with Farris's traditionalist understanding of family.[61]

[59] Alan Sears, *The Homosexual Agenda* (Nashville: Broadman and Holman.Sears, 2003) and *The ACLU vs. America: Exposing the Agenda to Redefine Moral Values* (Nashville: Broadman and Holman, 2005).

[60] Jay Sekulow, *From Intimidation to Victory* (Lake Mary, FL: Creation House, 1990). See also Jay Sekulow and Keith Fournier, *And Nothing But the Truth* (Nashville: Thomas Nelson, 1996); Farris, *Where Do I Draw the Line?*

[61] Michael Farris, *Anonymous Tip* (Nashville: Broadman and Holman, 1996) and *Guilt by Association* (Nashville: Broadman and Holman, 1997).

The phenomenon of the warrior-hero is not a repudiation of the existence of the culture war. Rather, the hero represents a perception that an insufficient number of combatants are fighting on the "orthodox" side. The hero motif also reinforces cross-cutting images of law and lawyering. The "law" and legal rights have been deeply infiltrated by secularist ideology, to the point that many conservative evangelicals view legal institutions with great distrust. Evangelicals, for example, are the least likely among all major religious traditions (Catholic, mainline Protestant, African American Protestant) other than Jews to assess the Supreme Court "warmly" on mass survey feeling thermometers.[62] That impression of the law has been vigorously advanced by evangelical cause lawyers themselves. Yet those same lawyers have cultivated a view of their own lawyering as noble – even heroic – action that acts as a bulwark against secularist success in the politics of rights.

V. Conclusion: The Culture War and the Politics of Rights

The metaphor of culture war, to the extent that it influences evangelical thinking, can be double-edged. On the one hand, it can be a spur to mobilization – including legal mobilization – by tapping into populist instincts and the perception of threat. On the other hand, it can be debilitating, especially when it appears that the strength of the movement is not as broad-based as it once seemed.

Lawyers, whose work is *relatively* insulated from the vagaries of mass politics, are perhaps best able to negotiate these two edges of the sword. Early in the movement of evangelicals into public life, lawyers, following the lead of clergy-activists, marshaled a collective fear of threat and transformed it into moral activism. At center stage in their efforts was the insidious and pervasive presence of secularism, which they argued had woven its way into all aspects of culture, as exemplified in (but not limited to) the politics of rights. The secularists were busy reshaping culture through assertions of abortion rights, gay rights, the right to die, and other rights claims that were anathema to traditionalist believers, and they did so with the aid of their willing accomplices in elite institutions. For evangelical elites, the rights claims of secularists simply reflected the primacy of culture, and

[62] Based on the author's analysis of National Elections Studies 2004 data.

called for an expansive strategy of countermobilization that would include deployment of the manifold instruments of culture itself, with a legion of attentive believers at the ready.

Even when the populist appeal of cultural conflict appeared to wane, evangelical attorneys managed to refashion their place in the war. The emergence of the warrior-hero heightened the importance of elite lawyering while diminishing the need for mass-based mobilization. This development has interesting connections with recent trends in political organization in general, which has generally moved toward a model of professionalized leadership at the expense of grassroots involvement.[63] What distinguishes the experience of evangelical firms and attorneys is that they have presented something like the professionalized model as not simply a practical expedient to ensure greater efficiency or expertise, but also as a necessity resulting from diminished support within a beleaguered and dispirited mass public. Without a serious army and in the face of a powerful enemy, the time was right for heroic action.

[63] Theda Skocpol, *Diminished Democracy: From Membership to Management in American Civic Life* (Norman, OK: University of Oklahoma Press, 2003).

3

Cause Lawyers and Cracker Culture at the Constructive Edge

A "Band of Brothers" Defeats Big Tobacco

Tim Howard

I. Introduction: Participant-Observer Scholarship at the Constructive Edge

This essay is new to cause lawyer project scholarship. It addresses a key question: Is there a story of cause lawyer heroism that can resonate with American culture? This case study provides numerous sources consistent with a heroic story of cause lawyers and Cracker political leaders at the constructive edge.

In answering this question, other questions are addressed as well. How do cause lawyers interface with culture, institutions of government, and media to effect strategic legal initiatives that obtain favorable media coverage and move public opinion? And how do these efforts ultimately lead to legislation and court rulings that advance their ideology and public policy goals? As part of their compelling story, Florida tobacco liability litigators implemented and accomplished each of these goals in one of the most successful cases in American history. This case study provides key source materials on how cause lawyers can successfully advance their ideology and public policy goals.

This descriptive and explanatory case study[1] of Florida tobacco liability litigation from 1993 to 1997 explores the central question of whether there

[1] Case study methodology focuses on developing a particular in-depth analysis of a single case or multiple cases. It is a study of a "bounded system" (bounded by time and place) or a case. The complexity of dynamics affecting public policy implementation by cause lawyers and Cracker political leaders of necessity requires a case study method. The case study discipline originated from political science, law, psychology, medicine, sociology, evaluation, urban studies and other social sciences (case studies, case law, etc). As such, one can take the case study and reason by analogy to different case studies for consistent patterns of causation of social phenomena to

is a culturally resonant story of cause lawyer heroism at the constructive edge. To answer this question, this case study "pentangulates" a limited portion of the data from five distinct data sources: (1) history of tobacco in the South; (2) courts and tobacco litigation from 1954–93; (3) participant-observer narrative of the processes involved in creating Florida's strategic tobacco liability initiative from 1993–95; (4) a ten-year quantity and content competing narrative frame analysis from 1987–97 of Florida tobacco litigation print media coverage; and (5) reference to key source documents.

The core data set comprises thick description from insider participant-observation of the complex interaction between bottom-up progressive cause lawyers and governmental institution leaders. These include such memorable characters as the "He-coon," Florida Governor Lawton Chiles, and the "Banty-Rooster," Dean of the Florida Senate W.D. Childers – to name a few. The insider data set discloses remnants of little-known "Florida Cracker" culture from 1993 to 1995.

The stealth tobacco liability law and strategic legal and legislative initiative emerged from this primal cultural and political *soup*. The ideological battle lines found in the constructed competing cultural narrative frames of Social Cost and Corporate Responsibility verses Economic Cost and Individual Responsibility were constructed and engaged in this *soup*. These ideologies then fought for prominence in the cultures of Florida, the

find causally valid *nomothetic* explanations. One use of the case study method is to identify *nomothetic* causal effects through empirical association, appropriate time order, and nonspuriousness. Is the association among ideology, culture, the dependent news reporting of competing narrative frames, and the independent strategic initiatives by cause lawyer and Cracker political leaders in the legislature and in the courts valid? Is this a tautology? Put another way, does public policy ever get implemented without alignment of these forces? It is believed that cause lawyers and Cracker political leaders could enact public policy without alignment with the dominant cultural narrative frame, but such policies will not last in the face of policy entrepreneurs competing for policies that align with the dominant cultural narrative frames and their interests.

A case study looks at the social unit as an integrated whole. As it relates to the participants, it tracks phenomenon research in that it attempts to understand a phenomenon from the standpoint of participants. This assists in also understanding why the phenomenon occurred, or its causation.

Consistent with applicable case study methodology, data collection in this study is from multiple sources, including documents, archival records, transcripts, personal observations, and quantitative data. Data analysis generally includes description, themes, and assertions, but quantitative coding and categorizing are available to quantify and measure the interaction of print media content dependent and independent variables. The internal and external validity of case study research can also be increased through data triangulation – use of multiple research methods to study limited research questions – as applied in this case study.

This is an *intrinsic case study* since the case itself has interest.

governor's office, the legislature, the courts, and the media. Cracker influence on southern culture is described to document some of the embedded ideologies and counterideologies coursing through the symbols and collective mind or spirit of the Florida Cracker leaders.

This essay is important because cause lawyer case study data add depth and texture to the evolving cause lawyer project literature. It also connects the cause lawyer project with the Western academic tradition of participant-observer scholarship that dates back to at least St. Augustine's *Confessions* and Machiavelli's *The Prince*. Case studies of this type, however, are limited. Despite the twentieth-century explosion of social science research and publications, there have been only a few noteworthy case studies of this type in social science disciplines over the past fifty years.[2] The combination of data sets and analysis is particularly rare because of the dual perspectives, demanding skill sets, tensions, and credentials that must be achieved by one person – those of a practicing cause lawyer and a PhD, and requiring application of knowledge creation craft to cause lawyer case study data.[3]

This essay is the first to apply this unique data set and "pentangulated" case study methodology to Florida Cracker culture and cause lawyer tobacco litigation. This essay is part of what I term postmodern *integration scholarship*: a scholastic effort that builds on legal realism's multidisciplinary integration, and reflective practitioner education – teaching practitioners and scholars the skills of "thinking what they are doing while they are doing it."[4]

I am an attorney with dual careers in small-firm cause lawyering and academia as a professor in Law and Policy.[5] Significant portions of the

[2] Examples include Herbert Gans, *The Urban Villagers, Group and Class in the Life of Italian-Americans* (New York, NY: The Free Press, 1982) (Gans and his wife were actual residents in the neighborhood studied, and they participated and observed the neighborhood's response to urban renewal); William Foote Whyte, *Street Corner Society: The Social Structure of an Italian Slum* (Chicago, IL: University of Chicago Press, 1955).

Street Corner Society (1955) (Whyte lived in Boston's North End and wrote on his sociological observations while living there); and Eric Redman's *Dance of Legislation* (1973) (Redman participated as a staff member and observed congressional actions).

[3] Current practicing lawyer/jurist scholars include, *inter alia*, Richard A. Posner (Chief Judge, United States Court of Appeals for the Seventh Circuit, and Senior Lecturer at the University of Chicago School of Law) and Laurence H. Tribe (Constitutional Law Practitioner and Professor at Harvard School of Law); however, practicing small-firm consumer cause lawyer scholars who apply participant-observer case studies to their scholarly work are little known.

[4] Donald A. Schőn, *Educating The Reflective Practitioner, Toward a New Design for Teaching and Learning in the Professions* (San Francisco, CA: Jossey-Bass, 1987).

[5] Small firm cause lawyers are aptly described in pages 88–95 of the collection of essays edited by Stuart Scheingold and Austin Sarat in *Something to Believe In, Politics, Professionalism,*

case study data were collected while I was the Florida Senior Health Care Attorney on a select inside team that advanced stealth legislative enactment of Florida's 1994 tobacco liability law. I collected other portions during my work on the Florida 1994 gubernatorial reelection campaign of Lawton Chiles, and from my small-firm cause lawyer litigation and coordinator role in Florida's legal action against Big Tobacco.[6]

Some data cited in this essay are drawn from real-time narrative. The narrative has been extensively reduced for this essay, yet is still lengthy. Although the length of the narrative and the use of other historical and documentary data sets limit the writing space available for analysis, they also provide depth of content and texture for innumerable insights and material for the cause lawyer project. The condensed analysis provided here is just a portion of what can be drawn from these data sets. Particular to this essay, within these unique data sources, we find Cracker culture, cause lawyers, and a heroic tale at the constructive edge.

II. Cracker Culture: Creation of a Heroic Band of Brothers Against Big Tobacco

"We're talking about a product that kills. It's pure and unadulterated money and power. It's too big to buck." Associated Press, August 28, 1987

It matters what we believe.
Some beliefs are like walled gardens.
They encourage exclusivity, and the feeling
of being especially privileged.

and Cause Lawyering (Stanford, CA: Stanford University Press, 2004, 88–95). I started my small cause lawyering firm after working as Florida Assistant Attorney General, Florida Senior Health Care Attorney, Special Counsel to the Florida Supreme Court, State Courts Administrator, and staff on numerous state and federal election campaigns. I represent consumer causes, and clients (including select criminal cases), that are disadvantaged in the legal system. Beyond being an originator of the crucibles and successes of tobacco litigation in the mid to late 1990s, I currently act as national co-lead counsel in six states addressing removal of potential benzene formation in soft drinks. I am also a Professor of Law & Policy at Northeastern University, directing and teaching in its Executive Doctoral Program in Law & Policy. The program emphasizes advancing professional competence in the student's respective domain, and doctoral knowledge-creation skills and publication. I was formerly a health law scholar and instructor in judicial process and constitutional law at Boston University.

[6] The participant-observer author disclosures and discussions are placed in the "I" format to provide a more personal, direct, and authentic ownership of the information, theory, and purposes behind this case study. This may concern some readers. It was felt that whatever disadvantages accrue from the personal "I" are outweighed by the power of commitment and acceptance of responsibility for the experience, data, research, and findings.

Other beliefs are expansive and lead the way
Into wider and deeper sympathies.

Sophia Lyon Fahs

People say that what we're all seeking is a meaning for life. I don't think that's what we're really seeking. I think that what we are seeking is an experience of being alive, that our life experiences on the purely physical plane will have resonances within our own innermost being and reality, so that we actually feel the rapture of being alive.

The new discoveries of science 'rejoin us to the ancients' by enabling us to recognize in this whole universe 'a reflection magnified of our own most inward nature; so that we are indeed its ears, its eyes, its thinking, and its speech – or, in theological terms, God's ears, God's eyes, God's thinking, and God's Word.'

Joseph Campbell (1988)

"*I've found the edge. Can you live there with me?*" asks the *fictional* young attorney Gavin Banek of his ethically compromised wife, in the 2002 hit movie, *Changing Lanes*.[7] This fictional story of finding the "constructive edge" mirrors the *true* story dynamic of Florida cause lawyers and their Cracker governmental allies as they "found" their constructive edge to successfully take on and defeat Big Tobacco.[8]

The "constructive edge" is where the forces of economics, nobility, law, culture, and story collide in dynamic real-time interface. Cause lawyers live the reality and humbly mediate[9] the crushing tension between the corporate and legal profession's low-road technical capitalism and high-road noble humanitarianism.[10] Cause lawyers individually and collectively

[7] *Changing Lanes*, Directed by Roger Mitchell, Screen Play by Chap Taylor (Paramount Pictures: 2002). Gavin defines and stakes out his moral and ethical center after a day of buffeting between legal technical corruptions, emotional confusion, and escalating revenge. Gavin's edge is formed after understanding the power and perversion of economics, social class, family relationships, and the courts. With this experiential knowledge and moral imperative to define himself and his role, Gavin ultimately commits his power to serve others and take steps to discipline and redeem the distorted souls around him.

[8] Note that just this simple term, "Big Tobacco" is an embedded term flipping Tobacco Power against itself – turning it into a heroic tale of the biblical archetype *David vs. Goliath*; a story that resonates with Florida Crackers.

[9] This mediation is a constant dynamic. Douglas Torgerson speaks to this stating,

> The dynamic nature of the [policy sciences] phenomenon is rooted in an internal tension, a *dialectic opposition between knowledge and politics*. Through the interplay of knowledge and politics, different aspects of the phenomenon become salient at different moments . . . the presence of dialectic tension means that the phenomenon has the potential to develop, to change form. However, no particular pattern of development is inevitable.

[10] Austin Sarat and Stuart Scheingold, *Cause Lawyers and Social Movements* (Stanford, CA: Stanford University Press, 2005, 450). Michael McCann and William Haltom observe that:

> Indeed, many trial lawyers routinely define their practices as committed to representing "the little person" and "equalizing" the contest against large corporations and faceless bureaucracies.

harness and engage in creative construction at that edge.[11] Constructing noble outcomes (i.e., "the Good" from this edge and the tension of existence) is not only the story of human identity formation; it is also the story of cause lawyer alignment[12] – of heroic, humble perseverance and resilience in a cause to redeem society.[13]

> In sum, such personal injury lawyers are transparently selective about: *the clients whom they represent*, namely injured consumers and other victims, including especially women and lower income citizens; *those parties whom they tend to challenge*, namely unaccountable business corporations, professionals, and governmental agencies; and *the larger social values* that they aim to serve in the process, which are access to social justice, the rule of law, civil rights, and democratic accountability. As such, the model personal injury lawyer "shares and aims to share with her client responsibility for the ends she is promoting in her representation . . . stretching those ideals from the representation of individual clients to causes."

Austin Sarat and Stuart Scheingold, *Cause Lawyers and Social Movements*, 431–432. *See also* Austin Sarat and Stuart Scheingold, *Cause Lawyering: Political Commitments and Professional Responsibilities* (New York, NY: Oxford University Press, 1998, 3, 7). This progressive cause lawyer motivation is described in this cause lawyer quote from McCann and Haltom's research:

> What really drives most trial lawyers that are successful in this business, and who are winning cases, is that they really have some underlying philosophy of good – and of outrage, disgust about what's going on with corporate indifference and abuse . . . I always had a real strong background in blue collar culture. And I was very aggravated at the way there's a lot of injustice in all phases of life. The way people abuse people. The way corporations abuse people . . . I have always had this sense that if you really worked something real, real hard and get to the truth and win, that's the right thing to do. That's what keeps me going.

Austin Sarat and Stuart Scheingold, *Cause Lawyers and Social Movements*, 431. See also William Haltom and Michael McCann, *Distorting The Law: Politics, Media, and the Litigation Crisis* (Chicago University of Chicago Press, 2004). Harold Lasswell provides a similar definition for policy sciences in that they are to provide the "intelligence pertinent to the integration of values realized by and embodied in interpersonal relations, "which "prizes not the glory of a depersonalized state of the efficiency of a social mechanism (such as technocratic application of law), but human dignity and the realization of human capabilities." Harold Lasswell and David Lerner, *The Policy Orientation, In The Policy Sciences: Recent Developments in Scope and Methods* (Stanford, CA: Stanford University Press, 1951, 2).

11 In 1832 Alexis de Tocqueville acknowledged the civilized embrace of this constructive edge recognizing that "scarcely any political question arises in the United States which is not resolved, sooner or later, into a judicial question." Alexis de Tocqueville, *Democracy in America* (1832).

12 Austin Sarat, *Between (the Presence of) Violence and (the Possibility of) Justice, Lawyering against Capital Punishment*, in *Cause Lawyering, Political commitment and Professional Responsibilities*, ed. Austin Sarat and Stuart Scheingold (New York, NY: Oxford University Press, 1998, 318–319). Stories, ritual, and mythology are at the core of law. For instance, judges wear robes for the purpose of ritual and mythology, so that the power of the law is not solely on coercion. Lawyers construct opposing stories and narratives out of facts and law to prevail in trials, appeals, and motions. Jerome Burke, *Making Stories, Law, Literature, Life* (Cambridge, MA: Harvard University Press, 2002, 37–41).

13 In story, heroes are not aggrandized. "The ultimate aim of the quest must be neither release nor ecstasy for oneself, but the wisdom and power to serve others" Joseph Campbell, *The Power of Myth*, ed. Bill Moyers (1988, xv). In story, a hero "acts to redeem society." *Id.*

Can American popular culture embrace cause lawyer alliance and nobility in "creative construction"[14] at the crushing edge? Is there a story[15] available in which cause lawyers align with public servants to create a heroic "band of brothers" to hold low-road corporate capitalists accountable for the sickness and death of Americans?

If so, it is important that such a story of victorious cause lawyer alignment be told. It should be told not to create celebrities, but to celebrate heroes and heroism, to advance our culture with a narrative that will celebrate and "give life to law's ethical aspirations."[16] The following participant-observer, thick description case source material constructs this story of cause lawyer nobility, one that, if properly presented, can resonate with American culture.

In March 1996, I was a small-firm cause lawyer coordinating the litigation, legislative lobbying, and grassroots campaign for Florida's historic multibillion dollar Medicaid third-party liability litigation against Big Tobacco. Just weeks before the Florida Senate's seismic vote to retain the tobacco liability law, which law was *sine qua non* for the cause lawyer and public servant alliance victory over Big Tobacco, I wrote in the *Journal of the Florida Medical Association*,

> Fortunes made from trading death for profits, deception, and addiction – for each crime to health by the cigarette industry, Florida law provides a remedy. These three intense legal offensives [Florida Medicaid Action, Engle Class Action, Individual Tort/Fraud Actions] are battling today to expose the truth of cigarette addiction, disease and death. These legal battles are fought to finally hold the cigarette industry accountable and obtain justice. Like the victorious warriors in Shakespeare's *King Henry V* on Saint Crispen's day, join "we band of brothers" in battle. Speak out in support of these legal battles against this loathsome scourge. Together we will leave a victorious mark in

[14] The term "creative construction" is a corollary to Joseph Shumpeter's "creative destruction" in that to create is the noble purpose of absolute Cartesian consciousness. The term "nobility" is the humble creative essence found as we smile with confident, resilient hope in the face of near certain oblivion, and the corruption from fear and decay that is faced daily.

[15] The crushing edge of imperfection, of conflict, tension, and purposeful resolution are also the *sine qua non* of great stories. Joseph Campbell, *The Power of Myth*, 4. Stories are ways we endeavor to fill the hole within us – to transcend pain, loss, and death Richard Kearney, *On Stories: Thinking in Action* (New York: Routledge, 2006, 159–160, n 7. Stories stir the absolute of Cartesian imagination and existential soul chords based on real human experience.

[16] Austin Sarat and Stuart Scheingold, *Cause Lawyering*, 1998, 319.

> history, save taxpayers hundreds of millions of dollars, and most importantly save this and future generations hundreds of thousands of lives.[17]

This prophetic plea describes the elements of a compelling story: Goliath corporate cartel spinning lies and causing sickness and death with addictive cigarettes solely for greed, a band of legal warriors applying law and government to expose the truth and exact justice, and a plea to adopt the narrative and take on this cause of justice. This story has not been told. As Haltom and McCann observed,

> Given the scope of harms inflicted by tobacco companies, their well-documented practices of deception, their general unpopularity, and the minimal regulatory actions of other governmental institutions, one might expect that successful litigation for injured citizens against tobacco giants would come to be considered a heroic public story for the civil legal system.[18]

It just so happens that creation of a heroic tale against Big Tobacco was exactly the motivation of the last leader of the fading Florida Scots-Irish Cracker culture – the late Florida Governor and U.S. Senator "Walkin" Lawton Chiles.

1. Florida Cracker Language and Heroic Legacy

It is the third day of the 1993 Florida health care reform workshop with Dr. David Brooks and the Jackson Hole Group, in Jackson Hole, Wyoming. As planned, Harold Lewis,[19] the General Counsel for the Florida Agency for

[17] Tim Howard and Paul Chmielewski, *Journal of the Florida Medical Association*, 1996: Vol. 83, No. 2, 126.

[18] Bill Haltom and Michael McCann, *Distorting the Law*, 228. Haltom and McCann go on to note that "observers have described the third tobacco campaign as 'dramatic' in both approach and outcome. Jurors who chose to punish defendants for spreading disease, dependency, and disinformation appeared little interested in what [cause] lawyers were paid to prosecute the cases in court" Bill Haltom, *Distorting the Law*, 240–241.

[19] Blood loyal since their ATO days at the University of Florida in the mid-1950s, in late 1994, just prior to his last term, the Governor appoints Harold as Chief Inspector General of Florida. Harold diligently tracks every step for the Governor. He would and ultimately will "fall on the sword" for him. In the July 1994 photograph of Lawton, Laurence H. Tribe, Harold, and me at the National Governor's Conference in Boston, where we met at the Boston Sheraton to finalize the tobacco complaint and litigation strategy, the Governor affectionately writes to his cowboy "Cracker" friend, "To 'Tom Horne' my favorite tracker, Lawton." Tom Horne refers to a famous western cowboy famed for his tracking ability.

Health Care Administration, has the horses saddled and the cowboy hats, boots, and lunches packed for their day of riding. "Governor, here's the white stallion, saddled up and ready. I've got the palomino." After several hours, they cross a stream below the Grand Teton. Harold and the Governor get off their horses and walk the field. "Governor, I'm with you walking or riding, walking or riding," Harold says. "Governor, in trying to get control of the Medicaid costs, there's a liability statute that requires third parties to pay before the State. Cigarettes are causing a lot of Medicaid costs. What do you think about having the tobacco companies pay for these costs instead of the State?" The Governor replies, "Sounds like they should be paying," Several hours after Harold's Dutch-Oven lunch – bacon pan-fried with onions and Worcestershire sauce, biscuits, tea, and chew – Harold pitches the tobacco idea as a heroic legacy builder: "**People remember Huey Long because he went to war and beat Standard Oil. To be remembered in history, you have to have your own Standard Oil. Governor, Big Tobacco can be *your* Standard Oil**."

The participant-observer, thick description case study data make it clear that taking on Big Tobacco was presented to Governor Chiles in the late summer of 1993 as a southern Cracker story of taking on a corporate Goliath and winning for the common folk. What was the motivation of the cause lawyers, and how were they involved?

Several weeks prior to the presentation to Governor Chiles, several highly successful small-firm consumer and personal injury cause lawyers took ideas from a 1977 *Emory Law Journal* article[20] by Southern Illinois

[20] After forty years of failed litigation efforts, in the third wave of cigarette litigation – from 1993 to 1997 – cause lawyers initiated a sea change in state and national cigarette policy, both private and public. They applied constructs of thought that had been developed through idealistic, missionary cause lawyers, such as Northeastern Law Professor Richard A. Daynard, and advocacy groups, such as the Tobacco Product Liability Project (TPLP) also at Northeastern University. The true "missionary" progressive cause lawyers advanced the cause prior to any "mercenary" cause lawyer involvement. They were voices crying in the wilderness.

These later, more mercenary, "progressive cause lawyers" picked up on an approach advanced by TPLP, as discussed in the 1977 *Emory Law Journal*. This was one critical source of the "policy" idea found stirring in the "policy soup," as described by Kingdon. John W. Kingdon, *Agendas, Alternatives, and Public Policies, Second Edition* (Boston, MA: Longman, 2003). The approach was to strategically change the instrumental narrative, legal normative and ideological framework, moving sharply from the framework of the first two waves. The idealists in the TPLP set the winning stage; the realists came to advance the cause driven by their embedded humanitarian philosophy and economic reward. This new instrumental narrative, legal normative and ideological framework avoided tobacco's jury defenses of assumption of risk and personal responsibility.

University Professor Donald Garner and started the initiative that led Harold Lewis to present this epic narrative. The concept was simple: the article proposed that states should seek compensation for smoking-related health care costs. "When an indigent smoker develops a cigarette-related illness his medical bills are often paid by the public through tax-supported hospitals and state-health care programs. Thus, the nonsmoking public indirectly subsidizes and promotes the consumption of tobacco products."[21]

State Medicaid programs, like Florida's had "clean hands." They did not manufacture Marlboro or Winston cigarettes, nor did they create a $45 billion industry with tentacles in significant facets and products in the world's economy. Nor did states kill 425,000 Americans from its cigarettes. It therefore violates common principles of justice as found in John Stuart Mills' "harm principle"[22] when Florida's Medicaid program is stuck with a $300 million bill each year to pay for the health care costs of poor Medicaid recipients who are sick and dying from cigarette-related diseases like lung cancer. Moreover, federal and state laws mandate recovery of this money from liable third parties.

Earlier that summer in 1993, at the Whistler Resort, seventy miles north of Vancouver, Canada, Fred Levin, a controversial and highly successful attorney with a medium-sized personal injury firm from Pensacola, Florida, attended a meeting of the Inner Circle of Advocates – 100 of the most powerful plaintiff lawyers in the world. These ninety-eight men and two women averaged total judgments in excess of $110 million each. A new member is taken only when an existing member dies. Another Inner Circle member, Ron Motley of Charleston, South Carolina, sidles up to Fred, and as they

The new narrative framework changed to a comparison of who is more appropriately liable between: (1) the wealthy tobacco companies that knew the harm and addiction their product would cause and made the profits from selling addiction and death, (2) the poor indigent Medicaid nicotine addict who cannot pay for their health care, and (3) the innocent state taxpayer nobly paying for the health care costs of the indigent? Figure 1.

21 Justin Castanoso, *Florida law targets tobacco industry*, News & Records, Greensboro, North Carolina, June 5, 1994, A-1, A-2.

22 Personal and in this instance corporate autonomy should be protected so long as it is not exercised in violation of the basic interests of others, such as dumping the medical costs of corporate-caused sickness and death upon the State. Montesquieu had a similar view in that liberty is to be limited by law in situations where some dominate others, such as when commercial interests harm consumers. The law would then be used to protect the common interest. Bailey Kuklin & Jeffrey W. Stempel, *Foundations of the Law, An Interdisciplinary and Jurisprudential Primer* (St. Paul, MN: West Publishing Co., 1994, 54, 57).

talk, Fred asks, "Mind if I smoke?" "Of course go ahead," Ron states. Fred complains, "It's too bad that individual cases don't work, this stuff is addictive and kills people. I can't quit." "As a matter of fact . . . ," Motley began:

> My mother Tease died[23] of that stuff. It slowly strangled her. She shrunk so much you couldn't recognize her. I promised her that I would get them. Dickie and I have been mapping out a plan to take on Big Tobacco. We got a Mississippi lawyer, Michael Lewis, to draft the complaint based on the idea that if innocent taxpayers were the plaintiff, the case might win. We've tried some focus groups in Mississippi and when the state was the one suing for Medicaid losses, the state won every time. It was a slam dunk.

Fred, who knew how to appraise a case's economic potential, perked up when he was told that focus groups and mock juries found for the state.[24] He calls W.D. Childers – the irascible 25-year Dean of the Florida Senate who is known as the "Banty Rooster" for his independent, quick-witted, and pugnacious style – to discuss how to get the litigation started in Florida.

Use of focus groups and mock trials permits a gauging of the dominant, embedded ideologies of the public and a typical juror. This assists progressive cause lawyers in grounding the *artisanality* of law into a structure that resonates with this sample of the public will.

By *artisanality*, I am referring to the unique construction and alignment of constituted knowledge found in the federal and state constitutions, legislation, and regulations with what elected officials in the executive and legislative branch consider wise policy, the building of external

[23] Ron details his mothers death, and reacts consistently with Scots-Irish "Cracker" cultural training:

> She actually would talk one of her sisters into sneaking her a cigarette. She would take the oxygen away from her and smoke a cigarette – which was, you know, very dangerous because it could have exploded. . . . It is deeply ingrained in my mind. Well, it is . . . To watch someone that you love very much die a slow miserable death, suffocating day by day, is a very unpleasant thing. . . . And to know exactly what caused it. And then when you hear the denials of the cigarette companies that they have never caused the illness or death of a single American citizen, having sat there and watched my mother suffocating. . . . **[I]t made me very angry. And when I get angry, I try to get even.**

Harold V. Cordry, *Tobacco* (Denver, CO: ABC-CLIO, Inc., 2001, 132).

[24] Don Yeager, *Where There's Smoke . . . The untold story of how the Inner Circle of powerful attorneys came up with a strategy to sue the tobacco industry, and why they chose Florida to be their client.* Florida Trend, October, 1996, pp. 62–67.

support through narratives, support from elected officials, advocacy groups, lobbyists, and use of media that also align with the internal capacity of the culture to effect the narrow, realistic range of achievable policies.

Richard Posner has a similar definition of *artisanality*. He describes *artisanality* as follows:

> Like an artist or artisan, the traditional legal advocate, professor or judge produced neither a replicable or otherwise verifiable argument or proof nor a standardized product that could be readily evaluated in the marketplace for legal services or academic scholarship. He produced an essentially literary product in which he displayed mastery of the rhetorical skills that are the distinctive fruit of the lawyer's talent, training, and experience.[25]

These cause lawyers are skilled participants in the risk analysis involved in the game of law.[26] As they play this game, they prepare and discuss legal theories aligned with legally relevant facts. They align the technical components of law with cognitive common sense from the embedded adoption of narrative frames and myths as indicated in focus groups and mock trials. They then take this constituted knowledge and legal skill and apply it to judges and juries that have the power to create law through their decisions.

Effective cause lawyering is "dissensual" in that it is rooted in conflict and power over the authoritative allocation of values for a society. Cause lawyering is "collective" in that it involves a leader-follower interaction. This concept parallels the pluralistic concept of distributed leadership – "one diffuses power without diluting it, one accrues power by sharing it."[27]

Here, there is a distributed cause lawyer leadership effort to align and share the power of their legal *artisanality* with Cracker political leaders to catch the next wave and advance the interests of both. John Kingdon

[25] Richard A. Posner, *Overcoming Law* (Cambridge, MA: Harvard University Press, 1995). The book *Law as Art* provides a comprehensive analysis of the similar cognitive and creative aspects of art and law. Gary Bagnall, *Art as Law* (Brookfield, VT: Dartmouth Publishing Company, 1996).

[26] The game of chess needs rules; otherwise it is not chess. The judicial game has rules that must abide by or it is not a judicial game. There are *activists* rules and *restraint* rules. By creating these rules and "games, people create a temporary refuge from, by imaginative transformation of, the sinister realities of ordinary life, the realities of hatred, disease, crime, betrayal, war, poverty, bereavement, despair." Richard A. Posner, *Overcoming Law*, 133.

[27] Leadership and Business Professor David P. Boyd, Northeastern University, Boston, Massachusetts, points out that "management literature today is replete with the importance of coalitions, alliances, lattice organizations, and webs of inclusion."

acknowledges the importance of leadership in his *interactional* model of public policymaking. He quotes an analyst for an interest group:

> As I see it, people who are trying to advocate change are like surfers waiting for the big wave. You get out there, you have to be ready to go, you have to be ready to paddle. If you're not ready to paddle when the big wave comes along, you're not going to ride in.[28]

Kingdon goes on to state, "Individuals do not control events or structures, but can anticipate them and bend them to their purposes to some degree."[29] These cause lawyers as leaders are watching, preparing, and ready for creating the next big wave.

"Doing well by doing good" is the common refrain of good capitalism and of economically successful cause lawyers. However, some members of the plaintiffs bar do so well and are so skilled and ruthless that doing good is perceived as an illusory pretext simply to do well. Although their capitalist drive may be similar to attorneys for Corporate America, the cause lawyer distinction is that these attorneys selectively apply their skills and drive for the "cause" of consumers and injured "one-time players." They choose to represent only consumers and personal injury cases and are not legal mercenaries-for-hire for any interest.

Because consumer, personal injury cause lawyers advance their own money and legal work, and are at risk in losing everything that is invested, they also use highly refined risk-benefit analysis to select profitable cases. Key methods to reduce their risk, mentioned in this description, are mock trials and mock juries. These exercises help determine if a case is worth taking on and refine case presentations to reduce the risk of loss in cases. Finally, the economic success of personal injury cause lawyers permits their alliance with populist political leaders who carry the same banner of consumer interests and advocacy for the weak and injured.

In this case, cause lawyer alignment with progressive, populist Cracker political leadership created a potentially potent "band of brothers." It became a cause lawyer juggernaut of political power and legal resources to challenge the dominant political and legal ideology of Big Tobacco.

[28] John W. Kingdon, *Agendas, Alternatives, and Public Policies, Second Edition* (Boston, MA: Longman, 2003, 165).

[29] John W. Kingdon, *Agendas*, 225.

But what is this Cracker culture from which the leaders and lawyers were fostered and in which they were aligning, and why was it important?

III. Florida Crackers

Florida Cracker wants are simple, garden, pigpen, chicken coop, and woods and streams. When the Cracker is full, he is heard saying, "I done et so free o' fish, my stommick rises and falls with the tide." Any small income is spent at the general store on Saturday to stock up on "bought vittles." His one luxury is tobacco, chew and snuff.

Federal Writers' Project 1976: 128–30

Florida Crackers were in part formed and woven in the womb of tobacco's southern soul[30] and have embedded instincts challenging injustice. Florida Crackers are descendants of the pre-Enlightenment, anti-intellectual, undesirable Scots-Irish Highlanders – the "Celtic fringe" who settled the frontier South.[31] "Florida Cracker" refers to "Florida's white backwoods settler who [has suffered] generations of hardship and poverty and appropriate the guile of the Negro. He drives a hard Bargain with soft words. The Cracker boasts, 'In the winter we live on the Yankee, and in the summer on fish.'"[32]

The dialect of Florida's original Scot settlers termed "Cracker" a person who talked boastingly.[33] "Cracker speech is a mixture of Old English

[30] Though their ancestors were white small farmers and laborers, these southern lawyers and Cracker politicians are not explicitly aware of the cultural abuses and centuries of injustice an economy based on tobacco fostered. Yet, when the opportunity of alignment came, these cause lawyers and the last post Civil War reconstruction populist "Florida Cracker" Democratic leaders took on their southern economic and hierarchical maker – Big Tobacco.

[31] Thomas Sowell, *Black Rednecks and White Liberals* (San Francisco, CA: Encounter Books, 2005, 8, 10, 22–23). "The Celts who settled in the South brought with them their non-English ways – including a pastoral economy based on open-range herding, a leisurely lifestyle and a distaste for hard work, rural values that stressed wasteful hospitality and outdoor sports, the reckless indulgence of food and drink, a touchy and romantic sense of honor, and a strong tendency toward lawlessness and settlement of disagreements by violent means – and they readily imposed these traditions upon their neighbors." Ste. Claire, *Florida Crackers* (Gainesville, FL: University of Florida Press, 2005: 62). "It is the western panhandle [of North Florida] that the Cracker is racially and culturally the least diluted. He is tall and rangy, with the angular bones of the Scot[s]-Irish and blue eyes of the Saxons and Celts acquired more than a thousand years ago when Vikings raided their villages." Ste. Claire, *Florida Crackers*, 62.

[32] Federal Writer's Project, *Florida Guide to the Southernmost State* (New York, NY: Oxford University Press, 1938, Republished in 1976, 128–130).

[33] Roots of the term Cracker are found in the sixteenth-century England term referring to a braggart or fast talker. "References to Cracker as a character trait appear as early as 1509, and was used in this context by William Shakespeare in King John, c. 1594: "What Cracker is this

provincialisms, local slang, and a variety of invented words, including 'Heifer on my haslet,' meaning, 'Well, I'll be damned!' Their humor originates from the limitations and hazards of existence, so he may declare, 'I done drunk outa fruit jars so long I got a ridge acrost my nose.'"[34]

In Florida, the name "Cracker" is also a cattle term. To communicate over miles of timber barrens, Florida's Cracker cowboys popped whips of braided buckskin, twelve to eighteen feet long. The "crack" over the ears of cattle sounded like a rifle shot and the sound carried as far. Harold Lewis was an authentic Florida cattle "Cracker."[35]

Cracker culture[36] socially supported "rough and tumble"[37] fights as personal demonstrations of courage and ferocity.[38] This cultural feature in part explains why football is almost considered a religion and professional wrestling is so popular in the South. This approach transferred to their justice system:

> To many rural southerners, rather than a set of legal statutes, justice remained a matter of societal norms allowing for the respect of property rights, individual honor, and a maximum of personal

same that deafes our eares with this abundance of superfluous breath?" Ste. Claire, *Florida Crackers*, 235. Allen Morris, *The Florida Handbook, 26th Biennial Edition* (Gainesville, FL: The Peninsular Publishing Company, 1997–1998, 292–293).

34 Federal Writers' Project, *Florida Guide*, 128–130.

35 At that time, Harold Lewis is Governor Chiles' handpicked General Counsel of the Agency for Health Care Administration. Harold is proud that his Florida roots go back to the six original Scottish families who arrived in North Florida in 1826. A true member of Florida's depression era "Cracker" network, Herald is a cowboy and outdoorsman. He lassoes cattle, hunts, owns horses, and owns part of "Big 9" – a million-acre Queen land grant hunting ranch and lodge in British Columbia, Canada. In fact, Harold participated in some of the last American western cattle drives. An Alpha Tao Omega president at the University of Florida, where Lawton was a fraternity brother, he worked on Florida Governor and former U.S. Senator "Walkin'" Lawton's first campaign for State House in 1958. Lawton and Harold share the love of Florida's "Cracker" cowboy roots, including chewing tobacco. Harold even names his personal horse "Cracker," and it has a direct lineage to De Soto's original Spanish horses from his 1539 exploration of Florida in search of gold.

36 The 1930s Federal Writers' Project reports that Florida Crackers are fond of social gatherings and kinfolk, chicken Palau is an appetizing excuse for an outing. The men build fires and put on large pots of rice, while the women cook, the men go hunting or fishing or sit and swap news. Their wants are simple, garden, pigpen, chicken coop, and woods and streams. When the Cracker is full, he is heard saying, "I done et so free o' fish, my stommick rises and falls with the tide." Any small income is spent at the general store on Saturday to stock up on "bought vittles." His one luxury is tobacco, chew and snuff. Federal Writers Project, *Florida Guide*, 128–130.

37 "Rough and tumble" fighting had no rules, and the goal, maiming of the opponent, was appropriate and expected. Thomas Sowell, *Black Rednecks and White Liberals*, 8.

38 Thomas Sowell, *Black Rednecks and White Liberals*, 8.

> independence. Any violation of this pattern amounted to a breach of justice requiring a specific response from the injured party.[39]

The courage and internal norms of individual honor also form the attractiveness of the Scots-Irish Cracker culture – "insistence on the dignity of the individual in the face of power, regardless of one's place or rank in society."[40] This populist libertarian, egalitarianism pervades Cracker culture and is found in their populist governmental leaders and southern cause lawyers.

Consistent with libertarian and egalitarian components of "Cracker" philosophy, Florida's Medicaid Third-Party Liability law was premised on the noble mission of Medicaid – medical payer of last resort for the poor as established in state and federal law and regulation. Florida Medicaid was an innocent party helping the poor, yet was paying the bill for Big Tobacco's profits. With John Stuart Mills' "harm principle" embedded in their sense of justice, it was intuitively unacceptable for innocent parties to bear the burden of other's abuses. Under Medicaid law, if any other party is more liable, it should pay the medical costs. In this case the party arguably most liable for these Medicaid costs was clear – **Big Tobacco** (see Figure 3.1).

IV. Dear Big Tobacco: One Stealth Missile, Compliments of Florida Crackers and Cause Lawyers

"Laws are like sausages, it is better not to see them being made."

Otto von Bismark

Smoking is an unhealthy habit with horrific consequences for which the tobacco industry should be held to account. A bill awaiting Gov. Lawton Chiles' signature would hasten the day. Unfortunately, it is the product of offensive political trickery and its terms are dangerously broad.

[39] Thomas Sowell, *Black Rednecks and White Liberals*, 9. "A lawman who was too diligent, or who offended the wrong family, could get himself injured or killed. Southern families, like those of their Celtic ancestors, were extended and clannish, and family feuds in the Old South were as easy to start and as difficult to stop as they were in pre-modern Scotland and Ireland." Grady McWhiney, *Cracker Culture: Celtic Ways in the Old South* (University of Alabama Press, 1989, 161–162).

[40] James Webb, *Born Fighting, How the Scots-Irish Shaped America* (New York: Broadway Books, 2004, 182).

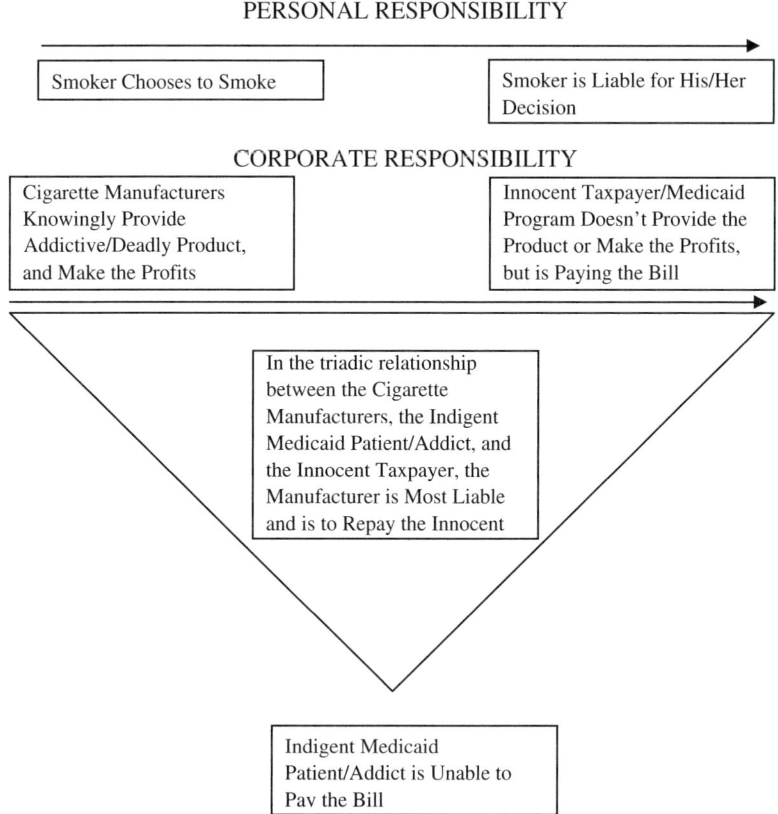

Figure 3.1. Third-Wave Legal Narrative and Normative Shift From Personal Responsibility to Corporate Liability.

. . . In the long history of "snookers," as legislative argot defines such stunts, this is the worst. Let it also be the last. *St. Petersburg Times*, May 6, 1994

"It's the definition of Lawton Chiles, how he operates. He gives an 'Ah shucks, you can trust me,' image, but underneath, he is manipulative and conniving."
Ash and Goldschmidt (1994)

"Legislation can neither be wise nor just which seeks the welfare of a single interest at the expense and to the injury of many and varied interests." Andrew Johnson

Cause lawyers and Florida Cracker legislative leaders took the Medicaid liability idea and crafted a stealth law and enactment strategy. Big Tobacco didn't see it coming.

Elected to the State Senate within two years of each other, Dean of the Florida Senate, W.D. Childers stays a Democrat in 1992 to vote North Florida Senator Pat Thomas[41] into the Senate Presidency. Pat and W.D. have historical and philosophical ties to the Florida's Democratic "Pork Chop Gang" heyday in the late 1950s and early 1960s, when conservative rural Cracker Democrats ruled state government. Split 20/20, Pat presides over the Senate in 1994, the last Florida "Cracker" Democrat to do so. Teamed with Pat, W.D.'s Senate Commerce Committee is the committee of reference for all bills before they go onto the Senate floor for approval. W.D. mused, "I've got the Legislature by the balls, and I know how to play them." Wary of W.D., Lawton assigns Harold, a thirty-year friend of W.D., to track him. They code name W.D., "Geronimo" to see if he's on the reservation.

None of the highly paid, political elite, sycophantic tobacco lobbyists, like Philip Morris's John French or the Tobacco Institute's Guy Spearman, knew the missile was coming. Crafted as a generic amendment, it was a stealth missile, launched below the radar screen. The secret is held so closely that Tom Herndon, a career state operator and the Governor's Chief of Staff, doesn't know anything about this tobacco liability bill. Besides all eyes are focused on the "joint and several" liability battle between Big Business and the trial lawyers.

Concerned that Governor Chiles would double-cross W.D. and not support the tobacco law, and that Attorney General Butterworth would not place the tobacco law amendments on Senate Bill 2110 (the Medicaid Fraud bill that I had help draft and advocated the House and Senate Health Care committees to pass), W.D. flexes his muscle: "Hell with them, they all lie, they're a bunch of lemmings. I'm shuttin' down the legislative beehive, no honey today." W.D. stops referring any bill to the floor, which effectively shuts down every piece of legislation. Harold reported to Lawton, "Geronimo's off the reservation."

The last days of every legislative session are always the most desperate and frenetic. Hundreds of millions of corporate and lobbying dollars are on the line. Through Harold, W.D. sends this message to the Governor and Speaker: "Until a green light is given for enactment of my tobacco

[41] Pat Thomas was born in the tobacco plantation region of Gadsden County, Florida, on November 21, 1933. Known for bringing home the bacon – road, building, and water projects aiding small town development, he rose as a Democratic Senate power from the late 1960s and early 1970s with Senator Dempsey Barron's "coalition"; a disciplined conservative band of Republicans and rural Democrats who kept liberal "Doghouse Democrats" of Southeast Florida at bay.

liability law, not another bill will pass this session." The $40 billion dollar annual state budget stalls in committee. As the hours pass, pressure builds. House Speaker, Bo Johnson, from Milton, Florida, a "Cracker" Democrat and protégé of Lawton, sends the Governor a message: "What's the hold up, are you behind this?" A true southern gentleman, Senate President Pat Thomas doesn't want responsibility either for holding the legislature hostage or for the political war against Big Tobacco: "W.D., please don't you get me tied into this thing. I've got too many friends that lobby for tobacco." Pat just wants his daughter's lobbying career to thrive, and Florida's last Southern Democrat Senate Presidency to go smoothly. The rest of the Senate leadership, including Rules Chairman Senator Kirkpatrick, Senator Toni Jennings, and Senator Jim Scott, know exactly what is happening. They keep silent.

Attorney General Butterworth's refusal to place the amendment on the bill weakens. Butterworth's cynical backdoor political operator, Karl Weckman, sits in W.D.'s waiting room with his head hung low. Butterworth agrees to put the amendment on his Medicaid Fraud bill, saying, "Go ahead, as long as you don't kill my bill."[42] W.D. tells his aide, "Bet, the bastards are getting in line. Pat's still whining." W.D. chuckles as he addresses the Commerce Committee Staff Director. Lawton calls W.D., saying, "Let it fly." W.D. directs the action: "Pat, walk when the joint and several vote comes up for reconsideration. Shebel and French will think they won. While they're celebrating at Clyde's we'll pass the tobacco law. They'll never know what hit 'em." W.D. sets the classic decoy before launching the missile.

On April 7, at 11:45 in the morning, W.D. takes the Senate President's gavel. He says, "Senator Forman, you are recognized. This Amendment expands the scope of liability payments that must be repaid." "Without objection," W.D. bangs the gavel. Amendment and bill pass the Senate 38–0. Watching the Senate chamber action from W.D.'s personal office, Harold and I shake hands, while Deputy Attorney General Pete Antonacci, and the baffled former Senator, and Secretary of the Department of Business, George Stuart and Professional Regulation, look on: "The missile is launched."

The next day, at 5:30 in the morning at the local "Whataburger" fast-food restaurant several miles from the State Capitol, W.D. asks, "Harold,

[42] Lucy Morgan, *How tobacco bill slipped into law*, St. Petersburg Times, March 7, 1995, 1B, 4B.

has Lawton called Bo or Peter [Bo is the Speaker and Peter Wallace is the Speaker designate]? I'm not budging until this is passed." Harold responds, "I'm checking with the Governor. He'll call Bo or Peter this morning." W.D. is firm, saying, "He better do his job. I ain't putting up with stonewalling." Harold calls the Governor at 7:00 in the morning, asking him, "How's my Governor?" The Governor's already in a frenzy. "God damn it Harold, W.D.'s got us shut down. You can't stop communicating with me just because W.D. and Pat want to put pressure on me. Now where are we on tobacco?" Harold responds, "You've got to call Bo and Peter and get it passed in the House before another bill moves." In response, Lawton says, "O. K. Harold, I'll call them now."

"Peter, W.D.'s got everything shut down. It is essential to pass this bill to bring the session to a conclusion."[43] "I thought so. W.D.'s been calling us to verify the status of the bill and wants to know when we are taking it up." Donnie Lamonica, lobbyist and friend of W.D., runs messages back from the Speaker's Office: "W.D., Bo's ready." On April 9, 1994 at 5:30 PM, Speaker Bo Johnson has the gavel. "Representative Graber you are recognized." "This is the transfer of the Medicaid Fraud Unit to the Attorney General's Office. It's come back with an Amendment that broadens principles of recovery, scope of the state's independent cause of action, and the ability of the state to consolidate cases." The House passes the bill 118–0.

The tobacco lobbyists knew of the bill, but were caught flat-footed. Guy Spearman, lobbyist for the Tobacco Institute, sent a copy of the bill to his Washington lawyers. They didn't give him their analysis in time. At "Clyde's", the local Bar across from the Capitol, the business lobbyists were giving high-fives and having drinks celebrating their defeat of the trial lawyers in their battle over "joint and several liability." They were so busy celebrating that they didn't focus on the minor Medicaid Fraud bill that had passed the Senate and was on the House calendar. "John, we kicked their butts. Have a drink on me." "Hey, the House just passed that Medicaid Fraud bill that Guy faxed to Washington for review." "I thought we had that bill held up, at least until we got the report from Washington? Well it's passed now. Let me know when we get the report from Washington. I'll call and let them know the bill passed."

[43] Lucy Morgan, *How tobacco bill slipped into law*, 1B, 4B.

The Washington report was not good. "What in the hell did you let get passed you down there? If this law is constitutional and doesn't get repealed, it could sink the industry. Keith Teel, with Covington & Burling will be down soon. We need to hire the best lobbyists and neutralize all the others. This law has to go!" By Monday, Chiles' former Chief of Staff and the individual who orchestrated his election and was his Campaign Manager, Jim Krog, now corporate lobbyist from Steel, Hector & Davis,[44] pays a personal visit to the Governor. Krog meets with him in his formal Capitol office. Harold and I are in the Governor's casual office adjacent to the formal office and can hear the conversation through the open door.

Krog places his 6′5″, well-fed frame in the chair in front of the Governor's desk, saying,

> Governor, you know if it was just tobacco it wouldn't be that bad. But this law can affect every industry and is not limited to tobacco. It's going to create a political firestorm and hurt your alliances with business in passing health care reform. Shebel and French are taking this personal and tobacco is not happy. This will also harm your chances for reelection. Don't let this one go into law. Let's go through the process next year and see if we can get a bill that goes only after tobacco.

Lawton clarifies:

> Tobacco's all we are going after. That's my intent and I will confirm it with anyone. This is the only chance at a bill we'll ever have. You know that. I tried for several years to raise the tax on cigarettes to cover juvenile justice reform and we got nothing. There's not a chance in hell that we could get a similar bill enacted, even if it was narrowed to tobacco. I do want health care enacted. If I get enough votes to pass that, and tobacco is the trade, I'd have to look at that. We'll take care of the campaign when it's time.

In the complex world of enacting law, the commitment it takes to hold steady in the face of numerous pressures and the corporate inside influence

[44] Not a cause lawyer firm, it lobbies and litigates for corporate interests, including the Florida sugar industry. Steel, Hector & Davis is one of the established and "wired" Florida law firms. It has public interest lawyers, but it is not itself a public interest firm. Lt. Governor Buddy McKay, U.S. Attorney Janet Reno, former Florida State University President, former Florida State College of Law Dean and former ABA President Sandy Talbot D'Alemberte, former Florida Comptroller Gerald Lewis, and former Florida Board of Regent appointee Steve Uhfelder all hail from this firm.

in almost every dimension make enacting corporate accountability laws extraordinarily difficult. This is true even when cause lawyers have the Governor, Senate, and House leadership in the same party and sympathetic to consumer interests. Then, even when such a law is enacted, it can be repealed. Corporate interests know how to fight and win this game.

Business has a privileged position in American politics. Corporations have pervasive influence and control over media, marketing, and the economic well-being of their shareholders, affiliates, and employees. Through the use of "motor-motives" – an embedded thought construct with a "spiritual" veneer, many of the "market" values, such as the quest to maximize one's own welfare and wealth = godliness, are found in significant segments of America's social consciousness. As a result, businesses are well represented in public and government debates, and often overpower any egalitarian-based constituted "common sense" that cause lawyers attempt to advance within the polis.[45]

The public relations machine of Big Tobacco and its business allies such as Associated Industries of Florida hit hard, and the press then adopts their narrative frame with editorials calling for repeal of the law. Already uncomfortable with their close alliance with trial lawyers, and sensitive to the press, the commitment of some of Chiles' staff weakens with each editorial. The Governor is open to a trade for health care.

[45] Aurther M. Okun, *Equity and Efficiency, The Big Tradeoff* (Washington, D.C: The Brookings Institute, 1975), explores the dyadic relationship between equality (polis) and efficiency (market). The tensions between the two can be understood and harnessed. The key question is whether through managing policy choices society can have the benefits of the market and the polis? Private policymakers and many economists generally take the view that there is a trade-off. Public policymakers and many other economists find that both goals can be met so long as each one does what they are efficient and good at. Aurther M. Okun, *Equity and Effiency*, 62–64.

"Economic well-being has been the most consistently important issue in American politics, and economic performance is both a cause and effect of government policy." Carl E. Van Horn, et al., *Politics and Public Policy*, Third Edition. (Washington D.C.: CQ Press, 2001, 50).

Income and wealth are distributed more unequally in the United States than in any country in Western Europe, and that unequal distribution of economic benefits is, at least in part, a matter of government policy. Van Horn, *Politics*, 46–48. Robert Kuttner's work has shown that there are many ways that society can pursue economic security, tax collection, full employment, economic development, and more equal income distribution. With a strong labor movement, political choices for economic policies "tend to reconcile equality with efficiency. The idea that the two are incompatible is a politically useful myth for the rich and powerful." Robert Kuttner, *The Economic Illusion: False Choices Between Prosperity and Justice* (Boston: Houghton Mifflin, 1984). Deborah Stone, *Policy Paradox, The Art of Political Decision Making* (New York, NY: W.W. Norton & Company, 2002).

When the word of the stealth missile gets out the Chairman of the Florida Republican Party, Tom Slade bristles. His comments mirror one hundred years of Yankee distrust of the Florida Cracker – now Governor Lawton Chiles: "It's the definition of Lawton Chiles, how he operates. He gives an 'Ah shucks, you can trust me,' image, but underneath, he is manipulative and conniving."[46] W.D.'s missile will ensure that tobacco, the maker of the anguished Southern soul, feels justice.

Like Bismarck's metaphor that laws are like sausage-making, *organized anarchy* aptly describes the competing interrelated dynamics that cause lawyers and Cracker governmental leaders must navigate to enact Florida's tobacco liability law. First, the Dean of the Florida Senate, W.D. wants the tobacco law and will use his power to get it enacted. Second, the Governor wants health care and will easily trade tobacco for it. Committee staff, and other agencies, such as the Attorney General's Office, all combine in this organized anarchy.

Progressive cause lawyer participants in the interrelationships of governmental and policymaking processes understand that policymakers draw on a variety of considerations in reaching decisions, and though some may be deplorable, others are on a sound basis in a pluralistic democracy.[47] "It is the very essence of democratic policymaking to draw on a range of sources in constructing the public interest on a particular issue."[48]

Study and modeling of dynamic processes, which incorporate randomness and chaos, are recent developments in both the natural and social sciences.[49] This essay on cause lawyers and Cracker culture demonstrates the

[46] Jim Ash and Keith Goldschmidt, *Chiles had active role in passing tobacco bill*, Florida Today, May 3, 1994.

[47] In determining public interest, policymakers may draw on the intensity of the problem, such as gun control and loss of jobs. They also may defer to the intuitive grasp of a situation by an experienced advisor or friend, as the late Florida U.S. Senator and Governor Lawton Chiles did in relying on his long-term friend and Florida's Chief Inspector General Harold D. Lewis's advice in pursuing Big Tobacco. Policy choices may be the result of compromise of numerous political, bureaucratic, and economic interests as well.

[48] Robert A. Heineman, et al., *The World of the Policy Analyst, Rationality, Values & Politics, 3rd Edition* (New York, NY: Chatham House Publishers, 2002, 24).

[49] Whether it is Gary Mucciaroni's *Garbage Can Model and the Study of Policy Making*, the fluid metaphors proposed by Gabriel Almond and Steven Genco, the chaos theories and fluid processes found in natural science study of cloud formation, air turbulence, whirlpools, or human consciousness research by Francis Crick and Christof Koch, the natural science and social science paradigms of analysis have striking similarities. John W. Kingdon, *Agendas*, 223. Gary Mucciaroni, *The Garbage Can Model of the Study of Policy Making: A Critique*. *Policy* (Spring, 1992) Vol. XXIV, 3:459–482. James Gleick, *Chaos: Making a New Science* (New York: Penguin Press, 1987).

random chaos at the constructive edge.[50] In fact, tracking natural science chaos theory, John Kingdon's term "organized anarchy" aptly describes the policymaking process streams interfacing at the constructive edge.[51] The relationship between structure and randomness in mobilizing trial courts and other institutions for social change is complex and fluid and is consistent with Kingdon's probabilistic model of analyzing components for social change and public policy[52] implementation.[53]

[50] Changes in society are a product of a multitude of factors and, in many cases, of the interrelationships among them. In addition to law, there are a number of other mechanisms of social change. All these mechanisms are in many ways interrelated, and one should be careful not to assign undue weight to any one of these 'causes' in isolation." Steve Vago, *Law and Society, Sixth Edition* (Upper Saddle River, NJ: Prentice Hall, 2000, 347).

[51] John W. Kingdon, *Agendas*, ix, 222–230.

[52] Public policy science while involving politics has an interdisciplinary definition that according to Thomas Dye is focused on "whatever governments choose to do or not to do." Thomas R. Dye, *Understanding Public Policy, 10th Edition* (Princeton, NJ: Prentice Hall, 2002, 25). The teaching of public policy in various fields emphasizes the distinct discipline in which it is taught. For instance, when public policy is taught as part of a law school curriculum "the emphasis is more on legal practice and on the underlying theories of law, litigation, and the search for legal meaning and legitimacy." Thomas A. Birkland, *An Introduction to the Policy Process, Theories, Concepts and Models of Public Policy Making* (Armonk, NY: M.E. Sharpe, 2001, 6).

The public policy definition has been refined to include, public concerns and "intentions that determine [government] actions." Charles L. Cochran and Eloise F. Malone, *Public Policy: Perspectives and Choices* (New York, NY: McGraw Hill, 1999, 1). The reality of scarcity of resources molds a public policy definition to be "the outcome of the struggle in government over who gets what." Charles L. Cochran, *Public Policy*, 1. Thus, public policies may "regulate behavior, organize bureaucracies, distribute benefits, or extract taxes." Thomas R. Dye, *Understanding Policy*, 1.

New paradigms of thought growing out of advances in science and technology, such as chaos theory and stream metaphors, permeate policy science studies. "Despite the growing hegemony of a scientific perspective in the policy arena, coordination of democratic processes with the contributions, methods, and challenges of the sciences remains an essential task for social scientists and policymakers." Robert A. Heineman, *Policy Analyst*, 15. An evolving theory of public policy science that incorporates developments in philosophy and natural sciences assists to create a shared set of principles, theories, and priorities.

One explanation for this inability to propose natural laws of public policy is the tension and terror of human consciousness. The tension of human existence drives humanity to both an art and a science, both free will and biology. Thus, societal consciousness levels can within a range be reasonably understood and predicted. In fact, there is historical evidence of generational cohorts and demographic societal patterns of coping with existence. In a general sense, the truth of the dynamic interaction of ingredients for public policy enactment can be discerned to structure a broad range of predictability.

[53] John W. Kingdon provides this description:

> Within the structure we can specify in the model and observe in the real world, processes like agenda-setting and alternative specification retain a degree of randomness. There is actually a lot of complexity and fluidity in this real world, and a model of that world should capture that complexity. One reason that a probabilistic model, such as the model used in this book,

Progressive cause lawyer involvement in this dynamic process to affect public policy[54] and effect social change is clearly culturally, politically, ideologically, and normatively integrated;[55] failure to integrate any factor can be a fatal flaw.[56] This aligns with multidimensional structural theories found in law and sociology, particularly those relating to the structure of the human spirit and the structure of human reality.[57]

This legislation and legal strategy had a goal of disrupting Big Tobacco's ideological dominance. Lawrence H. Friedman describes two types of change through law: planning and disruption: "Planning 'refers to architectural construction of new forms of social order and social interaction. Disruption refers to the blocking or amelioration of existing social forms and relations."[58] Once Big Tobacco and its big business allies understood the ramifications of the law and its disruption of their ideological dominance, an all-out war ensued for its repeal.

V. National Ideological War Waged on Florida Cracker Territory

This law by the Florida legislature takes on national prominence as the most powerful weapon in the legal and political arsenal to disrupt the economic

is more satisfying than a deterministic one is its recognition of that residual randomness. In fact, I tried my best along the way to specify necessary and sufficient conditions and to figure out some tight laws on causation. I found that there were too many exceptions, and that the specifications got unduly complex. I concluded that we do better to quote odds.

[54] John W. Kingdon, *Agendas*, 225.

[55] For instance, during the middle ages, the feudal customs and traditions found in the ideology of Christian paternalist ethic "could be, and [were] used to defend as natural and just the great inequities and intense exploitation that flowed from the concentration of wealth and power in the hands of the church and nobility." E. K. Hunt, *Property and Prophets, The Evolution of Economic Institutions and Ideologies, Seventh Edition*. (New York: Harper Collins College Publishers, 1998, 8). "Any economic system generates a class or classes whose privileges are dependent on the continuation of that system. Quite naturally, these classes go to great lengths to resist change and to protect their positions." E. K. Hunt, *Property and Prophets*, 19. Fundamental change in the feudal ideology and economic system, or any other system of power and wealth distribution, was achieved through traumatic and harsh social conflict. E. K. Hunt, *Property and Prophets*, 17–20.

[56] Cause lawyer leaders, politicians, bureaucrats, and judges have distinct premises and goals; the performance and quality of each are enhanced if they combine technical skills with an understanding of the normative and political context of the issues being considered. Distinct from any attempt at scientific objectivity and truth, public policy is immersed in cultural assumptions and tactical normative judgments relative to the methodology used, and these condition the range of alternatives that can be considered in any study. The *hegemonic lifeworld, metanormative*, and ideological frameworks limit the options available.

[57] Alan Hunt and Georges Gurvitch, *Sociology of Law* (New Brunswick, NJ: Transaction Publishers, 2001 [1942], 42–60).

[58] Lawrence M. Friedman, *A History of American Law* (New York: Simon & Schuster, 1977, 225).

and political dominance of tobacco. There is a real fear that Lawton may fold in the face of tobacco's full-court press and let the law be repealed. National elites, scholars, and media enter into the battle. There is also a need to develop a plan to manage the additional cause lawyers essential for a successful, limited risk, "band of brothers."

Once the rest of the nation got wind of the law's potential impact, lobbyists swarm and legislators flip. W.D. rants to the press, "We're in a hell of a war, and it's not with the process. It's with the tobacco companies and Senator Jesse Helms and paying them to grow tobacco and not grow tobacco. A half million people a year die, and they get people addicted, like me when I was 8 years old. They've got everybody addicted to this stuff, I think the sorry bastards ought to pay."[59]

It is far from certain whether Lawton will sign the bill. Various legislators, including former sponsor Democratic House member Ben Graber are now against the bill. To counter this pressure, I call Dr. Daynard and Northeastern law professor Beth Labasky with the American Lung Association to arrange for offensive support. They produce: first a May 25, 1994, letter from former President Jimmy Carter to Governor Lawton Chiles:

> I want to lend my voice and support to your and your efforts to recover Medicaid dollars from tobacco companies whose products cause diseases such as cancer, heart disease and emphysema. I applaud you and the Florida legislature for not only attempting to save tax-paying Floridians millions of tax dollars, but also by drawing increased attention to the perils of tobacco use. I have been watching with interest the recent congressional hearings during which evidence has come out that certain tobacco companies have long known of tobacco's addictive and deleterious effect on our nation's health. I understand the legislation that recently passed the Florida legislature is being touted as the most far reaching anti-tobacco bill in the country and accordingly, is something that our congressional leaders and other states may want to consider.
>
> Congratulations to you and the legislature on leading the fight against the ills of tobacco use for a healthier America.
>
> With best wishes,
> Sincerely,
> Jimmy Carter

[59] Keith Goldschmidt, *Childers defends*, May 6, 1994.

Similar letters come from current and former Surgeon Generals C. Everett Koop and Jocelyn Elders, M. D., as well as from Joseph A. Califano, Jr., former Secretary of Health and Human Services under President Jimmy Carter. The national media also enter into the fray, with national elites staking out their ground.

Several days after Lawton signs the tobacco law, on June 1, 1994, the *McNeil/Lehrer News Hour* on the Public Broadcasting System televises the conflict. Before the satellite broadcast I brief Harold on the ICD-9 (Medicaid diagnosis) codes, causation, and the innocent state, and personally escort him to the WFSU station in Tallahassee, Florida. John Shebel's pro-business political power vixen, Vice President Corrie Ruppt, escorts him. Shebel and Harold take their seats while Corrie and I go to the studio control center.

The show begins with testimony from Congressman Henry Waxman's 1994 Hearings on tobacco: "Do you believe nicotine is not addictive?" "I believe nicotine is not addictive, yes," replies William Campbell of Philip Morris USA. Jim Lehrer sets the stage: "Already defending themselves in Congress, tobacco companies are now faced with fighting a second front in state capitals like Tallahassee, Florida. Last week, Governor Lawton Chiles signed a bill allowing the state to file class action lawsuits against tobacco producers as Mississippi recently did. Florida estimates it has spent about $1.2 billion fighting tobacco-related illness in Medicaid patients in the last five years. Now it wants a refund."

Jeff Yasteen of public television's *Nightly Business Report* gives the background: "The new law was opposed by business lobbyists, who said it would make other manufacturers libel for similar claims by the state." "Citrus, milk, beef, chicken, toothpaste, Pampers, anything," adds John Shebel, President of Associated Industries of Florida, representing about 6,000 businesses in the state. "While Florida officials held the law as a breakthrough, it may not last long on the books. Tobacco industry and business groups are already moving to have the law rewritten or repealed when state lawmakers meet for a special session later this month."

Mr. McNeil: "Mr. Lewis, how did you calculate that $1.2 billion was incurred in medical expenses for tobacco-related diseases?"

Harold Lewis: "Thank you, Mr. MacNeil. First, let me say that Governor Lawton Chiles said it's time to take the Marlboro Man and Joe Camel to court to recover millions of dollars that Florida taxpayers have paid because of the tobacco companies. . . . We've taken the Medicaid disease codes and the costs attributable to smoking-related diseases as found by the Centers for Disease Control and the Congressional Office of Technology Assessment, and taken the dollar amount for each fiscal year.

Mr. McNeil: "So if you proceed with one of these suits, class action suits, what do you think you'd have to prove in court?"

Harold: "Well this is where some of these 'Chicken Little, Chicken Little, the sky is falling' argument being used by some in our state, where that comes from. We, as the state of Florida, as in any lawsuit, must show a cause of action. We must establish through a preponderance of the evidence at trial that, in fact, there was a causation between the product – in this case tobacco – and the injury caused by the particular ICD classification."

Mr. McNeil: "There's been some confusion over this. Would this law apply only to tobacco, only to cigarettes?"

Harold: "Governor Chiles made it absolutely abundantly clear when he signed the law last Thursday, May 26th, that this only applies to tobacco products."

Mr. McNeil: "Laurence Tribe in Boston, is this good law?"

Laurence Tribe: "I think it's a very intelligent and sensible legal approach. What it does is certainly not what Mr. Shebel describes. It doesn't presume the cigarette companies guilty. It doesn't take away all their defenses. I've read the law with some care. What it does is take away those defenses that have no application in a suit by an innocent third party like the state of Florida, namely defenses like assumption of risk. . . . And there's no good reason in the world in terms of sound economics or legal principle why taxpayers should subsidize the tobacco industry by absorbing these costs. The state is an innocent party and it makes eminent sense to have this kind of lawsuit."

Mr. McNeil: "Peter Huber, what is your view of this? Is this good law, and will it stand up, do you think?"

Peter Huber (a scholar with the Manhattan Institute): "I think it probably will not survive. Beyond that, the economics behind the law are silly. We're talking about a product, which undoubtedly does kill many poor people who are on public welfare in the state. Whatever else it may be doing, this product, it's almost certainly overall not costing the state money. Everybody dies sooner or later. If they die sooner and they happen to be on welfare and getting public housing and so on, the bottom line, the fact of the matter is that the state's almost certainly saving money here."

Laurence Tribe: "That is just not true. I can't believe, Peter, that you're saying that. . . . The U.S. Office of Technology Assessment in 1993 looked closely at the issue, concluded, first of all, even if a **ghoulish** argument like that, that we should be grateful that these people are being killed, even if we could accept that morally, it's not true economically, because what happens is people are cut down in their productive years."

Peter Huber: "No, you're wrong. Beyond that, under this law, one of those first defendants should be the state of Florida's own sunshine industry, every hotel that's peddling sunshine. We have 500,000 skin cancers a year in this country, 30,000 of those are malignant."

Mr. McNeil: "Mr. Lewis, what do you say to that argument, that Florida advertises its argument and sunshine causes cancer?"

Harold: "Well, that is certainly baloney, and we don't believe that for one minute. Sunshine is given to us by God and the universe, and that is certainly an inaccurate statement. I am an appointee for Governor Lawton Chiles for the health care administration representing the people of Florida. And for him to characterize me as the trial lawyers and not a state employee is part of the general misconception that they're trying to project to the people of Florida when we're trying to look out after the public dollar."

Mr. McNeil: "What's your view of that, Mr. Shebel?"

Mr. Shebel: "Well, I think the truth speaks for itself. Mr. Lewis and a trial lawyer and a state senator, all of whom are very good friends, slipped this bill through the legislature. Mr. Lewis misled the governor about the broadness of the bill."

Harold: "I think that Mr. Shebel's statement is totally inaccurate. The senator that he's referring to is a former President of the Florida Senate, the Dean of the Senate, having been in the Senate for 24 years, and the legislature had 29 hours from the time the bill passed the Florida Senate until it was enacted by the House. Mr. Shebel and his association have 16 registered lobbyists. The tobacco industry has 19 registered lobbyists, a total of 36 lobbyists that certainly are most sophisticated, highest paid in Tallahassee. They're not John Doe from Amokely. They are sophisticated, knowledgeable government specialists, and this bill sat in the legislature for 29 hours, and it passed the Senate 38 to nothing. It passed the House of Representatives 118 to nothing. And additionally after the regular session ended in and it passed on April the 8th, the governor extended the session for an additional week until April the 15th, and the bill passed and was part of that."

Mr. McNeil: "Mr. Lewis and Mr. Shebel in Tallahassee, Mr. Tribe, and Mr. Huber, thank you."

Cause lawyers and Cracker political leaders now receive legitimacy and support from academic and legal elites, such as Harvard's Laurence H. Tribe. In return, corporate lawyers and big business advocates receive academic support from their hired intellectuals, such as Peter Huber. In this televised skirmish, Peter Huber's "ghoulish" economic numbers argument that society saves money by permitting the premature killing of its citizens through cigarette addiction, sickness, and death is itself dead on arrival. That dog won't hunt.

With the elite "cause lawyer" and "Cracker political leader" battle engaged against Big Tobacco, other elite and progressive allies come to their aid. Letters from respected public policy elites, such as Jimmy Carter and C. Everett Koop, and televised advocacy from legal elites, such as Laurence H. Tribe, reinforce the nobility and legitimacy of this cause lawyer and Cracker political leader cultural vision of Big Tobacco liability. However, even the alliance with new national elite allies didn't appear to be enough.

VI. Special Session – Republican National Strategic Initiative Trumps Tobacco

"The first tobacco liability suit was filed 30 years ago. The Plaintiff gave up 12 years later, setting a pattern for hundreds of subsequent cases against cigarette companies. Though everyone knows smoking causes cancer, strokes and heart disease, no one has ever won a penny from those masters of denial and delay. The industry hires the best lawyers and spends whatever they need. Its victims have no such staying power.... [Beyond the flight attendant class action] the industry has an even bigger problem now thanks to the Florida Legislature's [Medicaid

Tobacco Liability Law]. . . . You don't win a fair fight with [tobacco]. This fight, as it happens, has only begun." *St. Petersburg Times*, May 4, 1994

"'These b-----s in the tobacco industry,' says Senator W.D. Childers, 'do you think they lose one minute's sleep over the fact that 400,000 people a year die over cigarettes?'" *St. Petersburg Times*, April 29, 1994

"When buying and selling are controlled by legislation, the first thing to be bought and sold are legislators." P. J. O'Rourke

The first opportunity for tobacco to show its political strength and end this threat is the special session on June 7–13, 1994, to enact health care reforms for Floridians. The opportunity would seem ideal. Big business has allied with the Democratic House and Senate leadership, the basis for repeal is reasonable, key legislative sponsors of the law are now opposing it, editorials are largely against the method of the law's enactment, and all immediate forces are advocating for a trade. Even the Governor is willing to trade. All that tobacco has to do is provide one vote for health care in the Senate in trade for tobacco repeal, and tobacco is off the hook. With all their resources it would seem an easy task.

In response to this law, tobacco firms unleash fifty lobbyists on the June 7–13 special session on health care. They are paid approximately $50,000 a piece for the six-day opportunity to fulfill their mission – trade health care for tobacco. Though the lobbyists represented Republican interests, they had one problem – the Republican leadership had a different plan. A century of minority party status had instilled Republicans with the sense to follow their leadership. The mission – no Democratic win on health care, period. The national elections come first.

This is what Harold, W.D., and I want as well. I give the grassroots advocates, and the Governor and Harold what they need to address the press on this subject. Fielding press inquiries, I provide an example: "We didn't buy the cigarettes, we didn't smoke the cigarettes, and we didn't assume the risk of smoking. Why should we get stuck with the bill? Let the tobacco industry be responsible for the damage they do . . . State taxpayers are now subsidizing tobacco industry profits by paying for these health care costs."[60] The Heart, Lung and Cancer associations put out their grassroots

[60] Justin Castanoso, *Florida law targets tobacco industry*, News & Records, Greensboro, North Carolina, June 5, 1994, p. A-1, A-2.

staff in full force, which was having an effect on lawmakers. Still, Lawton and the Democratic leadership wanted to trade tobacco for health care.

"We told them you won't get the tobacco law repealed without giving us health care. It was an all or nothing deal," said Representative Ben Graber, Chairman of the House Health Care Committee.[61] The Republicans held firm, not one vote went for the trade, and health care died. Tobacco liability lived for another day. W.D. gloats, "Tobacco sent 50 lobbyists, paid them tremendous amounts of money and gave them the sole assignment of repealing the cigarette bill. And you know what? They were so strong they couldn't get a single senator to file a bill to repeal."[62]

The unexpected standstill in the Florida Senate saved the tobacco law while ending the chance to expand health care coverage in Florida and nationally. Neither the cause lawyers nor the Cracker political leaders could have foreseen this dynamic. Yet, because of national political goals larger than the tobacco war, tobacco lost and health care reform lost too. Now that another tobacco liability hurdle was cleared, what about the upcoming challenge of creating and managing a posse of highly successful plaintiff attorney cause lawyers? How cannot one obtain the necessary insight to stake out a position prior to the maneuvering for power and control?

There are numerous fronts to address in constructing successful cause lawyer alignment with Cracker political leaders. There is a real need to understand and manage the complex group of highly successful cause lawyers that will advance the costs and litigate the case. Simply finding a reflective practitioner "cause lawyer" can be difficult, but once found, their insights are invaluable. In this instance, one such reflective practitioner cause lawyer, Northeastern Law Professor Richard A. Daynard, provides essential perspective and practical advice in structuring the more economically focused cause lawyer involvement in the "band of brothers" against Big Tobacco.

After the special session, Harold suggests to me, "We need our own accurate and honest information source on tobacco litigation, law firms, and how to manage them. We have Fred and Dexter, but we need someone who is focused on tobacco. We have Tribe and Massey on the constitutional

[61] William Booth, *Florida Refuses to Repeal Tobacco Liability Statute, Health Reform Stalls as Issues Are Intertwined,* The Washington Post, June 10, 1994, A-3.

[62] William Booth, *Florida Refuses to Repeal*, A-3.

battle, Dr. Daynard is the one for legislative, experts, trial team management, documents, factual history and strategy. He has lived and breathed tobacco for over a decade. He came through for us on the law, and he seems to have integrity." I agree and arrange to meet him in Orlando while I'm at the Florida Bar conference and he is attending an American Cancer Society annual meeting. We meet in Orlando on June 26, 1994, and I ask him, "Dr. Daynard, who are the best experts in the nation to use on liability, medical causation and damages?" He names Dr. Dorothy Rice at UCLA; Dr. David Burns, Senior Editor of many *Surgeon General Reports on Tobacco*; Dr. Jack Henningfield on addiction; Dr. Kenneth Warren on damages; Dr. Ronald Davis on medical causation; and Dr. Jeffery Harris on damages.

The dialogue continues:

Tim Howard: "We also have a public relations problem, what are your thoughts?"

Dr. Daynard: "I think that you need to show what value the case means to the average taxpayer, such as a $500 million drop in taxes, or the funding of health insurance for the working poor. Get neutral groups to support the effort. Focus on the pandering to our youth and its consequences for years and decades to come."

Tim Howard: "What do you think about Florida adding a RICO count to the action?"

Dr. Daynard: "That's a great idea. Massachusetts has a good RICO law, and I think that Florida's is even more aggressive. Millberg, Weis out of California has a good RICO complaint. Ness, Motley is involved in Mississippi and *Castano*. It's good to have several firms and their brainy heads working together. In the past tobacco has won because the Plaintiffs Bar was not unified. This entire wave of tobacco litigation will fail if we do not act in concert."

On the subject of contingency fees, Daynard advises, "Obviously it shouldn't cost the state anything, and the amount should be smaller as the recovery increases. The division of fees should be divided based on the time spent, with additional consideration for work on committees." He goes on to elaborate on how to manage the trial team: "Florida's team should be simpler than the organization in *Castano*. In *Castano* there are a lot of big egos who have battled before. They have no real client to deal with.

In your case you have the Governor and the state of Florida as the client. They will not be used to a sophisticated, strong client."

All legal and political cause lawyer projects need experienced advice from one committed to the noble purpose of the cause. In this instance, Professor Dick Daynard was this person and provided the guidance needed.

Despite their successful legislative results, this cause lawyer alignment with Florida Cracker populist governmental leaders will only work if the Cracker leaders are in power. If the Cracker governmental leaders lack instrumental power, namely, the Office of the Governor of Florida, the effort will fail. The next task of this cause lawyer "band of brothers" quest is to reelect "Walkin" Lawton Chiles as Florida's Governor.

VII. Florida Crackers' Last Leader – Populism, Personal History, and Symbols

In one of the closest Governor elections in Florida history, Chiles beat the petulant Jeb Bush by 75,000 votes out of nearly 1.5 million cast by tapping into Florida's roots in the last debate in Tampa. Lawton describes his prowess for humble Florida Crackers, saying, "The old He-coon walks just before the light of day."

Participant-observer data narrative

"Politics: A strife of interests masquerading as a contest of principles. The conduct of public affairs for private advantage." Ambrose Pierce

Florida's tobacco liability law survived the 1994 special session, its second challenge, but many more hurdles lay ahead, the most important of which was reelecting Governor Lawton Chiles. Lawton's leadership and the applied progressive philosophy behind it are the *sine qua non* of Florida's tobacco liability law. As the Dean of the Senate, "Banty Rooster" W.D. Childers has institutional power, prestige, and influence, but he is not the one who signs laws, trades for health care, has the media attention, and commands numerous state agencies. Progressive cause lawyers have to work with the culture of these institutions and institutional leaders to effectively use law and courts for their cause.

In one of the closest gubernatorial elections in Florida history, Chiles beat the petulant Jeb Bush by 75,000 votes out of nearly 1.5 million cast by tapping into Florida's roots in the last debate in Tampa. Lawton describes his prowess for humble Florida Crackers, saying, "The old He-coon walks just before the light of day." Knocked off his cadence of scripted lines and forced to deal with southern soul, Bush, a Florida resident for all of fifteen years, is baffled and off-balance. "He-coon" refers to the dominant male raccoon that protects the litter and takes on all challengers. Florida Crackers spent generations hunting raccoons for food under the moonlight. They understand the language. Lawton carries the day. For his last term, Lawton is known as the "He-coon." "He-coon" he is, yet like Cracker Florida, his days of cultural and political dominance are numbered.

Florida Cracker cultural language and communication carried the 1994 Governor's race for Lawton because in 1994, there were enough native Cracker Floridians left in the state who understood Cracker culture and identified with Cracker language. However, extraordinary demographic shifts and the daily immigration of nearly 800 generally conservative, retirees to Florida were changing the voting patterns toward Republican dominance. Demographic feedback loops influencing the direction of law and society must also be navigated by cause lawyers at the constructive edge.

Without support from those who wield the levers of power and institutional control, little policy can be made. Politics has been defined as "who gets what, when, how."[63] Being a governmental leader in command of institutions of necessity means that one's culture and philosophy of life influence the decisions, use of power, and social change *vel non* at the constructive edge of who gets what, when, and how. Leadership[64] is applied

[63] Harold Lasswell, and David Lerner, *The Policy Orientation, In The Policy Sciences: Recent Developments in Scope and Methods* (Stanford, CA: Stanford University Press, 1951).

[64] Leadership in its various forms is the *sine qua non* of civilization. Primordial in origin, leadership, narrative frames, myths, and God concepts interact, overlap, and often conflate in society and in civilizations. A nuclear reactor of social energy, to mix a metaphor, and just as deadly when misused, every human civilization, which must address the existential problems of life, death, comfort, security, is anchored in a God, narrative, myth concept, Spirit or *Geist*. The *Geist* is one of ideal existence, justice, peace, authority, hope, purpose, comfort, security, and transcendence. Karen Armstrong, *A History of God, The 4,000-Year Quest of Judaism, Christianity and Islam* (New York: Knopf, 1993). Samuel P. Huntington, *The Clash of Civilizations, Remaking of World Order* (New York: Touchstone, 1996). James Q. Wilson, *The Moral Sense* (New York: Alfred A. Knopf, 1993).

The God, narrative, and myth concepts elevate human consciousness from the abject and paralyzing terror of existence and survival. Armstrong, *A History of God* 28, 382–390). St. Augustine, *The Confessions* Book X, 2., *The Great Books of the Western World*, vol. 18 (Encyclopedia Britannica [1952] 1982). Paul Tillich, *The Courage to Be* (London: Oxford Press, 1962). Paul Tillich, *Theology and Culture* (New York NY: Oxford Press, 1963). Leadership incorporates the same social energy and volatile power. James MacGregor Burns, *Leadership* (New York: Harper

philosophy. It is ideologic consciousness – philosophy refined and empowered by the crucibles of experience – life at the constructive edge.[65]

& Row, 1978). In fact, often those who live lives worth emulating because of their integrated fulfillment of human existence, noble stories, and culturally aligning myths, such as the Moses, Buddha, Caesar, Christ, or Muhammad figures, are often referenced as God. Leaders, whether spiritual or political, generally transpose the "God" concepts to their own articulated medium and create narratives in order to personally embody its purposes. Thomas Hobbes, *Leviathan* (New York: Collier Books, Macmillan Publishing Company 1962, 394–395). Every human society has transcendent values, God concepts, narrative myths, and leadership. Bernard M. Bass, *Transformational Leadership, Industry, Military, and Educational Impact* (Mahway, NJ: Lawrence Erlbaum Associates, 1998, p. 5). Bernard M. Bass & Ralph M. Stogdill, *Handbook of Leadership* (New York: The Free Press, 1990). Bernard M. Bass & Ralph M. Stogdill, *Handbook of Leadership, Leadership Traits: 1904–1947* (New York: Free Press, 1974).

According to Jean-Jacques Rousseau, "leaders would be needed to help the masses understand God's justice." Jean-Jacques Rousseau, *The Social Contract* (New York: Hafner Publishing Company, 1947). David Cawthon, *Philosophical Foundations of Leadership* (New Brunswick, NJ: Transaction Publishers, 2002). The people should lead according to the "general will." According to Rousseau, in order to be successful in guiding the masses, leaders "must claim that God has sanctioned their judgment." David Cawthon, *Philosophical Foundations*, 69. Jean-Jacques Rousseau, *The Social Contract*, 38. Foreshadowing the importance of addressing the competing narrative frames and myths of a society, and following Aristotle's rhetorical principles of ethos and pathos, Rousseau alleges that leaders must create the illusion for followers that his ideas are their ideas, that his will is their will. David Cawthon, *Philosophical Foundations*, 70.

Moving from leadership based on democratic egalitarianism, *nihilism* challenges all previous ideas such as *idealism, realism, rationalism, and romanticism. Id.*, at 101. Nietzsche insisted that man was starkly alone and "God is dead." There is no *value, good, ideal, absolute, general will, or species being*, only a cruel and impersonal nature. Man's totality of existence is the struggle to live and his destiny is death. Friedrich Nietzsche, *Thus Spake Zarathustra* in Walter Kaufmann, ed. and trans., *The Portable Nietzsche* (New York: Penguin Books, [1882] 1976). Friedrich Nietzsche, *Twilight of the Idols*, in Walter Kaufmann, ed. and trans., *The Portable Nietzsche* (New York: Penguin Press, 1976). This approach changes the leadership dyad and the understanding of *rights, equality, justice, and liberty*. David Cawthon, *Philosophical Foundations*, 102. The *Will to Power* to rise above weakness, and the poverty and filth of the massive herd is what drives the "*ubermenschen*" or *overman*. The weak herd is subservient to the strong leader, and only the strong lead. Friedrich Nietzsche, *Thus Spake Zarathrustra*, 189. "The free man is a warrior." *Id.*, at 542. There is no rule by consent of the governed herd, no social contract, no limit to fear and violence. Leaders lead because they were born to lead. These "great men" are the result of historical and physiological conditioning. Nietzsche is a "might makes right" theorist; "power and right are synonymous." David Cawthon, *Philosophical Foundations*, 110. This narrative had a direct impact on Nazi Germany and aligns with the conservative "strict father" model of society. George Lakoff, *Don't Think of an Elephant! Know Your Values and Frame the Debate* (White River Junction, VT: Chelsea Green Publishing, 2004, 6–11).

[65] Warren G. Bennis and Robert J. Thomas, *Geeks and Geezers, How Era, Values and Defining Moments Shape Leaders* (Boston, MA: Harvard Business School Press, 2002: 14–21). Warren G. Bennis and Burt Nanus, *Leaders: Strategies for Taking Charge*. (New York: Harper & Row, 1985).

According to Warren Bennis, "Whether imposed or sought out, crucibles [life at the constructive edge]are places where the essential questions are asked: Who am I? Who could I be? Who should I be? How should I relate to the world outside myself? . . . Crucibles are, above all, places or experiences from which one extracts meaning, meaning that leads to new definitions of self and new competencies to better prepare one for the next crucible."[66] In fact, culture addresses these essential questions: Who am I? Who could I be? Who should I be? How should I relate to the world outside myself? Culture is formed from these collective crucibles. To affect law and policy, cause lawyers and Cracker leaders must understand and engage the culture and how these essential questions have been answered.

The late Florida "Cracker" Governor Lawton Chiles was known as "Walkin Lawton" for his "long-shot" successful 1970 U.S. Senate race when he personally walked across the entire state from Pensacola to Key West, meeting, understanding, and listening to everyday citizens along the way. As "Walkin Lawton" he symbolized patience, identification with, and commitment to understanding the average Floridian.

Folksy in style and moderate in his policies, during his last term, Lawton Chiles was now known as the "He-coon, that walks just before the light of day," in reference to his Cracker woodsman statement to Jeb Bush in the last and most critical debate during the razor-close 1994 reelection. He embodied cultural identity with and protection of his people when he took on the "He-coon" mantle in the language of native Cracker Floridians. The "He-coon" knew how to take care of his people – the core definition of a hero presented in a language that gets beneath their skin. Native and long-time Floridians identified with his deep southern Cracker roots, understanding, and humanitarian and egalitarian goals. Thus, the source of much of Lawton's political power ultimately came from the reality of *cultural symbols*[67] that his career embraced.

[66] Warren G. Bennis, *Geeks and Geezers*, 99.

[67] "The symbols are the inadequate sensitive expressions of spiritual meanings, taking the place between appearances and things themselves. They are the intermediary between those two and depend on both. They simultaneously reveal and conceal, or rather they reveal by concealing and conceal by revealing. What they express and what they hide is on the one hand the spiritual, on the other reality (physical, biological, psychological, sociological), in which the spirit partly embodies itself, partly reveals itself." Alan Hunt and Georges Gurvitch, *Sociology of Law* (New Brunswick, NJ: Transaction Publishers, 2001 [1942], 44).

VIII. Structuring Progressive Cause Lawyers for Battle

"'We're here to engage in a debate over whether trial lawyers will continue to pass laws that enrich them,' said Jon Shebel, President of Associated Industries of Florida."
Associated Press, February 21, 1995

"Litigation: A machine which you go into as a pig and come out as a sausage."
Ambrose Bierce

The "private attorneys general" hired by the state were not litigating to enrich individuals for their use of cigarettes. Rather, these progressive cause lawyers were litigating on behalf of innocent taxpayers who supported the services and salaries of government and government officials, including judges. The awards went not to individual plaintiffs, but to the state taxpayers for their Medicaid programs. Moreover, the awards were not diluted by contingency fees because the attorneys were not paid from the state recoveries, but directly from tobacco.

In the process of preparing for this battle, there was a conscious effort to aggregate plaintiffs and pool litigation resources to overcome the well-known facts about "why the haves come out ahead" in litigation.[68] Conceptualizing is easy; implementation of progressive cause lawyer mobilization can be complex and difficult.

After Lawton's reelection, Fred, Harold and I begin our formal search for the "posse." Fred calls more than thirty firms, including all the Florida Inner Circle members, all the Academy leadership, and any other firm that has expressed an interest. In late November of 1994, Lawton picks Harold as the State's Chief Inspector General. Lawton also wants Dexter Douglass to be his General Counsel. I call three law firms. By late December, Fred has a list of fourteen firms that want to be on the team, internally termed the "posse." He gives the list to Harold over the phone, who writes down the list of firms on a sheet of paper, showing it only to the Attorney General and Governor. On January 9, 1995, Fred, Harold, W.D., and Lawton meet at the Governor's Mansion in the formal room beneath Andrew Jackson's portrait. "Harold, Tim and I made the calls, and we've got a posse who'll put up the money and do the work. If it's okay, we'll formally organize a

[68] Mark Galanter, *Why the "Haves" Come out Ahead: Speculations on the Limits of Legal Change*. Law and Society Review, Vol. 9, 95–160 (1974).

trial team and get things ready to file." "Yep, let's do it. Have Harold review and coordinate the final team members." "Governor, I know that this is a Florida case with Florida counsel, but the team could benefit from the two out-of-state firms that are working on Mississippi and West Virginia's cases. Ness, Motley and Scruggs firms. It is okay to add them?" "That's okay with me, so long as Florida counsel are in charge."

Linked at the hip pocket, the rock star Ron Motley, the don-in-waiting Joe Rice, and the low-key Presbyterian Dick Scruggs are three faces of Eve. With slicked-black hair and southern drawl, the consigliore of plaintiff-bar assembly-line justice, Ron Motley brought in the wealth through his brilliance, manic dedication, home-cookin' justice, empathy, and insight. In 1993 alone, his personal income from the firm was more than $13 million. Unfortunately, these successes without personal order often bring excesses that lead to several marriages and substance abuse. "We did the asbestos cases in Pascagoula. These guys live like rock-and-roll stars, with women-groupies everywhere. They spent almost as much as they made on some of these cases. Over a million in jet flights, hotels, food, and entertainment," Dickie Scruggs confides to Harold and me.

Joe Rice, a self-styled rogue, is known among his peers and in legal publications as an "untrustworthy, cold eyed deal maker with the mind of an accountant."[69] Driven by the confluence of public good and personal wealth creation, Ron and Joe operate in sync, each with their unique skills and style. Ron prepares and tries the case, Dick supports and smoothes the way, and Joe cuts the deal.

At 9:00 the next morning, Fred and W.D. confer in the Senate Dean's office.

W.D.: "Fred, you're a lightnin' rod. You'll be the bulls-eye, and with the lobbyists and press targeting you, the law won't stick."

Fred: "W.D., who's going to manage this case? Lawton's relying on me. This is supposed to be run by Florida attorneys."

W.D.: "Hell, with you on the team, there'll be no case to manage, and Lawton will look like a fool. Make no mistake, Lawton will understand. Lawton knows how to take care of Lawton."

Fred: "I thought when we got the law passed the war was won. I guess it's only the beginning."

[69] Alison Frankel, *Smokin' Joe*, The American Lawyer, May, 1998, p. 53.

W.D.: "There's no question about it. You can't be on the team or State contract. Stay out of the spotlight. We put this together, and Fred you deserve to get paid. Lock-in your referral fee with the team, save your cash. If the law stays on the books, you win. If not, you're out nothing."
Fred: "I'll call Lawton and tell the rest at the meeting."

Here is how Fred's conversation goes with the Governor the next morning.

Fred: "Morning Governor. We're getting this tobacco case ready. After talking to W.D., we both feel that if I'm on the team, the law will be in jeopardy. You're already taking enough heat from Shebel and French on this."
Governor: "Who's going to coordinate the case?"
Fred: "You've got Tim trained and ready, Harold tracks the case's every move, and Dexter can corral the attorneys. Long-term, Governor, with Shebel breathing down your neck, if I'm on the team, people will believe that this is a political payoff for drafting the tobacco law. I've got to back out of direct participation."[70]
Governor: "I understand Fred, so long as we've got a team in place to keep the case on track you can be in the background. Let them know at the meeting."

Surrounding the executive tables in the Governor's Large Conference Room various Governor's staff and cause lawyers find their seats. Harold begins the meeting:

> The Governor has given a green light to file. Tim has refined the complaints he's drafted over the past several months with the review of Tribe, Levin and the AG, and has a copy of the Motley draft complaint. Each of you should have a memo describing their merits. Tim and I have been working closely with Ron Sachs in refining the pitch ever since the law passed and we've got it down. However, we are way behind the eight ball politically, and Shebel's 'chicken little, the sky's falling' pitch has got the legislators spooked.

[70] Judy Plunkett Evans, *The lawyer behind Florida's fight against the tobacco companies, Fred Levin wrote the law that gave the state grounds to sue and drafted the 13 firms taking the case to court*, The Daily Business Review, April 7, 1995, A12, A16.

Chief of Staff Tom Herndon elaborates: "We will face serious opposition starting in early March. Guy Spearman, John French, Shebel and fifty other well-paid lobbyists have been working to repeal this law for nine months without any serious opposition. We've got our lobbying and public relations work cut out for us. Beth Labasky will coordinate the support of the American Lung Association, and the Tri-Agency Coalition's support. They'll be out front."

"Tim, make sure we got the public relations paragraphs in the Complaint. Allen, make sure we have public relations paragraphs also in the fee contract." "We're on it." I confirm. General Counsel Jay Peterson asks, "Fred, how are we on finalizing the trial team members?" Fred responds, "We have our first formal invitational meeting February 6 in Fort Lauderdale, and should be able to lock-in those that want to be on the contract some time after that. I met with W.D., and conferred with the Governor, and we have determined that I will not be on the team. I'll be too much of a political liability."

The Governor's Communications Director Ron Sachs joins in: "Minnesota filed their Complaint several months ago and Tim got us a copy of their press packet. Tim's been working closely with us all along for the facts, law, and pitch. We'll be working from Minnesota's format for our press packet." Herndon presses the meeting, asking, "When can this be filed?" Harold details the next steps: "The Contract has to be completed, and Allen will be working from the other Medicaid Contingency Fee contract for estate recoveries that the State has with Teresa Cooper Ward." Fred follows, "I believe it'll take several weeks to get the team members committed, it should be done by mid-February." Deputy Attorney General Pete Antonacci stakes out his position: "We've got to have a team and contingency fee contract executed by them before filing; otherwise Butterworth is not on board and will not sign the complaint." Ron Motley describes his firm's participation: "We'll update our draft complaint and complete a study on the venue options. I understand that the State would prefer to have the action in Tallahassee, and is open to other venues. Our impression is that West Palm Beach is a good location due to the demographics and verdicts for Plaintiffs. We'll complete our analysis, provide it to Tim for circulation and final approval by the Governor and Attorney General's staff." Harold clarifies, "We need to make sure that we have a Florida Defendant for federal jurisdiction. We also need to limit the target to cigarette manufacturers. We already have all the convenience stores, and Publix Supermarkets attacking us, we don't need to make it worse."

Dr. Daynard again supplies key direction for the effort: "I recommend the focus on children and protecting them from tobacco. Counts on fraud should be included as well. This will help insulate the Governor from lawyer fee attacks." "Dr. Daynard is right on it, and this must be done," Harold agrees. "We have those counts in our drafts." Ron Motley affirms: "Great, now let's pick a date." Herndon takes the next step.

"Sometime in late February should give us enough time to get it all together. But no later since the Legislative Session starts the first week in March," Harold suggests. "I agree, how about February 21st? Any other suggestions?" Herndon offers. None being heard, he says, "Sounds like a date."

On the morning of February 6th, Dickie's limousine travels from his Hatteras yacht with several attorneys from Ron and Dickie's firms, along with Dickie and me, to Shelly Schlesinger's Ft. Lauderdale law firm – a huge white-domed atrium palace. Ron's limo follows. As they arrive, a chauffeured Bentley carries Bob Montgomery out of the parking lot. They park next to Shelly Schlesinger's black limousine.

Walking passed the bronze statute of justice beneath the glass ceiling, Dickie, Charles, Gus, and I take a left into the mock courtroom, Ron, Joe, and Charles follow. The courtroom gallery is filled with swaggering attorneys. All are deeply involved in one way or another with the Florida Academy of Trial Lawyers, most having held the presidency or leadership in the academy. Ron, Dickie, and I take seats behind the counsel tables facing the gallery. Viewing the twenty or so attorneys arrayed in various spheres of self-importance such as standing, sitting, and hands in one's pocket, I think to myself, "It looks like a scene of western gunslingers."

Joe puffs his authority, "The Governor has invited Ness, Motley to put this case together. We have Tim Howard from the Governor's Office and he's prepared a brief memo on the case. He will explain the damages and tobacco liability law. Dickie Scruggs is directing Mississippi's tobacco action, and will be working on how cigarettes cause injuries." "When Fred called me, he said that Florida counsel was leading the case and this was a Florida case," Phil Frieden challenges Joe. "We'll get to team organization and fees after we cover the merits of participation," Dickie helps cover. "Tim, why don't you review the memo."

The memo covers the legal aspects of the law and lawsuit, the contingency fee amounts, and the ethical compliance issues. I continue, "Thanks, if you could take out the memo handed out to everyone. What you'll see is the basic structure of team participation, the damages for the case, and the statute and rules on contingency for this case. Conservatively, damages for the four-year period amount to anywhere from $1.4 billion to over $6 billion if treble damages from fraud are proven. Using the commercially reasonable fee rate of 25%, this would generate fees of between $350 million and $1.6 billion."

"That's if the law stays on the books, and if the Supreme Court finds it constitutional. Which are long shots in my book," Asp Tong voices his concern. "You're right. We've got the legislative battles ahead, but there is good case law to support our market share approach to damages, consolidation of claims, and statistical evidence for causation. Since the statute is generic, they can't claim that we are violating equal protection and singling out an individual industry unfairly," I address the obvious. "We have Harvard Professor Laurence H. Tribe and his assistant Jonathan Massey on our team to give our best pitch. I've been working with them for over six months and all of us working the front line on this feel that the law will stick."

Phil Frieden gets to the meat, "Let's talk fees. Tim's shown the potential return. Now how do you propose splitting the fee?" Joe stands up and pulls a wall chart over and draws three steps as he speaks.

> Here's how we propose to split the fees. First 25 percent of the fees for compensatory damages go to organizing lead counsel – Dickie Scruggs' firm and Ness, Motley. Thirty percent of attorney's fees from treble damages also go to organizing lead counsel. Next, 33 and 1/3 percent of the fees, pro rata, go to all persons who contribute to the advancing of the costs on a pro rata basis, in addition to a reasonable rate of return by way of interest from the date of payment. $25,000 on or before July 1, 1995, and $25,000 on or before September 1, 1995. Thereafter up to $100,000 a year as needed, up to a total of $500,000. The balance of the fees, 41.6 percent, would be split 50 percent to organizing counsel and 50 percent to those persons who work on the case, in proportion to their contribution. An executive committee composed of two Florida counsel, organizing counsel and Dexter Douglass would oversee compliance with the fee division.

Phil Frieden replies, "Joe, excuse me, but when I put dollars into that formula, here's how it comes out. Starting with $100, your firms get $25 off the top. Then say another $3 on costs, and another $20.80 from the balance. It comes out to your two firms getting nearly $50 while the other 8–10 law firms put just as much work in, just as much money and get from $5–6. That's how this formula really plays out." Phil Frieden again cuts to the bottom line. "It's not fair." "Phil saw right through that shell game of Joe's," I thought to myself.

In response, Joe explains,"We'll be putting all our resources into this case, and taking most of the risk. We've been working with the anti-tobacco guru and head of the Tobacco Product Liability Project, Northeastern Law professor, Dr. Daynard, for months gleaning the law, facts, history, and strategy for the next wave of tobacco litigation. We've also joined several other current tobacco cases to get the benefit of documents and strategies. No doubt, you'll get your money's worth."

Ron tries to moves the meeting ahead, saying, "Gentlemen, you have our proposal. Why don't you select a chairperson and consider the next step. We'll wait in Shelly's kitchen." After walking into the kitchen, grabbing a Danish and juice, Joe is upset that he was not prepared going into the meeting. "Fred never told me that he said this was a Florida case with Florida counsel." After a twenty-minute delay, Dickie Scruggs, Ron, Joe, and I return to the mock courtroom. Mike Maher, the affable former president of the American Trial Lawyer's Association and a long-time Plaintiff Bar political operator, is the first to speak:

> I've been selected chairman, and I think that we have enough here with enough interest to develop a trial team. More than several firms think this case is an extreme long shot from almost every front, legislative, constitutionality, and at trial. We will need some time to coordinate the Florida participants. I suggest some conference calls and another meeting within the next week or so.

Keeping the effort in focus before the meeting breaks up, I remind them, "Gentlemen, please keep in mind that the filing date is February 21, and that a contract must be done prior to that date. We have only ten working days left."

The next day, in the Governor's large conference room, Ron Sachs and David White (public relations consultant for Ron Motley's firm) agree to coordinate their efforts, with the Governor's Office having the final say. David White makes "after the fact" efforts to dictate the state's public relations efforts and asks me to "smooze with Ron to get their view accomplished. Be sensitive, but remember, we're paying for Beth Labasky, Rick Oppenheim, and Betty Ray." I respond, "Look David, we're all on the same team, we want to protect the law, and win the case. I'm going to do what is right for the client first, that is what we all want." On this principle no one can object, but in reality a game is on for control and money. As for the public relations campaign, everyone agrees to build off of the Minnesota tobacco case public relations and media packet.

Managing these economically focused cause lawyers is a challenge. It is clear that they are well versed in economic risk/benefit analysis as applied to representing public and individual interests within the institution of the courts. They also have personal excesses that manifest in addictions and hubris as found in any elite group that takes on economic war with limited training or that lack peer examples in how to handle victories and the resulting economic rewards. This lack of prudence in engaging in an ostentatious demonstration of their wealth severely harms their public image, often overshadowing the public good that they accomplish.

With their motivation to take on the case being primarily economic, these lawyers intuitively apply an understanding of the relationship between private policy[71] and the strengths and weaknesses of the private economy. These cause lawyers, as described in the Inner Circle and those recruited to litigate Florida's tobacco war, are clearly closer to the economically motivated cause lawyer range of the spectrum. In any culture in which an economic and political alliance drives the rewards, a strong legal and ethical position must be staked out early so that it will not be lost when the struggles for control and wealth inevitably arise. Loyalty, personal judgment, and integrity assist in staking out such a position. As a more cause-focused cause lawyer, I formulated my skills and judgment in public service and election campaigns. By remaining independent from the "posse" with my own ethical and legal obligations to the client – the Governor and State

[71] *Private policy* is made by the business and financial elites through private decisions termed "boardroom politics" of those acting in their self-interest in the "free market" collective conduct super-structure. The free market "is a system that relies on voluntary exchanges between autonomous individuals to allocate goods and services in an efficient manner." Carl E. Van Horn, et al., *Politics and Public Policy, Third Edition* (Washington D.C.: CQ Press, 2001, 28–29). Efficiency is "getting the most output for a given input." Debra Stone, *Policy Paradox*, 37. These private decisions based on efficiency in the free market affect the wages, hours, working conditions, and health of millions of people and allocate vast resources, with little or no accountability. Carl E. Van Horn, et al., *Politics and Public Policy*.

of Florida, I am clearly shoring up my power base and legal, and ethical structure for the impending maelstrom.

There is an understanding of the political impact that the "greedy trial lawyer" narrative frame being used by corporate interests has on the media and legislators being lobbied to vote for repeal of the tobacco liability law. Fred Levin and W.D. take institutional and cause lawyer structural action to minimize this narrative attack and political fallout. Doing so also has the added benefit of reducing Fred Levin's capital and legal time exposure to zero while ensuring a good financial return if the cause prevails.

Control and spin are not only macro issues as found in metanarratives, strategic ideological initiatives, and distribution of wealth; they are also found in micro issues, such as which cause lawyer – more economic focused or more cause focused – is controlling the instrumental interface between the institutions of media, legislature, and the courts. There is an internal struggle for control and power over the instrumental direction. This is important to both the economic and ideologically motivated actors.

For those motivated by economics, if the cause is economically successful, instrumental control translates into wealth and increased fees through credit for work. The media can also advance the notoriety of lawyers, which can again translate into reputation, clients, and ultimately wealth. For those with ideological motivations, instrumental control ensures that the embedded narrative frame is consistent with the more missionary ideological goal of the strategic initiative, which is to keep the noble components of the cause first and foremost.

Nobility is the essential element of a story about cause lawyer and Cracker political leader alliance in taking the war to Big Tobacco. That war officially begins when Florida files its lawsuit. To resist the attacks that this story will receive, nobility must be directly embedded in the framing of that war.

IX. Florida Tobacco War's Face-to-Face Engagement – "Fix Bayonets!"

"'Anybody can declare war,' said John French, a Tallahassee attorney who lobbies for Philip Morris, the nation's largest tobacco manufacturer. 'The real test is who's left standing when the war is over.'" Associated Press, February 16, 1995

"The industry has responded with lobbying and ad campaigns and a full-scale legal defense." . . . 'While big tobacco goes to the bank and deposits enormous profits from the lives they're ruining, Florida's taxpayers consistently have to make withdrawals from their wallets to pay for the carnage,' said Florida Governor Lawton Chiles (D), a sworn enemy of cigarette manufacturers."

Washington Post, February 22, 1995

The legal and press *instruments* to begin the court conflict that leads to press coverage and transmission of knowledge through the print media are in place. This case study data demonstrate that there is a direct correlation between the court activities, media coverage, and the transmission of content as simplified by press releases and adopted almost wholesale by journalists.

On April 7, 1994, Harold, Fred Levin, and I brief Ron Sachs, the Governor's Communications Director, on the stealth tobacco law. Ron's prescient response is, "You've given the Governor the biggest ball in history, and we're going to knock it out of the park." From that day on, one of my daily assignments is to keep the Governor's Press Office informed about the case, legislation, facts, law, grassroots advocacy, and anything else they need in the war against Big Tobacco. The purpose of this assignment is to ensure that they remain strong in using the most compelling facts and narratives. On the day of filing the lawsuit, completing these tasks is of paramount importance.

After reviewing the press release and press packets, I go to Dexter Douglass's tapestry-walled office and we have this conversation:

Tim: "Good morning Mr. D, I've got the complaint done and need your signature. The *posse* completed their edits in Orlando late last night, and with their authority I placed most of their signatures on the contract early this morning. There are a couple of signatures we couldn't get on yet, but they'll be done soon. Greg Barnhart's firm, Searcy, Denny dropped out yesterday. Montgomery took their place and will sign the contract this afternoon in West Palm after I file the lawsuit."

Dexter Douglass: "Good job, where do I sign?"

Tim: "Mr. D, how's the draft speech for today? Here's a copy of the Q and A's and Press Release for the press packets. Remember, this pitch Mr. D.: 'tobacco is the only product when used as directed leads to sickness and death,' and 'tobacco may not have lost a case, but they haven't fought the 'He-coon.'

Dexter Douglass: "Fix Bayonets!" (Lawton, Dexter and others of their generation fought in the Korean War. The term that got their adrenaline flowing and instincts up for battle indicated that "hand-to-hand" combat was imminent – "Fix Bayonets." It was a term used in this battle, particularly in the legislative confrontations over the next three years.) "Got it" (Dexter winks).

Back at the press office, the tobacco press packets are stuffed. Ryan Banfill, from the Governor's Press Office, has left to ensure the sound system, camera location, and the thirty members of tobacco-free youth are arranged in the Lower Level Cabinet Meeting room. I have pushed for strong language and facts, and I am pleased with the pitch given in the final press release distributed to Florida's Capitol Press Corps:

STATE OF FLORIDA

OFFICE OF THE GOVERNOR

THE CAPITOL

TALLAHASSEE, FLORIDA 3239–0001

FOR IMMEDIATE RELEASE: CONTACT: Ron Sachs
February 21, 1995 (904) 488–4802 or
Jo Miglino
(904) 488–5394

STATE OF FLORIDA SUES TOBACCO COMPANIES

Chiles Leads Landmark Effort to Recover Taxpayer Dollars, Protect Teens

TALLAHASSEE – Under the direction of Governor Lawton Chiles, the State of Florida today is filing suit against the tobacco industry in order to recover billions of taxpayer dollars in Medicaid payments for health problems attributed to tobacco-related illness. The suit also aims to halt the industry's cold-hearted practice of selling its dangerous products through "Joe Camel" type marketing campaigns to teenagers.

"Tobacco is not cool, it's cruel. While tobacco goes to the bank and deposits enormous profits from the lives they're ruining. Florida's taxpayers consistently have to make withdrawals from their wallets to pay for the carnage," Governor Chiles said. "This suit sends a loud and clear message to the tobacco industry that it – not the taxpayer – will be held accountable for marketing sickness and death. We will protect our taxpayers and our most valuable citizens by ending tobacco's callous practice of hooking our children on a drug that's proven to be as addictive as heroin and cocaine."

. . . .

The press release continues: "Governor Chiles emphasizes that this is a pro-business lawsuit. The Florida economy loses $4.4 billion in direct and indirect costs (from premature death, lost work days, and prolonged illness) as the result of tobacco-related diseases. Recent studies reveal tobacco-related illnesses have directly cost the Florida taxpayer-supported Medicaid program more than *$1.4 billion* over a five-year period beginning in 1990–91.

In 1992, 28,212 Floridians died from smoking-related illnesses – that translates to *one out of every five deaths reported that year*. In 1992–93, Medicaid spent at least *$289 million* to treat Floridians suffering from smoking-related illnesses. . . . "

"We have the kind of weapons we need to win this case," Governor Chiles says. "We are using this law against the tobacco industry and only the tobacco industry. Contrary to the hysteria of some big business lobbyists, we are not coming after milk, beef, diapers or any other interests. Only the tobacco industry is targeted. This is the only product we know of that, when it's used as directed, leads to illness and death."

"According to the *ABA Journal*, the tobacco industry successfully spends *$600 million* per year to hire the world's top corporate law firms to defend itself from liability for the nearly 500,000 *deaths* attributed to tobacco use nationally and to protect their subsidy from state and federal taxpayers."

"Over the past forty years, there have been 300 suits filed against the tobacco industry over liability for the death and injury its products cause. The industry has never lost a case and has not paid one penny in damages.

The State of Florida has assembled a team of the best and private attorneys in the private and public sectors to argue, at no cost to the state, this landmark case. This suit is an effort to make the tobacco industry pay for the damage it does to Florida taxpayers and to stop the industry from enticing impressionable teenagers to use products known to lead to a lifetime of addiction, sickness, and eventually death."

"We are filing suit to protect the rights of Florida taxpayers and to protect future generations from falling victim to tobacco's cycle of death," Governor Chiles says. "Too many smokers addicted to tobacco products pay with their lives – and we all pay for their treatment. Now it's time for the tobacco industry to take responsibility for the damage it does."

It's now 8:50, and the press conference is ten minutes away. In the Cabinet Meeting Room, Jon Shebel, moribund President of Associated Industries of Florida, is busy arranging his visuals, cameras, and presentation of Big Tobacco's antilawyer, counterassault.

Dexter stands behind the State seal on the podium. Six television cameras and eleven reporters watch him and the thirty smoke-free members of the class of 2000 standing in front of no smoking in Florida placards.

He begins, "Today, Joe Camel is as recognizable to children as Mickey Mouse. In fact, the R. J. Reynolds' Joe Camel campaign has increased Camel's share of the illegal children's market from one-half of 1 percent to nearly 33 percent. Hooking children is not a cartoon and it's not funny.

. . . .

Each year Florida's Medicaid program loses $289 million treating smoking-related illnesses. This money could go to our classrooms to educate our children and hire more police officers to guarantee public safety.

. . . .

This is a product that when used as directed leads to sickness and death.

Tobacco companies can't hide from the facts, smoking kills. The number of people killed by tobacco each year is the equivalent of crashing a jumbo jet each day and killing all of its passengers. That's a chilling statement.

The governor hopes this sends a chill up the backs of lobbyists and corporate executives in their boardrooms. It's time for the tobacco industry to pay up.

. . . .

We know that tobacco has never lost a case, but they haven't fought the 'He-coon,' Lawton Chiles and the State of Florida."

With cameras rolling and reporters writing, Jon Shebel, the nemesis of the trial lawyers, launches his counterattack. Beginning with a personal attack, Shebel sarcastically describes Douglass as "one of the State's most distinguished trial lawyers," and says Douglass left his lucrative Tallahassee law practice to "walk down the street to orchestrate a suit for his trial-lawyer friends." Underlying his venom is the fact that Dexter represented Shebel's ex-wife in their divorce in which Shebel lost a lot of money.

> This lawsuit is nothing more than a bonanza for trial lawyers who will get as much as $350 million or more in contingency fees if they win. After the lawyers are paid and the federal government is reimbursed its share of the Medicaid payments, the State would receive only $214

> of a $1.4 billion judgment. This is a great lawsuit for plaintiff lawyers. That's what we think this is all about. It's $42 million a law firm.

Even using the state's numbers, Shebel distorts the state's return by nearly $700 million. Noting that Dexter raises beef cattle, Shebel asserts,

> The state will be attempting to file suit against the companies that sell alcohol or beef cattle. I have a basic problem with a law that basically strips all product manufacturers of their defenses . . . and allows the state to drag them into the courthouse and sues them for all they're worth.
>
> Shebel's gives his "chicken little, the sky's falling" pitch. Dexter responds: By having a private trial team, the State of Florida can take on the tobacco industry without depleting the treasury. Tobacco has had the edge in the past, but with the help of Florida's top trial lawyers and a new state law removing many of the defenses to such lawsuits, the state is in a position to win. These lawyers are even willing to give a portion of their fees to charity, and get nothing if they lose.

"Mr. Douglass, you don't give much to charity, in fact, I gave more than you last year," Shebel snarls. With a Cheshire grin Dexter retorts, "That's because you're richer."

After the press conference is over, I congratulate Harold, shaking his hand and saying, "The war's formally on. Dexter did great. Shebel's no match for Dexter's disarming Cracker humor and wit." Later that morning, Ryan Banfill and Dr. Joyner Simms, Director of Florida's Health Promotion and Wellness Program, accompany me on the Continental Airlines commuter flight to West Palm Beach, Florida.

Upon arrival we take the Avis rental car to Palm Beach County's old courthouse. CNN, WXEL, CBS, ABC, NBC all have satellite trucks lining the parking lot. The *Palm Beach Post, Miami Herald, Fort Lauderdale Sun Sentinel*, AP, UPI and reporters from twelve other news services mingle in the smoker's courtyard. I carry the box of complaints and summons, along with the three original contracts. Bob Montgomery greets me at the courthouse entrance: "Good mornin' my friend. I see you got it done! Welcome to Palm Beach. Let me take you to the clerk. As you can see, our new Courthouse across the street will be done soon." I reply, "Thanks Bob. Glad you're on board. I've got the three original contracts in my briefcase. I need you to sign them before I leave for Tallahassee." Jack Frost with the

Palm Beach chapter of the American Lung Association greets me, "The day's finally come! Glad you're here." A crowd of television cameramen and reporters engulf Bob and I as we enter the old courthouse and make our way to the clerk's counter. Meanwhile, Ryan goes to set up the podium and to hand out press packets. Dr. Sims assists him. Receiving the original complaint, the Clerk of the Court asks me, "Is the State asking for a jury trial?" With microphones dangling over my head, I respond, "Yes, we are. If you could, please stamp all the complaint copies and execute the summons for the twenty-one defendants. Bob, while she's doing that here's the three original contracts for your signature."[72]

After the Complaint is filed, we walk to the smoker's courtyard to hold a press conference. I begin,

> Governor Chiles is the only Governor in the history of the United States; in fact, he's the only Governor in the world with the courage and integrity to take on the tobacco industry.
>
> Each year the State spends $289 million treating Medicaid patients who are sick and dying from their products. Florida didn't smoke the cigarettes, sell the cigarettes or make the profits. We shouldn't be stuck with the bill.
>
> Cigarettes are as addictive as cocaine and heroin, and are the only product when used as directed produces only two results, sickness and death. More Floridians die from this scourge than from car wrecks, AIDS, drug abuse, and alcoholism combined. It's time to them to be held responsible.
>
> We aim to stop their callous pandering of cigarettes to children. With today's filing, Joe Camel's days are numbered.

Jack Frost follows, "The American Lung Association applauds Governor Chiles' action to bring Big Tobacco to Justice." When asked his role on the trial team, Montgomery responds, "I'm driving the bus. For every dollar tobacco spends, we'll spend ten, for every hour tobacco spends, we'll spend 20."[73]

This case study data demonstrate cause lawyer *artisanality* in their alignment of legal strategy and narrative framing of the facts and issues to create new legal thinking; moving from "individual responsibility" for the freedom

[72] Mary Ellen Klas, *State files $1.4 billion tobacco suit*, The Palm Beach Post, February 22, 1995, 1A, 6A.

[73] Mary Ellen Klas, *State files*, 1A, 6A.

of choosing to smoke to "corporate accountability" for purposeful and intentional conspiracy to addict Florida's indigent citizens to sickness and death.

Social change through litigation "has always been an important feature in the United States. Whether the change produced by such action is considered destructive or constructive, the fact remains that law can be a highly effective device for producing social change."[74] In this study, "bottom-up" progressive cause lawyer alignment with Cracker political leaders mobilized litigation to "disrupt" tobacco's crushing instrumental, institutional, and ideological dominance.

This suit is a prime example of progressive cause lawyers working in tandem with the culture, and public interest organizations, such as the heart, cancer and lung associations, which are generally seen by the public as positive forces.[75] We also observe the complementary tactics of media-oriented stagecraft and legal advocacy, effective tools of cause lawyer policy advocates.

In this case, litigation press coverage is a key element of the strategic effort to hold Big Tobacco accountable. In their effort to "name, claim and blame," cause lawyer and Cracker political leaders navigate the cultural tensions between facts and values, science and story.[76]

[74] Steve Vago, *Law and Society, Sixth Edition* (Upper Saddle River, NJ: Prentice Hall, 2000, 326).

[75] The prevalence of the cause lawyer as policy advocates is verified in interviews of over 140 pay equity activists in which "a huge majority of interviewees both ranked litigation as one of the several most effective tactics and identified its role in consciousness raising and movement building as the most important contribution." Michael McCann, *Rights at Work, Pay Equity Reform and the Politics of Legal Mobilization* (Chicago, IL: The University of Chicago Press, 1994, 83). In their complementary roles with social movements, cause lawyers often play a variety of roles, such as "movement publicity, rallying support from union members, coalition building, and political strategizing." Michael McCann, *Rights at Work*, 130.

[76] Cecil A. Gibb presented an "*interactional*" theory stressing the interplay between four components: (1) the leader, (2) the followers, (3) the situation, and (4) the goal. Cecil A. Gibb, *Leadership*, Handbook of Social Psychology, IV, ed. (1969). Cecil A. Gibb, *An Interactional View of the Emergence of Leadership*, Australian Journal of Psychology, Vol. 10:101–110 (1958).

The "*interactional*" model is elaborated by Fred E. Fiedler into a "contingency" model where the leader is dependent on two variables: (1) the leader's *goal structure* (task orientation vs. relationship orientation), and (2) the *situational controls* that enable the **leader** to influence the outcome of group activities. Fred E. Fiedler, *A Contingency Model of Leadership Effectiveness, Advances in Experimental Social Psychology* (New York: Academic Press, 1964). Robert J. House formulated a variant on the "contingency" model with a "path-goal theory." This model maintains that pursuits of organizational objectives are enhanced when the leader directs the followers to paths that are rewarding to both the followers and the organization.

The press release framed the suit as recovering innocent taxpayer money spent treating those sick and dying from cigarettes, and to stop the marketing of cigarettes to teenagers. Big Tobacco is named as the culprit. It avoids corporate responsibility for causing sickness and death and marketing to teenagers. Finally, Big Tobacco is blamed for the sickness and death of 28,212 Floridians annually, at a cost to the Florida treasury of $1.4 billion over a five-year period. The goal is to create a story that captures the public's imagination. The press release also counters the "greedy trial lawyer" argument by clarifying that these are "the best private attorneys in the private and public sectors to argue, at no cost to the state, this landmark case."

The press release is framed in moralistic terms with the "worthy" state and Governor fighting against "dangerous" big tobacco and its "dangerous" carnage. If one inserts the term "dangerous" and "worthy" in each applicable narrative frame, one can see the moral panic dimensions embedded in this press release. With the insertion, the press release reads,

> [Dangerous] Tobacco's not cool, it's cruel. While [dangerous] big tobacco goes to the bank and deposits enormous profits from the [worthy] lives they're ruining, Florida's [worthy] taxpayers consistently have to make withdrawals from their wallets to pay for the [dangerous] carnage," Governor Chiles said. "This suit sends a loud and clear message to the [dangerous] tobacco industry that it – not the [worthy] taxpayers – will be held accountable for marketing [dangerous] sickness and death. We will protect our [worthy] taxpayers and our most vulnerable [worthy] citizens by ending [dangerous] tobacco's callous practice of hooking our [worthy] children on a [dangerous] drug that's proven to be as addictive as [dangerous] heroin and cocaine.

James Morone, in his recent book, *Hellfire Nation*, describes the dynamic of narrative frames in moralistic terms driving America and its public policies.

> A new nation, drawn from many tribes and races, always faces the primal question, Who are we? . . .

Robert J. House, *A Path Goal Theory of Leadership Effectiveness*, Administrative Science Quarterly, Vol. 16, 321–38 (1971).

Fred E. Fiedler revised his model by joining the "contingency" approach with a "cognitive resource theory," emphasizing the leader's: (1) intellectual abilities, (2) technical competence, and (3) task-related experience. Fred E. Fiedler, and Joseph E. Garcia, *New Approaches to Effective Leadership: Cognitive Resources and Organizational Performance* (New York, NY: Wiley, 1987).

> If moral fervor stirs our better angels, moral fever spurs our demons. Frightening changes – a new economy, booming cities, still more strangers – rouse fears of decline. . . . Political life constantly gets entangled in two vital urges – redeeming "us" and reforming "them." The moral perspective revises all kinds of standard stories. . . . The nation develops not from religious to secular but from revival to revival. . . . In a nation made by immigrants, marked by social mobility, and home to a thousand religions, morality is dynamite. Visions of vice and virtue define the American community. They designate the worthy "us" (jammed into a Montgomery church) and finger the dangerous "them" (running brothels in the wicked cities). Moral fevers unleash our witch-hunts and racial panics. They inspire the dreamers who turn the nation upside-down in the name of social justice.[77]

In light of the moral panic component of American politics and policy, it is clear that the moral narratives must coordinate with problem, policy, and political alignment for implementation of policy. "As part of the 'package' containing the core frame, there are various framing devices (metaphors, exemplars, catchphrases, depictions, and visual images) and reasoning devices (causal attributions, consequences, and appeals to principles)."[78]

The tobacco story fits into the print media conflict format, and is prewritten and analyzed for efficient drop-ins to meet press deadlines. Although the media are independent and competitive, they have limited time and resources. Thus, if the analysis, facts, quotes, and important information are prepackaged for reporters, much more of the "framing, claiming, and blaming" content and narrative advocacy will be placed intact into their articles.

As an example, this is exactly what occurred in the *St. Petersburg Times* article covering the filing of Florida's Medicaid tobacco liability lawsuit. It incorporates whole portions of the Governor's press release, damages analysis, narrative, and ideological frames without change. The press simply amplified the societal consciousness impact of this lawsuit.

The Office of the Governor's Press Release dated February 21, 1995 – including graphic attachments of what diseases the $289 million in health care costs a year are spent on, the questions and answers for easy press

[77] James A. Morone, *Hellfire Nation, Politics of Sin in American History* (New Haven, CT: Yale University Press, 2004, 3–5).
[78] James A. Morone, *Hellfire Nation*, 3–5.

comprehension, and a simple fact sheet – sets the narrative frame that would be repeated and found at the core of most articles covering the subject over the next two and one-half years. The narrative frames of social cost, moral cause, and corporate responsibility infuse the press release and are repeated in nearly every news print article for the next thirty months. The February 22, 1995 edition of the *St. Petersburg Times* places the exact frame and data in its front-page article. In fact, most of the article uses the exact language and data supplied in the press packet. Key introductory statements and visual read,

> **Florida sues tobacco industry**
>
> Taxpayers have a right to reclaim
>
> Some $1.4 billion spent treating
>
> Medicaid patients for smoking-related
>
> Illnesses, Gov. Chiles says.

Tallahassee – Gov. Lawton Chiles filed suit Tuesday against the nation's cigarette companies in an effort to collect more than $1.4-billion the state has spent to provide medical care for smokers in the past five years.

The lawsuit also attempts to stop tobacco companies from using advertising campaigns that attract children to smoking.

"Today Joe Camel is as recognizable to children as Mickey Mouse.... Hooking children is not a cartoon and its not funny."

The article provides a pie chart of the division of $289 million in Medicaid costs from diseases such as lung cancer and the number of patients with each disease. This is an example of how both narrative truths and myths are transposed and produced in the "juridico-entertainment complex" of mass-mediated culture, often with little or no empirical basis.[79] In this case study, the print media often accepted "wholesale" the framing and data supplied by the Governor's Office and advocacy groups.

The methods to craft winning narratives to affect law, policy and society are demonstrated in this data set. Progressive cause lawyers allied with governmental leaders and their press platform are effectively interacting with the instruments, institutions, and ideologies to change the narrative

[79] Douglas S. Reed, A *New Constitutional Regime: The Juridico-Entertainment Complex*. Paper presented at the 1999 annual meeting of the Law and Society Association, in Chicago.

frame of Florida tobacco liability litigation. In this case, cause lawyers as public policy leaders are effectively working to modify cultural knowledge production and influencing the interrelated instrumental, institutional, and ideological factors affecting society, media, the courts, the legislature, and the executive branch.[80]

The data from this study demonstrate that changing the legal and narrative framework of the law, facts, and issues as reported in the print media assisted in shifting the "court of public opinion" and created new publics. It demonstrates that cause lawyers can participate and lead in reconstructing the public sphere where tensions between empiricism and norms generate the creative dialectic.[81] "Indeed, law itself, as a form of constituted knowledge, is significantly produced and reproduced by the narratives circulated by print and electronic news along with other forms of mass-produced entertainment."[82] Both general and focused media attention are likely to shape cause lawyer litigation by defining their 'social reality' and impact in mobilizing support and effecting social change. It is also believed that the news media are a "key institutional domain contributing to the mass construction specifically of legal knowledge and practical legal action."[83]

As stated by McCann,

> it is through the news production process of corporate mass media that legal 'naming, blaming, and claiming' are most broadly communicated among relevant actors and publics, especially on matters of general social concern. Indeed, the self-conscious effort to package legal knowledge and narratives for dissemination to the mass news media has been a hallmark of public interest litigation.[84]

Failure to project a noble, restrained image of consumer cause lawyers to the media harms the ability of consumer cause lawyers to advance public protection law. Failure of the news media to provide accurate facts and findings distorts legal policymaking and results in elected officials and the

[80] Austin Sarat and Stuart Scheingold, *Cause Lawyering: Political Commitments and Professional Responsibilities* (New York: Oxford University Press, 1998).

[81] Lance W. Bennett, *Constructing Publics and Their Opinions. Political Communication*, Vol. 10, 101–120 (1993). Jurgen Habermas, *The Theory of Communicative Action*, vol. 1, Thomas McCarthy, trans. (Boston, MA: Beacon Press, 1984). George Lakoff, *Know Your Values*, 99–119.

[82] Michael McCann and William Haltom, *Framing the Food Fights: How Mass Media Construct and Constrict Public Interest Litigation* (2004, 2).

[83] Michael McCann and William Haltom, *Framing*, 2.

[84] Michael McCann and William Haltom, *Framing*, 2.

public adopting a "common sense" view that there is an out-of-control jury lottery system. The effectiveness of this ideologically motivated, manufactured, and distorted "common sense" has recently led to state and national laws limiting consumer access to class actions in states, and limiting medical malpractice recovery for children and elderly because they are not worth as much for economic damages. This can be reengineered.

The engineered alignment of legal causation and the public causal story against tobacco is essential for the success of this multi-pronged legal, legislative, and political strategy. There are various dimensions of causal stories, and when causes are determined, blame and responsibility can be pinpointed, assigned, and solutions offered. Unlike the natural sciences method of determining causation by controlling dependent and independent variables *ceteris parabus*, in the polis "causes" are stories – cultural narrative frames and myths told carefully using symbols and numbers, which are ultimately "socially" created.

In Florida's tobacco liability cause, there were years of litigation, legislative battles, and media framing, naming, blaming, and claiming. Through perseverance, and embedded philosophic belief in their cause, Florida Cracker public servant and cause lawyer aligned leadership ultimately defeats Big Tobacco's legal and political ideological dominance.

1. Cause Lawyer Stories Worth Telling

This central question of whether there is a culturally resonant story of cause lawyer heroism at the constructive edge is answered in this essay using data from the descriptive and explanatory case study of Florida tobacco liability litigation. This case study provides numerous sources consistent with a heroic story of cause lawyers and Cracker political leaders at the constructive edge. Thus, I believe that this essay answers the question with a resounding yes.

In answering this question, we answered other questions as well. This essay gives examples of how cause lawyers successfully act at the interstices of culture, institutions of government, and media to create strategic legal initiatives that obtain favorable media coverage and thereby move public opinion. This essay also demonstrated how their successful cause lawyer *artisanality* ultimately leads to legislation and court rulings that advance their ideology and public policy goals.

The cause lawyer-Cracker political leadership "band of brothers" wins a national settlement, removing billboard advertising, ending marketing to teenagers, exposing the lies and dissembling found in their corporate and science research documents, and securing more than $200 billion in payments for state governments nationally. This is a story that can project a noble cultural image of progressive cause lawyers at the constructive edge.

The success of grossly inaccurate conservative, cultural manipulations of cause lawyer depiction is documented by Haltom and McCann in their 2004 publication, *Distorting the Law, Politics, Media, and the Litigation Crisis*. Compelling accurate cause lawyer narratives can also be constructed. In this essay alone, there are elements of a noble story of cause lawyers and Florida Cracker leaders that could resonate with the various cultures in America, accord with empirical data, and advance the legal ideals of accountability and compassion.

There are more such stories to be told about the lives of cause lawyers. These stories simply need to be researched, verified, analyzed and told to a national and world audience. When practitioners know that there are cause lawyers advocating for the legal ideal in the harsh real world, and obtaining success, such an effort can advance the ideals of justice, The Justice Project is such an example. Complacency needs to be challenged by the heightened consciousness found in the cause lawyer band of brothers. To constantly refresh our ideals and creativity, and apply these ideals to harsh realities, cause lawyers must continually hone their constructive edge, and continually ask the culture: "***We've found the edge. Can you live there with us?***"

THE CULTURAL CONSTRUCTION OF LAWYERS AND THEIR CAUSES

4

"They all have different policies, so of course they have to give different news"

Images of Human Rights Lawyers in the British Press

Richard J. Maiman

"What readers get when they pick up their newspaper – and what they miss when newspapers do not arrive – is a particular way of structuring events, of producing 'the news' as a coherent reality." ACH Smith, *Paper Voices*

"They all have different policies, so of course they have to give different news." Evelyn Waugh, *Scoop*

I. Introduction

It has been suggested that cause lawyers' moral commitments have the potential to legitimate and even enhance the public's view of the legal profession.[1] The likelihood of this occurring clearly depends on first, whether the public recognizes such a commitment in the work of cause lawyers, and second, whether the public subscribes to the particular moral principles underlying that work. These questions help focus our attention on the content of the messages about cause lawyers disseminated through the media. Recent developments in Great Britain provide an opportunity to examine in detail how one group of cause lawyers has been depicted by the nation's newspapers and to ask whether these depictions conform to a vision of the common good that is shared by newspapers and their readers.

The 1998 Human Rights Act (HRA) subjected all public authorities in the United Kingdom to the restrictions of the European Convention on Human Rights. The HRA greatly expanded the opportunities for Britons to challenge government officials in court; it also magnified the importance

[1] See Austin Sarat and Stuart Scheingold, "Cause Lawyering and the Reproduction of Professional Authority," in Austin Sarat and Stuart Scheingold (Eds.), *Cause Lawyering: Political Commitments and Professional Responsibilities* (New York: Oxford University Press, 1998): 3.

of lawyers who actually handle such cases.[2] The prospect of proliferating human rights-based litigation touched off vigorous debate about whether judicial involvement in policymaking enhanced or undermined British democracy. This argument, which had previously been confined to legal-academic circles, was now taken up by Britain's mass media as well. This essay analyzes the messages about human rights lawyers conveyed by leading British newspapers to their readers after the HRA came into force. Although it does not attempt to address how successful the papers may have been in achieving their purposes,[3] the picture that emerges from it – of a press, and perhaps a nation, highly polarized on the question of whether the work of human rights lawyers serves the public good – has important implications for the long-term efficacy of that work.

II. British Newspapers and British Politics

Since the rise of its popular press more than a century ago, Great Britain has been a nation of avid newspaper readers. Despite a decline in newspaper sales over the past forty years in response to the pressures of television,

[2] Rights-oriented litigation did not begin in Great Britain with passage of the HRA, of course. A number of advocacy groups such as Liberty, JUSTICE, the Child Poverty Action Group, the Society of Labour Lawyers, as well as numerous individual practitioners, had been engaged in such work for many years. Typically they used judicial review proceedings to challenge government actions in Britain's courts and took appeals based on the European Convention to the European Court of Human Rights. Some of these cases – for example, those involving the IRA, challenges to the Thatcher government, and prominent miscarriages of justice – were covered extensively by the newspapers. However, not until the Human Rights Act was passed did the media begin to give such legal work a collective label – "human rights lawyering" – and to vigorously contest its normative meaning. At the same time. the wide scope of the European Convention encouraged many lawyers with such disparate practices as corporate, criminal, immigration, and planning law (among others) to begin styling themselves "human rights lawyers." Within the fairly small cohort of "traditional" human rights lawyers – those with long experience with litigation before the European Court of Human Rights – concerns were raised about the cooptation – even corruption – of their unique identity. However, the term was now available to any lawyer who wished to apply it to him- or herself – and many clearly did. In 2003 the Human Rights Lawyers Association was founded in London with an initial paid membership of several hundred. By 2006 that number had grown to more than 1,000 (www.hrla.org.uk; accessed June 3, 2006). Because it is irrelevant to my purposes here, I make no attempt to draw any distinctions between "real" human rights lawyers and those who may have simply appropriated the title.

[3] There is a voluminous literature on the impact of the mass media on public opinion and electoral behavior in Great Britain and elsewhere. For a brief summary of the main lines of argument and a useful summary of some British data, see Kenneth Newton, "Mass Media Effects: Mobilization or Media Malaise?" *British Journal of Politics* 29 (1999): 557.

the Internet, and the pace of modern life, Britain remains a world leader in per capita newspaper readership.[4] Eleven daily newspapers compete in a national market consisting of about twelve million regular purchasers and an estimated thirty-six million readers.[5] More precisely, there are *two* distinct UK newspaper markets: one for the six morning "tabloids" or "popular" papers, with a total daily circulation in 2006 approaching nine million, and the other for the five "broadsheets," or "quality" titles, which have combined sales of just under three million.

In this crowded marketplace, one of the defining characteristics of the British press is its intense competitiveness. Although many readers, especially older ones, are intensely loyal to "their" paper, a substantial and growing number of younger people are not habitual readers of a particular title or indeed of newspapers in general. These "floaters" are ardently pursued by newspaper owners keen to expand (or replace) their aging reader base. Editors are sacked, replaced, and recycled with striking frequency as publishers search for a winning formula. Papers jostle for readers' attention with format changes, price wars, DVD giveaways, and multiple helpings of Sudoku. Their editorial ammunition includes generous helpings of checkbook journalism; shock-horror headlines; exhaustive coverage of sport, fashion, lifestyle, and entertainment news; highly sexualized subject matter; investigative stings; and public quarrels between rival columnists and even rival editors. Nor is such sensationalism confined to the world of the tabloids; the quality titles also compete aggressively among themselves with ever-splashier style and content.[6]

[4] One slightly ironic bit of evidence of the continued importance of newspapers in Britain is the perennial popularity of a fifty-year-old weekly television series, *What the Papers Say*. A newspaper columnist recently observed, "Nowadays no current affairs show, on radio or television, is complete without a trot through the day's papers" (Simon Hoggart, "The Ultimate Cuts Job," *Guardian*, October 30, 2006).

[5] The UK's population is about sixty million. Among modern industrialized nations, only Japan has a higher per capita newspaper readership than Great Britain. Paul Gordon and David Rosenberg, *The Press and Black People in Britain* (London: Runnymede Trust, 1989). In 1960 daily sales in Britain totaled around seventeen million: fifteen million in the popular category and about two million for the qualities. Comparing these figures to those of today probably overstates actual declines in tabloid readership because in past decades, when the papers were both slimmer and cheaper, people were more likely to buy more than one title a day. Even so, the proportion of adults in the UK who read a newspaper every day dropped from eighty-five to ninety percent in the 1960s to about forty percent in the 1990s. Jeffrey Tunstall, *Newspaper Power: The New National Press in Britain* (Oxford: Clarendon Press, 1996): 223.

[6] Two of the quality dailies, *The Times* and the *Independent*, have recently switched from the broadsheet format to the supposedly more reader-friendly tabloid layout. A former *Telegraph*

Another distinctive feature of British newspapers is their high level of political partisanship. As Hattersley (among many others) has observed, "[t]he ideological prejudice of the British Press is a fact of political life."[7] To a much greater extent than in, say, the United States, both the tabloids and the broadsheets in Britain wear their politics on their sleeves – not only in their leaders (editorials) and opinion columns but also in their selection and presentation of "news." The most conventional expressions of the papers' partisanship are their party endorsements during – and sometimes well ahead of – general elections. More unusual (at least by American standards) is the papers' often strikingly biased reporting of the election campaigns themselves. Some editors have unapologetically acknowledged that their coverage was deliberately crafted to influence an election outcome.[8]

The papers' political interventions are not confined to elections, however. Throughout the year British newspaper readers are treated to a rich diet of opinionated commentary on politics and politicians that ranges from high-minded to irreverent to downright raunchy. News stories habitually employ angled headlines and unflattering photos intended to deliver information wrapped in a point of view. The papers regularly mount campaigns to rally their readers behind favored policy changes.[9] This reflexive

editor recently asserted that by adopting not only the tabloid format but also the front-page editorialized headline, the *Independent* has surrendered its claim to "quality," reducing itself to a left-wing equivalent of the *Daily Mail*. Martin Newland, "Is the Indy Still a Quality Read?" *Guardian*, November 20, 2006. The qualities' editors vehemently deny accusations that they have succumbed to "tabloidization," claiming that they have made their papers more attractive and useful to their readers while expanding coverage of public affairs. Roy Greenslade, *Press Gang: How Newspapers Make Profits From Propaganda* (London: Macmillan, 2003): 626–27.

[7] Roy Hattersley, *Press Gang* (London: Robson Books, 1983): 9.

[8] The *Sun* famously headlined its first issue after the Conservative party's surprise victory in 1992: "IT WAS THE SUN WOT WON IT." The next day, after widespread criticism from politicians and pressure from publisher Rupert Murdoch, the Sun's editor changed his story and disclaimed any credit for the outcome. James Thomas, *Popular Newspapers, The Labour Party and British Politics* (Abingdon, UK: Routledge, 2005): 626–627.

[9] One of the earlier and best-known examples of a newspaper-led reform campaign was the *Sunday Times's* exposure in 1972 of the pathetically small settlements offered to thalidomide–damaged children by Distillers Ltd., the parent company of the drug's manufacturer. For an account of the campaign and its aftermath written by the then-editor of the *Sunday Times*, see Harold Evans, *Good Times, Bad Times* (London: Atheneum, 1984): 79–97. Recent examples include the *Sun's* "name and shame" campaigns in 2000 against convicted pedophiles released from prison and in 2006 against "soft" judges; the *Daily Mail's* demand in 2003 that the government hold a referendum on adopting the proposed European Union constitution; the *Daily Telegraph*'s effort to "save" the Royal Unionist Constabulary in 2003; the *Independent's*

partisanship is so pervasive that looking only at the electoral endorsements of some newspapers would give a distorted picture of their real politics. For example, three of the papers studied here – the *Guardian*, the *Daily Mirror*, and the *Sun* – have formally supported Tony Blair in three successive general elections, despite giving aspects of his government's performance extremely negative reviews in their day-to-day coverage. Addressing this apparent anomaly, Koss has observed that Britain's old-style party-political press has virtually disappeared, and that newspapers have "substituted what may be called political dispositions for what had been formal party allegiances."[10] In eschewing such traditional allegiances, the newspapers resemble an increasing number of their readers, whose strongly held political convictions (one of which may be an abiding cynicism about politics and politicians) do not necessarily lead them to identify with, much less belong to, a party organization.

Koss's notion that Britain's newspapers now have general "political dispositions" rather than "party allegiances" is related to Lacey and Longman's contention that public opinion in the UK can be seen as "a series of overlapping cultures of understanding, each sustained and dependent upon a major national newspaper."[11] Their argument rests on two kinds of empirical evidence: data showing that Britain's national newspaper readerships are sharply differentiated in socioeconomic terms[12] and striking variations

long-running campaign to decriminalize the use of cannabis; and the *Guardian's* periodic efforts since 2000 to rally its readers behind abolition of the monarchy and its unsuccessful legal challenge in 2002 to an historic statute prohibiting a non-Protestant from assuming the British throne.

10 Stephen Koss, *The Rise and Fall of the Political Press in Britain* (Volume 2) (London: Hamish Hamilton, 1984): 680.

11 Colin Lacey and David Longman, *The Press as Public Educator: Cultures of Understanding, Cultures of Ignorance* (Luton: University of Luton Press, 1997): 76.

12 Readers of the five quality dailies – the *Financial Times*, the *Times*, the *Independent*, the *Daily Telegraph*, and the *Guardian* – are overwhelmingly middle class; two of the tabloids – the *Daily Mail* and the *Daily Express* – have readerships divided between the middle and the working classes; and the readers of the other four tabloids – the *Daily Mirror*, the *Sun*, the *Daily Star*, and the *Daily Record* – are predominantly working class (Tunstall, *Newspaper Power: The New National Press in Britain*: 77). However, these categories are somewhat misleading because the relatively large circulations of the *Daily Mirror* and the *Sun* mean that more middle-class people read these papers than read the smaller circulation broadsheets. This segmentation of "upmarket," "midmarket," and "downmarket" readerships has persisted over the last century, though with varying numbers of titles in each category. Today the downmarket tabloids account for about fifty percent of total daily circulation, with the other half divided equally between the broadsheets and the midmarket tabloids.

in the reported political views of readers of different papers.[13] Although these findings are far from definitive,[14] they are in accord with a popular perception that there is such a thing as a typical "*Guardian* reader," "*Daily Mail* reader," and so on. Lacey and Longman themselves acknowledge that the various cultures of understanding in Britain may actually overlap, but they conclude that each leading newspaper performs a crucial role "of defending and maintaining the myths of the culture of understanding of its readers, enticing into readership similarly minded individuals and deriding the myths of opposing groups."[15]

This study loosely employs the concept of "cultures of understanding" as it examines the various meanings that newspapers have given to a relatively new phrase in their lexicon: "human rights lawyer." It is irrelevant for my purposes whether the papers' readerships are completely distinct demographically and ideologically – though this seems highly unlikely – or whether the papers are perfectly attuned to their readers' views. What I am seeking to determine is whether discernible differences can be found in the stories that various papers tell their readers about human rights lawyers. To help set the stage for the analysis that follows, I begin with some brief remarks about the overall "political dispositions" of the newspapers involved in this study. First, the tabloids:

- The *Daily Mail*, currently ranked second among UK newspapers in daily circulation, is the only tabloid whose sales have risen in the

[13] They base their "cultures of understanding" argument largely on data from a 1991–92 MORI survey asking respondents about "the most important problem facing Britain today." The most frequent answers to this question, grouped according to the newspaper respondents said they were most likely to read, showed some striking variation (Lacey and Longman, 81). For example:

Guardian: Education, Housing, National Health Service
Daily Telegraph: Common Market (*sic*), Defense, German unification, Race/race relations
The Times: Economic situation, Common Market
Daily Mail: Crime, Race/relations
Daily Mirror: Privatization, Pensions, Nuclear fuels/power, National Health Service
Sun: AIDS, Taxes, Don't Know

[14] For example, despite the fanfare surrounding the papers' endorsements and campaigns, there is considerable evidence that many readers are either unaware of or indifferent to their paper's political views. Some surveys have shown that only about half of newspaper readers can correctly name the party preference of their paper and that a quarter to a third of readers support a party other than the one endorsed by the newspaper they read most frequently (Colin Seymour-Ure, *The British Press and Broadcasting Since 1945*, 2nd Edition (London: Blackwell Press, 1996): 216.

[15] Lacey and Longman, 76.

last decade, thanks in large part to its success in attracting female readers. Long opposed to the policies of the Labour party, the *Daily Mail* has been an unrelenting critic of both the style and substance of the Blair government. It has also been scathing about Conservative leader David Cameron's recent efforts to reposition his party closer to the political center.

- The *Daily Mirror* is the tabloid traditionally aligned most closely with the labor movement and the Labour party. The paper has moved somewhat to the right on some social issues in recent years in what some see as an attempt to keep its readers from defecting to the *Sun*, but it still is essentially centrist on issues like immigration and European unification. Although the *Daily Mirror* has opposed Tony Blair over the Iraq War, it has expressed its criticisms in a moderate tone that is perhaps intended not to offend its pro-Blair readers.
- The *Sun* is a relative newcomer among Britain's daily papers. It became the national circulation leader in 1978, less than a decade after its founding, thanks in part to an uninhibited style typified by its daily topless "Page Three Girl" and its front-page coverage of television soap stars. A strong supporter of Prime Minister Thatcher on domestic issues such as the miners' strike, the *Sun* broke with the Major government in the 1990s partly over its pro-Europe policies. The newspaper's endorsements of Tony Blair in 1997 and in the two subsequent general elections probably were based less on political affinity than on owner Rupert Murdoch's desire to back (and exercise influence over) a winner. The *Sun* has strongly opposed Blair's European policies and criticized his government's failure to stem the tide of asylum seekers and illegal immigrants.

And the qualities:

- The *Guardian*, a descendant of the *Manchester Guardian*, has long been associated with left-wing values and policies, though during the 1970s and 80s the paper was closer in its politics to the Social Democrats than to Labour (in 1983 four *Guardian* columnists were Social Democrat Party candidates for Parliament). A strong backer of New Labour in 1997, the *Guardian* has been less enthusiastic about Blair in each succeeding general election, chiefly because of Iraq, and can now be described more accurately as anti-Conservative than as pro-Labour. The *Guardian* is a strong supporter of European integration and critical of what it sees as draconian government efforts to discourage asylum seekers from coming to the UK.

- The *Daily Telegraph* is Britain's best-selling quality paper (and except for the *Financial Times* the only remaining full-sized broadsheet), though for more than a decade it has been rapidly losing its predominantly older readers. The *Daily Telegraph* traditionally has been right-of-center, but at the same time always careful not to be too close to the Conservative party. However, in the late 1990s the paper was nicknamed "The Torygraph" by some critics because of the uncompromisingly anti-Blair views of its crusading editor Charles Moore. It has been highly skeptical about the wisdom of forging closer connections with Europe and strongly critical of the government for failing to get a handle on the immigration/asylum crisis.
- *The Times* has made no secret of its goal of overtaking the *Daily Telegraph* as the qualities' circulation leader, and its recent switch to tabloid format was intended to hasten that day. *The Times* has been Britain's most prestigious newspaper for most of the past two centuries, but since being acquired by Rupert Murdoch in 1981 its successive editors have struggled to demonstrate that they remain free of his editorial control. Today the paper occupies a moderately conservative niche – skeptical about, rather than stridently opposed to, many of the Blair government's constitutional reforms, concerned but far from hysterical about the immigration issue, and essentially supportive of the European Union while opposing Britain's signing on to the single currency.

III. The Frequency of Human Rights Lawyer Stories

My research began with keyword searches in the online archives of six daily newspapers – three tabloids (the *Daily Mail*, the *Daily Mirror*, and the *Sun*) and three broadsheets (the *Daily Telegraph*, the *Guardian*, and *The Times*), identifying every instance in which the phrase "human rights lawyer" or its plural form appeared between January 1, 2001 and December 31, 2005. These are hereafter referred to as HRL stories. The beginning of 2001 was chosen as a starting point because the Human Rights Act had come into force just a few months earlier (in October 2000). Data for the *Guardian*, the *Daily Mail*, and the *Daily Telegraph* were obtained through those

Table 4.1: *Frequency of British 'Human Rights Lawyers' Articles by Year, 2001–05*

	2001	2002	2003	2004	2005	Percentage Increase from 2001–05	Total
TABLOIDS							
Daily Mail	8	11	20	24	34	325	97
Daily Mirror	11	12	12	7	20	95	62
Sun	4	5	17	17	25	525	68
TOTAL	23	28	49	48	79	243	227
BROADSHEETS							
Guardian	31	29	37	73	96	210	266
Daily Telegraph	13	13	14	20	35	169	95
The Times	15	14	29	26	26	73	110
TOTAL	59	56	80	119	157	183	471

newspapers' online archives. Records for the other papers were accessed through the LexisNexis system online.[16]

Until the late 1990s most of the relatively small number of HRL stories found in the British press involved lawyers from countries other than the UK.[17] After the passage of the Human Rights Act the newspapers' coverage of Britons identified as human rights lawyers increased exponentially, but in the broadsheets stories about non-British human rights lawyers continued to appear (the tabloids all had quite limited foreign news coverage). Because the focus of this research is on the meanings attached to the term "human rights lawyer" in the *British* context, I decided to exclude from my analysis all HRL stories involving *non-British* lawyers; this eliminated about thirty percent of the broadsheets' and about eight percent of the tabloids' HRL stories. Table 4.1 reports on the frequency with which the phrase "human rights lawyer(s)," referring to British women and men, appeared in these papers during the five-year period covered by this study. It shows a steady

[16] The three tabloids in this study accounted for seventy-eight percent of the total daily popular circulation (using December 2006 figures), whereas the three broadsheets comprised seventy-three percent of the daily quality sales (Jim Bilton, "Grave New World," *Guardian*, November 13, 2006).

[17] Newspapers in the United States still apply the term "human rights lawyer" predominantly to foreign lawyers. For example, the phrase appeared 159 times in *The New York Times* between January 1, 2000 and December 31, 2004. Only twenty of these references were to American lawyers, nearly all of whom were representing non-American clients and/or working abroad. *The Times* more commonly described attorneys situated in the United States as "civil rights lawyers" (213 references during this period) or "civil liberties lawyers" (eighty-four references).

rise in the overall coverage of the activities of human rights lawyers between 2001 and 2005. It also shows that the three broadsheets together published more than twice as many HRL stories as the three tabloids during the five-year period. (Moreover, the broadsheets' articles were considerably longer: the average length of an HRL story in the *Times*, at 656 words, was exactly twice that of the average *Sun* story, at 327 words.) There also were significant disparities within both categories of newspapers. The *Guardian* carried almost three times as many HRL stories as the *Telegraph*, and more than twice as many as *The Times*, whereas the *Daily Mail* printed around fifty percent more HRL pieces than either the *Daily Mirror* or the *Sun*. Thus readers who relied on a single paper for their news during these years were exposed to widely varying amounts of coverage of the activities of human rights lawyers.

IV. The Tone of Human Rights Lawyer Stories

To analyze the various papers' presentations and interpretations of the term "human rights lawyer," I classified each story by its tone; the classification was based on whether the content of the article was positive, negative, or neutral toward the lawyer or lawyers. These data are presented in Table 4.2. Positive stories were those in which lawyers or their activities were reported favorably or which exclusively or predominantly reflected their points of view. Because the majority of HRL stories involved some sort of conflict between individuals (or groups) and governments, the crucial question often was whether the story sided either explicitly or implicitly with the lawyer's client or cause. In some cases such a preference occurred by default; simply by omitting any coverage of the opposing position, the story reflected favorably on the lawyer's side. Other stories covered both sides of a conflict, but presented the human rights lawyer's position more sympathetically. Negative stories were those in which a lawyer's activities were shown in a pejorative light. Many of these stories depicted individuals described as human rights lawyers, or human rights lawyers as a group, as engaged in activities that were either self-serving or dishonest or unpatriotic. Finally, stories were classified as neutral if they presented information and a point of view that on balance were neither favorable nor unfavorable toward the lawyer or lawyers. Some of these stories described conflicts between a human rights lawyer and others in which the opposing positions

Table 4.2: *2001–05 British Human Rights Lawyers' Articles by Tone*

	Positive	Negative	Neutral	Total
TABLOIDS				
Daily Mail	7 (7.2%)	64 (66.0%)	26 (26.8%)	97
Daily Mirror	32 (51.6%)	11 (17.7%)	19 (30.6%)	62
Sun	9 (13.2%)	41 (60.3%)	18 (26.5%)	68
TOTAL	48 (21.1%)	116 (51.1%)	63 (27.8%)	227
BROADSHEETS				
Guardian	160 (60.2%)	20 (7.5%)	86 (32.3%)	266
Daily Telegraph	20 (22.7%)	31 (35.2%)	37 (42.0%)	88
The Times	58 (52.7%)	12 (10.9%)	40 (36.4%)	110
TOTAL	238 (51.3%)	63 (13.6%)	163 (35.1%)	464
ALL PAPERS	286 (41.4%)	179 (25.9%)	226 (32.7%)	691

were given more or less equal weight. Another typical neutral HRL story was one in which a reference to a human rights lawyer was only incidental to the storyline (for example, the subject of an interview or profile might be described as being married to a human rights lawyer). I employed the "neutral" category whenever I had any doubt about an article's predominant point of view.

Most of the stories were relatively easy to classify. Simplest of all were opinion columns, especially those in some of the tabloids, in which the words "human rights lawyer(s)" typically were accompanied by adjectives like "greedy," "arrogant," "high-earning," or "parasitic." The tone of the broadsheets' coverage was usually more subtle, but as Table 4.2 shows, their stories were only slightly more likely than those of the tabloids to be classified as neutral. Table 4.2 also reveals significant variations in the six newspapers' points of view on Britain's human rights lawyers and their activities. Among the tabloid papers, the *Daily Mirror* had by far the most favorable coverage of human rights lawyers; HRL stories in the *Daily Mail* and the *Sun* were overwhelmingly negative. Among the tabloids as a whole, there were more than twice as many negative HRL stories as positive ones.

Among the broadsheets, the *Guardian's* coverage of human rights lawyers was highly favorable, *The Times'* slightly less so. Although a reader of *The Times* would have encountered far fewer HRL stories than a *Guardian* reader during this five-year period, the content would have been nearly as positive as that in the *Guardian*. The *Daily Telegraph's* HRL coverage was fairly negative, but less so than that of the right-wing tabloids. Because of the *Guardian's* comparatively heavy HRL coverage, the total number of favorable stories in the broadsheets outnumbered the unfavorable ones by a ratio of almost five to one.

V. Narrative Frameworks

The data thus far have told us that in the post-HRA period, as the story of human rights lawyering became increasingly newsworthy, Britain's leading newspapers varied considerably in how they covered that story. Combining these findings with what we already know about the papers suggests that the way each paper depicted human rights lawyers – whether in a positive or a negative light – was hardly a matter of chance. Rather than fashioning their coverage out of whole cloth, each newspaper largely incorporated the HRL story into preexisting narrative frameworks, giving readers a picture of human rights lawyers consistent with the particular "culture of understanding" within which the paper operated. Thus, what each newspaper had to say about human rights lawyers derived much of its shape and substance from the paper's established editorial views. A close reading of the papers' HRL coverage identified four such narratives that played particularly significant parts in determining how the papers depicted human rights lawyers and their work. In order of their relative importance, these four established story-lines can be described as "New Labour," "the Human Rights Act," "immigration and political asylum," and "Britain's relationship with Europe." Elements of these four narratives could be found, either separately or in combination, in about two-thirds of the papers' positive and negative HRL coverage, although their importance varied both overall and from paper to paper. (They were found infrequently in their neutral HRL stories, however.) In this way, the messages that the papers were already conveying to their readers about these four matters – messages embedded in the newspaper's "cultures of understanding" – affected in a major way what they told their readers about human rights lawyers. The sections that follow illustrate more specifically just how those stories were told.

1. New Labour

The tone of the papers' HRL coverage was shaped to a considerable degree by their attitudes toward the Blair government, particularly toward what might be called New Labour's culture or, more plainly, its style. This was especially true of the negative HRL coverage in the *Daily Mail*, the *Sun*, and the *Daily Telegraph*, all of which found the comportment of Blair's government highly objectionable. These papers especially enjoyed demonstrating that Blair's team, for all of its claims to be practicing a "new" politics, was in fact carrying on just as governments always had – using its power to reward its allies, punish its opponents, and generally protect its interests. The fact that many of the leading members of Blair's government, including the prime minister himself, were lawyers by profession occasioned many sneering tabloid references to "fashionable" Blairite lawyers. Gradually, the hostile papers began to focus on one *particular* group of lawyers as exemplars of what was wrong with the government. These were human rights lawyers. As a *Daily Telegraph* columnist wrote in 2003,

> If you question their beliefs, they will express disdain, mock you for being old-fashioned, suggest you are immoral or dim, and – their trump card – racist. But the truth is they are, for the most part, members of the government salariat, who live off taxpayers' money.... This allows them to indulge in their I-feel-your-pain rhetoric and to posture as understanding, while at the same time living a prosperous life, taking off the whole month of August, before returning to their practice as a spin doctor, 'human rights lawyer,' broadcaster, 'chief executive' of a council, or backbench Labour MP. It goes without saying that their leader and the chief protector of their interests is Tony Blair.

According to these newspapers, Blair's support for the Human Rights Act was a sophisticated form of cronyism, a cynical scheme for helping lawyers sympathetic to New Labour get rich – or richer – through legal aid, which the *Sun* in 2004 termed a "massive earner for human rights lawyers."[18]

[18] The charge that human rights lawyers were exploiting government legal aid was similar to an accusation that the right-wing papers had been using against lawyers in general since the 1980s. See Richard Abel, *English Lawyers Between Market and State: The Politics of Professionalism* (Oxford: Oxford University Press 2003): 279–80. However, directing the complaint against human rights lawyers seemingly ignored the fact that in its first term Blair's government had imposed new restrictions on legal aid and made virtually all cases involving money damages conditional fee cases. Moreover, the Human Rights Act itself included a notably ungenerous scheme (modeled after the practice of the European Court of Human Rights) for figuring damage awards. In fact, most of the work of human rights lawyers was directed *against* the government and indeed caused successive Home Secretaries of the government acute distress. In 1999, for example, Jack Straw lashed out at "the lawyers and so-called legal experts" who had charged that the government's policy of issuing antisocial behavior orders violated the European Convention. Straw said that there was "a huge issue of hypocrisy here. They represent the perpetrator of the crime and then get into their BMWs and drive into areas where they

According to the *Daily Mail* in 2003, the "human rights culture" that the government had pledged to foster was "nothing more than a "compensation culture [that] grows ever more malign, while human rights lawyers grow rich." As a *Sun* columnist put it in 2002, "We are breeding a nation of wimps, through political insanity and fear of greedy 'human rights' lawyers suing for millions because a child scratched his knee playing football in the playground."

Another strand of the papers' case against what they depicted as an unholy alliance between the government and human rights lawyers was the charge that, like the government itself, these lawyers were biased and hypocritical in determining the interests they represented. A *Daily Telegraph* columnist in 2002 criticized "conceited human rights lawyers who could not give a damn about the human rights of white racists." Another *Daily Telegraph* column in 2004, referring to a judgment against Israel handed down by a Chinese judge in the The Hague, suggested that "China's atrocities, whether now or in the past, are not a modish subject among human rights' lawyers. They prefer the subject of Israel's, though Israel's have been few compared with China's." In 2005, responding to the government's plans for policing the World Cup tournament, yet another *Daily Telegraph* columnist complained that "[w]hen it comes to football hooliganism, fashionable concerns about human rights fly out of the window." Those who would loudly object to government surveillance of young Muslim men had nothing to say about the

> extraordinary battery of measures that governments have deployed against the minor problem of fat men misbehaving at football matches." It seems strange that these "very firm measures" are deemed more legitimate than draconian anti terror laws. After all, the "various sickening ills of football violence" do not include suicide bombings. The difference is that "potential football hooligans" tend to be white working-class men. And most judges, human rights lawyers, liberal journalists and MPs tend to despise those whom they see as white trash every bit as much as the Government does. "Chav scum" are the one minority it is legitimate to give a good kicking to.

are immune from much crime" (Alan Travis, "Straw Attacks Hypocrisy of 'BMW Lawyers,'" *Guardian*, September 15, 1999). Similarly, in 2003 Straw's successor David Blunkett attacked human rights lawyers for challenging his efforts to reduce crime, telling a reporter, "I'm looking forward to the day when John Wadham, head of Liberty, comes to my constituency and sets up a surgery designed to liberate and protect the victims of crime" (Rachel Sylvester, "Slimline Blunkett Targets the Flash Group," *Daily Telegraph*, February 21, 2003).

The Cherie Booth Factor

The various elements of the newspapers' case against the Blair government for inflicting human rights lawyers on the British public were crystallized in the extensive coverage of one such person in particular: Cherie Booth Blair, the wife of the prime minister. A prominent Queen's Counsel (QC) specializing in employment law, Booth (as she wishes to be called in her professional capacity) was an outspoken supporter of the Human Rights Act from the time of its introduction. In 2000 she helped organize a group of high-powered barristers into a new chambers called Matrix, which announced that it would specialize in litigation under the Human Rights Act.[19]

Of the eighty-three individual Britons identified as human rights lawyers by at least one of the newspapers in this study, Booth's total of ninety-four references was more than twice that of the nearest runner-up, with forty-three.[20] Overall, Booth accounted for about fifteen percent of the six newspapers' specific human rights lawyer references. Her name was particularly prominent in the *Daily Mail* and the *Daily Telegraph*, appearing in twenty-five and thirty-one percent, respectively, of those papers' total HRL references. Booth's name, of course, also appeared in countless other articles without the keywords "human right lawyer."[21]

For the *Daily Mail* and the *Daily Telegraph* in particular, Cherie Booth conveniently personified all of the negative qualities they ascribed to human rights lawyers as a group. Booth was situated at the center of power without being accountable to the electorate herself. She had decidedly liberal opinions on many issues that she expressed forthrightly. She was an

[19] Critics were quick to cite Matrix as Exhibit A for their claim that well-connected lawyers were using human rights to make their fortunes. See, for example, Kristin Sellars, "How to Make a Killing Out of Human Rights," *The Spectator*, April 8, 2000: 10.

[20] This finding is consistent with the results of a survey of coverage of British lawyers by national and regional newspapers published in September 2005 by Sweet & Maxwell. The report showed Cherie Blair Booth by a large margin with the largest number of newspaper mentions between July 2004 and June 2005. Although the Sweet & Maxwell survey was not limited to human rights lawyers, there was a close correspondence between its results and those reported here: the persons occupying second, third, and sixth places on the Sweet & Maxwell list were in second, sixth, and third places, respectively, in this survey. (www.sweetandmaxwell.co.uk/pressroom/2005. Visited April 11, 2006).

There was surprisingly little consensus among the newspapers about who should be called a human rights lawyer. Of the eighty-three Britons so identified, only four were named by all six papers. There was more agreement among the broadsheets, where sixteen lawyers were identified by all three papers and another eleven by two of the three.

[21] For a comprehensive study of media coverage of Booth in her various roles, see Ruth E. Page, "'Cherie: Lawyer, Wife, Mum:' Contradictory Patterns of Representation in Media Reports of Cherie Booth/Blair," *Discourse and Society* 14 (2003): 559.

enthusiastic champion of the principles enshrined in the HRA, and she had a lucrative legal practice based partly on litigating under the act. Moreover, in her dual roles as spouse and advocate, Booth was an especially inviting target, a character literally of Shakespearean dimensions: when she supported her husband's policies (or he supported hers) she could be portrayed as a Lady Macbeth exercising malign influence; and when she publicly opposed his government (as she occasionally did, both in court and in public) she could be accused of Gertrude-like betrayal.[22]

A 2005 *Daily Mail* column shows how effectively criticism of Blair, Booth, and human rights lawyers could be combined in a single story. The prime minister had recently criticized a House of Lords judgment restricting the deportation of terrorist suspects, whereas his wife had defended it. The *Daily Mail* columnist told her readers that this "perversity" was directly attributable to Blair's decision to introduce the Human Rights Act, with the consequence that the "government is clamped in the vice-like grip of human rights lawyers" – most notably his wife, who "is acting as a kind of shop steward of human rights lawyers." The column concluded by suggesting that the prime minister instruct his wife to "put a sock on it" – although "that might risk a human rights action brought against him by Cherie Booth QC, defending her freedom of speech. This would doubtless be funded by Legal Aid and bring still more lucre to Matrix's chambers."

A *Sun* columnist in 2004 had produced a similar broadside, aiming jibes simultaneously at Blair, Booth, and human rights lawyers in general:

> NOW that the Tipton Taliban are safely back home, Tony Blair is pleading for the release of the other British prisoners at Guantanamo Bay. Be honest, do you know anyone apart from their immediate families and the usual procession of bleeding-heart "human rights" lawyers who want them back here? Most of us would have been more than happy if they had taken a bullet to the temple in Afghanistan. No doubt when they fly home in triumph, Left-wing briefs will be queueing up to file huge compensation claims on their behalf. With the Wicked Witch and her mates at Nonces 'R' Us first in line. On legal aid, natch.

[22] Despite its formidable reputation for news management, the government apparently was not always aware in advance of the content of Cherie Booth's speeches and other public remarks. See Lance Price, *The Spin Doctor's Diary: Inside Number 10 with New Labour* (London: Hodder & Stoughton, 2006): 243–44.

Table 4.3: *2001–05 Articles about Cherie Booth as Human Rights Lawyer, by Tone*

	Positive	Negative	Neutral	Total
TABLOIDS				
Daily Mail	0 (0.0%)	20 (83.3%)	4 (16.7%)	24
Daily Mirror	3 (42.9%)	4 (57.1%)	0 (0.0%)	7
Sun	0 (0.0%)	9 (90.0%)	1 (10.0%)	10
TOTAL	3 (7.3%)	33 (80.5%)	5 (12.2%)	41
BROADSHEETS				
Guardian	8 (40.0%)	4 (20.0%)	8 (40.0%)	20
Daily Telegraph	4 (14.8%)	11 (40.7%)	12 (44.4%)	27
The Times	4 (40.0%)	1 (10.0%)	5 (50.0%)	10
TOTAL	16 (28.0%)	16 (28.0%)	25 (43.9%)	57
ALL PAPERS	19 (19.4%)	49 (50.0%)	30 (30.6%)	98

Booth's high profile as a human rights lawyer would have made her an easy target for detractors under any circumstances, but her negative press coverage was compounded by two misadventures that, though they had no direct connection to Booth's human rights work, nevertheless gave newspapers an opportunity to suggest that the hearts of human rights lawyers might be less than pure. The first story, which some papers liked to call "Cheriegate," grew out of Booth's friendship with Carole Caplin, a "new-age lifestyle guru" who provided Booth with advice on fashion and exercise. In 2002 it was reported that Booth had asked Caplin's boyfriend, an Australian businessman with a criminal fraud conviction, for assistance with a property purchase and that a short time later Booth had interceded for him in an immigration matter. The second story arose when Cherie Booth embarked on a highly paid speaking tour in the United States. According to her office, Booth was speaking as a well-known lawyer and not as the wife of Tony Blair; thus she was not profiting personally from her relationship with the prime minister. Both of these stories were covered by all the papers, but most extensively by the *Daily Mail* and the *Daily Telegraph*; those papers in particular, by repeatedly referring to Booth as a "prominent" or "leading" or "distinguished" or "brilliant" human rights lawyer, implied that Booth's denials and explanations were skillful evasions of the truth.

Table 4.3 summarizes the tone of the papers' HRL stories involving Cherie Booth. Exactly half of Booth's total HRL coverage was negative in tone, whereas less than twenty percent was positive. Table 4.3 also shows

Table 4.4: *Frequency of Negative References to Cherie Booth as British Human Rights Lawyer*

	Total Neg HRL Refs	Neg Refs to Booth as HRL	Neg Booth Refs as Pct of Total
TABLOIDS			
Daily Mail	64	20	31.3%
Daily Mirror	11	4	36.4%
Sun	41	9	22.0%
TOTAL	116	33	28.4%
BROADSHEETS			
Guardian	20	4	20.0%
Daily Telegraph	31	11	35.5%
The Times	12	1	8.3%
TOTAL	63	16	25.4%
ALL PAPERS	179	49	27.4%

that Booth's coverage by the six papers, unlike their HRL coverage overall, cannot accurately be described as "polarized." Although Booth was demonized by some of the papers, she was hardly deified, or even defended, by the others.[23] Blair's overwhelmingly negative treatment by the *Daily Mail*, the *Sun*, and the *Daily Telegraph* was not offset by equally favorable coverage elsewhere: even in the pro-HRL *Daily Mirror* and *Guardian*, fewer than half of the Booth stories were classified as positive. The *Daily Mirror*, *The Times*, and the *Guardian* all gave Booth much less positive treatment than they gave human rights lawyers generally.

Table 4.4 shows how the newspapers' depictions of Booth affected their overall HRL coverage: in five of the six papers (the only exception being *The Times*), a substantial percentage of the total negative HRL references involved Cherie Booth. Overall, negative references to Cherie Booth accounted for more than one-quarter of all the negative HRL stories. It is

[23] For example, the *Guardian* published several negative articles about Booth in the aftermath of the Caplin story. In one, a columnist outlined the charges in her multiple-count indictment against Cherie Booth: "[1)] her exploitation of her husband's public position for private gain; 2) her undignified enthusiasm for anything gratis or discounted; 3) her worrying reliance on individuals of extreme flakiness; and 4) the Blairs' numerous taste issues including the deployment of their family life for promotional purposes, and apparent delusion that they constitute some sort of royalty" (Catherine Bennett, "I Was at a Party When I Got the Summons... Cherie Wanted to Know Why I'd Written So Many Horrible Things About Her," *Guardian*, November 17, 2005).

not clear whether the primary target of the most hostile papers' vitriol in these stories was Cherie Booth in particular or human rights lawyers in general. What seems plain is that the connection between their two targets was close enough that they could hit both (and sometimes Tony Blair as well) with the same shot.

2. The Human Rights Act

A second major news story that helped shape the newspapers' HRL coverage from 2001 to 2005 was the adoption of the Human Rights Act itself. Although the HRA was debated and passed by Parliament in 1998, its implementation was delayed until October 2000 to give the legal system, and particularly the judiciary, time to prepare for its new demands. During this unusually long gestation period the papers had ample time to develop and articulate strong views about the effects they foresaw the HRA having on Great Britain. These expectations ranged from highly positive (*Guardian*, *Daily Mirror*) to cautiously hopeful (*The Times*) to extremely negative (*Daily Telegraph*, *Daily Mail*, and *Sun*). Once those editorial positions were set, they remained essentially unchanged. How each newspaper depicted human rights lawyers and their work reflected to a large degree its opinion of the HRA itself.

The *Guardian*, a strong supporter of incorporation of the European Convention since the early 1980s, was enthusiastic about the Act's potential to act as a check on official power. An October 2000 leading article, titled "A Warm Welcome for the Human Rights Act," predicted that "sooner or later the Home Office will feel the pain of the rights act and Mr Straw's [the Home Secretary's] head will be demanded. It is not often politicians deliberately make rods for their own backs. . . . Foolhardy or brave, its authors deserve much credit."

The *Daily Telegraph* took a very different view, characterizing the HRA as a serious threat to democratic principles. A leader asserted in October 2000, "The Act settles, for the first time in our history, the long-running dispute between judges and Parliament as to who is the supreme authority. From now on, the judges will be in charge." Two months later, another *Daily Telegraph* leader revisited the issue of judicial authority, suggesting that future judicial appointments might need to be scrutinized by Parliament to ensure proper accountability. The gravity of the paper's concern may have caused it to state – incorrectly – that "[j]udges can – indeed, must – now strike down legislation they deem incompatible with the ECHR, and return it to Parliament to consider fast-track amendment."[24]

The Times' view of the HRA was much less positive than the *Guardian's*, but not nearly as critical as the *Daily Telegraph's*. Like the *Guardian*, *The Times* had supported incorporation of the European Convention into British law for some time; however, it considered Blair's bill too expansive in defining the "public authorities" that would now be subject to the European Convention. A leading article in 2000 expressed concern that "a document designed to prevent the rise of a secret police has become a vehicle for disputing decisions made by bodies such as the Sports Council." Asserting that many such bodies "have little or absolutely no idea of what is about to hit them," *The Times* criticized the government for its tendency "to legislate now and contemplate later." Without attacking the law directly, the paper observed that the government's approach to constitutional reform "lacks coherent central principles."[25] On October 2, 2000, a *Times* leader lead article entitled "Best of Rights" reviewed the major arguments for and against the new law and concluded that "there are still reasons for disquiet about where the law goes from here," including the possibility that "the role of 'unelected' and 'unaccountable' judges" would begin to be

[24] In a letter published in the paper two days later, Home Secretary Jack Straw pointed out that the Human Rights Act "does not allow the courts to strike down an Act of Parliament." He was referring to the fact that the law deliberately does not enact American-style judicial review. It requires that judges issue a "declaration of incompatibility" if they are unable to interpret a statute to be consistent with the European Convention. The decision to either rewrite the law or allow it to stand then lies with Parliament. This point apparently still confuses many in Great Britain. Prime Minister Blair himself recently wrote in a newspaper article, "The point about the Human Rights Act is that it does allow the courts to strike down the act of our 'sovereign Parliament'" (*Observer*, April 26, 2006).

[25] In contrast with the uniformly pro- and anti-HRA coverage in the *Guardian* and the *Daily Telegraph*, respectively, *The Times* published a rich and varied mix of opinions about the new law. Shortly before the Act took effect in October 2000, the newspaper presented "point-counterpoint" pieces setting out contrasting views of the impending change. The Shadow Lord Chancellor, Christopher Kingsland, expressed Conservatives' concern (once shared by the Labour party) that by giving judges new authority the Act would reverse "the classic roles of legislator and judge in our constitution." Defending the Act was Anthony Lester, a Liberal-Democratic peer and for decades one of the most important supporters of Convention incorporation. Lord Lester argued that under the HRA "ministers are made more accountable to the rule of law administered by the independent judiciary and to Parliament itself." On the same day *The Times* also published an article by John Wadham, director of the pro-HRA pressure group Liberty, explaining some of the legal changes that would – and would not – occur under the law.

examined more closely. Although the new law "could be a force for great good," by expanding judicial authority it might have the unintended effect of "extending the power of the State," which would be "the very opposite of what human rights campaigners can have intended."

The tabloids essentially ignored the Human Rights Bill Act during its passage through Parliament in 1998 and for some time thereafter. Their silence ended emphatically in mid-2000, however, when the *Daily Mail* and the *Sun* began warning their readers about the dire consequences of the HRA when it came into force in October. A *Daily Mail* story described the frightening results the HRA already had produced in Scotland, where as part of the devolution process the law had already been in effect for a year. The article went on to predict a long list of dangerous results from the act: the asylum system "could be brought to the verge of collapse by legal challenges"; "it will soon become a 'human right' not to wear a suit to work"; "even convicted murderers" could claim the right to have children by artificial insemination; and "the police will no longer be able to use 'reasonable force' during violent struggles or arrests." Similarly, the *Sun*, in a story headlined "Courting Disaster," predicted that "Labour's Euro-style Human Rights Act will swamp our legal system. . . . " When the HRA came into force, the *Sun*, quoting the Lord Chief Justice out of context, had him predicting that one of the first effects of the new law could be to force the release of a notorious child murderer.

The only tabloid expressing enthusiasm for the Human Rights Act was the unshakably pro-Labour (though some would say anti-Conservative) *Daily Mirror*. In a 2000 leader entitled "The Rights Stuff," the *Daily Mirror* heralded the arrival of the Act HRA as "the most significant change in the law in more than 300 years." Describing the HRA as a populist triumph, the paper asserted that it would give "ordinary people a real chance to fight back" against "outrageous laws," such as Margaret Thatcher's poll tax. An October 2000 column applauded the fact that "the government has given up a huge amount of power without a war or an uprising."

The tone of the newspapers' subsequent HRL coverage closely tracked the positions each had taken on the Human Rights Act itself. The anti-HRA papers often depicted the activities of human rights lawyers as fulfilling their most dire predictions about the act's damaging effects. For example, in 2002 a *Daily Mail* columnist called a successful challenge by human rights lawyers of a provision of the government's antiterrorism legislation "typical of the many malign, unintended effects which have followed from the Human Rights Act." In 2005 a *Daily Mail* leader lead article attacked a government proposal to establish an Equality Commission, which the paper described as "a vast 'equality' superquango licensed to poke and pry into every corner of national life."

> Stamping out bigotry may be a worthy aim, but this is positively Orwellian: an army of Thought Police to snoop on businesses and individuals, power to summon suspects before tribunals, the right to lay down the law and push our lunatic Human Rights Act to the limit. . . . The only beneficiaries will be the usual pack of well-heeled human rights lawyers (step forward, Cherie Blair's Matrix chambers) who will now grow even richer.

After 9/11, for the newspapers opposed to the Human Rights Act, the threat of terrorism quickly came to exemplify the law's disastrous impact on British life. In 2005, for example, a *Daily Mail* columnist described a Web site with content, written in part by a specialist in human rights, advising young Muslims on their legal rights under the HRA and other statutes if they were detained by the police. He concluded that such advice "by respected human rights lawyers" is "actively fuelling the discontent of Islamic radicals." In a similar tone, a *Sun* columnist commented in 2004 on the government's failure to either detain or deport foreign terror suspects:

> Ideally, I would like to think they will ALL have been deported by the time you read this. But their "human rights" lawyers won't let that happen. . . . They have the Law Lords to thank for their release from Belmarsh Prison five months ago. If the human rights industry hadn't managed to secure its stranglehold on Britain, they would have been kicked out years ago. Now, hand-wringing civil rights lawyers and like-minded judges will go into top gear to keep them here. For the Human Rights Act (born of the European Human Rights Convention) offers fanatics comforting assurance that we cannot just deport them.

Another *Sun* correspondent wrote in 2003 that "if Osama bin Laden turned up at the Finsbury Park mosque tomorrow there would be a queue of 'human rights' lawyers the length of the Seven Sisters Road ready to argue – on legal aid, natch – that he shouldn't be extradited to the USA because he might, poor lamb, face the death penalty." The following year the same commentator observed: "Even when we do round up a few terror suspects, the 'human rights' lobby goes apoplectic and demands their instant release.

And who is the most famous 'human rights' lawyer in Britain? Correct. The Wicked Witch, wife of our own Prime Minister."

The *Daily Telegraph*, which had based its opposition to the Human Rights Act largely on its concerns that it would shift power from politicians to judges, often returned to that theme in its HRL coverage. In 2005, for example, one of its columnists discussed the ongoing conflict over antiterror laws, with judges supported by human rights lawyers on one side and government ministers on the other. The columnist concluded that, although a proper debate "about the proper balance between freedom and security" was worthwhile,

> that debate will be pointless if judges assume, automatically and without reflection, that all measures proposed by the Government to fight terrorism are, ipso facto, disreputable attempts to increase State power and to rob citizens arbitrarily of their liberties.

On the other side of the ledger, the *Guardian's* overwhelmingly positive HRL coverage was of a piece with its strong support for the Human Rights Act. In 2001 a columnist made no secret of his views in describing a human rights awards ceremony at which he had just presided:

> What a difference a year makes! A year ago, just after Human Rights Act came into force, all seemed bright and hopeful. Who could doubt that Britain would become a more just and a fairer place? Then came September 11 and suddenly human rights are on the defensive, and there's a home secretary who describes civil liberties concerns as airy-fairy. What struck me, though, reading the nominations for the various awards, was that all around the country committed people are working very hard, for little or no pay, to promote the human rights they believe in.

The linkage between a favorable view of the Human Rights Act and a positive depiction of human rights lawyering was also explicit in the argument made by a *Guardian* columnist in 2001 that the HRA should be used to challenge discriminatory government practices including the granting of visas:

> Leading human rights lawyer Keir Starmer says: "The whole point of the Human Rights Act is to give protection against discrimination – and discrimination against those with less money could come within the prohibitions set out in article 14."...At the very least, it would force the discriminating authority to explain why they favoured one

> set of individuals over another. The experts always told us this new law would make a big difference. In the US the bill of rights has long been used to advance civil rights, from abortion to women's status at work, that were too hot for the politicians to handle. Now it can be our turn.

The *Guardian* columnist's last sentence removes any possible doubt about his personal identification with the aims of the Human Rights Act and with the efforts of lawyers to fulfill its potential.

3. Immigration and Political Asylum

The third established story-line affecting the tone of the newspapers' HRL coverage was their coverage of immigration and political asylum, which during the 2001–05 period were among the most contested issues on Britain's political agenda. The asylum issue had come to the fore in the late 1990s when a sudden spike in the number of asylum applications filed in the UK resulted in a significant backlog of unresolved cases. At the same time, the public's attention was drawn to the large number of refugees remaining in the UK after their asylum applications had been rejected. The issue was not a new one, however. What the conservative papers regarded as the flaunting of Britain's immigration and asylum laws had been a matter of controversy for some time. In 1995, for example, a *Daily Mail* leader charged that "Britain's asylum laws are being systematically abused" and described "the overwhelming majority" of political asylum claims as "bogus." In that same year a columnist wrote in that paper that "Middle England is tired of . . . granting legal aid to Algerian terrorists and handing out money and a free council flat to bogus asylum seekers."

Between 2001 and 2005 the asylum issue featured prominently in many HRL stories, as efforts by the government to toughen its asylum policy were challenged aggressively by advocacy groups. For example, in 2003 a leading article in the *Daily Mail* asserted that the government's efforts to improve the system had been thwarted by the "voracious, greedy asylum industry," and it concluded,

> While the liberal consensus that dominates the BBC, the civil service and local authorities is mindlessly determined never to criticise endless immigration or the number of bogus asylum seekers, 'human rights'

> lawyers prosper on asylum cases, as do the social workers whose jobs depend on the refugee business.

That same year, after the government announced that it would grant indefinite leave to stay to some persons earlier denied political asylum who were still in the country, a *Daily Mail* columnist predicted that "since many more asylum seekers have arrived since October 2000, it can't be long before human rights lawyers are bringing yet further time wasting claims that it is discriminatory not to give them an amnesty, too."

The *Daily Mirror* and *The Times* both took a more moderate position on the asylum issue, criticizing economic refugees who tried to take advantage of Britain's reputation for tolerance but opposing demands to close the borders to all asylum seekers. Still, the asylum issue was troubling enough to both papers to help shape the tone of a number of their relatively few negative HRL stories. For example, writing shortly after the 2005 London suicide bombings, a *Daily Mirror* columnist castigated "[t]he libertarians and the human rights lawyers (who earn a tidy living protecting the rights of people who shouldn't be here)," for

> screaming that Tony Blair's latest crackdown will curtail liberty and democracy in this country. Well good! Because the kind of democracy we have now has put each and every one of us in danger. And the fact is there isn't one of those people who, had they played by our rules, would be in jail now. It's time the British people stopped beating themselves up over how we treat people who come here from abroad. We have nothing to castigate ourselves for because we couldn't have done more to make them welcome. We have bust a collective gut to accommodate their creeds and their cultures.

In a lengthy 2003 article on the asylum system, *The Times* characterized many of the lawyers who defended refugees as either hopelessly naïve or deeply cynical when they resorted to technicalities to defeat an ineffective bureaucracy:

> The asylum system has become increasingly constipated because the Government has vastly increased the legal rights of asylum-seekers. For example, the Human Rights Act has so many different provisions, so widely defined, that lawyers say there are almost always ways in which it can be cited, whatever the case.

The *Guardian* traditionally had treated the political asylum issue with a good deal of sympathy for asylum seekers. This attitude persisted even after the problem became a political hot potato; indeed, it contributed to the strongly positive tone of the paper's HRL coverage. In 2003, for example, a *Guardian* columnist provided readers with the following "bleak glimpse into the world of asylum . . . from human rights lawyer Louise Christian:"

> Prompted by our look at the Iraqi paradox – whereby most of those fleeing a man Mr. Tony Blair rightly describes as a monstrous tyrant are turned down – Louise reports a client who fled Kirkuk, outside the autonomous Kurdish area, whose application was refused the very day Mr Tony Blair published his dossier on Saddam's human rights abuses. Last week, Louise took part in a C4 televised war debate, after which she asked fellow guest and foreign office minister Mike O'Brien if, since he'd just adduced the hellishness of life in Iraq in favour of war, he could do anything to help this poor chap. The ex-immigration minister said it was no longer his brief, and he never wanted to deal with an asylum case again. Enchanting. As for Louise's client, since the FO's (Foreign Office) planned removal of Iraqis to the Kurdish north has yet to begin, he must stay here with no legal employment status (i.e., he cannot work) and no benefits – a truly ghastly non-existence, and a very odd way for a Labour government to treat refugees from our most mortal enemy.

Also in 2003, another *Guardian* columnist applauded a high court judgment that the government's treatment of destitute asylum seekers had violated their human rights:

> Thankfully, in a robust judgment yesterday, Mr Justice Collins ruled the new procedure "inhumane" and a breach of human rights laws. . . . The Home Office is appealing. The home secretary returned to a familiar theme: "Frankly, I'm fed up with having to deal with a situation where parliament debates issues and judges then overturn them." Mr. Blunkett should not have been surprised. He was warned what would happen by human rights lawyers, refugee groups and a cross-party committee of MPs and peers opposed to this part of his shameful asylum bill. . . . True, Home Office lawyers inserted new clauses in last year's bill to handicap court challenges, but such a blatant breach of human rights was never going to survive challenge.

4. The United Kingdom and Europe

In some of the newspapers' stories about human rights lawyers, particularly in the negative ones, there were trace elements of a fourth narrative line: the story of the UK's relationship with the institutions of the European Union and the Council of Europe. Construction of that narrative had begun in the 1960s, when Britain made its first faltering efforts (twice vetoed by France) to enter what was then the European Economic Community, before finally being admitted in 1973. By the 1980s Europe had become a hot-button issue in Britain, especially for the political Right, which strongly condemned what it regarded as the surrender of the nation's economic and political sovereignty to "Brussels bureaucrats." (The Left, including the Labour party, was much more divided on the question.) The *Daily Mail* and the *Sun* were particularly outspoken in their anti-Europe views, reaching new heights of indignation in the later 1990s over Tony Blair's apparent inclination (never actually implemented as policy) to "ditch the pound" and join the European common currency.

A second dimension of the issue was Britain's relationship with the Council of Europe, more specifically with the European Court of Human Rights (ECHR). The UK's refusal (until 1998) to incorporate the European Convention into its domestic law (though it had agreed by treaty to abide by the Convention itself) meant that its own courts for many years were unable to decide EC-based cases or contribute to Convention jurisprudence. This contributed to Britain's being on the losing end in a higher percentage of ECHR decisions than almost any other member state. Such outcomes, coupled with an ever-increasing flow of European Community/Union directives, provided Britain's anti-Europe newspapers with plenty of evidence that the nation was being damaged by its "submission" to European institutions. For example, after a 1995 Court of Human Rights ruling that the killings of some IRA members by British intelligence forces were "unlawful," the *Daily Mail* charged that the decision "put a civilized government in the dock and gave terror the benefit of the doubt."

> More than a generation ago, when there was still a Cold War and an Iron Curtain, the European Court of Human Rights was set up with noble ideals to protect all on this Continent from the totalitarian excesses of Communism or resurgent Fascism. These days, its rulings

> veer crankily from the tragic to the farcical, giving comfort here to terrorists, drug barons, gipsy squatters and transsexuals. Why should Britain continue to bow to the superior pretensions of this perverse court? The case for remaining within its outrageously meddlesome jurisdiction is now more than ever hard to justify.

The *Daily Mail* returned to the attack a few days later, publishing a list of the ECHR's previous rulings against the UK government, along with an angry lead article titled "Taking Orders from a Foreign Court":

> Bad enough that we have to submit to that other European Court, which is the judicial arm of the Brussels bureaucracy. But when we also feel obliged to swallow the most crass decisions of the entirely separate Court of Human Rights, the limit has surely been reached. When there are cases of deep concern to the British people, involving the British way of life and British customs, the Government should insist on judgment in the proper place. Before the British courts.

The influence of this highly negative view of European institutions can be detected in some of the tabloids' HRL coverage. Both the *Daily Mail* and the *Sun* carried stories accusing human rights lawyers of contributing to the imposition of European values on Great Britain through their litigation under the European Convention. For example, a *Daily Mail* columnist in 2004 asserted that by incorporating the European Convention into British law the Human Rights Act had fortified Europe's domination of Britain:

> Once our courts were bound by the decisions of foreign judges in Strasbourg, they found themselves repeatedly at odds both with public opinion and Parliament.... Meanwhile, the compensation culture grows ever more malign, while human rights lawyers grow rich.

The *Sun*, displaying confusion about the difference between the Council of Europe and the European Union, commented in 2005 that Tony Blair was reported to be

> "tearing his hair out" over the way liberal judges are interpreting this EU-based legislation. He is furious that dangerous terrorists are set free instead of being locked up or exiled. That's pretty rich. He was warned by us and others about the consequences of enshrining this barmy European charter into British law. But, in thrall to his wife Cherie, herself a human rights lawyer, he refused to listen.

The *Guardian's* pro-Europe views were only occasionally explicit in its HRL coverage. One such linkage, a rather awkward one to be sure, was found in a 2003 leader criticizing the prime minister's decision to include in the government's newest antiterror bill a derogation from a provision of the Human Rights Act:

> Mr Blair's willingness to tamper with the Human Rights Act in order to send deportees to countries known to practice torture is alarming and could even jeopardise Britain's adoption of the European Convention on Human Rights. These measures could have just as easily been drafted as a job creation scheme for the Society of Unemployed Human Rights Lawyers, if such a thing existed.

VI. Conclusion

This detailed look at the messages that leading British newspapers offered to their readers over five years about human rights lawyers and their work makes it clear that the normative content of the term "human rights lawyer" is highly contested. Three of the papers – the *Daily Mail*, the *Daily Telegraph*, and the *Sun* – have given their readers a steady diet of negative messages about human rights lawyers, whereas in three others – the *Daily Mirror*, the *Guardian*, and *The Times* – the HRL coverage has ranged from moderately to highly positive.

The impact of these messages on their intended audiences is unknown, though surely we can reject a crude stimulus-response conclusion that *because of* the papers' HRL coverage, the twenty million or so readers of the "negative" papers view human rights lawyers as villains, whereas the approximately ten million consumers of the "positive" papers see them as heroes. It may be, in fact, that the influence mainly flows the other way: successful newspaper editors, as Lacey and Longman put it, "take note of the different world views, skills, abilities and perspectives of potential readers and construct their paper to appeal to a definable targeted audience."[26] Similarly, Smith has said, "Newspapers must continually situate themselves within the assumed knowledge and interests of their readership, consciously or unconsciously adopt modes and strategies of address.... Language, style

[26] Lacey and Longman, 79. When I asked a reporter why his newspaper carried substantially fewer HRL stories than another paper had, he said that the other paper's readers simply were more interested in human rights than his were.

and format are therefore the products of a process of reciprocal symbolic interaction between the newspaper and its audiences."[27] If the papers indeed are reflecting rather than (or as well as) shaping public opinion, then we might conclude that a substantial number of Britons already have a notably jaundiced view of human rights lawyers, whereas many others are quite favorably impressed by them.

However, it is also possible – in fact, it seems quite likely – that at this point in time, public perceptions of the work of human rights lawyers are still not particularly well developed. The term itself is still rather new, and even within the legal profession it connotes different things to different people. It would not be surprising if the phrase "human rights lawyer" was still largely unknown to most members of the public. After all, the most observant daily reader of the *Daily Mirror* or the *Sun* would have encountered the term only about once a month between 2001 and 2005, and even in the *Guardian* it appeared only about once a week.

It likely is the case, then, that what the British public knows and thinks about human rights lawyers and their work is still in the early stages of construction. If anything, this underscores the importance of the finding that the construction of its meaning has taken place not in a vacuum, but in close connection with other ongoing stories that have much higher salience. Although the typical British newspaper reader today may not have a fixed image or opinion of human rights lawyers, he or she is much more likely to have a point of view about Tony Blair's government, immigration and asylum, Europe, and perhaps even the Human Rights Act. It also appears to be the case that opinions in Britain on these (and other) issues tend first to cluster together and then to divide into two broad "cultures of understanding" – two familiar narratives that provide competing accounts of the general health of the body politic. By situating the work of human rights lawyers within one or the other of these story-lines, newspapers help give that work different and distinct meanings. They also lay the groundwork for what may over time develop into highly polarized views of whether or not human rights lawyers are associated with a commitment to the common good.

These findings may have important implications for the long-term success of human rights lawyering in the UK. Political developments in the last

[27] A. C. H. Smith, *Paper Voices: The Popular Press and Social Change, 1935–1965* (London: Chatto and Windus, 1975): 22.

decade, most notably the adoption of the Human Rights Act, have greatly improved the outlook for lawyers associated with this particular cause. But the HRA came about through elite pressure, not popular demand, and it is by no means clear that since 2000 the law has developed a broader constituency. If public opinion were ever successfully mobilized behind its repeal, human rights lawyers in Britain would be deprived of a resource that many have come to regard as critical to their work. In the meantime, it is ironic but inevitable that many of the victories won by human rights lawyers under the HRA will be interpreted by hostile newspapers as doing further damage to the body politic, thus perhaps hastening the day when public opinion turns decisively against their work.

Acknowledgments

I wish to thank Richard Abel and Colin Seymour-Ure for their detailed and perceptive readings of earlier versions of this chapter. Thanks are also due to the editors of this volume and to my colleagues in this collaborative project for their generosity of spirit.

5

Ed Fagan and the Ethics of Causes

Who Stole Identity Politics?

Valerie Karno

How can we understand the cultural life of any group? Where in culture do we find such life? The answer lies partly in the query, What is actively "living" in the nominal repository of "life," and how do representations of that living cohere with or distend from the "lived"? For as culture is that realm that is always in circulation, moving and shifting amidst people even as it is created and remade through repetitive channels, locating in and across groups a cultural life is an arguably formidable task. Nevertheless, media representations certainly influence the transmission of cultural ideas. The media, as a series of vessels, assist in perpetuating the ways in which representative notions and images "live" as they are distributed daily. To some degree the cultural life of any group must exist in an eternally suspicious mimetic relation to its members. As each member's unique lived performance may or may not correspond with media representations of the group's lived condition, the cultural life of a group must necessarily be a partial figment of imagination and a rhetorical strategy. Because of its link to representation, the cultural life of any group can only be that which becomes a normative measurement device against which active lived performance is ascertained and judged. There may, however, be utter incommensurability between the cultural life of images taken as reflective of the "real" and the lived events of bodies.

In the instance of cause lawyers, though they are certainly not always depicted as saintly, scholarship has generally represented the profession as maintaining some alignment between lawyers' moral principles and their work product. As Sarat and Scheingold have suggested, for example, "cause lawyers . . . reconnect law and morality, and make tangible the idea that lawyering is a 'public profession'..."[1] Cause lawyers have been seen as aiding those who cannot help themselves.[2] Working as a cause lawyer "is attractive precisely because it is a deeply moral or political activity, a kind of work that encourages pursuit of the right, the good, or the just."[3]

Yet, let us question some key assumptions about cause lawyers – that they are working for the "good," as scholars Sarat, Scheingold, and Menkel-Meadow have suggested,[4] and that they mimetically reproduce their own belief systems through their work.[5] The reason for challenging these rather fundamental presuppositions is to open the distinction between the representation of cause lawyers themselves, as people with fixed identities, and the *doing* of, or the performance of, cause lawyering. This distinction is crucial for considering the popular representations of cause lawyers, because the doing of acts and the status of identities involved in doing those acts are often unnecessarily or confusingly conflated. As Sarat and Scheingold have argued, "Cause lawyering is ... more than a story that lawyers can tell themselves about how their work comports with their beliefs. It is a *way of doing things* that takes time, money, and strategic ingenuity as well as moral and political commitment."[6]

The case of Ed Fagan poses an ideal opportunity to examine the discrepancy between working for the "good" and reproducing the "good" as an

[1] Austin Sarat and Stuart Scheingold, "Cause Lawyering and the Reproduction of Professional Authority: An Introduction," in *Cause Lawyering: Political Commitments and Professional Responsibilities*, eds. Sarat, Scheingold (New York: Oxford University Press, 1998), 3.

[2] Scholar Richard Abel has suggested, for example, that "the moments when law offers leverage to the relatively powerless...when it is wielded, or trumped, by power.... These are the occasions for cause lawyering." See Richard Abel, "Speaking Law to Power: Occasions for Cause Lawyering," in *Cause Lawyering: Political Commitments and Professional Responsibilities*, 69.

[3] Austin Sarat and Stuart Scheingold, "Introduction: The Dynamics of Cause Lawyering – Constraints and Opportunities," in *The World Cause Lawyers Make*, eds. Sarat, Scheingold (Stanford: Stanford University Press, 2005), 1.

[4] Sarat and Scheingold write that "causes offer lawyers the chance to enlist in a partisan pursuit of the good while refusing completely to commodify their professional skills." Sarat, Scheingold, "The Dynamics of Cause Lawyering," 1. See also Carrie Menkel-Meadow, "The Causes of Cause Lawyering," in *Cause Lawyering: Political Commitments and Professional Responsibilities*, 31.

[5] Sarat and Scheingold claim, for instance, that "Cause lawyers ... bring their beliefs to bear in their work lives.... In this sense they are neither alienated from their work nor anxious about the separation of role from person." See "The Dynamics of Cause Lawyering," 1.

[6] Stuart Scheingold and Austin Sarat, *Something to Believe In: Politics, Professionalism, and Cause Lawyering* (Stanford: Stanford University Press, 2004), 95.

identificatory stance. It is very difficult if not impossible to locate Ed Fagan's intentions in his life within the bounds of what many have argued form cause lawyers' identities – an aspiration for the good. As this essay discusses, media representations of Fagan help illuminate the ways in which the distinction between cause lawyers and cause lawyering offers critical commentary on ever-evolving identity politics. Through the disgust generated by numerous insistent accounts of Fagan's inconsistent behaviors, the media contribute to the ways in which the cultural life of cause lawyers is created and circulated through idealized and contemptible representations.

Arguably emblematic of one type of democratic advocacy – in the form of working for the good – cause lawyering has been considered by previous scholarship as one form of democractic process. To understand cause lawyers' practices as existing in relation to a general democratic lawyerly disposition, scholars have invoked Tocqueville as a historic commentator on democracy. He has been referenced, for instance, as thinking about lawyers' "habits of order, a taste for formalities, and a kind of instinctive regard for the regular connection of ideas."[7] Cause lawyers' habits, taste, and instinct have been generally assumed to take particular forms – a habit toward advocating for certain types of "justice," a taste for rewarding those disenfranchised or oppressed, or perhaps an instinct about who deserves compensation for a prior harm. But rather than assume these qualities and their relations to "goodness" in cause lawyers particularly, let us first examine their socioeconomic and professionally dependent contexts.

Habit as a class and social phenomenon has been considerably theorized by scholars like Pierre Bourdieu who posited social class as being based in "class habitus" – "the internalized form of class condition and of the conditionings it entails."[8] Bourdieu speaks of the

> set of agents who are placed in homogeneous conditions of existence imposing homogeneous conditionings and producing homogeneous systems of dispositions capable of generating similar practices; and who possess a set of common properties, objectified properties, sometimes legally guaranteed (as possession of goods and power) or

[7] Alexis de Tocqueville, cited in *Something to Believe In*, 98.

[8] Pierre Bourdieu, *Distinction: A Social Critique of the Judgement of Taste*, (Cambridge, MA: Harvard University Press, 1984), 101.

> properties embodied as class habitus (and, in particular, systems of classificatory schemes).[9]

In its application to cause lawyers, this analysis would suggest that the profession of cause lawyer will produce and be produced by similar conditions of being and modes of practice across the constituents comprising the field of cause lawyering.

Bourdieu stresses, however, that the "habitus" is linked to ways of acting – modes of *doing* – rather than simply ways of identifying (without subsequent actions) in the world. Habitus for Bourdieu is

> a system of practice-generating schemes which expresses systematically the necessity and freedom inherent in its class condition and the difference constituting that position; the habitus apprehends differences between conditions, which it grasps in the form of differences between classified, classifying, practices (products of other habitus).... While it must be reasserted ... that ordinary experience of the social world is a cognition, it is equally important to realize ... that primary cognition is misrecognition, recognition of an order which is also established in the mind. Life-styles are thus the systematic products of habitus....[10]

This attention to practice-generating schemes and lifestyles is helpful for thinking through the distinctions between the doing of cause lawyering, and the status of being a cause lawyer. To unpack the disparity between the two categories, let us consider the case of Ed Fagan.

Ed Fagan, the noted and infamous reparations lawyer, has advocated a litany of cases for a range of clients. The New-York-based Jewish lawyer is known for having won a $1.3 billion settlement for Holocaust victims from Swiss banks and also having rallied for apartheid and tsunami reparations. He further insisted that the Polish government pay roughly 600 Polish-born holders of pre-World War II T-bonds (issued before Germany occupied the country in 1939) sums of more than a billion euros, or more than a billion dollars.[11] According to the *Warsaw Business Journal*,[12] Fagan estimated that around 5 percent of all bonds issued before the war still exist and has

[9] Bourdieu, 101.
[10] Bourdieu, 172.
[11] *Edmonton Journal*, 6/24/06, Cracow-Life.com, 6/22/06.
[12] *Warsaw Business Journal*, 6/24/2006.

demanded that Poland respond in thirty days as to whether it will negotiate to pay Fagan's clients (descendants of World War II victims who had their property taken and bonds rendered useless) or be sued. Most recently, two villagers of Glod have hired Fagan to sue the makers of the *Borat* film for $30 million for human rights abuses. Fagan intends to submit lawsuits in New York and Florida state courts, as well as in Frankfurt, Germany against those involved in making *Borat*.[13]

With his history of fighting on behalf of victims of atrocity or wrongdoing, Fagan stands on one leg as the prototypical cause lawyer seeking reparations for those abused. Moreover, as a self-identified Jewish man, he seems to choose at least some of his cases based on the causes with which he identifies religiously and culturally; he further aligns himself to serve those groups (like South African blacks who were subjected to apartheid) who have also arguably been similarly systematically mistreated and killed.

But unlike cause lawyers whose identity politics has conveniently mimetically reproduced that of their clients, Fagan's public image has been marked by a series of seemingly unethical scandals. In October 2005 Fagan had to defend himself against published accusations that he hired an underage prostitute (Inga) in Austria. Initially he responded by saying that first she had told him she was twenty-two, and more importantly, "It would have been an offense to not sleep with her. Later we slept with each other without payment."[14]

Before this incident, Fagan was charged by the New Jersey Office of Attorney Ethics with "looting more than $400,000.00 from the trust accounts of two survivors he represented."[15] He was also cited for malpractice in a judgment on behalf of a Brooklyn man, Hector Ortiz. Fagan had filed a $35 million lawsuit in 1994 on behalf of the injured truckdriver, but in 1998 the case was dismissed because as the judge said, "Mr. Fagan had failed to prosecute it for 3 years and had ignored court orders."[16] Several other suits against Fagan based on client neglect ended similarly.[17]

[13] Pancevski, Bojan. "Villagers to sue 'Borat,'" *Los Angeles Times*, 11/20/2006.

[14] Fagan has commented on the problem with the German translation from his English interview, as well as the timeliness of this scandal being linked to his filing of a lawsuit against the Austrian government in an American court accusing it of complicity in a ski resort fire in 2000 that killed 155 people. See Nathaniel Popper, "Holocaust Lawyer Fights Accusation He Hired Underage Austrian Hooker," Forward.com, 10/7/2005.

[15] *Jewish Week*, 1/7/ 2005.

[16] Theawarenesscenter.org/Fagan_Ed.html.

[17] Theawarenesscenter.org/Fagan_Ed.html.

Critical to the media depictions of Ed Fagan is *how* he is represented: headlines consistently scrutinize him for the inconsistencies between his character and the causes he represents. *ABC News* and *20/20* conducted a report on Fagan's negligent treatment of many of his clients. The headline to an article about Fagan on ABC News online reads, "abcNEWS Reports on the Great Holocaust Industry Shakedown and the Shysters Running it for Money."[18] Another headline regarding Fagan reads, "A Case of Self-Promotion? Prominent Holocaust Claims Lawyer Accused of Neglecting Clients."[19] Yet a third news headline reads, "Holocaust Lawyer Fights Accusation He Hired Underage Austrian Hooker."[20] Additionally, the Jewish Coalition Against Sexual Abuse/Assault compiled numerous news accounts of Fagan on their Web site, listing further headlines like "Holocaust Lawyer in Austrian Sex Scandal" and "Lawyer in Holocaust Case Faces Litany of Complaints."[21] Quoting Bella Ross, a woman whose family Fagan was to represent in gaining reparations and who claims Fagan missed the deadline for filing their request, an online Action Report disseminated by the controversial David Irving highlights the woman's outrage. It quotes her as saying, "How could somebody with such high ideals step on them and step on the people involved. Just to champion himself, for a paycheck? There are lots of other ways to make money, not to take advantage of people who suffered."[22] Fagan is thus repetitively represented by the media for his interest in capital gain, rather than moral justice.

These headlines and interviews are designed to unearth contradictions between personal life and work product. The image of this contradictory figure embodied by Fagan is held up as contemptible; it is demeaning to an otherwise idealized higher unity between person and work. The media representations beg us to rigidify the category of cause lawyer as one whose image relies on the unification between personal motives and professional outcomes. The headlines subtly encourage readers to disallow the misalignment between person and work, insisting on a singular linear purity between mind and action.

One might, however, inquire why Fagan's personal life is even being discussed; why, as a public figure is his personal life relevant to the news?

18 See abcnews.go.com.
19 www.fpp.co.uk.
20 See www.forward.com/articles.
21 See www.theawarenesscenter.org/Fagan_Ed.html.
22 See www.fpp.co.uk.

Do his physical ailments, his dietary regimen, or other mundane aspects of his daily life get reported? Solely because certain behaviors are seemingly inconsistent with his causes do media representations insist on noting them. In this way, the cultural life of cause lawyers becomes reinforced in a series of repetitive circular notions: the image of person and work as unified daily toward particular long-term goals becomes an expected demand.

Focusing then on the contradictions between Fagan's personal character and work product, the public is led to ask the definitional question asked before of other cause lawyers: is Ed Fagan a cause lawyer if his wide and varied actions do not support a unified intention toward a moral imperative? To answer in the affirmative, that Fagan does belong in the group named cause lawyers, we might say he has argued for and won Holocaust reparations – and so is a cause lawyer indeed. He has "done" the practice of classifying oppressed groups, and strived to provide a financial remedy for the atrocities and wrongdoing committed toward them. Yet, the impulse to refuse Fagan membership in the highly regarded cause lawyer group is strong, because doing so enables cause lawyers to maintain the image of propriety and idealized moral ground so often afforded them. For those wishing to maintain the shroud of respectability attached to many cause lawyers, dumping Fagan from the membership list, or never allowing him entry at all because of his seeming misuse of the position for his own gain, can be a quick decision. Given Fagan's history of personal and professional ethical scandals, it is tantamount to overstatement to claim that his motives singularly or in any unified way exist in relation to the achievement of "good" in the world. Arguably the court of public opinion depends in part on the cultural life of cause lawyers being one that shows this subset of the profession to uphold high standards. By disallowing him from the group, the public can endorse causes without the inconvenience of questioning inconsistencies or motives of those representing the victimized.

In part, linking "goodness" with detectable motivations is an interpretive stretch in any event. Motives, if they can be found at all, are at best shifting and malleable. As Laura Hatcher has stated, lawyers' motives *change* (emphasis added).[23] But if motivations can be understood as distinct from practical habits – as related to but not dependent on or caused by

[23] Laura Hatcher, "Economic Libertarians, Property, and Institutions: Linking Activism, Ideas, and Identities among Property Rights Advocates," in *The Worlds Cause Lawyers Make*, 114.

practices – then conceptualizing the category of "cause lawyer" and interpreting popular representations of cause lawyers become more complex and comprehensive tasks.

The lifestyle of Ed Fagan serves as a suitable example of how class and social positioning as cause lawyer allows for a wide and multifaceted series of actions that do not all neatly correspond with equally difficult-to-name notions of the "good." Cause lawyers' actions do not in all events, as Sarat and Scheingold have noted, "reconnect law and morality, elevat[ing] the moral posture of the legal profession beyond a crude instrument where lawyers sell their services without regard to the ends to which those services are put."[24] Quite to the contrary, cases like Ed Fagan show that identities are multifaceted rather than static, and people can choose at one moment to behave in ethical ways and at the next moment to counteract the impression of ethical actions. Identities formed around habitus, or, as Hatcher has claimed, around professional identities morph in context.[25] Ed Fagan's identities, numerous and shifting depending on his transitional professional and personal modes, are emblematic of how his, and perhaps other cause lawyers' habits are determined in numerous ways.

Then, in addition to the important legal and political work being done by cause lawyers like Fagan, they are also contributing to a more refined understanding of identity politics *precisely* because some of their motives *do not* neatly cohere with the identities painted for them in the media. When cause litigation is championed by cause lawyers who are representatives of their clients' demographic, that cause lawyer work stands as a form of identity politics. Ed Fagan serves, for instance, as an emblematic example of a Jewish man who has fought for Jewish victims of the Holocaust. His being Jewish likely aided in his client relations with those Jews he represented, as well as gave him a certain sort of credibility in the public eye to aid Jewish victims in seeking reparations. Yet, Fagan's personal and professional conduct severs a tidy allegiance with those victims, ruptures a mimetic sympathy for those oppressed, and calls into question the role of cause lawyers in producing cause litigation ostensibly subject to the pitfalls of identity politics.

[24] "Cause Lawyering and the Reproduction of Professional Authority: An Introduction," 3.

[25] Hatcher claims that "identity takes shape in specific institutional spaces and during particular professional practices (rather than {being} shaped by motivations)." Hatcher, 114.

It is in this space of identity, and of identity politics, that media representations of cause lawyers like Ed Fagan (who some see as repugnant) are offering a fascinating new view on staid identity politics – it is where we can see how the notion of motivation gets unshackled from a unified notion of the self and can be seen as an impulse leading toward a range of ethical possibilities. Instead of mimicking identity politics – where personal identity and coalitional identity often merge – media coverage of Ed Fagan shows us that cause lawyers represent much more than another day of identity politics. Rather, as this essay will ultimately consider, the media might be contributing to one of several first steps toward dismantling the identity categories that bind so rigidly daily classifications and the processes of legal decision making.[26] The case of Ed Fagan as we know him through the media might be a way that the law is loosening its grip on governing through identity categorization. The cause lawyer here stands as a monument not to always preserving "the good" necessarily, but to arguing for ethical claims at some moments while undermining other ethical impulses at other moments. In this way, the cause lawyer has co-opted an aged version of identity politics, using it to unwittingly point the way toward a potentially reimagined legal sense of identity born not of holistic components, but of mutable ones that the law might later take into account.

The media, popular culture, and popular reception have a large part to play in demonstrating the dilemmas inherent in identity politics. They seem especially adept at showing the vast and numerous disparities between coalitional and personal politics, and in so doing function to dismantle many cause lawyers' static public images as benevolent creatures working for the good. In the recent anthology, *Identity Politics Reconsidered*, Linda Martin Alcoff and Satya Mohanty, two of its editors, claim that

> activists involved in successful social movements who self-consciously invoked the concept of identity in their struggles for social justice held at least two beliefs: 1) That identities are often resources of knowledge especially relevant for social change, and that 2) oppressed groups

[26] Here I refer to the need to fit into an identity category to be considered under the law. See for instance the question of "what constituted a tribe" in the *Mashpee v. New Seabury Corp.* case, which was dismissed because the court could not come up with a palatable definition of a tribe (592 F.2d 575, 1979). Also see the historic need to sue for discrimination under the category of being a woman or African American for discrimination cases, but being unable to claim a hybrid category between the two as a basis for a lawsuit.

> need to be at the forefront of their own liberation.... Crucially, these successful social movements were led, never exclusively, but primarily, by the oppressed themselves. And they have profoundly transformed society for the better.[27]

Cause lawyers like Ed Fagan seemingly support this claim while also demonstrating the reasons why identity politics has, in many minds, failed to achieve its goals. As a Jewish man, Fagan seems to be at the forefront of advocating justice through reparations for Holocaust victims and their descendants. Fagan himself has said that, despite negligently handling some smaller cases, "I know for a fact that the majority of these cases wouldn't have happened without me. That's not, that's not from bravado, it's just a fact."[28] But Fagan's own personal life, which then gets translated by others into his identity – an identity that he neither endorses nor disclaims – shows the fissures and inconsistencies inherent in cause litigation itself. In a June 20, 2004, interview with the South African magazine *Carte Blanche*, Fagan had to address why he was removed from representing clients in an apartheid lawsuit. He had been working, according to some in name only, with local lawyer John Ngcebetsha, but was fired and then fought to retain the clients. Asked by the interviewer, "Isn't what you're doing just grandstanding?" Fagan replied, "No. I built the grandstand. I don't have to do grandstanding." He went on to say, "I'm here because I feel guilty as a Jew. That's why I'm here. I did all this work for the Holocaust victims. The cases didn't just stand for justice for Holocaust victims; the cases stood for justice for victims." When asked if he is a "knight in shining armor?" Fagan replied, "No. I'm just a guy who's passionate. I happen to believe very strongly in some things and I will fight to the death. To the death! I hope they're ready to fight this to the death because the only way they'll stop me is to kill me. And no one's been able to kill me yet. They've tried, but they haven't been able to. Maybe one day."[29] Here, in the same interview Fagan identifies as a guilty Jew, as someone who is "just" passionate because he believes in some things, and as one who takes credit for building a grandstand on which he now sits. It is challenging to locate any one stance of

[27] Linda Martin Alcoff and Satya P. Mohanty, "Reconsidering Identity Politics: An Introduction," in *Identity Politics Reconsidered*, eds. Alcoff, Hames-Garcia, Mohanty, Moya (New York: Palgrave Macmillan, 2006), 2.

[28] See www.fpp.co.uk.

[29] See www.carteblanche.co.za.

identification for him, as he only partially embraces identity politics, and his discourse shifts between ideas. He seems unwilling to claim any one identificatory position to explain his actions or his history, but rather calls on numerous stances of identification to do so.

Identity politics has been heavily criticized for numerous reasons, including a questioning of identity itself as being fluid rather than static, as being a set of shifting and unpredictable practices rather than as naturally determined, and as being not essentially capturable by anything called identity politics. Editors Alcoff and Mohanty, acknowledging that identity politics has been attacked both by the Right and the Left, try to rehabilitate identity politics, claiming that "identity politics in itself is neither positive nor negative. At its minimum, it is a claim that identities are politically relevant, an irrefutable fact. Identities are the locus and nodal point by which political structures are played out, mobilized, reinforced, and sometimes challenged."[30] "Identities matter politically," they say.[31] But in the case of cause lawyering – and particularly in representations of cause lawyers and their practices – locating an identity for the cause lawyer both within and outside of the profession becomes highly difficult and problematic.

Identities certainly do matter, because acts of atrocity or oppression are often committed in the shallow, misguided name of harming group identities. "Being" a "Black South African," in cases of apartheid, or a "Jew," in cases of the Holocaust, subjected one to being treated appallingly solely on the basis of being construed within that category. Personal acts, individual history, and shifting identifications were of no import or consequence against the backdrop of group marking. Atrocities, then, have often been and continue to be committed in the name of identity-based difference. As a result, causes are often a reflection of that very identity-based difference, and class action lawsuits are even dependent on the very mass identification that has been used to harm so wrongly. The question then becomes, How can one rally on behalf of members of these groups – who have been arguably victimized solely on the basis of belonging to a particular group category – without rigidifying the very category that so ineptly describes a human in all of its parts and arguably would be better dismantled as a totalizing idea? How can one "be" a cause lawyer, fight for reparative justice,

[30] "Reconsidering Identity Politics: An Introduction," 7.
[31] "Reconsidering Identity Politics: An Introduction," 8.

and yet not reproduce the very structures endemic of, if not at the base of, the harm?

The cause lawyer example of the categorization conundrum demonstrates one of the main problems of law today that operates not only in the cause lawyer realm but also in multiple forms of lawsuits. How can law account for the multiplicity of human "being," given its limited categories of understanding and redress? The case of cause lawyer Ed Fagan strangely and surprisingly serves to demonstrate that identities are not static, but conflicting. Rather than concretize or further codify identity categories, the Fagan case shows the necessity for recognizing how habitus and practices are contextual and mutable. Fagan reveals the inconsistencies inherent in identity categories through his own example of seemingly irreconcilable ethical choices.

In opening new avenues for thinking about how notions of malleable identities can be understood and integrated into legal processes, it is useful to consider the ways in which "experience" has been accounted for as a mode of being. Dominick LaCapra has helped elucidate the ways identities can be understood not through their ontological totality, but rather through their links to both imagined and actual ongoing experiences. LaCapra claims that "identity . . . involve[s] modes of being with others that range from the actual to the imagined, virtual, sought-after, normatively affirmed, or utopian."[32] Experience, then, comprises the continuum between what would be called "the real" and the "imagined." It is in this continuum that identities are continually reformed. Identities do not stagnate, but are rather perpetually regrown and reinvented. As LaCapra postulates, "Identity-formation might even be defined in non-essentialized terms as a problematic attempt to configure and, in certain ways, coordinate subject positions-in-process."[33]

This emphasis on process and on constant configuration in relation to others underlies one of the dilemmas inherent in cause litigation. When harms have been committed in the name of a staid, essentialized group identity, identity formation often takes a particular turn toward reinforcing the dichotomy between victimizing and victimized group, whether or not individuals entirely aligned their identities with a collective before the

[32] Dominick LaCapra, "Experience and Identity," in *Identity Politics Reconsidered*, 228.
[33] "Experience and Identity," 238.

harm was committed. Cause lawyers seeking reparations most often for traumatic events might have multiple identificatory relationships to the trauma. They might relate personally and professionally in numerous striated ways. They might, for instance, hold one imaginative family relationship to the trauma and several professional judgmental relations to it based on socioeconomic habitus. As LaCapra discusses, "With respect to identity-formation, one should make special mention of the founding trauma in the life of individuals and groups. The founding trauma is the actual or imagined event . . . that poses in accentuated fashion the very question of identity yet may paradoxically become the very basis of an individual or collective identity."[34] Cause lawyers may engage in the profession because of this "founding trauma," whether cognitively concocted, lived through the body, or some combination of the two. Whichever way they come to the profession, the "experiential" facet of their identity formation is significant because it likely stems from multiple sources – sources that when translated into action provide potentially opposing outcomes.

To highlight how the scope and breadth of "experience" create identity, LaCapra analyzes the various *Oxford English Dictionary* definitions of experience. Revolving around actual practices and epistemological conditions, definitions range from "proof by actual trial," "practical demonstration," "the state of having been occupied in any department of study or practice . . . the aptitudes, skill, judgment, etc. thereby acquired" to "the events that have taken place within the knowledge of an individual, a community, mankind at large."[35] The dictionary presents a wide range of options to consider the multifaceted realm of experience, involving practice, judgment, and knowledge. These help form pivotal foundations for the ways in which identity politics circulates, though the foundations born of imagination or alliance might create highly divergent behavior from those emerging out of bodily interaction.

The Ed Fagan representations help highlight the ways in which cause litigation – as it is heralded by its representative lawyers and circulated in the popular imagination – comments on the evolving status of identity politics. Representatives like Fagan threaten and challenge what is in part rooted in identity politics: a legitimacy given by the public to the cause based on a

[34] "Experience and Identity," 236.

[35] "Experience and Identity," 231–32.

perceived allegiance between representative advocate (lawyer) and victimized group. This allegiance can be formed through mimetic representation, a sense of there being parallel victimhoods, or a perceived sympathy generated for those having suffered a wrong. The contradictions of someone associated with identity politics who nonetheless does not uniformly fall into one identification category might serve to reduce the potency of the lawyer's public advocacy; additionally, though, they might also reduce the success of the cause being advocated *because* inconsistencies diminish a certain inflexible notion of the way identities and politics are supposed to uniformly collude.

Because cause lawyers represented in newspapers and other media like television become scrutinized as public agents, releasing news of Ed Fagan's seemingly illegal or unethical persona ostensibly derails the legitimacy of group claims of victimhood he is arguing for by dismantling the unified correlation between cause and representative. As Stuart Hall has previously theorized, mass communication operates as a series of connected, circulating practices.[36] Images of cause lawyers already circulating in the public sphere help determine how individual cause lawyers are then represented and perceived against a preconditioned norm. Arguing that "the moments of encoding and decoding" the discursive form of messages "are determinate moments" in the communicative process, Hall claims that an event "must become a story before it can become a communicative event."[37] A narrative must be generated around an "event" before that "event" can be discursively disseminated. Narratives are constructed through and within a discursive community, however, and are then similarly distributed through that same shared community. Thus, the narratives likely to be generated are those already predisposed to draw from or be totally encompassed by a previous context.

In the case of Ed Fagan, media communication is likely to draw from prior understandings of cause lawyers in its depictions. It is no wonder, then, that Fagan appears scandalous when his noncompliance with cause lawyers' understood allegiance to identity politics becomes visible. Though speaking primarily about television, Hall's theorization also works well for

[36] Stuart Hall, "Encoding/Decoding," in *The Cultural Studies Reader*, 2nd edition, ed. Simon During (New York: Routledge, 2003), 508.
[37] "Encoding/Decoding," 508.

considering newspapers, and particularly their representations of Fagan. Suggesting that "unless they are wildly aberrant, encoding will have the effect of constructing some of the limits and parameters within which decodings will operate,"[38] Hall articulates some of the reasons why newspaper readers will interpret Fagan's acts within the "accepted" paradigms of cause lawyers through which we already think. Readers will "decode" reports of Fagan's activities through the same lens of "encoding" that generated the newsworthy narrative. In this case, readers will, perhaps unwittingly, note the disparity between Fagan's personal and professional ethics. They will suspect him of a disingenuous legal practice because he stands not as one devoted to identity politics, but as one engaging in disparate, inconsistent acts. They will expect a cause lawyer who behaves uniformly out of one set of guiding motives, and be disappointed and even disgusted by the cause lawyer who behaves differently depending on milieu. These reactions are all predictable and expected given Fagan's deviation from the historic representations of cause lawyers.

But it is this communicative response to Ed Fagan that, if noticed, can open possibilities for rethinking how law oversimplifies identity categories. It is this reaction that can potentially create space for the public to engage in a more complex relationship to causes and to personal and professional identities. It is this moment that holds the potential to recognize the ongoing process and vitality of democratic difference as it manifests in recognizable changes within single identities. Embracing these notions might offer our legal systems, as well as our personal mores, enhanced flexibility in interacting with ourselves and others.

Ultimately, this essay is neither condoning nor condemning the representative acts of Ed Fagan. Rather, instead of engaging in judgment about his acts, it is more fruitful to analyze the ways in which the representations of Ed Fagan serve a role in our ongoing deliberations about identity politics. Fagan's representations of one doing cause lawyering potentially open up avenues for rethinking the old categories of identity that still operate – explicitly, rigidly, and often insufficiently – in the law today. And, equally importantly, by fixating on troubling inconsistencies between personal life and work product, media representations of Fagan contribute to the cultural life of cause lawyers as being deeply embedded in ideals of unity. Ed

[38] "Encoding/Decoding," 515.

Fagan serves as just one example of the way media accounts demonstrate our fervent cultural need for cause lawyers to act "purely." Deviation from a clear alignment between advocate and cause creates distress that resonates far beyond the mistrust of one lawyer. Media foci reveal the discomfort many around the world feel toward cause lawyers who do not traverse a linear moral path. The cultural life of cause lawyers is thus made up of those images that live in constant danger of being undermined or overthrown by that which is less than ideal; it is constituted by representative standards that are already crumbling at the time they are depicted. The case of Ed Fagan reveals for us this dilemma.

6

Of Windmills and Wetlands

The Press and the Romance of Property Rights

Laura J. Hatcher

I. Introduction

I began this research when I was asked to consider whether I could think of any place in popular culture in which conservative cause lawyers – or more specifically, the property rights lawyers I have been studying for the last several years – have a life. Where were they represented? How were they represented?

After much thinking and rereading the press narratives that I describe here, I began to discern a very important pattern in the stories of cases about property rights: they tend to discuss the lawyers very little and instead focus much of the attention on their clients. Most of the time, the lawyers come into the narratives only to bring necessary legal information or to clarify a point made by their clients. They are, in a sense, a form of citation to the law. The absence of lawyers in some places and their presence as citation in others are not surprising as the plaintiffs in these cases quite often have very compelling stories to tell. With clients such as these, the lawyers can stand back and let the story of the case persuade their audience while bringing in legal matters when they want to validate something their client has said about rights and law, or to provide additional information about past precedents and the arguments they will make in the courtroom. What I find intriguing, however, is that the journalists who write these stories are very rarely interested in the larger political narrative in which the lawyers themselves do their work. Instead, they, too, are swept up in the stories the clients tell, and present them in their newspaper articles in ways that leaves out any connections the case and the lawyers have to the larger conservative movement – nor do they investigate whether the clients of these lawyers maintain the same political perspective as their lawyers.

In this essay, I argue that in press stories property rights lawyers are very carefully situated as the defenders of disadvantaged property owners. They are generally placed outside the discourse their work produces around key cases, effectively erasing their identities as activists within the larger conservative movement, while maintaining them in the narrative as sources of legal authority and additional information. I do not argue that this placement is consciously arranged by the lawyers because, at this, point I have scant evidence to suggest this to be true. Rather, the narratives that are told by the press fit commonly held beliefs about the way in which "the little guy" can eventually come before the U.S. Supreme Court and thus ultimately reinvent what Stuart Scheingold has termed "the myth of rights" (Scheingold 2004). This reinvention accords with narratives spun around litigation and the individuals involved in litigation and thus is not surprising to sociolegal scholars. The newspaper articles discussed here are part of knowledge production in a manner very similar to the way in which Haltom and McCann (2004) find the mass media to be involved in knowledge production in tort reform, in which the framing of stories is informed by the expectations of the audience and of the reporters who produce them.

The reinvention of the myth of rights occurs *because* of, rather than despite, the mixed rulings and losses suffered by clients of property rights lawyers before the Supreme Court. The absence of the lawyers' connection to the conservative movement and their presence only as a citation to the authority of the law enable this mythmaking by creating representations of litigants who fight with the odds against them, lose, then live to fight on despite the odds. These representations are tropes that run deep in the consciousness of our culture: the persons who tilt at windmills – the Don Quixotes of the world – who always lose yet live to fight another day. These are compelling romantic figures that fit a cultural narrative about lost causes and idealism in which the lawyers themselves do not fit. In fact, if the lawyers were made the focus of attention, the deregulatory activity of this movement would not only be a much less romantic tale; it would feature an understanding of the law that would highlight the complex and often obscure relationship that politics and law have to one another. Instead, my analysis suggests that the news reports serve in part to "create the nation as an imaginary community" (Sarat and Simon 2003, p. 5), a community that produces romantic heroes who often fight losing battles in the name of justice and their ideals. It is in this imaginary community that the myth of rights is reborn and reworked on behalf of deregulation.

II. Finding the Stories

There are several reasons to choose the story of Anthony Palazzolo and his thirty-year fight to build a housing development along the Rhode Island coast. Mr. Palazzolo's case was covered in both the state and national press before, during, and after his Supreme Court case was argued and decided. He was also explicitly labeled a Don Quixote by the attorney general of the State of Rhode Island (now U.S. Senator Sheldon Whitehouse) in a newspaper article. Although the reference to him as "a Don Quixote" was intended to diminish his claims (as being unrealistic, imaginary), it also invoked the romanticism that is so important here. It suggested that Mr. Palazzolo was motivated by his ideals and that those ideals were based on unrealistic expectations of the possible. Indeed, in the stories about the case, more than one reporter described Mr. Palazzolo in a way that suggested he was determined to fight regardless of the odds against him, pointing to his idealistic understanding of private property rights. These were ideals he maintained, despite the reality of environmental regulation along the Rhode Island coast.

My discussion here is based on textual analysis of newspaper articles from both state-level newspapers and the national press covering the story of *Palazzolo v. Rhode Island* as it made its way to the U.S. Supreme Court, as well as subsequent action by the state court of Rhode Island. I found the newspapers stories using LexisNexis Academic Universe®, searching among major U.S. newspapers, the news wires, news transcripts, as well as state and local newspapers in Rhode Island, Massachusetts, and Connecticut. These searches yielded several hundred newspaper articles. My research assistant and I then sorted through them to find those that substantively discussed the court case and/or property rights. This process yielded approximately 140 news stories. Once this subset was put together, I read and analyzed them to determine how characters were developed in the narratives, as well as who was left in and who was left out of the story. I whittled this subset down to a few dozen articles, looking for articles that treated the case substantively. This meant that they discussed the case beyond merely stating the particular claim Mr. Palazzolo was making in court. Perhaps not surprisingly, most of these articles came from local New England press. They represent original research on the part of the reporter that went beyond the superficial discussions of claims and litigants that was prevalent in much of the rest of the press. Largely due to space limitations here, the articles discussed here represent a subset of this group that I believe are representative of them. In addition, as part of a larger project, I traveled to Rhode Island in the summer of 2005 and the spring of 2006 to discuss this case with environmental activists, political actors, and others concerned with the case in the state. I have also collected documents related to the history of the case and about the Rhode Island Coastal Management Resource Council (CRMC), which is the agency charged with the permitting and regulation of the coastal lands in the state. The CRMC material, although not always drawn on for this analysis, certainly informs my understanding of the background of the case and the political culture of Rhode Island.

As I worked through the news articles, I often set Cervantes' *Don Quixote* (2003) next to the newspaper text and tried to unearth what it was about Cervantes' work that seemed to be informing the way the stories were arranged and the individuals involved in the case were characterized. The story of Don Quixote is one that many have heard about, but fewer have read. As I argue here, it is striking that Don Quixote, as created by Cervantes, does not map easily to the press stories, yet a cultural representation of him – the crazy gentleman who tilts at windmills – lurks there in the background, occasionally emerging when Mr. Palazzolo's idealism seems to be presented at its strongest. This happens most often after Mr. Palazzolo's Supreme Court case has been decided, and is especially prevalent in the local press in New England. Particular scenes of the novel often seem to inform the notion of a modern-day Don Quixote, specifically and most frequently the story of his windmill tilting.

One could imagine that the lawyers who sponsor these cases, rather than their clients, could be thought of as Don Quixotes. However, in these newspaper articles this was not the case. For the most part, as stated above, the lawyers tend to come in only to provide additional information. At times, they provide additional reason to believe that Mr. Palazzolo is a Don Quixote. Therefore, I focus much of the essay on describing the narrative as it was developed to highlight the *absence* of the lawyers in the larger story told to the public. In this way, I hope to provide evidence for my case that the lawyers are not present in these newspaper depictions, and that this absence makes it very difficult to understand what the politics of property rights are in Rhode Island. Because this case is part of a larger litigation movement, there are indeed broader ramifications if other cases are handled in similar fashion.[1] Before making this broader case, however, I reassemble the story of *Palazzolo v. Rhode Island* as it was told in the newspaper stories.

III. Wetlands and Rights

In a state that is roughly 48 miles long and just over 37 miles wide, with an area of just more than 1,200 miles total, Rhode Island has a remarkable amount of coastline: more than 400 miles in all. This is partly because of its location, cornered between Connecticut and Massachusetts along the coast of the Atlantic Ocean; but in addition, the state has a large cleft in its eastern side that is a result of rivers flowing through the land and into the ocean, producing the Narragansett Bay and the Mount Hope Bay, which is shared with Massachusetts and connects Rhode Island to Nantucket Sound. These bays contain various islands, including the historically important Jamestown Island, Aquidneck Island,[2] and Block Island and more coastline along the various rivers, including the Seekonk River and the Sahkonnet River (all of which empty into the Narragansett and Mount Hope Bays). Its appellation as "the Ocean State" is quite appropriate. Its coastal areas are at the center of many discussions within the state concerning wetlands, beach erosion, and the appropriate means for regulating them. Regulation is particularly important because the rivers in the area have all suffered from heavy pollution from industrialization and the heavy shipping industry that was once a major element of the area's economy.[3]

[1] Such evidence does exist, though at this point the findings are very preliminary. In addition to *Palazzolo*, we have been gathering data on several other takings cases. Not surprisingly, we see the pattern play out again and again.

[2] "Aquidneck Island" is the appellation Rhode Islanders give to the large island on the eastern side of the state that the US Geological Survey labels "Rhode Island" on their maps, which often will give the full name of the state as well: "The Great State of Providence Plantations and Rhode Island." The irony of having the longest official name and being the smallest state is cause of many a smile in the area.

[3] According to regional sources, the Port of Providence is the oldest port in the United States.

According to newspaper reports, in 1959 Anthony Palazzolo, a lifelong resident of Westerly, Rhode Island, and owner of a junkyard, joined in corporate partnership with some others and bought eighteen acres of land along the southern coast of Rhode Island in his native county. The land had been zoned several years earlier for a residential subdivision. His property is on a thin bar of land that sits between Winnepaug Pond and the Atlantic Ocean, near what was then a newly created beach. According to court documents, most of the eighteen acres designated as wetlands are submerged under water during most of the year. Nearly two acres are "upland," however, and could potentially be developed.

Mr. Palazzolo, it appears, was aware at the time of purchase that the land was mostly wetlands. However, in 1959, and throughout much of the 1960s, the area stretching along the southern coast of the state was filled in and dredged so that in Mr. Palazzolo's mind, there was no concern that he would not be able to use the land as he hoped at some point.[4] During the 1960s, Mr. Palazzolo's building permits were denied for various reasons and by various state agencies. Mr. Palazzolo's problems became far worse in 1971 and over the course of the next fifteen years as the state of Rhode Island began to work to solve its pollution problems and protect its coastal lands from further erosion within the frameworks of federal laws and increasing state regulations. The reasons why Mr. Palazzolo's building permits were rejected are as yet unclear. Officially, it appears that they had largely to do with concerns about the appropriate type of buildings to be constructed on such land, but this is only implied by the information so far available.[5]

[4] This date is somewhat misleading – the issue of whether Mr. Palazzolo owned all the land in 1959 was something the Court had to decide. The corporate partnership in which Mr. Palazzolo initially participated acquired the land in 1959; however, he became sole owner in 1978 when the partnership dissolved. Based upon the various dealings he made, the state argued that he did not own the land in full title until 1978 – after the regulations were in place, and therefore he could have no expectations of building along the original plans. The PLF lawyers argued before the Court that the ownership rights were handed down from partner to partner, and that since, historically, building had been permitted in the area, Mr. Palazzolo had every right to expect he would be able to build. At oral arguments, however, it became clear that this would not be the take of at least some of the justices. J. Souter asked, "If the rights to land use pass from owner to owner, how far back does it go? There is no logical stopping place until you get back to Roger Williams and the 17th-century settlement" (quoted in Greenhouse 2001).

[5] "Officially," i.e., that is according to the arguments made by the Attorney General on brief, and according to press reports. Yet, during fieldwork this past spring, several sources suggested (hesitantly) that these permits may have been denied because the Coastal Resources Management Council (CRMC), the organization in charge of granting the permits, was less likely to grant

Finally, in *Lucas v. South Carolina Coastal Commission* (1992), in which David Lucas claimed regulation that kept him from using his land in an economically viable way resulted in a taking even though there had been no physical taking, the Supreme Court agreed with Mr. Lucas. In the wake of the case, Mr. Palazzolo demanded that the state pay him $3 million for the property. He alleged that the various regulations amounted to a regulatory taking, like the one in *Lucas*, of his property. Both national and local reporters covering this case refer to *Lucas* many times, and Mr. Palazzolo makes reference to it himself in several interviews. The symbolic importance of *Lucas* to the Rhode Island case seems very strong, at least at the time the reporters interviewed the Pacific Legal Foundation (PLF) lawyers and Mr. Palazzolo together in 2001.

As the case made its way through the Rhode Island courts, the press reported that Mr. Palazzolo's arguments were rejected again and again. Initially, the State Superior Court upheld the Coastal Resources Management Council's (CRMC) decision not to allow Palazzolo to fill in the salt marsh on his land. The CRMC had denied his permit, arguing that the eighteen acres of land that Mr. Palazzolo wanted to fill in amounted to 12 percent of the marshes surrounding Winnapaug Pond and that filling this area in would jeopardize the pond's future. Ultimately, the Rhode Island Supreme Court rejected his appeal, arguing that the case was not ripe as Mr. Palazzolo had not yet "explored development options less grandiose than filling 18 acres of salt marsh" (quoted in Levitz 2000). The case eventually made its way to the U.S. Supreme Court, but only after the Pacific Legal Foundation stepped in and sponsored the litigation in 2000.

According to newspaper accounts leading up to and around the time of the U.S. Supreme Court decision, an odd turn in this story is that Mr. Palazzolo is not your typical property rights advocate (Flint 2002). According to the *Boston Globe*, Mr. Palazzolo is "an unabashed New Deal Democrat, and says he has no problem with regulation in theory." The reporter, Anthony Flint, describes him as "a regular guy caught in one of the most complex areas of law today." He goes on to write that "Palazzolo is an unlikely champion of the property rights cause, which is generally

them to individuals who were not well connected to the political and business establishment in Providence. At this point, this is only an "educated guess" and one that those who were making it were unwilling to make too strongly. Further research will be done this summer to determine whether there is evidence that this may be true.

associated with conservatives and wide-open spaces in the West. He appreciates the government lending a hand to people in need – but not when they give others the runaround" (Flint 2002). His property is characterized in the article as bought "at the beach to make some money for his family – that was all it was, back in 1959, when junkyard owner . . . purchased 18 acres on Winnapaug Pond that had been zoned for residential subdivision years before." Flint quotes Palazzolo as explaining in the interview, "I never got one penny off this land. All I got is tax bills. . . . You think those guys fighting the Revolutionary War wanted us to have to ask the next person, 'Can I do this with my land?' [Expletive]. They were tough" (quoted in Flint 2002).

Later in the article, Anthony Palazzolo explains that the Rhode Island Attorney General (Sheldon Whitehouse) and state administrators "are not people you can sit down and talk with. They just keeping rubbing my nose in it." Finally, "I wanted to build a nice project. . . . The kids had to go to school. We had to eat. It wasn't like this, the way it is now – I wouldn't have bought the frigging land." His sense that the regulations were unfair seemed deeply rooted in the changing nature of land use policy over the course of the forty years in which he had battled with state regulations. But he also seems to think that this case and property rights in general, are a "cause":

> "I'm just the vehicle, you know," Palazzolo said. "This isn't just about me, or even about the land. What happens to me will happen to everyone in Rhode Island. They could go downtown and take a bank building down because it blocks the sun" (quoted in Flint 2002).

Mr. Palazollo is also frequently credited in press reports for having developed a great deal of knowledge about property rights and property law. His lawyer was quoted in the *Providence Journal-Bulletin* as describing his knowledge as "amazing": "For a non-lawyer, he has amazing legal knowledge" (Lord 2001a). This is one of the few references to the PLF lawyers made in the press. Though this particular article does situate the case in terms of "a growing national debate between environmentalists and governmental officials," it does not connect this debate to the broader conservative legal movement.

The Pacific Legal Foundation (PLF) entered the picture in 2000. Eric Grant, one of its staff attorneys, was assigned to the case, and later it was turned over to James Burling. It was Burling who eventually argued the case before the Supreme Court. According to the *Providence Journal-Bulletin*, which is the paper of record in the state, had it not been for their sponsorship, it is unlikely the case would have made it to the federal courts (Lord 2001a and Lord 2001b). Yet, very little is said in the local newspaper accounts about the PLF itself. One writer describes the organization as a "conservative advocacy group" (Denniston 2001), whereas an article in the *Providence Journal-Bulletin* characterized it as "a western property rights group" (Levitz 2000). The PLF is both of these things, yet it also is more than that and is certainly situated in a network of lawyers whose work goes well beyond this particular issue.

Yet, Rhode Island Attorney General Sheldon Whitehouse declared a victory when the U.S. Supreme Court rejected some of Mr. Palazzolo's claims. He said, "The important point is that under the theory Mr. Palazzolo pursued, he lost, and he lost flat out" (Lord 2001c). In the press reports, Whitehouse only receives a few lines and does not explain what this theory was or why its defeat was so important to environmental regulation. Moreover, Whitehouse appears only to provide a summary of the decision, without giving any context or explanation as to his particular interpretation of the outcome, given that the decision was, in fact, more mixed than this suggests.

Meanwhile, a commentary published in the *Providence Journal-Bulletin* and written by Brian Bishop, a local Wise Use Movement activist and radio talk show host, chastises Attorney General Whitehouse for not understanding that the action of remanding the case while simultaneously setting a particular precedent concerning ripeness did not amount to a "win" as claimed on the Attorney General's Web site, but instead was a loss (Bishop 2001). Bishop argues that Whitehouse's claim of victory belongs "to the list of infamous premature announcements in the vein of *Dewey Defeats Truman*, lengthened recently by network predictions that *Gore Takes Florida*." He goes on to point out that the national press had declared this case a "victory" to property owners (in fact, the national press was mixed on who had won this case) and that many environmental lawyers had been disappointed by the result. Invoking the *Lucas* case several times, Bishop argues that Mr. Palazzolo may yet win compensation in state courts, as Mr. Lucas had (in fact, Palazzolo lost on remand and has since dropped all appeals). He then argues that regulation had become akin to slavery: "perhaps the closest experiences to slavery in today's America." Mr. Bishop does not discuss the role of property rights movements in antiregulation activities more broadly, nor does he discuss these efforts as an element of the conservative legal movement.

And yet, to truly understand the politics of law in this arena and even in this case, it helps to understand what the PLF is and to place it in the broader politics of property rights playing throughout the United States.

IV. Property Rights as a Movement Activity

The property rights movement is not one single movement. Rather, there have been a number of mobilizations at the state and national level in the United States aimed at increasing the level of protection afforded to individual private property rights. Interest groups, such as the various farm bureaus and the National Home Builders Associations; corporations as well as small businesses; and individual private property owners who are affected by governmental regulation of their property, usually land use regulations or environmental protection regulations, make up the movement. Some of the better known mobilizations include the activism around the spotted owl in the Pacific Northwest and, more recently, in Klamath Falls in Oregon. These mobilizations make similar claims about rights to private property and demands that the government respect and protect those rights, despite the variations in the situations of those whose rights have supposedly been violated and the different forms of regulation involved.

At the state level, the variations in the property rights movement efforts are particularly intriguing and seem tied to the political culture as well as the particular institutional structures of each state. The ability of property rights advocates to have their claims addressed in state legislatures and state courts appears, in this preliminary investigation, to be influenced by the level of support they find in the governor's office, as well as the degree to which the environmental lobby in the state also has ties to these state institutional structures. Another factor that I touch on here but will require much more rigorous analysis in future research concerns the degree to which multinational corporations are involved with property rights activism. For example, when large extractive industries, such as forestry and mining, are involved, the degree of conflict seems greater than when smaller businesses and more local property owners are involved. Similarly, when national property rights groups filled with lawyers, such as the Pacific Legal Foundation, are also present, the disputes appear to generate greater political heat.

When these property rights mobilizations occur at the state level, they usually involve state attorneys general who have the responsibility, among other things, to represent state agencies in land use and environmental regulation issues. As they stated in their amicus brief in *Nollan v. California Coastal Commission*, the attorneys general have the responsibility "for ensuring that the natural resources within their borders are not over-used or overdeveloped to the detriment of the health, safety, and welfare of their residents..." (*Nollan* SAG Brief: 1). Over time, the takings challenges have posed a challenge to governmental planners and administrators in part because they tend to require factual inquiries that often seem ad hoc and seem to produce unpredictable outcomes.

Of course, part of the story about property rights at the state level has to do with whether states have strong environmental regimes in place. For example, California, like Rhode Island, has a fairly strong environmental regime while also having multinational corporations within its borders. These corporations have been involved in property rights disputes, particularly in Northern California where the forests are thick and the forestry industry has much at stake.[6] These multinational corporations have been deeply involved in attempting to curb state-level regulations of the redwood forests in the northern part of the state. However, small property owners are also involved in property rights mobilizations in California. California has, among other state-level environmental regulations, its own Endangered Species Act that protects species for the region that are not listed under the national Endangered Species Act. This has been a point of contention, especially with regard to the cougar, the population of which has grown considerably but remains protected in the state (though it is not protected in the other states in the area).[7]

In terms of national politics, the Pacific Legal Foundation (PLF) is important for several reasons. It was the first organization involved in conservative public interest law and remains one of the most active conservative/economic libertarian groups. It has been active in the area of property

[6] It should be noted that it's not only extractive industries that make property rights claims. Methanex Corporation, a Canadian multinational, has made similar claims under NAFTA regarding the sale of a gasoline additive said to be a water contaminant and therefore regulated by the State of California. This case is currently in international arbitration, but it is significant as it takes issue with a state regulation by invoking an international trade agreement.

[7] According to the Fish and Wildlife Service, the cougar is protected under national law only in the Southeastern United States.

rights protection for nearly three decades and recently has expanded its scope both in terms of specific strategies and other areas of law. Case sponsorship was not a part of their strategies until changes in the judiciary created a hospitable environment for their efforts (Smith 1993).

According to the PLF, its founders wanted "to preserve the basic freedoms set out by the U.S. Constitution and to reverse the growing trend toward greater government control and influence into American lives. [The founders of the PLF] also saw an increasingly politicized judiciary tending more and more to *make* laws rather than to interpret them" (PLF, 2003). Rather than advocating specific causes, the PLF's goal at the beginning was to address particular legal issues, mostly in California where its base of operations was, with particular attention to the legality of environmental impact reports. Today's PLF litigates cases throughout the country and has offices in Washington state, Florida, and Hawaii.

If a case is one the PLF would like to see brought before the Supreme Court, the PLF assists the plaintiff by petitioning the Supreme Court for a writ of certiorari. However, its primary litigation strategy is the amicus brief (O'Connor and Epstein 1983). Through a careful process of monitoring cases around the country, the PLF files as amici in cases reaching federal appellate or state supreme court review (Kendall and Lord 1998). The PLF claims its work has affected many areas of law, including land use, endangered species, agricultural development, public finance and taxation, education, welfare, public contracting and employment, energy development, national defense and tort liability. The list suggests the degree to which PLF's litigation activity has expanded well beyond its initial narrow scope. Yet, the PLF remains focused on economic interests, informed by its belief that economic liberty remains at the heart of individual freedom (PLF 2003).

V. Why the Absence Matters

The press, because it is focused on the story of the lawyers' client, generally does not examine who the lawyers are or how they have shaped the perceptions of their clients. Instead, they identify the lawyers only as "property rights activists" (and sometimes associated with "the West") and do not link them more explicitly to the broader property rights discourse and conservative legal movement. I argue here that this effectively erases the lawyers, their legal activism, and the politics of law from the broader political discourse concerning land use management and development, placing the focus on the clients who are, by and large, less empowered than many in their communities.

This erasure appears to rely on distancing both the lawyers and the state regulators from the property owners. The property rights lawyers are thus placed outside the realities of the conservative legal movement more generally. When the lawyers are left out as movement actors involved in a much larger, national political scene, their roles disappear from the political discourse – despite the fact that their work is constitutive of it. Meanwhile, the stories of their clients reinforce long-held beliefs about law and justice, despite the losses their clients have suffered before the U.S. Supreme Court.

I began this essay by suggesting that the not quite complete erasure of the lawyers involved in this case meant that the broader political and legal movement they are a part of is forgotten in the political discourse. Local press coverage in particular is very important to the way in which individuals understand the workings of their state governments. Yet these state governments operate within and often react to broader national politics. Rather than providing accounts of how this case fit into those national politics, the local press stayed focused on the local actors, particularly the plaintiff, and either ignored or oversimplified the workings of regulation.

Two other important characteristics stand out in the press accounts in southern New England. The first is that Palazzolo's age and the amount of time and energy he put into the case by himself – before the PLF became involved – are referred to frequently. The PLF comes in almost as a knight in shining armor, saving the case from drowning in state courts and keeping it alive for this elderly gentleman who, at the very least, has ideals that transcend his own personal involvement in the case. The reporters do not, as part of this story, explain in detail why the permits were denied over four decades, nor do they expend much energy in determining whether Mr. Palazzolo followed state law in filing these permits or in exploring the politics of the regulatory process in Rhode Island.

Second, though the PLF lawyers, the state attorney general (AG), and various environmental lawyers and activists are interviewed and discussed, rarely are they much beyond supporting characters in the story of this case. Rhode Island's AG at the time, Sheldon Whitehouse, does receive attention in the *Providence Journal-Bulletin* through a detailed description of his preparation for his first (and only) U.S. Supreme Court case (Lord

2001b). Intriguingly, this article opens with the lead, "When Atty. General Sheldon Whitehouse appears before the U.S. Supreme Court to argue a major property rights case, should he tone down his legal language and be a bit more informal? Should he talk about salt marshes, for instance, instead of 'lands below the mean high water mark'?" The rest of the story is about the preparation for the AG's *performance* rather than an explanation of why he is so worried about this particular performance or what sorts of arguments might be made before the Court. The politics of the law, in this instance, is reduced to rhetorical style and the ability to fire back answers in the face of potentially hostile justices. The PLF is mentioned, but as its lawyer was unavailable to be interviewed, is not discussed in detail. In contrast, Mr. Palazzolo is discussed in reference to his case, his various press interviews, and the fact that he will be present with his wife and three of his children (all grown, though this is not mentioned).

Ultimately, the Supreme Court sent the case back to the Rhode Island courts to be reviewed again under tough standards concerning the economic impact of land use regulations on a property owner. However, while they were considering the case, the Supreme Court managed to set a precedent concerning ripeness that was understood by many property rights advocates to be a "win" for their cause.[8] Once again, the symbolic significance of a case mattered to the movement more than the particular outcome. The PLF lawyers turned the case over to local counsel once the Supreme Court had made its ruling. Mr. Palazzolo continued to litigate the case until the

[8] In essence, the Court decided the issue of whether an owner can claim a regulatory taking of property subject to wetlands regulation *after* the acquisition of the property. In a 5–4 decision authored by J. Anthony Kennedy, the Supreme Court found that the Rhode Island Supreme Court had erred in determining that the case was not ripe for judicial review, though they had been correct in asserting that Palazzolo had not yet established a deprivation of all economic value in his claims. As for the state's responsibility toward a land owner when a regulation is passed after acquisition, Kennedy explained:

"Were we to accept the State's rule, the postenactment transfer of title would absolve the State of its obligation to defend any action restricting land use, no matter how extreme or unreasonable. A State would be allowed, in effect to put an expiration date on the Takings Clause. This ought not to be the rule. Future generations, too, have a right to challenge unreasonable limitations on the use and value of land." (533 US 606 at 613).

For this reason, Kennedy explained, the state courts will need to consider whether a regulatory taking has occurred in this case through tests set out in various precedents. The property rights advocates and other observers, particularly the Pacific Legal Foundation, clearly felt this to be a win for their cause. In January of 2002, in a New Year's update posted on their Web site, Frank Shepherd of the PLF wrote that the victory here amounted to a major loss to bureaucrats nationwide who would no longer be able to argue that compensation was not required when a regulation was already in place at the time of purchase.

Superior Court told him, once again, that the permit denials were legal and he would not be able to develop his land. He then let the case drop. For Mr. Palazzolo, who had a moment of fame in the press, the case has been a source of frustration for over 35 years.

REFERENCES

Associated Press. 2001. "Westerly Man, State to Argue Today Before U.S. High Court," *Providence Journal-Bulletin*, February 26, 2001, p. 8B.

Bishop, Brian. 2001. "Commentary: Whitehouse Loses War on Property Rights," *Providence Journal-Bulletin*, July 17, 2001, p. 4B.

Brief for the Commonwealth of Massachusetts et al. *Nollan v. California Coastal Commission*, 1986 U.S. Briefs 133, October Term 1986.

Cervantes Saavedra, Miguel de. 2003. *Don Quixote*. Translated with introduction and notes by John Rutherford. New York: Penguin Books.

Denniston, Lyle. 2001. "Landowners Gain New Weapon Against Zoning," *The Boston Globe*, June 29, 2001, p. A14.

Flint, Anthony. 2002. "Landlocked on the Coast for 40 Years, Anthony Palazzolo Has Battled RI over Property Rights, All the Way to the Supreme Court," *Boston Globe*, November 3, 2002, p. B1.

Haltom, William and Michael McCann. 2004. *Distorting the Law: Politics, Media and the Litigation Crisis*. Chicago: University of Chicago Press.

Kendall, David T. and Charles P. Lord. 1998. "The Takings Project: A Critical Analysis and Assessment of the Progress So Far," 25 *Environmental Affairs* 509.

Levitz, Jennifer. 2000. "U.S. Supreme Court to Hear RI Land Case," *Providence Journal-Bulletin*, October 12, 2000, p. 1B.

Lord, Peter. 2001a. "Battleground – Westerly Landowner's Fight Headed for Highest Court," *Providence Journal-Bulletin*, January 21, 2001, p. 1C.

Lord, Peter. 2001b. "Whitehouse In Training for High-Court Fight," *Providence Journal-Bulletin*, February 20, 2001, p. 1A.

Lord, Peter. 2001c. "Turf Battle Supreme – Property Rights Affirmed; Payment Denied," *Providence Journal-Bulletin*, June 29, 2001, p. 1A.

O'Connor, Karen and Lee Epstein. 1983. "The Rise of Consservative Interest Group Litigation," 45 *The Journal of Politics* 479.

Pacific Legal Foundation. 2003. www.pacificlegal.org, downloaded February 21, 2003.

Palazzolo v. Rhode Island, 533 U.S. 606 (2001).

Sarat, Austin and Jonathan Simon. 2003. "Cultural Analysis, Cultural Studies, and the Situation of Legal Scholarship," in *Cultural Analysis, Cultural Studies, and the Law: Moving Beyond Legal Realism*. Austin Sarat and Jonathan Simon, editors. Durham, NC: Duke University Press.

Smith, Christopher E. 1993. *Justice Antonin Scalia and the Supreme Court's Conservative Moment*. Westport: Prager Press.

Scheingold, Stuart A. 2004. *The Politics of Rights: Lawyers, Public Policy, and Political Change*, 2nd edition. Ann Arbor, MI: University of Michigan Press.

7

"The Kids are Alright"

Cause Lawyering on Television in 1960s America

Thomas M. Hilbink

I. Introduction

CBS's advertisement in *Variety* touted that its new series for the fall 1970 season, *The Storefront Lawyers*, would "capture the whole spirit of an exciting, significant movement."[1] The ad assumed readers would know what this movement was. It wasn't an unreasonable assumption. The movement – the "exciting, significant" movement – had been building over the course of a decade. Beginning in the early years of the 1960s, when lawyers became involved in large numbers with the direct action phase of the civil rights movement, and growing exponentially with the creation of the Legal Services Program, this movement only continued to expand and grow in the later years of the decade. This cause lawyering "explosion" – as I have elsewhere labeled it – neared its zenith in 1970. As the sixties became the seventies, more and more legal professionals were involved in battles against the war in Vietnam, racism, and sexism, as well as with such issues as civil liberties, consumer rights, the environment, and government accountability.

The explosion was the product of an era in which people were questioning the fundamental assumptions of American life and institutions. Many have noted the ways the sixties constituted a period of inquiry about structures of race, of sexuality, of modernity. But the sixties also marked the period in which assumptions about law, lawyers, and the legal profession – law's role in democratic society, lawyers' relationships with clients and to social change, and the legal profession's definitions of how attorneys

[1] Michael M. Epstein, "Young Lawyers," in *Prime Time Law*, ed. Robert M. Jarvis and Paul R. Joseph (Durham: Carolina Academic Press, 1998), 254.

should do their work – came up for debate and challenge. That the debates occurred in Supreme Court arguments, law reviews, and bar associations was not surprising, but that these debates were also happening in congressional hearings, in foundation boardrooms, in social movement strategy sessions, and in general interest periodicals demonstrates the seeming ubiquity of the discussion. *The Storefront Lawyers* and two other hour-long dramatic series that aired in the 1970–71 television season – *The Young Lawyers* and *The Bold Ones: The Lawyers* – further extended the realm of these debates, bringing them into the homes of millions of Americans. At a time when cause lawyering was – according to Sarat and Scheingold – "making peace with the organized bar" and "becoming a substantial presence within the profession," it was also negotiating for acceptance in American society more generally.[2]

In the wake of a series of highly publicized trials, such as the Chicago conspiracy trial in 1969, many Americans were deeply anxious about this emerging subculture within the generally tradition-bound and well-established legal profession. Radical political activists and lawyers in such trials had rejected the "basic house rules" (as Yippie leader Abbie Hoffman labeled them), using the courtroom as just another venue for protest and street theater.[3] Such behavior in the sanctified space of a courtroom suggested that the most fundamental underpinnings of society were under assault. The three television shows about new lawyers reflected that anxiety, challenging the idea of radical politics and lawyering while offering a reassuring portrait of young lawyers working out of storefront offices in American cities who did not pose a threat to the professional, political, social, cultural, or legal status quo.

This essay looks at cause lawyering as it appeared in popular culture at the end of the "long 1960s" (delineated here not as a decade, but as an era that stretched into the mid-1970s). It does not aim to establish the extent to which television shows of the era did or did not represent accurate portrayals of cause lawyering. Like Mezey and Niles, in their analysis of ideologies of law in television and film, I am "decidedly uninterested in whether popular

[2] Austin Sarat and Stuart A. Scheingold, *Something to Believe In: Politics, Professionalism, and Cause Lawyering* (Palo Alto: Stanford Law & Politics, 2004), 40.

[3] Abbie Hoffman, *The Autobiography of Abbie Hoffman* (New York: Four Walls Eight Windows, 1980), 161.

culture gets law 'right.'"[4] Nor am I interested in understanding the success or failure of these shows with audiences (they were all relative ratings failures).[5] Rather, the essay takes as a jumping-off point the idea expressed by Jim Cullen, in his book *The Art of Democracy*: "[I]f the study of popular culture is surrounded by a great deal of uncertainty, even mystery, it also affords valuable clues – about collective fears, hopes, and debates."[6] Indeed, the three aforementioned shows airing on each of the major networks during the 1970–71 television season reveal "collective fears, hopes, and debates" over the idea of cause lawyering and the perception that radical lawyers were threatening to destroy the legal system itself. Analysis of these shows demonstrates the extent to which they reveal the concerns Americans had about instability in the legal profession and the lawyering process in the wake of the radical challenge to traditional law and lawyering.[7]

The sixties, writes legal historian Pnina Lahav, "were marked by a massive challenge to the conventional conception of American identity."[8] Although this challenge presented itself in the legal profession, *The Young Lawyers*, *The Storefront Lawyers*, and *The Bold Ones: The Lawyers* offered an alternative vision of cause lawyering that situated it well within the traditions and control of the mainstream legal profession. In other words, the shows suggest that the challenge to conventional conceptions of American lawyering did not pose a significant threat of succeeding. According to these shows, cause lawyering might challenge the dress codes or the gender makeup of the profession, might take on some controversial subjects, but that by and large such lawyers worked within the traditions and rules of the profession and the legal system and, most importantly, repudiated radicalism in both its political and legal manifestations. Lawyers – be they young, storefront, or

[4] Naomi Mezey and Mark C. Niles, "Screening the Law: Ideology and Law in American Popular Culture," *Columbia Journal of Law & the Arts* 28 (2004–05): 95.

[5] Epstein, "Young Lawyers."

[6] Mezey and Niles, "Screening the Law," 106; Austin Sarat, Lawrence Douglas, and Martha Umphrey, "On Film and Law: Broadening the Focus," in *Law on the Screen*, ed. Austin Sarat, Lawrence Douglas, and Martha Umphrey (Stanford: Stanford University Press, 2005), 3.

[7] I watched all episodes of the three shows available in the collection of the Museum of Television and Radio in New York City. These included two episodes of each television show discussed (see bibliography). I also based my conclusions on discussions of other episodes discussed by other authors; see Epstein, "Young Lawyers"; Mezey and Niles, "Screening the Law."

[8] Pnina Lahav, "The Chicago Conspiracy Trial as a Jewish Morality Tale," in *Lives in the Law*, ed. Austin Sarat, Lawrence Douglas, and Martha Umphrey (Ann Arbor: University of Michigan Press, 2006), 21.

bold – may have challenged the limits on hair or skirt length, but they would not go far beyond the limits of traditional practice. *At a time when radical lawyers were making a splash in the news, this was surely a reassuring vision.*

II. Understanding the Historical Moment

To understand the extent to which these television shows reflected "collective fears" about the changing identity of American lawyers at the dawn of the 1970s, it is essential to comprehend the concerns voiced elsewhere about the destructive impact of cause lawyering – and specifically what I call "grassroots" cause lawyering – in American law and society more broadly.[9] What becomes clear is that these three shows mirror concerns about the behavior and work of lawyers that were part and parcel of a larger set of concerns within America's liberal establishment.[10]

By the fall of 1970, Americans were well acquainted with disruptive actions taken by lawyers and defendants in courtrooms around the nation. Radical lawyers and their activist clients challenged legal procedures, legal institutions, and the law in instances that had become a staple of news coverage and the publishing world during the previous years. The events of 1968 generally, and in Chicago surrounding the Democratic National Convention specifically, had a significant impact on many fronts. Americans watched the events in horror (though what horrified them varied). The conduct of the police, the actions of elected officials, and the reactions of protesters demonstrated the deep chasm separating elements of the American body politic. The Chicago conspiracy trial, alternately known as the Chicago Seven or Chicago Eight trial, put those divisions on stark display. For the Right, represented by the recently elected Nixon administration, the Chicago trial was an opportunity to make good on promises of bringing law and order to the nation, punishing the leftists whom it blamed not only for the disorder in the streets that summer but more generally for

[9] Thomas M. Hilbink, "You Know the Type . . . : Categories of Cause Lawyering," *Law & Social Inquiry* 29, no. 3 (2004).

[10] Cynthia Lucia labels as expressions of "Hollywood liberalism" those productions that while "appearing to mount an ideological critique often end up supporting the very systems they call into question"; Cynthia Lucia, *Framing Female Lawyers* (Austin: University of Texas Press, 2005), 3.

the breakdown of so-called traditional American values (including legal values). For the Left, specifically those indicted in Chicago (a group that included the leaders of major factions of the antiwar movement), the trial served as an opportunity to use the courtroom as a stage to speak to the American public at large in hopes of exposing as repressive and reactionary the political and legal systems of the nation.[11]

Most (in)famous in attacking the sanctity of courtrooms, law, and the legal system was William Kunstler, the lead attorney in the Chicago conspiracy trial.[12] It was there that Kunstler – influenced by his radical clients – abandoned his commitment to lawyering within the parameters of mainstream professionalism and began to position himself both politically and professionally in opposition to the legal system itself. "I started out seeing myself as a sort of middleman – the traditional lawyer's role of interceding between the system and the client, without really being a part of either, almost like a eunuch," said Kunstler in an interview.[13] "Lawyers who can no longer remain their society's most complacent eunuchs must pass from passive or active acceptance to open resistance."[14] The idea of lawyers engaged in "open resistance" was indeed radical, for it violated the very idea of the lawyer as an officer of the court and a steward of the legal system. Perhaps more significant was the rejection by Kunstler and his colleagues of the assumption that a lawyer should control his client in the courtroom. The defendants in Chicago "wanted to decide for themselves what happened during their trial. They wanted our legal strategies to reflect their political philosophies. After a time, I began to understand their point of view and act on it."[15] Kunstler, like lawyers in the Oakland Seven and Panther 21 trials, became "the political agent of his client in the courtroom."[16]

Kunstler's actions in the Chicago trial marked the high point (or low point) in the use of American courts to challenge the status quo. Lawyers

[11] David Farber, *Chicago 68* (Chicago: University of Chicago Press, 1988); David Langum, *William Kunstler: The Most Hated Lawyer in America* (New York: New York University Press, 1999).

[12] Walter Schneir, "Desanctifying the Courts." in *Radical Lawyers*, ed. Jonathan Black, 297–301. New York: Avon Books, 1971.

[13] Jonathan Black, "An Interview with William Kunstler," in *Radical Lawyers*, 301–02.

[14] Ibid., 268.

[15] Kunstler, quoted in Langum, *William M. Kunstler*, 123.

[16] Ibid.

and defendants alike wore black armbands into court to protest the War in Vietnam; this was seen as a breach of courtroom decorum, particularly by the lawyers who were supposed to appear as neutral and objective officers of the court.[17] Defendants Abbie Hoffman and Jerry Rubin, founders of the Yippies, wore judges' robes to court one day to challenge Judge Julius Hoffman's authority.[18] The lawyers called to the witness stand such cultural figures as poet Allen Ginsberg (who chanted "Om" from the stand while bailiffs wrestled with one defendant), protest singers Phil Ochs and Judy Collins, and civil rights activist Julian Bond (to name a few). The lawyers and defendants repeatedly challenged and ridiculed the judge's authority in front of the jury, refusing to offer the typical deference accorded to court officials. Perhaps most glaring (at least to the judge) was the defense counsel's refusal to quiet or rein in their clients. As noted by radical lawyer Carol Goodman, "Lawyers are supposed to keep their clients quiet, in the name of professionalism."[19] But that was precisely what lawyers in these cases refused to do.

Most dramatic at the trial was the struggle between Judge Hoffman and defendant Bobby Seale. Seale, co-founder of the Black Panther Party, wished to represent himself after Judge Hoffman refused to grant a continuance that would have allowed Seale's long-time lawyer to handle his case. Seale, not accepting Hoffman's imposition of Kunstler as his attorney, defied the judge and repeatedly attempted to represent himself by addressing the jury and cross-examining witnesses. Seale simultaneously challenged and worked within the legal system, refusing to accede to the authority of the judge while attempting to assert his legal and constitutional rights. At one point, Seale argued for his due process rights:

> You are denying them. You have been denying them. Every word you say is denied, denied, denied, denied, and you begin to oink in the faces of the masses of the people of this country. This is what you

[17] Ibid.

[18] As Pnina Lahav rightly points out, the challenge of this protest was heightened by the fact that the defendants, both Jewish, affixed gold Jewish stars to the robes, both calling attention to their Jewishness (and suggesting their persecution *as* Jews) and to the Jewishness of Judge Hoffman; Lahav, "The Chicago Conspiracy Trial as a Jewish Morality Tale," 33–34.

[19] Carol Goodman, "On the Oppression of Women Lawyers and Legal Workers," in *Radical Lawyers*, 250.

> begin to represent, the corruptness of this rotten government of four hundred years . . . [20]

Seale pulled no punches in letting those involved in the trial know what he thought of them, the law, and the legal process; for instance, calling the prosecutor a "rotten racist pig, fascist liar" in open court.[21] After multiple verbal and physical skirmishes with court officers, Hoffman ordered Seale bound and gagged in a chair, prompting tears and protests from his co-defendants.

Through these actions and many, many more, the defendants and lawyers sought (intentionally or not) to pull back the curtain from the legal system, challenging its façades of blind justice and neutrality and unveiling its true inner workings. In the words of Gerald Lefcourt, a member of the Chicago legal team and one of the most prominent radical lawyers in the era, "the court system operates to oppress, and operates as an arm of the government to maintain the status quo and the class interests of society . . . "[22] In conjunction with their clients, radical lawyers used courtrooms (often, but not always) to expose the oppression and bias in the courtroom.

But Chicago was hardly the only example of real or perceived "disorder in the courts."[23] The trial of the Oakland Seven in 1968 stemmed from the defendants' blockade of the Oakland Armed Forces Induction Center. The activists did not offer a legal defense but a political one. According to one journalist, "The defendants were not saying that they had a right to do what they did, but that what they did was right. What was on trial was not the First Amendment, but the War in Vietnam and the movement against it."[24] The Panther 21 trial in New York involved members of the Black Panther Party charged with conspiracy to bomb public places around the city. Lawyers in both trials worked closely with the defendants to challenge the authority of the court and publicly question their prosecution in particular and the legal

[20] Mark L. Levine, George C. McNamee, and Daniel Greenberg, *The Tales of Hoffman* (New York: Bantam Books, 1970), 56.

[21] Ibid., 59.

[22] Jonathan Black, "An Interview with Gerald Lefcourt," in *Radical Lawyers*, 311.

[23] Norman Dorsen and Leon Friedman, *Disorder in the Court: Report of the Association of the Bar of the City of New York Special Committee on Courtroom Conduct* (New York: Pantheon Books, 1973).

[24] Elinor Langer, "The Oakland Seven," *Atlantic Monthly*, October 1969.

process more generally.[25] The judge eventually suspended the hearings until the defendants each gave him a signed note promising "to behave properly in the courtroom."[26] In reply, the defendants wrote,

> Accusations of contempt for the "dignity" of and respect for, the court indicate to us, the defendants, that a devious attempt by the court prevails, to obscure the truth of these proceedings. There is a note of glaring distinction between the theory and practice within the "halls of justice" which is consistent with the judicial history as it pertains to Black and poor people.... What fool cannot see that the "justice" of which you speak has a dual interpretation quite apart from the legal definition and is in keeping with "slave-master" traditions.[27]

Radicals attempted to use trials as public platforms, explicitly violating the legalist separation of law from politics to call attention to their political claims while simultaneously exposing the political agenda they saw cloaked by law's formality.

In reaction to these events and others, many in the American establishment began to speak out against radical (ab)use of the courts, seeing such actions as undermining American democracy. Chief Justice Warren Burger, for instance, decried the "unseemly, outrageous episodes" in American courtrooms that served to undermine "some of the public confidence in the entire system."[28] Burger advocated for ABA recommendations that would place stricter limits on attorney behavior in the courtroom.[29] A committee of the American College of Trial Lawyers asserted that lawyers should be cited for contempt when they "misbehave" in court. Disruptive tactics, they wrote, threatened "to become systematized and popularized among a small but militant segment of the profession and the general public."[30] ABA

[25] For instance, defendants maintained "a stream of invective toward [the judge] and witnesses until [the judge] halted the proceedings"; Edith Evans Asbury, "Police Spies Due at Panther Trial," *New York Times*, March 10, 1970.

[26] Ibid.

[27] Panther 21, "Statement to Judge Murtagh," in *Radical Lawyers*, 130.

[28] Fred Graham, "Burger Finds Courts Imperiled by Breaches of Civility at Trials," *New York Times*, August 8, 1970.

[29] Michael Tigar, present at the same ABA Convention as Burger, decried the Chief Justice's position as an attempt to declare "martial law" in courtrooms and thereby silence unpopular clients. Ibid.

[30] "Stronger Action Urged Against Unruly Lawyers," *New York Times*, July 23, 1970. A committee of the Association of the Bar of the City of New York (ABCNY), headed by former Assistant Attorney General and LCCRUL co-chair Burke Marshall, issued another report (co-authored

President William Gossett denounced left-wing "mock trials" of police and government officials.[31] Gossett's successor, Bernard Segal, argued that the legal profession had a duty to combine preservation of the system with attempts to reform the nation, "so that America can move forward again within the confines of its basic institutions."[32] Reform, as Segal suggested, was the only appropriate approach. And the courts were the forum for such reform, so long as courts were used in "legitimate" ways. The line between radical and liberal use of the law was clear. Radical lawyers were evoking a strong reaction from the upper reaches of the profession.

Politicians as well spoke out against what they believed was happening in the courts and the profession. New York City Mayor John Lindsay, a leading liberal figure, observed of the Chicago trial, "We all know the danger of using courtrooms as political forums. And it is important to oppose political extremists who make illegitimate use of our courts."[33] Yet no one used lawyers as a rallying point more than then-California Governor Ronald Reagan who, along with his allies, railed against the federally funded Legal Services Program (LSP). Galled by the successes of California Rural Legal Assistance (CRLA), an LSP program closely allied with Cesar Chavez's United Farm Workers union movement, Reagan demanded that the Nixon administration rein in the lawyers whom Vice President Spiro Agnew labeled "ideological vigilantes" while Senator Jesse Helms called LSP a "distortion of the democratic process."[34] In short, cause lawyers were becoming political and cultural bogeymen. Between the realities of the Chicago trial and the distortions of political opponents, there existed a

by civil libertarian Norman Dorsen and LCDC alum Leon Friedman) stating that the "problem" of disorder in the courtroom had been vastly overblown; Norman Dorsen and Leon Friedman, *Disorder in the Court: Report of the Association of the Bar of the City of New York, Special Committee on Courtroom Conduct* (New York: Pantheon, 1973).

31 William T. Gossett, "The Rule of Law or the Defiance of Law?," in ABA *Annual Report* (Chicago: American Bar Association, 1969), 434–35.

32 Bernard G. Segal, "The Tasks of Law in a Troubled Time," Gossett, "The Rule of Law or the Defiance of Law?," 434–35, Bernard G. Segal, "The Tasks of Law in a Troubled Time," in *ABA Annual Report* (Chicago: American Bar Association, 1970), 661. These leaders were not only critical of those on the Left. They also challenged the authoritarian and lawless tendencies of those on the Right (including in the White House); Gossett, "The Rule of Law or the Defiance of Law?," 434–35, Bernard G. Segal, "The Tasks of Law in a Troubled Time," 656.

33 Levine, McNamee, and Greenberg, *The Tales of Hoffman*, ii.

34 Spiro Agnew, "What's Wrong with the Legal Services Program," *ABA Journal* 58 (1972): 930; Sen. Helms. "Legal Services Corporation Act," *Congressional Record* 119, December 10, 1973, p. 40459.

view that cause lawyers were undermining law and legal institutions' role in maintaining social stability.

In April 1970, Ford Foundation President McGeorge Bundy announced a $1 million grant to study (and seemingly help shore up) the administration of justice in America due to a "concern over what has been perceived as a growing question of public confidence in the law."[35] One part of the grant went to the Association of the Bar of the City of New York (ABCNY) to fund a report on the "disruptive tactics" of defendants in the Chicago Eight and Panther 21 trials.[36] Among leading newspapers, the *Wall Street Journal* wrote of the troubling fact that the "strategy of provocation" employed by the defendants in Chicago was "not aimed at winning the trial, but at manipulating the media. It is, in fact, a courtroom version of the radical strategy at the Democratic convention itself."[37] In agreement was a bastion of liberal journalism, the *New York Times*, as it wrote in an editorial in February of 1970:

> If the Chicago Seven and the Black Panthers have become so intoxicated with their own rhetoric as to believe that they are acting out a prelude to massive revolution, it is more than ever essential for responsible citizens not to be deluded by so suicidal a strategy. Those who defile the courts with obscenities and threats of violence are not defending their right to think or even preach revolutionary thoughts and doctrine; they are engaged in an illegal action – punishable by law under the Constitution – whose sole purpose is to discredit and destroy the judicial process.[38]

By 1970 – when the three new lawyer shows were on the air – people across the political spectrum, but particularly in the liberal middle, saw in challenges to the legal system a serious threat to national stability. The events of the preceding years, in courtrooms and law offices, but particularly those beamed through the news media into American homes, demonstrated the ways in which the legal profession was undergoing its own version of the "massive challenge to the conventional conception of American identity" and the anxiety that challenge produced.[39] In this

[35] Martin Arnold, "Faith in the Law Subject of Study," *New York Times*, April 3, 1970.
[36] Dorsen and Friedman, *Disorder in the Court*.
[37] "The Strategy of Provocation (editorial)," *Wall Street Journal*, November 11, 1969.
[38] "Disorder in the Courts (editorial)," *New York Times*, February 11, 1970, 46.
[39] Lahav, "The Chicago Conspiracy Trial as a Jewish Morality Tale," 21.

context, *The Young Lawyers*, *The Storefront Lawyers*, and *The Bold Ones* appeared to offer a reassuring palliative to viewers by portraying young, activist lawyers as working within the accepted bounds and traditions of the profession and distinguishing their work from that of political activists: Don't worry about the lawyers. They're under control.

III. "What are you rebelling against?" Legal Liberalism on the Small Screen

Writing in the *California Law Review* in 1971, Boalt Hall Law School Assistant Dean David Averbuck noted, "During the past three years, while university graduates have flocked in greater numbers to join the legal profession in an attempt to bring about 'meaningful social change,' the three commercial national television networks have responded with hour-long programs which attempt to interpret this collegiate legal mania."[40] The networks' interpretation, in the form of *The Storefront Lawyers*, *The Bold Ones*, and *The Young Lawyers*, portrayed a system that worked and that the threat (perceived or otherwise) to the law and legal institutions by "ideological vigilantes" was nothing to worry about. Although the attorneys in these shows might talk and dress differently from the three-piece suit and Brylcreemed lawyers of another generation, they were nonetheless constrained by conventional concepts of professionalism and legal precedent, guided by more conventional older attorneys, and ultimately contemptuous of radical politics and its lawyering equivalent. These lawyers may have been cause lawyers, but they hewed close to the traditional conception of the legal professional.

The Storefront Lawyers aired on CBS.[41] Three young lawyers, presumably recently out of law school, worked for a major Los Angeles law firm (presumably with the salary that entailed), but spent most or all of their time operating a "storefront" law firm in a poor neighborhood far from the gleaming towers of Century City. The scenario mirrored what seemed to be a somewhat common way in which big name firms were attracting

[40] David Averbuck, "Television Review," *California Law Review* 59 (1971): 1081.

[41] The pilot of the television show was titled *Men at Law* – a more or less accurate portrayal (gender wise) of the show. Once aired it was retitled *The Storefront Lawyers*. After its first season, however, the show was retitled *Men at Law* and, after that season, was cancelled.

top students at a time when many were eschewing private firm practice.[42] As the managing partner of the firm told a colleague in the pilot episode, "They didn't come to this firm because we offered them more money. They came because we promised to open that store and let them staff it."[43] As this piece of dialogue suggests, these were lawyers who could have worked anywhere, for large sums of money, but followed their moral and ethical compass to assist those in need. They worked independently at "the store," but returned to their managing partner for guidance as needed.

The Young Lawyers debuted the same season on NBC. It portrayed the lawyering of third-year law students working in an off-campus clinical law office. The clinical law office concept had blossomed over the course of the 1960s and, like the storefront law office, was an innovative practice setting. The voiceover introducing the show laid out the premise: "Every law student wants real action and he's getting it. Not in the classroom but in our courts, helping people who need legal services. These students are doing it at the neighborhood law office. They're lawyers. They're young lawyers."[44] Like *The Storefront Lawyers*, this show portrayed students as driven not just by a desire for "real action" but also by a moral and ethical commitment to help people in need. As clinical law students, they worked under the tutelage of an older, well-seasoned attorney.

The Bold Ones: The Lawyers was one of four thematically linked series that debuted on ABC in 1969. Each of the four shows (appearing in the same time slot on a rotating basis) centered on crusading men (women seemed to lack boldness, it seems) in various careers: law, politics, law enforcement, and medicine. It featured two brothers working in a more traditional small law practice setting in Southern California, led by a portly, soft-spoken, but authoritative elder. Unlike the lawyers in the shows on the other networks,

[42] The storefront concept was relatively widespread by 1970. Piper Marbury – a firm in Baltimore – ran such a storefront. MFY Legal Services (and other legal service groups) began operating storefront service offices in poor neighborhoods to break out of service models that located lawyers far from the communities with which they worked. And the Ford Foundation funded the Neighborhood Law Office in Harlem that was staffed by attorneys lent out to the NLO by large firms around the city; Derek Curtis Bok, "New Lawyers in Old Firms," *New York Times*, February 3, 1971; Anthony Lukas, *Common Ground* (New York: Vintage, 1985), 6; Raymond Marks, Kirk Leswig, and Barbara Fortinsky, *The Lawyer, The Public, and Professional Responsibility* (Chicago: American Bar Foundation, 1972).

[43] In 1968, the Ford Foundation funded a Community Law Office that operated along the same lines as the fictitious storefront: a storefront (this one in Harlem) that served a poor community and was staffed by lawyers from large private law firms from around New York City.

[44] *Is There a Good Samaritan in the House?* (1970).

these lawyers accepted money for their services, which they did not limit to the poor. Their docket included criminal defense in cases involving major political matters.

According to press reports at the time, by airing these shows the networks were attempting to bring emissions of "social significance" to prime time, celebrating "socially involved" characters and plots in the hopes of capturing the youth demographic.[45] Although these shows challenged some aspects of the ideal lawyer and concepts of professionalism, primarily they challenged the physical image of what constituted a lawyer. Whether it was in magazines such as *Student Lawyer* or on television shows such as *The Defenders*, in the early 1960s the image of a lawyer was of a clean-cut, white, Anglo-Saxon Protestant. Older lawyers wore three-piece suits; younger lawyers "rebelled" by wearing two-piece suits. In all cases their hair was very short. All spoke with clear diction.

Lawyers on these three shows broke those molds in many ways. Their style of dress was quite different. Men wore blazers (often tweed) and sometimes wore tight pants; perhaps with a tie, but sometimes not. Women were present in small numbers, wearing short, mod skirts. The young lawyers generally wore their hair longer, a particularly striking fact for men. Aaron Silverman, the leading character on *The Young Lawyers*, with his mop of hair down to his eyes, hands thrust deep into his pockets, had the mien of a surfer at times, mumbling softly and gently to witnesses in the courtroom. He was hardly the clean-cut and articulate attorney seen on such shows as *Perry Mason* or *The Defenders*.[46]

Most significant, however, was the racial, ethnic, and gender makeup of the attorneys on such shows. Lawyers on these shows shared backgrounds with those groups who had been traditionally excluded from the upper echelons of the bar.[47] *The Lawyers* featured two Catholic brothers. Their boss was a self-described "backcountry Protestant" who raised the question

[45] George Gent, "TV Will Drip Social Significance," *New York Times*, September 7, 1970; Jack Gould, "TV: Socially Involved "Storefront Lawyers" Bows," *New York Times*, September 17, 1970.

[46] For an excellent analysis of *The Defenders* in the context of the sixties of Kennedy's New Frontier, see Steven Classen, "Lawyers Not in Love: *The Defenders* and Sixties TV," *Television and New Media* 8 (2007): 144–68.

[47] Jerold S. Auerbach, *Unequal Justice: Lawyers and Social Change in Modern America* (New York: Oxford University Press, 1976); Harry T. Edwards, "A New Role for the Black Law Graduate – A Reality or an Illusion?," *Michigan Law Review* 69 (1971); Peter Irons, *The New Deal Lawyers* (Princeton: Princeton University Press, 1982).

of their Catholicism when they took on a client who had performed an abortion. *The Storefront Lawyers* featured two men and one woman, all seemingly WASPs, but the presence of a woman was a departure at a time when women still constituted less than 5 percent of the profession.[48] In creating *The Young Lawyers*, Paramount Pictures suggested that the show include a Jewish man, a black woman, and a white actor "who would represent Anglo-Saxon Protestants."[49] The character of Aaron Silverman represented "the first overtly Jewish leading man in any American television series."[50] This mixed race and gender casting caused controversy when one scene on the show portrayed the Jewish male and black female together in a bar. The writer of the show protested when Paramount Pictures, the backer of the show, suggested that the woman in the scene be white so as to avoid controversy.[51] Yet apart from these factors that showed how the lawyers were different from the "typical" lawyer of the era (though they did show vague similarities to the demographics of cause lawyers working at the time) and though they may have rebelled against the dress codes of the older generation, the young prime-time lawyers were hardly rebelling against the profession itself.

On all three shows the lawyers appear guided or constrained by traditional expectations of professionalism that emphasized a lawyer's neutral, passive, dispassionate, yet zealous representation of a client.[52] As an ethical obligation, neutrality and "nonaccountability" assume that lawyers remain removed from their clients, taking cases regardless of whether or not they agree with that client's actions or views.[53] William Simon calls this the "ideology of advocacy," the idea that lawyers are "neutral but partisan."[54]

[48] Cynthia Fuchs Epstein, *Women in Law* (New York: Basic Books, 1981), 4.

[49] Jack Gould, "Writers Attack Censorship of TV Scene," *New York Times*, February 11, 1971.

[50] Bob Shayne, "Leading Man Named Zalman?," *New York Times*, February 28, 1971.

[51] Gould, "Writers Attack Censorship of TV Scene."

[52] Thomas M. Hilbink, "Defining Cause Lawyering: *NAACP v. Button* and the Struggle over Professional Ideology," *Studies in Law, Politics, and Society* 26 (2002).

[53] Sarat and Scheingold, *Something to Believe In: Politics, Professionalism, and Cause Lawyering*, 3; Ronen Shamir and Sara Chinski, "Destruction of Houses and Construction of a Cause: Lawyers and Bedouins in the Israeli Courts," in *Cause Lawyering: Political Commitments and Professional Responsibilities*, ed. Austin Sarat and Stuart Scheingold (New York: Oxford University Press, 1998), 235.

[54] Stuart Scheingold, "Cause Lawyering and Democracy in Transnational Perspective," in *Cause Lawyering and the State in a Global Era*, ed. Austin Sarat and Stuart Scheingold (New York: Oxford University Press, 2001), 386; William Simon, "The Ideology of Advocacy," *Wisconsin Law Review* 1978 (1978).

Ultimately lawyers are to maintain a stance whereby they are unconcerned about the substantive outcome of their client's case, driven instead by a commitment to "technical competence."[55] Cause lawyering challenges the "ideology of advocacy."

In the lawyering shows of the 1970 season, however, the attorneys appear committed to the "ideology of advocacy," the traditional norm of neutrality and nonaccountability, rather than a deviation from such. In one episode of *The Bold Ones: The Lawyers*, the firm represents a doctor charged with performing illegal abortions. A discussion ensues as to whether or not the two Catholic lawyers will take the case despite their religious opposition to abortion. They do so and, in closing arguments, distinguish between their personal beliefs and those of their clients in order to persuade the jury to do the same.[56] Their conduct in representing a Black Panther Party member accused of murdering a police officer emphasizes even more the idea of distance between attorney and client. The camera work offers images of lawyers independent from their client. In shot after shot, the lawyers express disgust or annoyance at their client's racial and political diatribes. They separate themselves both physically and verbally from their client, remaining on one side of the room while their client paces or pulls back into a corner. Shots do not show lawyer and client in any way physically connected as the plot focuses on how far the lawyers will go in representing the radical activist in resisting the power of the court.[57] The lead character in *The Storefront Lawyers* exemplifies the ideology of advocacy when he defends his handling of cases involving poor people and people of color to a partner at his firm: "So long as my name is on that flyer I'll handle any case. Whatever I'm called upon to do, I'll do."[58] Far from being political collaborators with clients or only representing those with whom they agree – as was the stated case with radical lawyering – these lawyers demonstrate neutrality and independence.

The above quotation also expresses another prominent ideal in conventional lawyering: that lawyers are to be passive actors in their acquisition of

[55] Austin Sarat and Stuart Scheingold, "Cause Lawyering and the Reproduction of Professional Authority: An Introduction," in *Cause Lawyering: Political Commitments and Professional Responsibilities*, 3.

[56] *The Verdict* (1970).

[57] *Panther in a Cage* (1970).

[58] *A Man's Castle* (1970).

cases. The traditional model of lawyering assumes that lawyers sit idly by in their offices waiting for clients to approach them. Yet over the course of the 1960s, one critique of cause lawyers – starting with opponents to school desegregation in the years after *Brown* and continuing with right-wing opposition to Legal Services and "public interest" law – was that they sought out clients to advance lawyer-determined ends.[59] Again, on these shows, lawyers behave in the most traditional of ways when it came to the formation of lawyer-client relationships. Wives and fathers of the accused seek out the lawyers, coming to their offices for assistance. In touting "Whatever I'm *called upon* to do, I'll do," *The Storefront Lawyers* emphasizes that passivity, suggesting that lawyers do nothing unless called on. Given anxiety over lawyers trolling for clients, this portrayal suggests there is nothing to worry about. From the viewer's perspective such things simply do not happen.

Most significant and dramatic on the shows is the *Sturm und Drang* surrounding the place of passion in the lawyering enterprise. Sarat and Scheingold also focus on the way in which legal education makes the privileging of rationality and the purging of morality and emotion from the act of lawyering into a central underlying lesson.[60] In his analysis of *The Defenders* – the popular and critically acclaimed lawyer show that aired from 1961–65, Steven Classen sees the question of passion in lawyering as a trope. The sixties TV lawyer prototype, he writes, was "fatherly, noble, rational, and wise." The ideal lawyer – such as Kenneth Preston on *The Defenders* – demonstrates "detachment and emotionless problem solving" abilities.[61] One sees similar portrayals and themes animating some episodes of the three new lawyer shows from 1970.

In both *The Storefront Lawyers* and *Men at Law* the protagonists are highly "rational" men.[62] They lay out facts and make arguments in a

[59] Thomas M. Hilbink, "Constructing Cause Lawyering: Professionalism, Politics, and Social Change in 1960s America" (PhD Dissertation, New York University, 2006); Hilbink, "Defining Cause Lawyering: *NAACP v. Button* and the Struggle over Professional Ideology."

[60] Sarat and Scheingold, *Something to Believe In: Politics, Professionalism, and Cause Lawyering*, 9.

[61] Classen, "Lawyers not in Love," 154. Carolyn Blum makes this point in her discussion of lawyering in the film *In the Name of the Father*: "From law school forward, law is presented as a system based on rational thinking. Emotions are banned from this arena"; Carolyn Patty Blum, "Images of Lawyering and Political Activism in *In the Name of the Father*," *University of San Francisco Law Review* 30 (1995–96): 1075.

[62] The sole female character on *The Storefront Lawyers* is shown to question the assumed rationality of law in "A Man's Castle," when she gets in the district attorney's face and questions the idea that *any* person who commits murder could be considered sane; *A Man's Castle*.

courtroom in methodical and unemotional ways. Even when they appear to be filled with passion for their argument – as is the junior attorney on *The Lawyers* when he presses the judge to inform the jury about the possibility of jury nullification – it is clear that their arguments are highly strategic and calculated. They may believe in the idea, but they use that belief only when necessary to defend a client.

The Young Lawyers makes the tension over the place of passion in the work of lawyering a central theme. The lead character, Aaron Silverman, a third-year law student, serves as a reflection on the relation of cause lawyers to the concept of professionalism. Silverman comes in repeated conflict with the ideology of advocacy. In a case involving an anti-Vietnam War activist, his supervisor reprimands him for lacking the necessary distance from the substantive political issues and the client: "Aaron, you don't have a grasp on this case. You're too close to it."[63] In another case, the junior attorney's opposing counsel objects to his examination of a witness because it was "insensitive and melodramatic."[64] An episode in which Aaron represents a daring, maverick doctor pits two visions of professionalism against each other: one is medical and one is legal. The doctor is willing to take risks while the young lawyer shows that he believes in and hews to more conservative professional expectations. The doctor prods the lawyer as to whether he would take a chance and break the rules to do the right thing. Aaron's anguish is palpable: "Yeah, I personally would probably do that. But as a lawyer, especially a student lawyer, I have to play it pretty much by the book."[65] If he does bend the rules, it is only at the margins. "I play it by the book, except sometimes I don't read the fine print," he adds.[66] What the viewer sees is a young man who wants to break the rules, who wants to push the limits, but is restrained by the idea of legal professionalism and its norms.

Aaron's anguish and struggle with the limits of professionalism and the balance of passion and rationality are most vividly on display when he represents a radio show host who is fired for speaking out against the War in Vietnam. Aaron – who is visibly anguished by the war and very much wishes to get involved in opposing it – is in the studio and on the air with the deejay when the deejay (soon to be his client) makes the offending comments. The deejay unsuccessfully prods Aaron to make similar comments denouncing

[63] *I've Got a Problem* (1971).
[64] *Is There a Good Samaritan in the House?*
[65] Ibid.
[66] Ibid.

the war and encouraging a young man to resist the draft. Once back at the office a fellow student – the WASP character who is more "by the book" and more "lawyerly" (if not more conservative) – praises Aaron's restraint as "entirely proper." Aaron lashes back, "Well, you see, I don't think I did the right thing. I had something very important to say, something specific to say and I didn't say it." "But you exercised good judgment," his colleague suggests. "Oh yeah, I did, I exercised very good judgment," he replies caustically. "When that kid asked me those questions I wasn't thinking about him or the war in Vietnam. I was thinking about myself, I was thinking about Aaron Silverman. How I would salvage, how I would endanger my reputation, how I would endanger the reputation of the [Neighborhood Law Office]."[67] At another point in the episode, Aaron tells his supervisor, "I assure you that the NLO board has cause to be proud because I didn't stick my neck out, didn't commit myself. I copped out." Being a good lawyer means copping out politically, but that is what Aaron does.

Aaron resents the idea that "good judgment" as a lawyer requires staying silent, remaining neutral, and working within the limits of the law rather than allowing morality and politics to color the advice he gives the young man seeking help. He also resents that being "entirely proper" also means thinking about his reputation as a lawyer and the best interests of the firm first and foremost. The most he could do for the young man is suggest that he come to the law office for a consultation. This seems inadequate to him in the face of a war that he opposes deeply. Yet by the end of the episode – as discussed in greater detail below – Aaron has come to believe that he could help a person more in the apolitical role of the lawyer than he could as an unfettered activist. Silverman strains at such limits, but slowly learns to channel his energies and control his emotions in ways that appear to benefit him as a lawyer.[68] Given the national tensions over the War in Vietnam and the worries over lawyers rejecting law's (and the profession's) limits, Aaron's behavior comes across as particularly reassuring. Even a "radical" like Aaron could be tamed by the law.

Facilitating the taming process of professionalization are what David Averbuck, in his review of the three shows, refers to as the "older, tough, and respected" lawyers who "guide" and "shepherd" the young attorneys.[69]

[67] *I've Got a Problem.*

[68] Thus, in another episode, Aaron's supervisor praises the teaming of Aaron with another student who is far more "law" oriented (focused on precedent and the black letter law).

[69] Averbuck, "Television Review," 1082.

On *The Young Lawyers*, Lee J. Cobb plays the "shepherd" as a gruff and gritty, cigar-chomping well-seasoned professional. When Silverman lashes out in frustration at the legal system his shepherd quickly puts him in check, yelling, "Aaron! Cool it! Because unless you do, unless you put your years of experience and training behind this case, unless you function at your very best [your client will suffer]."[70] Burl Ives fills the role of the "vest-wearing old guard" on *The Lawyers*.[71] Here Ives tends to sit back and offer guidance to his two younger partners, allowing them to battle it out on one issue or another before offering gentle guidance to resolve the dispute. The "old guard" on *The Storefront Lawyers* is a partner in the tony Los Angeles law firm. He defends the young attorneys against attacks from outside, offers generic advice when necessary, and brings coffee and hamburgers when the three work late.

In all three shows, the "shepherds" serve to calm the tension and demonstrate that a strong controlling presence is watching over these young attorneys. Many shots portray the "shepherds" doing just that: watching. The camera draws the viewers' eye to this surveillance. The elder lawyers sit behind their charges while in court; they sit back and watch as the young attorneys argue with one another. Yet their presence portrays a solid authority, a check on the young. The shows' visual cues call attention to the fact that the elders are sitting patiently just behind their charges, ready to act and rein in the young lawyers when they go too far.[72]

Such visual and written portrayals of the elders bring to mind Jerome Frank's idea of the father: "To the child, the father is the Infallible Judge, the Maker of definite rules of conduct. He knows precisely what is right and what is wrong and . . . sits in judgment and punishes misdeeds."[73] Although Austin Sarat uses Frank's quote to different effect, the idea holds here of a

[70] *Is There a Good Samaritan in the House?*

[71] Averbuck, "Television Review," 1083.

[72] In one scene from the *Young Lawyers*, the older opposing counsel speaks with the "shepherd" character after trial. "Yes, David, he's more than competent. I say he has excellent potential as a lawyer. But for his own sake I wish you'd remind him not to take so many chances." David (the shepherd) replies, "Well if a man's reach didn't exceed his grasp, aren't we lucky that he's a young man. Gutsy young men willing to put their dreams, their principles on the line. Ready to take risks. Knowing they might be hurt but taking them anyway"; *Is There a Good Samaritan in the House?* Averbuck makes a similar argument that "the vest-wearing Old Guard assures the viewer that despite the emotional and erratic behavior of the young protagonists, they will be controlled and steadied by the wise hand of the elder learned counsels"; Averbuck, "Television Review," 1083.

[73] Austin Sarat, "Living in a Copernican Universe: Law and Fatherhood in a Perfect World," *New York Law School Law Review* 43 (1999).

trusted and faultless father figure who knows and hands down the rules of conduct, sitting in judgment of the child. The programs depict the older attorneys as "the more stable and cautious practitioner, constantly deflating the idealistic balloons of his younger cohorts."[74]

Michael Epstein finds the significance of the mentor-apprentice dramas in the "complex depiction of masculine values and ideology as they apply to lawyers.... [T]he lawyers on these shows acted to reinforce the status quo of patriarchy, just as they seemed at the same time to be trying to subvert that status quo."[75] Epstein is certainly correct about the ways in which these shows demonstrate the restraining influence of the mentors as well as their maintenance of the masculine hegemony within the profession itself. And although Epstein is on the right track in noting the disjuncture between such a patriarchal and status quo-oriented show emerging "in the midst of a culture that, at least in popular consciousness, was becoming more egalitarian, free-spirited, and youth oriented," he misses the particular significance of these shows at the end of the 1960s. Epstein loses sight of the fact that the massive social, cultural, and political upheaval and anxiety went far beyond gender and patriarchy. The programs are of a piece with a wide range of anxieties of an older generation. The shows appear to address the anxieties of the age – anxiety about the generation gap, anxiety about the threatened traditions of an older generation, and anxiety about the threat to justice posed by the antiprofessional actions of radical lawyers – by portraying young lawyers who, despite their passionate opposition to the war, or restrictive abortion laws, or racial inequality, are constrained by their work as lawyers.

Although the mentor-apprentice relationships do much to illustrate the restraints of professionalism and the processes of professionalization, the ways in which lawyers on the shows interact and are contrasted with radical activists say much about the wider anxieties of the era in which these shows emerged. Particularly disturbing for bar leaders and others offended by the behavior of lawyers in trials of political radicals was the fact that lawyers were allies with their clients (rather than remaining aloof and nonpartisan) and that they refused to quiet clients who attacked the courts. Thus, what best demonstrates the legal liberal anxiety exuded by the lawyer shows of

[74] Averbuck, "Television Review," 1083.
[75] Epstein, "Young Lawyers," 251.

1970–71 season are the ways in which the attorneys on those shows demonstrate scorn for radicalism and disdain for activism.

Many episodes of these shows deal with contemporary political struggles. *The Storefront Lawyers* and *The Young Lawyers* take on opposition to the War in Vietnam. *The Lawyers* series takes a case challenging California's abortion law and another defending a Black Panther Party member accused of murdering a police officer. Activists appear selfish and rude, driven by something other than idealism. They want to use the courts not to establish legal facts or resolve a legal dispute, but for publicity or to "expose" the system. The protagonists, by contrast, are sympathetic and idealistic characters dedicated to law and the legal system on its terms. Activists are in it for their egos, whereas lawyers are in it to help people. Lawyers will help their clients, yet believe in and remain committed to the health of the legal system.

Attorneys on the shows either believe at the outset or come to believe that courtrooms should not be used to gain publicity for their clients or a cause. On *The Storefront Lawyers*, the attorneys speak with an activist from the radical Military Resisters League in connection with a court-martial of a young soldier.[76] The activist offers his organization's assistance: "Anything I can do [to help]. Not for your rotten legal system, but you're the people we need on this case and 1000 more." After their meeting, one attorney tells the other, "There is a witness to blow the military mind. But he's just after publicity and I'm not going to help him."[77] In an episode of *The Lawyers* about the case of a Black Panther Party member, the elder attorney admonishes the firm's new client: "Stop striking poses, Miller. I'm an attorney and not a TV interviewer. Now if you want us to help you you've got to cut out your propaganda speeches."[78] And on an episode of the *Young Lawyers* in which the NLO takes on the defense of an antiwar activist, the young attorneys come to realize that their client is not interested in winning in court. "He wanted to make sure he wouldn't win," says the more conservative student. A colleague responds incredulously, "You're saying he was using the trial as an extension of the radio broadcast?" "Well, why

[76] The disdain for the activist – who is played by an African American man dressed in a paramilitary fashion suggesting the Black Panthers – is set from the first mention when one attorney asks if the man is from the Communist party. "Much further to the left than that," his colleague snarkily replies.

[77] *One American* (1971).

[78] *Panther in a Cage*.

not? The press was covering the trial, the whole city was watching it."[79] In each instance, the lawyers are disturbed or disgusted by the behavior of their clients. They make implicitly clear the idea that the courts are not to be used in such a way. Again, this stance distinguishes the prime-time lawyers from the radical lawyers on display on the nightly news. Attorneys like William Kunstler or Gerald Lefcourt were willing to stand aside or participate, while clients openly used their trials to gain publicity for their larger political agenda. The viewer troubled by such behavior on the evening news could find comfort in the more traditionally professional performances broadcast later in the evening.

On these shows, behavior in the courtroom space further distinguishes lawyers from activists. Lawyers on TV go to court to win the case for their clients. Radical activists on the shows – and like their counterparts in the real-life Chicago Eight, the Oakland Seven, and the Panther 21 trials – are far more interested in making political points and, as these shows portray it, grandstanding. The allusion to those real-life trials is quite striking. One episode of *The Lawyers*, "Panther in a Cage," involves a client whose behavior bears a striking resemblance to Bobby Seale in Chicago: he challenges the authority of the court, making speeches about racism and bias. The parallels could not have been lost on those familiar with the events in the Chicago courtroom one year earlier.[80]

Given their contempt for the use of trials as platforms for publicity, it is not surprising that the young lawyers portrayed on TV generally depoliticize their legal practices in the courtroom. Though they may have been selective as to what cases they would take – acting as defense lawyers rather than prosecutors, for instance – they do not flaunt their politics in the courtroom.[81] On *The Lawyers*, when the team of attorneys meets with the Black Panther defendant, they roll their eyes when the client rails against the racism of the justice system. Finally, the "old guy" (Burl Ives) stops the defendant: "We aren't interested in your politics, we're just interested in your rights."[82] The attorney tries to depoliticize the case, distinguishing

[79] *I've Got a Problem*.

[80] Bobby Seale was bound and gagged by the U.S. District Court on October 29, 1969. "Panther in a Cage" aired on October 18, 1970; Levine, McNamee, and Greenberg, *The Tales of Hoffman*, 63.

[81] Elayne Rapping, *Law and Justice as Seen on TV* (New York: New York University Press, 2003).

[82] *Panther in a Cage*.

law from politics, lawyers from broadcast journalists, and propaganda from facts. In that same exchange the distinction between lawyer and activist is further clarified. The client describes the case through a political lens – "A pig's dead and they want a brother to burn for it" – and the attorney translates it through an "apolitical" legal lens: "A policeman's dead and they think they have the man who killed him."[83] Law and politics represent separate realms for these attorneys, and the lawyers work to make sure it stayed that way. They police the boundary rather than blurring it.

The policing of the law/politics divide is nowhere as sharp as in the courtroom. In the "Panther in the Cage" episode of *The Bold Ones*, one young attorney makes this point explicit: "Ken, if all you want to do is to commit suicide in public, to use this court to make a martyr of yourself, then we're off the case. We won't help you do that because it is pointless for you. It's completely futile.... Either we're in charge of your defense, which means you listen to our advice and instructions, or we'll just have to step aside."[84] This intolerance for political action in the courtroom deepens when their client speaks up in court, yelling at the judge in front of the jury about the "fascist power structure" represented in the courtroom. Rather than supporting the client's clear attempt to make explicit the political undertones of the proceedings, the attorney apologizes for his conduct: "He's under very great stress." When the judge asks that the attorney control his client, the Panther activist explodes again: "He don't tell me what to do. Nobody tells me what to do." But the lawyer pushes him back in his seat. "I'm supposed to take that. Is that it?" the defendant asks. "That's a fact. Let us do the objecting," the lawyer responds.[85] In these moments, the separation between attorney and client is a stark one. Activists are excitable, emotional, and uncivilized, refusing to play by the rules that society has laid out.[86] Attorneys operate in the realm of the calm, the rational, the

[83] Ibid. The younger attorneys share their elder's perspective as well, with the youngest attorney defending the system and the judge against the Panther's derisive attacks: "Now come off it, Ken. We've got a good case and Wiley's a fair man. But you're going to end up in the gas chamber if you try to turn this trial into a political spectacular"; *Panther in a Cage*.

[84] *Panther in a Cage*.

[85] Ibid.

[86] The link between prime time and the nightly news was most glaring in "Panther in a Cage," the episode of *The Lawyers* with the Panther member who would not quiet down in court. The judge, portrayed as a reasonable and patient man (in contrast with the judge in other episodes), calls counsel to the bench and tells them that he doesn't want to gag the defendant, but he will if there are more outbursts. At the Chicago trial, Judge Hoffman told Bobby Seale

"civilized" (as the judge in the episode puts it). And when an activist gets out of line and brings politics into the courtroom, the lawyers are quick to clamp down.

Further separating lawyers from clients (and from radical lawyers) is the fact that attorneys in these shows wish to control their clients. William Kunstler made clear that he would not restrain his clients in such circumstances, telling William F. Buckley in an interview after the Chicago trial, "No, I did not restrain a single client because I don't believe I have that obligation.... It may be in the opinion of most judges, but I'll tell you this, if I believe the client were justified..."[87] Yet, the lawyers on television in 1970 reassert traditional lawyer-client power relations. Prime-time lawyers tell the client to sit down; they push him back into his chair. They tell him to let them do the objecting, that either they're in charge of the defense or they're off the case. Lawyers are firmly in control.[88] The same is true of Aaron Silverman on *The Young Lawyers* when he tries to keep his client, the antiwar activist, from speaking out against the war on the stand. Aaron objects when his activist client, Billy, begins to rail against the war, hoping the objection will stop his client. "Oh, now I'm supposed to be careful what I say?" the defendant asks his lawyer. Aaron replies, "Billy, that's enough." But Billy won't be silenced: "If justice means I have to become a party to this conspiracy of silence, then I say, to hell with it."[89] Billy challenges the very idea of justice, confronting the legalistic law-politics separation. In the end, Aaron buries his face in his hands, hardly the expression of a lawyer who wants to support his client's use of the courtroom for public and political ends.

"the Court has the right to gag you. I don't want to do that... But under the law you may be gagged and chained to your chair." In both cases, the Panther defendant was finally bound and gagged. Given that the binding and gagging of Bobby Seale was perhaps the most famous single incident in the Chicago trial, the similarity could not have been lost on viewers. The other factor, however, was the contrast between the show and the Chicago trial. In the Chicago trial, Kunstler and others objected to the treatment of Bobby Seale; Levine, McNamee, and Greenberg, *The Tales of Hoffman*, 63. On *The Lawyers*, in contrast, Kenneth Miller's attorneys seemed to support the action; *Panther in a Cage*.

[87] *The Lawyer's Role* (1971). In the Chicago trial, Kunstler sparred with Judge Hoffman over Kunstler's refusal to control his clients. Kunstler at one point told the judge, "They are free and independent and they have the right to do what they please"; Jason Epstein, *The Great Conspiracy Trial* (New York: Random House, 1970), 248.

[88] *Panther in a Cage*.

[89] *I've Got a Problem*.

In the end, the prime-time lawyers come to understand that politics has no place in the courtroom. Some believe this from the outset. But for Aaron, struggling with the bounds of professionalism (the dispassion, the nonpartisanship, the apoliticism) the lesson is more difficult. In defending his antiwar client, the attorney fights the constraints of traditional lawyering. He is pained when he stays silent rather than speaking out against the war. He caustically tells his boss that he "just sat there. Like a good boy I didn't say anything, I didn't do anything."[90] He sits with his activist client in press conferences, eager to be a part of a case that involves questions of free speech and the war that he loathes. Yet in the end, he is convinced by his shepherd and his more traditionalist colleagues that it is wrong to use the courts to speak out against the war, that lawyers can do more good representing clients than taking on causes, that they can accomplish more staying within the bounds of professionalism. Thus, after losing the case, Aaron and his colleague refuse to accept the accolades of their client at a party celebrating the end of the case. Billy introduces them as "two guys who think that winning a cause is a lot better than winning some lousy case." Such a statement would place Aaron and his co-counsel firmly in the realm of cause lawyering. Thus, by rejecting the statement he rejects the role. Aaron's further interaction with Billy cements his understanding of the role of the lawyer in relation to activism. (Clove is another activist.)

Aaron: [Y]ou could have beaten him in a court of law if you had trusted in the law.
Billy: Counselor, I think you forgot one thing: I lost the case.
Aaron: No, you didn't lose the case, you blew the case because you wanted to blow the case.
Clove: Who do you think you are, knocking Billy for speaking out?
Aaron: Oh, I'm not knocking Billy for speaking out. I'm the man that defended him. I'm his lawyer, remember?
Clove: Don't do us any favors. We don't want your repression disguised as law. Or your handouts masquerading as social justice.
Billy: Hey, counselor. Do you really believe your naïve faith in the system is going to save it from destruction?

[90] Ibid.

Aaron: No, I don't think my naïve faith in the system is going to save it from destruction, but you're not interested in saving anyone. You're interested in confusion. You talk about humanity, but when a human being comes here for help what do you do? You use him.

Clove: What are you going to do for him?

Aaron: (*whispering*) Listen.

Clove: And save the world . . .

Aaron: No, no. I'm going to try to help him. Just one person.[91]

The definition of a "good" lawyer (particularly in contrast with an activist) is laid out in this one dialogue. A lawyer believes in and trusts the law. Radical activists see law as repression in disguise. Activists want to spread confusion and fail to practice what they preach. They use people. But lawyers help people. When a frightened young man seeking help in dealing with his draft status called on Billy, Billy used him to advance his opposition to the war. Aaron had at first wished he had done what Billy did: speak out against the war. But by the end of the episode, Aaron realizes that he could serve people better by listening rather than speaking out. And as a lawyer, his job is not to place a cause above a case, but a case above a cause. He isn't out to save the world; he is just going to help one person at a time. In other words, lawyers keep law and politics separate and *individualize* justice. Aaron embraces liberal legalism's proceduralist focus, seeing change at the level of the client rather than the larger systemic problem.

In the closing frame of what would be the final episode of *The Young Lawyers*, Aaron and his more traditional young colleague are shown sitting in their law office with the young man, listening to him and finally telling him: "You're not alone, Walter. There are lots of us struggling to find an answer, an honest answer."[92] On *The Young Lawyers*, *The Storefront Lawyers*, and *The Lawyers*, the characters are struggling with the bounds of professionalism to a greater or lesser extent, but they are all looking for "honest answers" within the bounds of the system. For that is what "honest" seems to connote in this context: that those who deal with their problems through the legal system, and use that legal system in the way it had traditionally been used, were honest. The shows portray such "honesty" – and those guided by it – as close to heroic.

[91] Ibid.
[92] Ibid.

The prime-time lawyers of the 1970–71 season may still have been cause lawyers, but they are what I have called "proceduralist" cause lawyers. They treated law and politics as separate and distinct, they believed the legal system to be essentially fair and just, and they tackled social ills at an individual level. Their cause was delineated by the professional ideal of providing legal assistance to all those in need, and they took on cases in a passive manner (when clients approached them). Finally, they acted as neutral representatives of their clients, ultimately owing fealty to the legal system and its institutions. They may have taken on specific causes, but this was by happenstance only.[93]

Of all the types of cause lawyering one observes in the 1960s, proceduralist lawyering was the least controversial. It had little in common with "grassroots" or radical lawyering that dominated American media and was inflated and distorted beyond recognition in American politics. This seems to be the point. In his discussion of *The Defenders*, Classen argues that the New Frontier era show showed deference to "liberal legalism's 'rule of law'" and offered viewers reassurance that the disruptive potentials of subjectivity and partiality would not sway those working in the courts.[94] Such reassurance may have been significant amidst the perceived social ills of the Kennedy years such as rising crime rates and the sense of social instability that many white people felt in the face of racial change. But by the end of the 1960s, with its massive social and political upheaval, urban riots, violent radical opposition to the War in Vietnam, and disorder in the courts, the contrast was much more significant and far more urgent. Law's provision of stability in a time of uncertainty was practically quaint. After the Chicago Convention, the conspiracy trial, the Panther 21 trial, and other attacks on the system, what many wished for was not law's stability, but law's social control. With worries about the role lawyers were playing in the disorder swirling about, *The Storefront Lawyers*, *The Young Lawyers*, and *The Bold Ones* appear to tell viewers not to worry – "the massive challenge to the conventional conception of American identity" was not going to disrupt the traditions of the American legal profession.[95]

93 Hilbink, "You Know the Type . . . : Categories of Cause Lawyering," 664–73.
94 Classen, "Lawyers Not in Love," 151.
95 Lahav, "The Chicago Conspiracy Trial as a Jewish Morality Tale," 21.

8

Nothing to Believe In – Lawyers in Contemporary Films About Public Interest Litigation

Michael McCann and William Haltom

I. Introduction

"Ya know why everyone thinks that all lawyers are back-stabbing, blood sucking scum bags? Because they are." (Julia Roberts, *Erin Brockovich*)[1]

"If somebody like her came to see me back in New York with this dogshit case . . . you know what I'd do? I'd take it. Settle quick, pocket the contingency . . . make more money than her, never see a courtroom." (Woody Harrelson, *North Country*)[2]

A cavalcade of American films over the last fifteen years has addressed legal challenges by lawyers representing ordinary citizens who have been harmed by products or practices of large private corporations.[3] The types of legal actions featured in these films are very much like one familiar form of public interest litigation that we ordinarily associate with cause lawyering. According to some critical observers, these films reflect a strong liberal and

[1] See http://imdb.com/title/tt0195685/quotes (accessed June 14, 2007). Throughout this chapter, we usually leave spelling and punctuation as found at the Internet Movie DataBase (IMDB) and correct quotations only when the IMDB diverges from the soundtrack of the DVD. The script called for Ms. Roberts to say "BECAUSE THEY ARE!" rather than "cause they are!" (Susannah Grant, *Erin Brockovich – The Shooting Script* [New York: Newmarket Press, 2000], p. 111), but both the DVD subtitles and the DVD soundtrack go with "Because they are."

[2] See http://www.script-o-rama.com/movie_scripts/n/north-country-script-transcript-theron.html (accessed June 8, 2006).

[3] This includes *Class Action, A Civil Action, The Insider, The Rainmaker*, and *Runaway Jury*.

Our title inverts the title of the classic book on "cause lawyers" by Stuart Scheingold and Austin Sarat, *Something to Believe In: Politics, Professionalism, and Cause Lawyers* (Stanford: Stanford University Press, 2005). We imply both that cinematic lawyers representing wronged clients do not seem highly motivated by social values and, consequently, that the viewing public has little reason for faith in them. Plaintiffs' attorneys have and are nothing to believe in.

pro-lawyer bias. These films, we are told, portray modern mass corporations and other large entities as lawless symbionts driven by the amoral and immoral pursuit of profits and awash in reckless and unaccountable perfidies. At the same time, these films purportedly portray the "trial lawyer as (the) hero" who most successfully challenges the corporation, its unlawful practices, or its owners.[4] In this common reading, contemporary films offer simplistic narratives celebrating left-wing cause lawyering on behalf of victimized American consumers and workers.[5]

Such "good press" for cause lawyers would, if plausible, be a novel development in U.S. cultural history. For one thing, abundant scholarship has documented that Americans long have tended to be ambivalent about lawyers, especially civil attorneys.[6] This ambivalence has been reflected and expressed especially in feature films about civil lawsuits, which for the most part have traditionally sided both with litigators and with critics of litigiousness.[7] Plots and characterizations in classic American films have tended to track predictable beliefs and attitudes among movie audiences habituated to positive and negative characterizations of lawyers in U.S. society. Long-standing love-hate attitudes imbued classic films long before class action suits became common: across from Atticus Finch in *To Kill a Mockingbird*, a prosecutor snarls sexual innuendo at an innocent defendant; in *Counsellor at Law* (1933) John Barrymore's character is part-shyster and part-shrink for his clientele; Henry Drummond and Matthew Harrison Brady are each heroes and villains in different sections of an audience for cinematic renderings of *Inherit the Wind*.[8] Such ambivalence has arguably

[4] See: Larry E. Ribstein, "Wall Street and Vine: Hollywood's View of Business" (September 14, 2005). *University of Illinois Law & Economics Research Paper No. LE05–010*. Available at SSRN: http://ssrn.com/abstract=563181 or DOI: 10.2139/ssrn.563181; 1999; Richard Chase, "Civil Action Cinema." *Michigan State University Law Review* (1999):945; Philip Lopate, "The Corporation as Fantasy Villain," *New York Times*. April 9, 2000, p. 24.

[5] In presenting findings about cultural bashing of litigation and lawyers in our recent book (William Haltom and Michael McCann, *Distorting the Law: Politics, Media, and the Litigation Crisis*, Chicago: University of Chicago Press, 2004), the most commonly raised question concerned how the movies we address here seemed to counter other press. This was one motivation for writing this essay.

[6] Haltom and McCann 2004, Ch. 4; Marvin Mindes and Alan Acock, "Trickster, Hero, Helper: A Report on the Lawyer Image," *American Bar Foundation Research Journal* 6 (1982):177–233.

[7] Chase 1997; Michael Asimow, "Bad Lawyers in the Movies," *Nova Law Review* 24 (Winter 2000):533–84; Richard Sherwin, *When Law Goes Pop: The Vanishing Line between Law and Popular Culture* (Chicago: University of Chicago Press, 2000).

[8] Note that we here use two examples from films about *criminal* trials, not civil actions.

intensified in the last few decades. Civil litigators and litigation in general have taken a beating in multiple media.[9] Scurrilous jokes about predacious lawyers, fraudulent claimants, credulous jurors, permissive judges, unpredictable standards, and unconscionable costs have saturated the public space as rules, precedents, and practices have opened courthouses to plaintiffs and exacerbated long-standing pejorative characterizations of Bench and Bar.[10]

Cued by these contradictory readings of recent cultural trends, we offer a complex and decidedly ambiguous interpretation of two recent, and we think representative, films about public interest litigation challenging corporate power. In these films, corporations and conventional lawyers alike are portrayed negatively as heartless, profit-driven monoliths. By contrast, ordinary people emerge as sympathetic, innocent victims wronged by the large institutions. Yet, as the epigraphs from the two movies above suggest, lawyers[11] and lawyering for these victimized consumers take very serious lumps on the screen. Popular films render in simplistic, mostly unflattering terms the lawyers' motives, skills, connection to the legal profession, and relations with clients – all features of cause lawyering that scholars treat complexly and often sympathetically. Attorneys who represent injured

[9] See www.overlawyered.com; http://www.pointoflaw.com; http://cgood.org; Max Boot, *Out of Order: Arrogance, Corruption and Incompetence on the Bench* (New York: Basic Books, 1998); Patrick M. Garry, *A Nation of Adversaries: How the Litigation Explosion is Reshaping America* (Boulder, CO: Perseus Publishing, 1997); John Stossel, "The Trouble with Lawyers," ABC Special, 1997; Lester Brickman, "On the Relevance of the Admissibility of Scientific Evidence: Tort System Outcomes Are Principally Determined by Lawyers' Rates of Return," *Cardozo Law Review* 15 (1994):1755–97; Philip K. Howard, *The Death of Common Sense: How Law Is Suffocating America* (New York: Random House, 1994); Peter W. Huber, *Liability: A Legal Revolution and Its Consequences* (New York: Basic Books, 1990); Mary Ann Glendon, *Rights Talk: The Impoverishment of Political Discourse* (New York: Free Press, 1991); Walter K. Olson, *The Litigation Explosion: What Happened When America Unleashed the Lawsuit* (New York: Truman Talley Books, 1991).

[10] Marc Galanter, *Lowering the Bar: Lawyer Jokes and Legal Culture* (Madison: University of Wisconsin Press, 2005).

[11] Although we are mindful of the problems in defining the label "public interest lawyers," the lawyers in the films discussed here fit common usage. The films that we consider in the chapter feature lawyers who self-consciously represent victims injured by negligent, harmful practices of large entities. The lawyers have chosen to direct their practices to helping these underrepresented denizens of small means, often for quite small or uncertain monetary return. The motives and tactics of the lawyers are often mixed, but that reflects real-life complexities (see Scheingold and Sarat 2005) and provides fodder for often exaggerated or simplistic cinematic dramatization.

victims in movies are framed in terms familiar for private attorneys generally; they tend to fit right in with officials who injure citizens and societies, defense attorneys who are cunning when not sleazy, judges who are corrupt or incompetent, and other archetypes of cinematic civil justice run amok. Repeatedly, lawyers battling for some public interest are portrayed on celluloid as incapable of securing any semblance of justice or satisfaction for their clients or for anyone else. Only through the interventions of "outside" agents – almost always morally upright, ordinary people who are not lawyers and frequently are female – are plaintiffs' attorneys in most films saved from their ineptitude and judicial institutions saved from imminent injustices. *In sum, although these films offer up images of victims, causes, lawyers, and idealistic heroes, they do not include what many of us might recognize as idealistic* ***cause lawyers*** *whose campaigns for victims are worthy of study, much less celebration as heroes.*

The essay begins with extensive analysis of the most prominent public interest litigation film, *Erin Brockovich*, to establish in detail how it derides lawyers for the underdogs in the United States, even while it endorses the responsiveness of the larger legal system to good, ordinary Americans victimized by corporate greed and to one extraordinary outsider to law who fights for them. A less detailed look at a more recent film, *North Country*, confirms the general themes but also reveals some interesting variations. Taken together, these analyses cast doubt on any claims that contemporary cinematic outputs make up for the poor press under which the system of civil justice in general and cause lawyers representing ordinary victims in particular labor. We conclude the essay with some more complex reflections on the implications of our argument.

II. *Erin Brockovich* as Populist Cartoon

> Brockovich: "I admit I don't know shit about shit but I know right from wrong!"[12]

Critics of civil justice in the United States would not be vigilant if they failed to notice the popularity of *Erin Brockovich* and the massive payouts

[12] See http://imdb.com/title/tt0195685/quotes (accessed on June 2, 2006). Quotation from the IMDB slightly corrected to match DVD release.

that the Pacific Gas and Electric Company (PG&E) issued plaintiffs and their lawyers. Advocates who routinely brandish "tort tales" to lampoon public interest causes and class action lawyers could scarcely be indifferent to a toxic tort tale in which sympathetic, hard-working victims reluctantly agree to sue a deep-pocketed, powerful corporation that injured them and their children and deviously and duplicitously sought to avoid responsibility for poisoning the water supply. Even worse for critics, this cinematic narrative featured an Oscar-winning turn by Julia Roberts and worldwide distribution via cable and satellite, VHS and DVD. Might this narrative shape attitudes toward public interest groups and cause lawyers or pollute future jury pools?

Setback for jural critics that *Erin Brockovich* may have been, the movie does not praise trial lawyers or cause lawyering so much as it scorns them. On screens, the unwavering common sense and unyielding common decency of a courageous, dedicated newcomer to civil litigation win the day and the case. A feeling but flawed everywoman wrests case and cause from unfeeling, ineffective barristers on every side and at every turn. Ed Masry (Albert Finney) never asks why and perhaps never knew that medical records were interspersed in a real estate transaction between PG&E and his client, Donna Jensen (Marg Helgenberger plays this focal victim and plaintiff); it is his eponymous file clerk who knows and asks why. Brockovich, not any lawyer, catches PG&E concealing its introduction of hexavalent chromium into the local water supply. Despite Masry's energetic efforts to abandon the case, Brockovich reveals why and for what PG&E should be named and blamed. Little wonder that victims and plaintiffs credit Brockovich, believe in her because she believed in them, and distrust the ineffective, unsympathetic, often diffident Masry. Whatever encomia *Erin Brockovich* offers to civil justice, the film offers almost none to Masry or other plaintiffs' attorneys.

Jensen: "You're a lawyer?"
Brockovich: "NO, no. . . . I hate lawyers. I only work for them."[13]

Lead attorney Masry bumbles into the movie as an overconfident, incompetent ambulance chaser. He evolves through the plot from frivolous solicitor to feckless barrister to fatuous advocate saved from his lawyerly

[13] See http://imdb.com/title/tt0195685/quotes (accessed on June 2, 2006).

ineptitude and moral indifference by the "tutelage" of plucky tyro Brockovich. Brockovich surmounts procedural and tactical obstacles that daunted Masry, then explains to Masry the facts of the case and justice of the cause. Far from a noble cause lawyer, Masry resembles through most of the movie a pejorative stereotype, a lawyer joke.

> Dallavale: "Okay, look, I think we got off on the wrong foot here . . . "
> Brockovich: "That's all you got, lady. Two wrong feet and fucking ugly shoes."[14]

And Masry gets off easier than trial lawyers in general and other lawyers on the plaintiffs' side. The former beauty queen and single mother of three acquaints a high-powered class action veteran (Kurt Potter, played by Peter Coyote) with the bare-bones, back-breaking researches that many moviegoers might have expected lawyers to undertake or to oversee. Lawyer Potter is genially baffled until Brockovich wises him up. Potter's young, female assistant counsel (Theresa Dallavale, played by Veanne Cox) is battered gratuitously and repeatedly by Brockovich.[15] The film first accentuates the young attorney's shortcomings as confidante and as champion of the Hinkley victims – talents and traits that an empathetic layperson would be expected to bring to the team; it then trumpets Brockovich's manifest superiority in researching the case and preparing the clients – talents and traits that lay moviegoers would expect of a lawyer.

Of course, corporate defense attorneys generally and PG&E lawyers specifically take harder lumps, so to that extent critics of cause lawyering have a point. The victims' lawyers are inept; PG&E's lawyers are venal. Brockovich and Masry confront PG&E representatives who are by turns callow, dismissive, patronizing, and frightening. In one sly scene, Brockovich bests and berates a female lead attorney. Throughout the movie, Masry denigrates corporations' and their attorneys' motives and methods.

[14] See http://imdb.com/title/tt0195685/quotes (accessed on June 2, 2006).

[15] Ms. Brockovich and the screenwriter may be protected by their sex from suspicions of misogyny, but the director is not. Brockovich abuses the lead defense attorney, another woman, later in the film; explains her success in securing clients' cooperation by stating that she performed sexual favors; and calls a heavy-set female superior at Masry's office "Krispy Kreme." This thread of woman-bashing may make Brockovich seem more common or even vulgar and may build some identification among some moviegoers. Nonetheless, it seems unnecessary and distasteful at multiple places.

If we restrict our gaze to women in *Erin Brockovich*, the rout of jural insiders by an ordinary outsider stuns us. Brockovich combines brassy jewelry and sassy outfits, moral outrage and mother courage. By contrast, female attorneys Dallavale and Sanchez are reserved, formal professionals seemingly lacking in conscience, common sense, or the human touch. The appearances and wardrobes of the two female attorneys most prominent in the film are reduced absolutely, not merely relative to the heroine's flashy flesh. Brockovich's combination of sexuality and humanity with street smarts overwhelms the female attorneys' professional distance, book learning, and icy, desexualized demeanors.

Brockovich: "All you lawyers do is complicate situations that aren't complicated."[16]

Denouncing plaintiffs and defendants alike, *Erin Brockovich* provides barristers almost no opportunities to strut their stuff in courtrooms. So completely do laypeople dominate the film and power the lawsuit that lawyers square off in a courtroom for a mere 100 seconds of screen time.[17] Once an erstwhile PG&E employee provides Brockovich documents that prove that PG&E managers knew that its Hinkley operations had created a poisonous chromium plume, the results ($333,000,000 for the plaintiffs) issue from arbitration so quickly as to be almost anticlimactic. No adroit tactics or courtroom theatrics force Brockovich and other laypersons to share the spotlight with lawyers. The film leaves no doubt that its title identified the most valuable player.

Brockovich: "Annabelle Daniels . . . 10 years old, 11 in May. Lived on the plume since birth. Wanted to be a synchronized swimmer so she spent every minute she could in the PG&E pool. She had a tumor in her brain stem detected last November, an operation last Thanksgiving, shrunk it with radiation after that. Her parents are Ted & Rita. Ted's got Crohn's disease, Rita has chronic headaches, and nausea, and underwent a hysterectomy last fall . . . "[18]

16 Derived by the authors from the soundtrack and captions of the DVD.

17 This figure was created via a laptop counter from a DVD release. Counters may vary, so perhaps the more precise figure would be from 95 to 105 seconds. The preliminary hearing regarding PG&E's 84 motions was the only action, other than Brockovich's automobile case, in a courtroom, although negotiations and meetings were dramatized.

18 See http://imdb.com/title/tt0195685/quotes (accessed June 2, 2006). Spelling and punctuation as at the IMDB.

The merest beginning of Brockovich's improbable total recall of maladies and tragedies presumably generates sympathy for victims and plaintiffs and anger against PG&E. Worse for critics, *Erin Brockovich* contradicts decades of complaints about frivolous litigation and fraudulent litigants to show working people injured by corporations and their legal mercenaries. Donna Jensen as the plain-spoken, plainly dressed, just plain good lead plaintiff is the opposite of a greedy, malingering plaintiff playing the victim for attention and profit. Annabelle Daniels is the quintessential innocent battling the consequences of toxic torts and corporate cover-ups thereof. Probably necessary to ensure that moviegoers root for the plaintiff, such identification of common heroes and corporate villains is as much a feature of *Erin Brockovich* as of most dramas about class actions. In this respect and to this degree, those who claim that Hollywood assists trial attorneys and obstructs reform of civil justice may be correct. Such critics' reliance on "common sense" legislation, moreover, may be inverted by this movie. In the film injured innocents receive recompense due solely to the efforts of a lay, unemployed, vulgar former beauty queen who averted family catastrophes via common sense when the ordinary workings of the civil justice system would have foredoomed the victims.

Potter: "Wha . . . how did you do this?"
Brockovich: "Well, um, seeing as how I have no brains or legal expertise, . . . I just went out there and performed sexual favors. Six hundred and thirty-four blow jobs in five days. . . . I'm really quite tired."[19]

Nonetheless, *Erin Brockovich* posited that innocent victims of immorality and bottom-lines who named the blameworthy and claimed some recompense would be set upon by cold, adversarial, cunning, and amoral attorneys on every side. That plaintiffs were innocents afflicted by merciless mercenaries and that corporations employed lawyers to press "Scorched Earth, Wall of Flesh" tactics[20] suited an expectation that Hollywood tends to lionize civil plaintiffs and to demonize civil defendants (and their attorneys) more than print or broadcast news media tend to do. By contrast, critics seem to have missed that *Erin Brockovich* also scored trial attorneys as faint-hearted advocates who often betray the interests of ordinary people (such as those in theater seats), as feckless bumblers as likely to harm as to

[19] See http://imdb.com/title/tt0195685/quotes (accessed June 2, 2006).
[20] We derived the name for this second motif from Zegart (2000:85).

help victims, and as privileged profiteers so imbued with their own learning and importance or greed that they can neither serve their clients nor even socialize with them. No cause lawyers or public interest attorneys or plaintiffs' lawyers would welcome this portrait. Nor is it likely to please advocates for public interests to see that one of their own must be saved from surrender or defeat by a foul-talking, flesh-baring, poorly educated everywoman blithely ignorant of legal doctrines and jurisprudential theories but proudly possessed of decency and common sense.

III. *North Country*: Lawyer Without a Cause

We have elsewhere demonstrated that the motifs outlined above are common in contemporary films about public interest litigation.[21] We turn here to just one of these films, because it complicates the image of lawyers for causes yet further and so deserves focused scrutiny. *North Country* (2005) provides a loose account of *Jenson v. Eveleth Mines*, the first sexual harassment class action lawsuit. This dispute involved harm to female workers rather than to innocent consumers, but the legal struggle against unaccountable corporate power is parallel to *Erin Brockovich* in many ways. Compelled to employ women, some mine executives make more miserable the already difficult conditions under which the women have to work, whereas other executives look the other way as male miners embarrass, intimidate, assault, and otherwise degrade women who dare to work alongside the men.

After employee Josie Aimes (Charlize Theron) is stymied through every official channel and shunned by other miners, including female miners, she pleads with attorney Bill White (Woody Harrelson) to take her case. Cynical, fatalistic, and worn down by earlier litigation that failed to help victims, Mr. White agrees to do so. Ms. Aimes's father, her co-workers male and female, company executives, and defense attorneys vie to be viler to Ms. Aimes than others.[22] Only when ordinary people, especially women in the

[21] See our longer essay, "Ordinary Heroes vs. Failed Lawyers – Public Interest Litigation in Eight Contemporary Films," forthcoming in *Law & Social Inquiry*, 2008.

[22] In this respect and others, *North Country* goes far easier on the female attorney for the defense of Eveleth Mines than the book did. The original book version (Clara Bingham and Laura Leedy Gansler, *Class Action: The Story of Lois Jenson and the Landmark Case That Changed Sexual Harassment Law*, New York: Anchor, 2003) makes Mary Stumo a horror. In comparison to the nonfiction book, then the movie lets the defense off lightly, just as studies have found that newspaper reports do.

courtroom, begin to stand beside her does the plaintiff gain the small class action that the professional but heartless lead attorney for the mines (chosen for her gender) forewarned the company head that the company must lose.

North Country is, as its closing credits declaim, "inspired by the book titled *Class Action: The Landmark Case That Changed Sexual Harassment Law*" and dedicated to the women who began a fight in the Mesabi Range that resonated around the world. But the movie diverges sharply from the book in ways that are much more likely to make it resonate throughout the legal culture.[23] Some divergences bear on the general points of this chapter, but do not directly concern cause lawyers. In the book, which purports to be the true story,[24] the will-be plaintiff is a more complex working-class woman than the angelic victim portrayed by Charlize Theron[25]; the lead attorney for the defense of Eveleth Mines is more loathsome in her efforts to win at any costs – especially costs to the plaintiffs or their attorneys – than the determined but professional defense attorney who leaves most of the perfidy in *North Country* to executives at the top and co-workers at the bottom of the company; the formation and maintenance of the class of plaintiffs are far more difficult than getting two women to agree with the singular plaintiff that harassment was persistent and pervasive; and judges and arbiters are far less tolerant of circus stunts in court than the cheesy tactic with which the movie climaxes. Some such changes, of course, are to be expected when a nonfiction book is transformed into a highly fictionalized Hollywood film, especially one with two previous winners of the Oscar for Best Actress.[26]

> Josey Aimes: "I need a lawyer. I wanna sue the mine. The company. All of them."
> Bill White: "Well, good luck with that."

[23] Near the opening of the film, words in the center of the screen state that the movie is "inspired by a true story," which hyperliteralists among the audience may take to imply that what follows is hardly true.

[24] Bingham and Gansler 2002.

[25] We acknowledge and thank Professor Susan Sterrett for alerting us to this discrepancy.

[26] Nonetheless, we note that the script and film truncate if not attenuate the abuses and indignities that the women suffered, bowdlerize the behavior of the lead defense attorney, and omit the foibles of one or more adjudicators. Perhaps necessary for marketing the movie or making it seem realistic, these choices at the very least ill-favor trial lawyers or those opposed to reform of civil justice in the United States. If the plaintiff is "cleaned up" for the movie, that may make her a more welcome plaintiff from the points of view of trial lawyers and opponents of most reforms. We see little evidence, in sum, that *North Country* remedies disadvantages that plaintiffs and their lawyers endure in news media.

Aimes: "I'm saying I wanna hire you."
White: "Sorry, don't do that anymore."
Aimes: "That sucks, because you're the only lawyer I ever met."
White: "Well, the good news is, all roads lead to lawyers."[27]

However, the particular logic of the fictional transformation fits and fortifies simplistic stereotypes and popular scripts. The transformation of the real-life plaintiffs' lawyers who sustained the first class action sexual harassment suit[28] into loner-lawyer Bill White (Woody Harrelson) partakes of the pattern we have derived and defined already in *Erin Brockovich*. Through most of the movie, White is the epitomic cinematic trial lawyer: battered and beaten by the legal system, cynical and pessimistic about obtaining justice through litigation, uninterested in if not indifferent to the women's travails, and dubious about his ability to do anything heroic or good outside a hockey rink. The first attorney to take up Lois Jenson's real-world cause, by contrast, was an idealistic, energetic lawyer working in the Minnesota Attorney General's Office who eventually was driven out by the vileness of the miners and executives and by the viciousness of the first defense attorney for the mines.[29] The lead attorney who pushed the landmark case after the state of Minnesota largely let it go was an accomplished specialist in employment discrimination litigation, sought after by victims and feared by the mines and their lawyers. When real-life plaintiffs Lois Jenson (to be transformed into Charlize Theron's character) and Pat Kosmach (Frances McDormand's character) drove to consult with Paul Sprenger, he was listed in *The Best Lawyers in America* (Bingham and Gansler 2002: 141–155). No viewer would imagine Bill White was so listed.[30] Any of these real-life attorneys might qualify for cause lawyer status. We learn that White himself once championed causes as a progressive lawyer,

[27] We derived the dialogue from http://www.script-o-rama.com/movie_scripts/n/north-country-script-transcript-theron.html (accessed June 8, 2006). Punctuation and spelling follow that source.

[28] As filed in U. S. District Court in Minnesota on August 15, 1988, the case was styled *Lois E. Jenson and Patricia S. Kosmach v. Eveleth Tacomite Co.* (Bingham and Gansler 2002: 163). The larger corporate entity involved was Oglebay Norton.

[29] Bingham and Gansler 2002: 115–35.

[30] In addition to lawyers in his own firm, Sprenger brought in Greg Wolsky, a specialist in malpractice litigation, to handle Oglebay Norton's unremitting depositions to discover any health or other information that might tamp down what each member of the class could recover. See Bingham and Gansler 2002: 286.

but a costly loss soured him on idealistic legal crusades. He is less a "lost cause" lawyer of the sort Sarat identifies than a cause lawyer who has lost his way in life.

> White (on Aimes's doorstep): "Can you get the other women? (at her kitchen table) You know what a class action is? It's when a bunch of plaintiffs have the same issue. File a claim on behalf of the whole group, the class. It's tough for the company to argue that you're all lying; you're all crazy. It's why you have to get the others."
> Aimes: "Why'd you change your mind?"
> White: "It's never been done before. Sexual harassment class action."
> Aimes: "So you'd be doing this just because it's never been done."
> White: "Yeah. Can you live with that?"[31]

After one minute and twenty-five seconds (screen time) of barroom banter about how herds increase the longevity of their members who otherwise would perish separately, White darkens Aimes's doorstep with an offer of legal assistance premised on the novelty of the class action. This scene flatters neither White nor cause lawyers nor class actions. Lest that disparagement be lost on any viewer, White's barroom discussion makes his shyster, as opposed to resigned, side explicit.[32] White's crass motive differs greatly from the motives attributed first to Helen Rubenstein, the lawyer in the Minnesota AG's Office, and then to Paul Sprenger, Jane Lang, and Jean Boler, the team that waged the class action.[33] These lawyers believed that the abuses were extreme,[34] that the union and the executives were at best indifferent to the hostile environment and at worst sympathetic to the abusers, and that without legal representation the hostility and abuses would increase. Viewers well informed about the actualities of litigation would likely regard White's barratry as a filmic flourish utterly unrepresentative

[31] As above, punctuation and spelling follow http://www.script-o-rama.com/movie_scripts/n/north-country-script-transcript-theron.html (accessed June 8, 2006) except that "You're all crazy" was treated as a discrete sentence in that script, but in apposition to "you're all lying" in the DVD release.

[32] See the second epigraph for this essay.

[33] Bingham and Gansler 2002:112–51.

[34] In fairness to the makers of *North Country*, their decision to tone down the loathsome, despicable, depraved acts and words that unrelentingly wracked the women at the mines may have limited Bill White's understanding of just how hostile the environment was and of just how abused the women were. See Bingham and Gansler (2002:116–17) for a brief summary of the outrages.

of the rigors of pursuing cases through either bureaucracies or courts. Less informed viewers, however, might accept it as fulfillment of a hoary stereotype about trial lawyers.

Leslie Conlin (lawyer for the mining company): "... how do you know who to believe in a situation like that?"
White: "Your honor, is she kidding with that question? Maybe she could ask if he likes piña coladas and walks in the rain."
Judge: "Are you kidding with that objection, Mr. White? Because it's denied."

Before playing on his long-ago experiences as a hockey star to set up a cowardly predator and perjurer, White lurches from sardonic comments sarcastically rejected by the reasonably tolerant judge to desperate arguments and objections. To be sure, the proceedings in *Jenson v. Eveleth Mines* took many turns and challenged Lois Jenson's attorneys. As should be expected by now, however, those lawyers manifested exactly none of the world weariness or scorn for the proceedings that White exudes. The closest approximation to this dramatization would have been Helen Rubenstein, who was worn down by unrelieved baseness from executives and employees of the mines and by unrelenting delays and subterfuges by the legal representatives for the mines.

White: "Look, Josey, the illusion is that all your problems are solved in the courtroom. The reality is that even when you win, you don't win."
Aimes: "I know, but I'm right."
White: "I'm sure you are, but right has nothing to do with the real world. Look at Anita Hill. Because she's you. You think you're outgunned at the mine, wait till you get to the courtroom. It's called the 'nuts and sluts defense.' You're either nuts and you imagined it, or a slut and you asked for it."[35]

No reasonable analyst would expect a feature film to capture the nuances of a lawsuit bifurcated into a judge's finding of a hostile work environment for the class followed by a special master's determination of damages due each member of the class and so on. That concession to the exigencies

[35] From http://www.script-o-rama.com/movie_scripts/n/north-country-script-transcript-theron.html (accessed June 8, 2006).

of movie-making, however, must be accompanied by the acknowledgment that *North Country* shows neither Bill White nor anyone else patiently engaged in the arduous and arcane processes of determining damages,[36] then pursuing appeals, all the while striving to induce the parent corporation to settle out of court. As in so many (but not all) civil justicc films, the celebratory ending of the movie was far from the ending of the dispute. In this sense, *North Country* specifically and Hollywood generally make litigation look easy, short, and revelatory, once the ordinary heroes stand up together for the cause.

Having defined the path along which *North Country* diverges from the nonfiction book that inspired it, we should not be surprised that the movie follows the formula of *Erin Brockovich* and other Hollywood movies. We nonetheless can and do underline that the cinematic formula followed in *North Country* is utterly at odds with the facts that presumably "presold" the plot, the types of facts that lead socio-legal scholars to nuanced, respectful, politically acute analysis. As lawyer Ransom Stoddard (James Stewart) learns in the movie classic, *The Man Who Shot Liberty Valance*, when the legend has become fact, market-savvy producers publish the legend.

IV. Variations on Class[ic] American Populist Romance

Films are cultural artifacts that reproduce yet often complicate and even disturb prevailing cultural narratives. We agree with many other scholars that films are indeterminate constructs that are open to competing interpretations and normative assessments or inferences. At the same time, we tend to think that the dramatic motifs identified in this essay are potentially significant because they resonate with classic themes in the American tradition of populist social romance. Our analysis here considers the profound fidelity to these themes and their complex implications. The exploration in this section takes us deeper into the ambivalences and ambiguities about law, lawyers, and romantic desires for alternative heroes with which we introduced this essay. It may help explain why cultural representations fail to imagine cause lawyers in the ways that scholars do.

[36] Note that *Erin Brockovich* skips the calculus by which Donna Jenson and her husband received $5,000,000.

The romantic tradition suggests both a literature of artistic production and critical perspectives toward it. The critical tradition has emerged from exchanges among writers themselves as well as from scholars; it is identified in the last century with D. H. Lawrence and William Carlos Williams, was amplified by Cold War scholars like Leslie Fiedler and Richard Chase, and diversified by later feminist, critical race, postmodern, and other perspectives.[37] This tradition has tended to provide a counterpoint to the alternative traditions in social science analysis that celebrate American pragmatism and borrow from the logics of interests, markets, and rationality they claim to find through study.[38] The classics of the American literary tradition tend instead to describe fantasies, but they often are fantasies deeply embedded in and enacted through actual collective life. In this sense, we join others urging the forging of connections between these traditions in efforts to understand American politics and law.

Scholars make sense of those romantic fantasies in a variety of ways. An earlier generation of scholarship began with Marx, who showed how bourgeois society divides citizen life between self-interest and the communal aspiration, between commodity logic and civic virtue.[39] Each of the former is concrete and deeply embedded in material practice; each of the latter an abstract ideal that dominates the heavenly domain of ideology, routinely legitimating and normalizing the gross asymmetries of organized power in material life. Other scholars have drawn on Freud, feminism, critical race theory, and poststructural theory, among other traditions, to make sense of populist fables. The fantasies themselves take many familiar forms – regenerative violence, homoerotic bonding, commodity fetishism, wilderness escape. The triumph of the heroic outsider to law who can reconcile heavenly ideals with egoistic practice, communal virtue with material interest, the garden with the commodity machine in its midst, has powered our popular literature in the last century – from the classic pioneer frontiersman to the cowboy western to the detective story to superhero fables to the contemporary films we analyze here. Such fantasies often reproduce and confirm dominant ideological constructs, but they also often expose

[37] Michael P. Rogin, *"Ronald Reagan," the Movie, and Other Episodes in Political Demonology* (Berkeley: University of California Press, 1987).

[38] Rogin 1987: Ch. VI.

[39] "On the Jewish Question," in Lawrence H. Simon, ed., *Karl Marx: Selected Writings* (Indianapolis: Hackett Publishing Company, 1973).

clashes between prevailing cultural narratives and actual practices as well as among conflicting ideas and cultural norms themselves. Both words and images in cinematic texts often generate great emotional power as well as thematic substance meriting intellectual reflection.

1. Cinematic Heroes and the Individualization of Struggle

Populist romance tends to be inherently ambiguous about politics. On the one hand, romances simplify the contemporary social world into a dramatic moral battle of heroes vs. villains, saints vs. sinners, and in recent decades, workaday Davids vs. corporate Goliaths. "She brought a small town to its feet and a huge company to its knees," proclaims the tagline for publicity of *Erin Brockovich*. There is something to be said for this moralistic populism. The films we have examined display the workings of institutional power in corporations and governments in bald and bold fashion. Indeed, they identify manifestations of hierarchical power on a level that makes most social science and professional legal scholarship look innocuous if not complicit, while making corporate apologists nearly apoplectic. Large institutions are portrayed as causing massive harm, including death, and then rigging the legal system to protect the status quo. We rarely see corporate executives,[40] but their legal representatives tend to be as cold, smug, and deceitful as they are well coiffed. Most defense attorneys are portrayed similarly, the symbols of the corporate greed and reckless disregard for others that they represent in law. In these stories, commodification, the profit motive, and patriarchy run rampant at cost to the natural environment, human bodies, and civil society. We should not overlook the degree to which these feature films speak some semblance – however moralistic, simplistic, and self-righteous – of truth to power in ways that cause lawyers on the Left might celebrate.[41]

[40] Exceptions include *Class Action* and *The Rainmaker*. The latter film features insurance executives as slimy and sociopathic as the defense attorneys. *Class Action* features a defense attorney who is the moral-legal heroine surmounting unethical defense attorneys and Fred Dalton Thompson as an executive indifferent to human suffering.

[41] Critics whom we cite at the start of this essay are on firm ground in alleging the simplistic terms of corporation-bashing in these films, especially regarding the source of evil (executives? capitalists? middle management? corporate bureaucracy itself?). Given the scale of corporate, material, cultural, and ideological power that renders consumers and workers so thoroughly dependent on them in modern society, the critical messages that the films convey may offset advantages little.

Moreover, such films at least indirectly register the failures of the official political system (legislatures, executives) and the scarcity of organized social groups (unions, social movements) to demand change, effectively promote justice, and aid victims, leaving litigation as one of the few avenues of action for relief. The startling lack of political mobilization from above or below in these films well captures the barren political landscape of modern mass society. Indeed, the most populist-oriented of these films express their starkly apolitical, or politically unorganized and unresponsive, contexts quite vividly in their portrayals of the physical landscape. *Erin Brockovich* repeatedly portrays the colorful heroine against sun-bleached images of the arid, baked, infertile, poisoned landscape of southern California, whereas *North Country* is shot in oppressively depressing gray tones that hover over the barren, snow-covered landscape or haunt interior scenes of underground workplaces. Legal action is highly fallible and the legal system highly flawed in these films, but there are few alternatives to litigation for the most palpable victims of unaccountable, reckless power. If there is a surprise in these legal dramas, it is that actual courtroom trials and jury deliberations – the fertile ground for individualized heroic duels in older films about law – are scarce and somewhat peripheral, with most of the action taking place in pretrial maneuverings among attorneys, clients, and adversaries. This too, it strikes us, is a small advance in portrayals of law in action.

On the other hand, by focusing narratives on individual villains and lone heroes, and specifically on professional elite sinners and innocent saints free or freed of professional roles and positioned outside of law, these movies reduce complex dimensions of social power to moral battles between individuals, where character determines outcomes and natural virtue assures success. "In a world where heroes are often in short supply, the story of Erin Brockovich is an inspirational reminder of the power of the human spirit," preaches the film's Web site. Innocence and purity of purpose demonstrated by lone outsiders to law alone enable justice to prevail in nearly every case. Such odes to innocence for the most part exclude cause lawyers, who, scholars reveal, must negotiate tensions between professionalism and politics, procedural convention and substantive transformation, law and justice. Moreover, movies reproduce and exaggerate the constraining tendencies of law itself to individualize struggles as dyadic disputes and morality plays in ways that fail to confront the multiple layers of power relationships at stake. While displaying the anemic political options for obtaining justice, these films thus ignore or erase the complex processes of group mobilization that are characteristic of most "politics of rights." At once reflecting and normalizing the larger social context of contemporary society, these movies look to moral purity for deliverance and away from politics for transformation.

2. Gender Play

The preceding points reflect a familiar set of observations about the political myopia of American populist romances.[42] But recent films represent several other novel, quite contemporary twists on traditional literary romance that deserve nuanced attention. Again, these novel dimensions are highly ambiguous in their implications.

The first theme we address concerns gender, especially the roles of women and their relationships to men. It is, perhaps, not surprising that these movies tend to feature women prominently as the primary victims of corporate harm. In both films we consider, women are the injured parties to whom lawyers and lawyer surrogates like Erin Brockovich speak to learn of physical and emotional injury. Whether they are cast as directly afflicted or indirectly suffering as mothers and widowed wives, female victims capture the actual indignities and physical travails often experienced in private, typically invisible lives. The focus on women underlines the dependence and relative powerlessness of citizens in a society organized by mega-corporate institutions. Moreover, these films clearly draw on traditional images of women, and their children, as dependents excluded from public roles to enhance the dramatic effects in promoting audience identification with victims of reckless power.

In classical American romance, of course, men typically have been the heroes who deliver such women from danger or harm (usually caused by other men). Classical American political romances have been written by men about men and for men; they are boys' fantasies. Men are, by contrast, usually the problem in contemporary films about law and lawyers challenging corporate-caused harms. Indeed, corporate boardrooms and the legal

[42] See Rogin 1987; Diane Waldman, "A Case for Corrective Criticism: A *Civil Action*," in Austin Sarat, Lawrence Douglas, and Martha Merrill Umphrey (eds.), *Law on the Screen* (Stanford: Stanford University Press, 2005):201–30.

profession alike tend to be portrayed as inherently men's worlds, motivated by heartless greed, duplicity, and reckless indifference to social welfare. The guys in the expensive suits and elevated suites run rampant above the law, often manipulating legal processes like puppeteers. Similarly, select (mostly professional) women, especially in *Erin Brockovich*, are skewered for becoming masculinized, or at least desexualized, giving into the male cultures in order to succeed. The one sphere of professional life dominated by men that does get good press is that of scientific health experts in *Erin Brockovich* and other such films about environmental contamination. Such specialists, usually working in university labs or hospitals, prove to be critical if not always effective allies of the forces promoting health and challenging corporate greed in all the films. This no doubt pleases liberal academics as much as it outrages defenders of corporate America who decry "junk science."

Most curious and important, we think, is that women are often the heroic outsiders to law who win the day for justice in recent films. Erin Brockovich and Josie Aimes (*North Country*) are heroines who completely dominate their films; Julia Roberts won an Academy Award for the former film, by far the highest profile role and most profitable movie that we consider, and Charlize Theron was nominated for an Academy Award in her role as the latter heroine. In each case, women play roles as skilled, resilient, resourceful, disciplined, and sympathetic agents who force the legal system to respect rights and do justice, outwit and undo corporate foes, and succeed where lawyers cannot or will not for victims. The emergence of female heroines in legal films follows or parallels larger changes in cinema and society over recent decades, of course. Feminists no doubt have found reason to cheer most of these heroic depictions. The story of Josie Aimes in *North Country* is the most clear-cut second-wave feminist parable, although the tale of heroic triumph produced surprisingly mixed reviews from critics (often claiming that males are portrayed too negatively) and mediocre box office returns. By contrast, Erin Brockovich's shameless use of sexual display to wield influence, her merciless assault on female lawyers and fellow women workers alike, and her self-righteous arrogance surely lace her heroic image with contradictions or at least ambiguities associated with third-wave feminism. In both cases, though, extraordinary ordinary women triumph over men who traditionally hold the reins of power above or within the law.

3. Redemption . . . Righting the Legal Fall from Grace

American populist romances inevitably culminate as dramas of redemption, especially in the salvation or transformation of flawed individuals who depart from core virtues. And in these films salvation does arrive. Most obviously and materially, the victims of corporate abuse extract some sort of material return and partial justice by film's end. Their innocence is repaid, and the system works, once the virtuous ordinary folk can make it live up to its promises. But equally interesting and perhaps more important, we think, is the process of conversion and/or redemption that these dramas imagine for flawed lawyers, usually as a result of contact with victims and/or ordinary heroes, again mostly women. This is quite palpable in *Erin Brockovich*, where the male lawyer, Masry, is "rehumanized" by Erin's tireless efforts; in the end, he recognizes her worth, pays her a huge bonus, and renews his own commitment to doing good while he is doing well as a personal injury attorney. The disillusioned, resigned lawyer in *North Country* is similarly saved from both his general cynicism and specific missteps at trial by the eventual legal victory, in the end emerging with renewed commitment to using law to do good. Similar themes imbue other films in this genre – *The Verdict*, *A Civil Action*, *Class Action*, *Runaway Jury*, and *The Rainmaker* are examples. These many variations on a theme add up, we note again, to a very powerful pattern of redemption in law wrought by (female) outsiders to law.

We offer one final point about this redemptive process. Ever since John Winthrop celebrated the "marriage bond" that united citizens and sanctified their brave venture on the Arabella, the idol of the family has been celebrated as a source of virtue and a metaphor for love or commitment in American culture. And so are family bonds the source of moral regeneration in most of these films. Virtually every female victim and heroic mother, with Erin and Josie in the lead, does all she can for her own and others' children.[43] If men are the sources of corrosive irresponsibility that weakens bonds, the mothers' union of private and public virtue rebuilds community on the foundation of familial care. Redress for widows

[43] We note, however, that Josie's commitment is far more consistent and credible than that of Erin, who leaves her children for long periods of time with virtual strangers and surrogate parents. Josie's heroic struggle is indistinguishable from her role as mother, whereas Erin's struggle to help other families leads her to neglect her own.

and parents, especially again for the virtuous female survivors, plays a role in many civil justice films. This is especially powerful in *North Country*, where Josie's case is won once her metaphorical sisters from work and her real father stand up on her behalf, inspired to make the real, proximate, and imagined communal family whole again. Indeed, the specific theme of daughters transforming or redeeming father figures looms large in *Erin Brockovich* and *North Country*.[44] In no other regard are the films considered here more typical of classical romances than in the fantastic portrayals of how private family bonds nurture, transform, and redeem the public life of law, regenerating virtue and triumphing over violence by the power of love. The films are complicated with regard to how they deal with the traditional, patriarchal foundation of liberal families, to be sure.[45] And there is some potential power in calls for familial love to infuse heart into the cold procedures of law, of course. But in the context of these films, audiences again are invited to indulge more personal wish fulfillment than sober reflection about the challenges confronting real-life advocates for social justice.

V. More Ambivalence: Scholarly Reflections on the Politics of Rights in the Mega-Corporate Age

American films generally promote ambiguous images and ideas about lawyers and the legal system. In the films we reviewed, citizens seek and usually win legal justice that redresses harms caused by corporate greed, but the legal system generally and defendants' and plaintiffs' attorneys specifically are portrayed in mostly derisive terms. Films reduce to simplistic, unflattering cartoons matters of lawyer motivation, professional identity, relationships with clients, and tactics of advocacy that socio-legal scholars have identified as far more complex, variable, and worthy of respect. Such demeaning cinematic images thus tend to confirm rather than complicate or challenge the undignified images of plaintiffs' attorneys representing ordinary people that we regularly see in news reporting, paid ads from

44 *The Sweet Hereafter*, of course, offers moviegoers very different interactions between daughters and fathers.

45 Erin Brockovich's persistence in building the case for suffering victims leads her to neglect her children considerably, often leaving them for long periods of time with nannies and then a male neighbor with whom she strikes up a curious, fleeting romance.

corporate groups, books by hired public intellectuals, and jokes or cartoons that saturate mass culture. Meanwhile, these films indulge in many other dimensions of romance – especially the faith that ordinary heroes and family values can make law deliver justice – that make cause lawyering both elusive and unnecessary. In such narratives, scholarly understandings of cause lawyers find little resonance and, in fact, make little sense.

Our position about the significance of our argument is ambivalent and admittedly unsettled. We cannot say with any confidence how these cinematic images and narratives are interpreted by most people in society. The ubiquity of the patterns is hard to ignore, but we can only speculate about the implications of such imagery and narratives that flood mass culture. On the one hand, to the extent that these films undermine a simplistic "myth of rights"[46] that lawyers and litigation can successfully render corporate power accountable and beneficent, we applaud them. If these films undermine faith in lawyers as unqualified moral heroes and nurture faith that ordinary people can struggle successfully for social justice, that is probably a good thing. If they support a more complex insight that lawyers and the legal system generally are most effective when they learn to understand and respond to the different worlds of meaning that their disadvantaged clients inhabit, we sing "Amen."

At the same time, these films express a moralistic populism that is simplistic, naïve, and bordering on reactionary. The tendency to focus indiscriminate attention on all professionals as heartless, often feckless villains or at least as small-minded hypocrites radically individualizes understandings about the multiple dimensions of hierarchical instrumental, institutional, and ideological power in modern society.[47] Treating select corporate managers and their legal defenders as cartoon villains reduces matters of corporate accountability to the moral failures of select "bad apples," whereas equating lawyers who challenge privilege with such privileged elites obscures the former's distinctive aspirations and variable achievements. Together, such individualistic obsessions erase attention to the complexities of political power and struggle in contemporary society. Indeed, these films fit easily with the familiar apolitical and antipolitical biases that

[46] Stuart A. Scheingold, *The Politics of Rights: Lawyers, Public Policy and Political Change*, 2nd ed. (Ann Arbor: University of Michigan Press, 2004).

[47] See Haltom and McCann 2004.

are deeply entrenched in American culture. Civil justice films thus are likely to encourage not only simplistic understandings but also cynicism about the type of complex collective action and committed legal activists necessary to narrow the huge gap between law and its promises of justice. That said, what else might we expect from the contemporary producers of commodified mass entertainment in the United States?

Acknowledgments

The authors wish to thank Howie Erlanger, Richard Sherwin, and everyone in the cause lawyering group – especially Austin Sarat, Stuart Scheingold, and William MacNeil – for comments on variants of this essay.

9

"Of course he just stood there; he's the law"

Two Depictions of Cause Lawyers in Post-Authoritarian Chile

Stephen Meili

"Of course he just stood there, he's the law."

– Paulina Lorca, *Death and the Maiden*

I. Introduction

Paulina Lorca's comment about Gerardo Escobar, her husband and a human rights lawyer in Roman Polanski's 1994 film *Death and the Maiden*, succinctly captures one way that cause lawyers have often been viewed within Chilean popular culture: they just stand there. This essay explores whether this cynical critique of cause lawyers has endured the decade of political upheaval, social transformation, and legal reform that followed *Death and the Maiden*, using the recently produced Chilean television drama *Justicia Para Todos* ("Justice for All") as a vehicle for comparison. In so doing, it focuses on two dilemmas consistently encountered by the cause lawyers in these fictionalized accounts: law vs. social justice and professionalism vs. public service.

This essay begins with a brief review of the legal reforms (primarily in the criminal law field) that followed the end of the Pinochet regime in Chile. It then describes the history of legal culture in Chile. The bulk of the essay analyzes *Death and the Maiden* and *Justicia Para Todos*, comparing the ways in which they depict the cause lawyers who figure prominently in the plots of each.[1] The essay concludes with a series of observations about cultural depictions of cause lawyers in post-authoritarian Chile that relate

[1] In their compelling essay on *Death and the Maiden* in this volume (see Chapter 10), Fleury-Steiner and Fichtelberg assert that Paulina Lorca, wife of human rights lawyer Gerardo Escobar, is a cause lawyer. This essay instead focuses solely on a more traditional category of cause lawyers: those who are licensed to practice law.

to the overall themes of this book. Throughout, the essay refers to enduring themes of the Cause Lawyering Project that these depictions bring to mind.

II. Post-Authoritarian Chilean Legal Reforms

The end of Chile's military dictatorship in 1990 brought about numerous changes in civil society, including a series of reforms within the nation's legal system. The most significant of these occurred in criminal law and procedure, which is hardly surprising given the military regime's brutal violation of human rights and systemic denial of due process.[2] For the vast majority of the twentieth century, criminal prosecution in Chile was conducted according to the inquisitorial system inherited from the postcolonial era. Under this system, judges both investigated and ruled on criminal matters. All proceedings were conducted via written submissions rather than arguments in open court. The entire process was secretive and "flew in the face of due process and a fair trial."[3]

In 2000, after nearly a decade of legislative debate, Chile adopted a series of criminal law and procedural reforms that were phased in over the ensuing four years. The result is a system that would look familiar to many Americans: separate functions for judges and prosecutors and the creation of two new institutions: (1) the office of the Public Prosecutor, which investigates crimes with the assistance of the police (and enjoys the discretion to choose which cases to prosecute); and (2) the office of the Public Defender, which represents defendants through all aspects of the case. The reforms also include public, pretrial hearings and trials before judges. All criminal defendants are entitled to legal representation and must be brought before a judge for a preliminary hearing within twenty-four hours of their arrest. Preventive detention is the exception rather than the norm. Defendants (or their attorneys) are permitted to produce, review, assess, and object to evidence, as well as cross-examine adverse witnesses. Victims are also afforded greater rights under the reforms: they have the right to contest the proposed resolution of a case and may agree to reparations.[4]

[2] Lisa Hilbink, "An Exception to Chilean Exceptionalism? The Historical Role of Chile's Judiciary," in *What Justice? Whose Justice?*, ed. S. Eckstein and T. Wickham-Crowley (Berkeley: University of California Press, 2003).

[3] Diego Portales School of Law, *Annual Report on Human Rights in Chile 2003*.

[4] Id.

The overall purpose of these reforms appears to be twofold. First, and most obvious, was the need to change the structure of the Chilean legal system. Yet perhaps just as important, given the nation's recent history, was the desire to emphasize the importance of human rights in a newly emerging democracy whose citizens would prefer to erase the memory of that history. As Diego Portales Law School's 2003 *Human Rights Report* in Chile puts it:

> While opinion polls would appear to indicate that human rights issues now rank low in the minds of Chileans, to a large extent this is due to the fact that in the public mind the concept tends to be almost exclusively associated with the massive, systematic rights violations of the past.
>
> [This] Report seeks to revert this trend by showing that human rights lie at the core of a democratic society and are inextricably linked to the lives of all individuals and groups.[5]

Thus, one view of the new criminal law system is that it is designed not only to protect the rights of the accused but also to serve as a bulwark against future authoritarian regimes and other state incursions against civil rights and due process.

III. Legal Culture in Chile

Any discussion of the cultural depiction of cause lawyers in Chile must be framed by two underlying observations about Chilean legal culture. First, Chileans – like many Latin Americans – harbor negative views of the judiciary and the overall legal system of which it is a part. They tend to see it not as a means of redress of individual grievances or protection of civil and human rights, but rather as another arm of official state repression, corporate control, and protection of private property.[6] After all, when the

[5] Id.

[6] Javier Couso, "The Changing Role of Law and Courts in Latin America: From an Obstacle to Social Change to a Tool of Social Equity." Paper presented at the Annual Meeting of the Law and Society Association, Baltimore, July 2006; Stephen Meili, "Latin American Cause Lawyering Networks," in *Cause Lawyering and the State in a Global Era*, ed. A. Sarat and S. Scheingold (New York: Oxford University Press: 2001); Yves Dezalay and Bryant Garth, "Chile: Law and the Legitimation of Transitions: From the Patrimonial State to the International Neo-Liberal State," *American Bar Foundation Working Paper*, 9709 (1998).

military overthrew the democratically elected government of Salvadore Allende in 1973, it explicitly did so in the name of the rule of law.[7] This negative perception is also based on Chile's civil law system, under which judges have traditionally (save for the decade from 1964 to 1973) exhibited little independence from the executive or interest in protecting or extending rights or striking down government policies.[8] The structure of the judiciary was top-down and hierarchical, virtually guaranteeing that judges would remain passive. Many Chileans have also historically believed that the judiciary is both inefficient and corrupt.[9]

Public opinion polls reflect this skepticism. In June of 1990, the first year of Chile's post-Pinochet era, 41% of the population had confidence in the judiciary.[10] Although low, this figure was higher than in most Latin American countries. However, the level of public confidence declined even as democracy and criminal laws became more entrenched. In 1998, the year that Pinochet was detained in London, the figure plummeted to 22%, 7 points lower than the military. By 2002, it had dropped to 14%, though it climbed to 19% the next year. Similarly, in a 1993 survey of low-income Chileans, 83% expressed a negative opinion about the justice system in general, frequently referring to its discriminatory character.[11]

The second underlying observation is that there are very few cause lawyers in Chile.[12] Indeed, there is no consensus about whether "cause lawyering" or "public interest lawyering" even constitutes separate branches of the profession in Chile. Accordingly, one must be very guarded in drawing conclusions about cause lawyering in Chile, ever mindful that the assumptions underlying this form of lawyering, based largely on the U.S.

[7] L. Hilbink, "An Exception."

[8] L. Hilbink, "An Exception"; Austin Sarat and Stuart Scheingold, "Cause Lawyering and the Reproduction of Professional Authority," in *Cause Lawyering: Political Commitments and Professional Responsibilities*, ed. A. Sarat and S. Scheingold (New York: Oxford University Press: 1998). 3–28.

[9] Sarat and Scheingold, "Cause Lawyering and the Reproduction of Professional Authority,": 3–28; Joseph Thome, "Searching for Democracy: The Rule of Law and the Process of Legal Reform in Latin America." Paper prepared for the Workshop on Reforma Judicial, Motivaciones, Proyectos, Caminos Recorridos, Caminos por Reorrer, Instituto Internacional de Sociologia Juridica, Onati, Gipuzkoa, Spain, April 6–7, 1998.

[10] Alexandra Huneeus, "Between Deference and Responsive Law: The Dynamics of Judicial Stasis & Pinochet-Era Cases (1998–2005)." Paper presented at the Annual Meeting of the Law and Society Association, Baltimore, July 5–9, 2006.

[11] Michael Samway, "Access to Justice: A Study of Legal Assistance Programs for the Poor in Santiago, Chile," *Duke Journal of Comparative & International Law* 6 (1996): 347–69.

[12] Meili, "Latin American Cause Lawyering Networks": 307–33.

experience, may not apply in the Chilean context. Thus, for example, it was not surprising to find few stories about cause lawyers within the popular culture of Latin America generally, much less in Chile in particular. As such, the sample from within which to view popular culture depictions of Chilean cause lawyers is small indeed.

With these frames and caveats in mind, this essay uses two vehicles for analyzing the portrayal of cause lawyers within Chilean popular culture: the film version of *Death and the Maiden* and the recent television series *Justicia Para Todos*.

IV. *Death and the Maiden*

Death and the Maiden, the film adaptation of the play by Chilean writer and former exile Ariel Dorfman, was released in 1994, only a few years after the fall of Pinochet and well before the enactment of the criminal law reforms outlined above. It is set in an unidentified Latin American country, widely assumed to be Chile, shortly after the fall of a brutal military dictatorship. It features three main characters in a claustrophobic environment. Paulina Lorca is a former political prisoner who was tortured and raped following her abduction by the recently deposed military. Gerardo Escobar, Paulina's former boyfriend and current husband, was a student activist during the regime but was never arrested, thanks in large part to Paulina's refusal to disclose information about him to her torturers. Gerardo is now a human rights lawyer, recently appointed by the democratically elected president to head a national commission investigating past abuses by the military. And Dr. Roberto Miranda is a physician whom Paulina believes is the man who raped her in prison.

Some might question the premise that *Death and the Maiden* is part of (or a product of) Chilean popular culture because the film was produced in the United States and Dorfman had lived in exile for so long prior to its release that he was arguably out of touch with its culture. Moreover, both the play and the movie were far more popular in the United States and Britain than in Chile, though this may have more to do with what Dorfman recently observed as Chileans' unwillingness or inability to confront the horrors of the dictatorship so soon after its demise.[13] In any event, *Death's*

[13] Ascen Arriazu, "Democracy with Blood on its Hands: A Interview with Ariel Dorfman," from http://www.threemonkeysonline.com (2006).

comparatively tepid reception in Chile underscores the distinction between "text as produced" and "text as read" and the different ways in which texts are read in different cultural contexts.[14]

Death and the Maiden is an extremely complicated story that can be viewed and critiqued on numerous levels, though conventional, linear "cause lawyer seeks justice" is surely not one of them. As Fleury-Steiner and Fichtelberg note in Chapter 10, *Death* is a "complex morality tale about the long slog from authoritarian rule to a democracy characterized by equal rights." They place Paulina in the role of cause lawyer, both because she is seeking justice for her own victimization at the hands of the dictatorship but also as a symbol of the endless struggle for equal justice under the law and against what they call "second rapes" by newly created democracies that refuse to "attend to the messy work of confronting atrocity." My essay, in contrast, examines *Death* as one interpretation of the conflicts that plague – and immobilize – more conventional cause lawyers in post-authoritarian civil society.

Most of the film takes place over the course of a single evening and the following morning in Paulina and Gerardo's secluded seaside home, after Dr. Miranda finds Gerardo beside his car with a flat tire and gives him a ride home in a downpour. Once Miranda is inside the home, Paulina immediately suspects him and eventually conducts her own investigation and trial, mimicking the inquisitorial system of which she has recently been a victim. Eventually, Miranda confesses to his atrocities, but only after Paulina persists in her interrogation, threatening to throw him over a cliff into the ocean unless he talks. Having finally received what she wanted (the truth), Paulina releases him, as Gerardo can only stand by with an expression of what appears to be equal parts horror, remorse, and powerlessness.

Through complex and multilayered interactions among its three central characters, *Death* casts post-authoritarian Chilean cause lawyers in an unflinchingly dark and cynical light. Chief among its critiques is that such lawyers, personified by the human rights attorney Gerardo, are immobilized by the tension between law and social justice, as well as between professionalism and public service. As Kamir notes in her critique of the film, Gerardo wants a smooth social transformation, with the law as facilitator.[15]

[14] Richard Johnson, "What is Cultural Studies Anyway?," *Social Text* 16 (1986–87): 38–80.

[15] Orit Kamir, "Cinematic Judgment and Jurisprudence: A Woman's Memory, Recovery, and Justice in a Post-Traumatic Society (A Study of Polanski's *Death and the Maiden*)," in *Law on*

In Gerardo's view, the law must adapt to political considerations. This view is most notable in Gerardo's defense of the charge given to the human rights commission to investigate only those former regime members who murdered their victims, as opposed to all torturers (such as the one who raped Paulina). Paulina, on the other hand, demands justice. She focuses on her personal needs as a victim of state violence.[16] The human rights commission, of which Gerardo is now chair, is deaf to her concerns.[17] Gerardo consistently attempts to chart a middle ground between the determined, revenge-seeking Paulina and the accused but as yet unconvicted Miranda. His inertia during the struggle over the gun that Paulina uses to threaten Miranda is what leads Paulina to utter the condemnation that serves as the title of this essay. In the end, he pleases neither Paulina nor Miranda and is mostly an onlooker to the action created by them.[18]

The film also portrays Gerardo as an incrementalist rather than a radical. He tries, unsuccessfully, to convince Paulina that society must move slowly in investigating perpetrators of state violence, beginning with the most egregious cases. Through that process, he argues, more perpetrators' names will be revealed, and those guilty of less heinous crimes will also be prosecuted. When he tells her that those who are proven to be former death squad members will be turned over to the courts, Paulina laughs derisively, referring to a previous case in which a judge rejected accusations against a torturer.

In addition to being portrayed as denigrating the abuse suffered by Paulina and other victims of rape and other forms of nonmurderous torture, the incrementalist approach seems to ring hollow even to Gerardo. Later in the evening, soon after Miranda makes his surprise visit to the house (while Paulina is in another room, yet to confront him), Gerardo confides in Miranda that the human rights commission is a *step* in the right direction that *might* result in some change in the country. In this depiction,

the Screen, ed. A. Sarat, L. Douglas, and M. Umphrey (Stanford: Stanford University Press, 2005).

16 Id.

17 As Fleury-Steiner and Fichtelberg note, rape has historically been excluded from redress by human rights institutions. See Chapter 10.

18 Gerardo's privileging of professionalism over the needs of individuals (most notably his wife) is illustrative of what Scheingold and Sarat have observed as the importance of professionalism to lawyers of all political persuasions. Stuart Scheingold and Austin Sarat, *Something To Believe In* (Stanford: Stanford University Press, 2004).

the human rights cause lawyer is portrayed as almost wistfully hopeful, rather than determined or passionate, about the likelihood that the law will bring about effective social change. Gerardo seems to agree with Miranda's conclusion that the only justice likely to be achieved by the human rights commission will be of a personal nature, because most perpetrators had received amnesty but will nevertheless have to "face their own flesh and blood." Of course, such a "sentence" can be delivered without the formalities of a human rights commission. As we learn later in the film, this is the only sentence Miranda will receive. The movie's final scene, in which all three of the main characters listen to the same orchestra in an ornate concert hall performing Paulina's beloved *Death and the Maiden* (which Miranda played on a tape deck while raping her), strongly suggests that this "sentence" is an insufficient punishment, except perhaps to Gerardo.

Similar to the film's critique of the incrementalist approach is its portrayal of cause lawyers as measured and unemotional. When Miranda, obviously pandering to Gerardo in order to conceal his true identity, advocates killing perpetrators, Gerardo responds that killing by either side won't help. This is a far cry from the passion one might assume Gerardo exhibited in his earlier days as a leader in the student protest movement. Indeed, another criticism that the film seems to level at human rights cause lawyers is that, by adopting the professional mien of attorneys in service to the rule of law, they have abandoned the idealism that led them to pursue a cause lawyering career in the first place. This criticism is related to the well-documented observation that many idealistic law students retreat from cause lawyering during the course of their legal education.[19]

Another negative aspect of the professionalism adopted by cause lawyers as depicted in *Death* is the chasm it creates between lawyers and the clients for whom they are supposedly advocating. At best, they are naïve about their clients' situations; at worst, they have completely lost touch with the "real world," unable to sympathize with their clients' fate. Thus, after Paulina abducts Miranda and ties him to a chair with a gun to his head, Gerardo tells her that, even if Miranda is guilty, she cannot torture him. She scoffs at his analysis: "You call this torture? . . . you know so little about your subject."

The film's critique of cause lawyers extends from the professional to the personal. It portrays Gerardo as more concerned about his own career

[19] Id.

advancement than the injustice suffered by his wife. When Gerardo returns home from work on that rainy evening, Paulina is obviously upset by the radio report she has just heard indicating that the human rights commission will only investigate murderers. Gerardo is oblivious, focusing on the importance of his appointment as head of the commission (he says it is "*a* peak, not *the* peak" of his career), as well as the disabled car he left on the road. Paulina refuses to stroke his ego. In response to Gerardo's claim that heading the commission is "a job worth doing," she replies, "I don't exist." He further reveals his self-centeredness later in the film when, waking up from a drunken slumber and seeing that Paulina has tied Miranda to a chair, he asserts (perhaps reflecting on his infidelity to Paulina), "This is about me. You're angry with me." Tellingly, the task of professional ego gratification falls to Miranda, the torturer. After learning of Gerardo's professional identity, Miranda tells him, "I'm such a fan of yours" and "You're doing such important work."

These exchanges might be interpreted as Dorfman's critique of the conventional cultural division between the public and the private. As Johnson notes, popular culture privileges the male-dominated public sphere, with its emphasis on the heady issues of the day, over more personal concerns such as family life and sexuality.[20] Thus, by depicting Gerardo as obsessed with the public (masculine) issues of human rights and the rule of law, while oblivious to the personal issues of his relationship with Paulina and her desire for retribution, Dorfman reflects – and appears to criticize – the gender-based cultural bias of the mass media.

Much has changed in Chilean public life since *Death* was released. Before his death in December 2006, Pinochet's amnesty was revoked (he was twice excused from trials for personal health reasons before being prosecuted a third time), a former political prisoner (Michelle Bachelet) is now president, and sweeping criminal law reforms have been implemented. But have media depictions of cause lawyering, as reflected and refracted through film and television, changed accordingly?[21] To the extent that cause lawyers are depicted in Chilean popular culture at all, are they portrayed as "just standing there," immobilized by their adherence to the rule of law and professionalism to the point that they cannot effectively bring about justice

[20] R. Johnson, "What is Cultural Studies Anyway?": 38–80.
[21] Orit Kamir, "Cinematic Judgment and Jurisprudence."

or effective social change? Are they depicted as privileging the public over the private? For some answers to these questions, we turn to *Justicia Para Todos*, a television series that premiered in 2004, fourteen years after the fall of the dictatorship, ten years after the release of *Death and the Maiden*, and at roughly the same time as the implementation of the post-authoritarian criminal procedure reforms.

V. *Justicia Para Todos*

Justicia Para Todos (*JPT*) is a television dramatic series set in Santiago that aired during the 2004–05 season. It was produced by Chilean public television and portrayed the activities of several lawyers on both sides of Chile's new criminal law system (i.e., prosecutors and public defenders).

I assume for purposes of this essay that all of the lawyers in *JPT* are "cause lawyers": the prosecutors are portrayed as lawyering for the cause of punishing criminals and keeping society safe for law-abiding citizens; the public defenders as lawyering for the cause of exonerating the falsely accused and protecting the rights of all criminal defendants, guilty and innocent alike. Both sets of lawyers, in their own way, are depicted as upholding the rule of law.

Any reader of even a small portion of the cause lawyering literature is likely aware that the definition and scope of both "cause lawyer" and "cause lawyering" are enduring and perhaps unsolvable riddles. Indeed, as noted above, some have expanded the scope of cause lawyer to include nonattorneys (see Chapter 10). Nevertheless, it is not difficult to place criminal defense lawyers in the cause lawyering camp, given their representation of individuals against the power of the state.[22] This is especially true in the case of the Chief Public Defender in *JPT*, Esteban Perez, who sees his work as a continuing battle to even a playing field systematically skewed against his clients.

Categorizing prosecutors as cause lawyers is more problematic because they are the embodiment of state power against the individual. But the chief prosecutor in *JPT*, José Luis Orrego, who is so devoted to the post-authoritarian criminal justice reforms that he left a lucrative job with

[22] Richard Abel,"Speaking Law to Power: Occasions for Cause Lawyering," in *Cause Lawyering: Political Commitments and Professional Responsibilities*.

a private firm to assume his new post, appears to fall within McCann's description of those procedural rights cause lawyers who emphasize what he terms "procedural liberalism"[23] (i.e., cause lawyers upholding the cause of the rule of law). He also fits Thomas Hilbink's definition of the proceduralist cause lawyer ("Proceduralist lawyering is marked by a belief in the separation of law and politics, and a belief that the legal system is essentially fair and just").[24] Moreover, prosecutors may be more easily labeled cause lawyers in a post-authoritarian society. This may be particularly true in Chile, which ranks above nearly every other country in the world for incarcerating members of a prior regime for human rights crimes.[25]

Even before analyzing the depiction of the cause lawyers in *JPT*, there are three elements to it that are worth noting in the cause lawyering context. The first is that the show is intentionally educational. The official description of the series, which is a production of Chilean public television, indicates that it combines "information with entertainment."[26] Thus, one of the show's explicit purposes is to educate people about the new criminal law reforms and the role of lawyers within it. Interestingly, the 2003 *Human Rights Report* from Diego Portales School of Law in Santiago, which includes a section on the criminal procedure reforms, also explicitly assumes an educational purpose.[27]

Second, large portions of *JPT's* episodes are devoted to the personal lives of the main characters. As the official description put it, "We also learn, in the beginning of the series, about the relations established between characters and about their surroundings. There will be romance, humor and much action." This creates a telling contrast with *Death and the Maiden*, in which nearly the only relevant information provided about the background of any of the characters (lawyers or not) is where they stood in relation to the military dictatorship: for or against it? In *JPT*, produced fourteen years after the end of the dictatorship, the background descriptions of the main characters provided by the producers of the series are

[23] Michael McCann, comments at the cause lawyering conference at Bellagio, Italy, June 1999.
[24] Thomas M Hilbink, "You Know the Type . . . : Categories of Cause Lawyering," *Law and Social Inquiry* 29 (2004): 657–98; Yves Dotan, "The Global Language of Human Rights: Patterns of Cooperation Between State and Civil Rights Lawyers in Israel," in *Cause Lawyering: Political Commitments and Professional Responsibilities*.
[25] A. Huneeus, "Between Deference and Responsive Law."
[26] *Justicia Para Todos* website (http://www.tvn.cl/programas/jpt/).
[27] Diego Portales School of Law, 2003 *Annual Report*.

replete with personal information (family relationships, love interests, professional troubles, domestic violence, etc.), but devoid of their attitudes toward the former military regime.

One might interpret this phenomenon in several ways. For example, it may reflect the desire of many Chileans to leave the authoritarian past behind and focus instead on the future.[28] Alternatively, it may reflect the difference between the two forms of media involved. As McCann has noted, filmmakers and playwrights might be considered "cause writers," using film or plays to assert a political point, knowing (or perhaps at least hoping) that it will challenge, or even offend, some audience members. Television, on the other hand, is more likely to pander to its audience, providing it with entertainment rather than challenging political or social messages.[29]

Finally, the title of the series, whether intentional or not, is instructive from a cultural studies standpoint. As many students of American film are aware, the 1979 U.S. movie starring Al Pacino with a very similar title (*And Justice for All*) depicts a corrupt criminal justice system in which wealthy defendants buy their way out of convictions while innocent but poor defendants rot in prison. The title is also ironic because, as noted below, most episodes of the show are decidedly ambiguous about whether all parties received or otherwise experienced justice. On the other hand, the title is consistent with the notion in the cultural studies literature that the law has a role in the cultural construction of identities.[30] Thus, by using the title "*JPT*" the producers of the show may have consciously aimed to construct the identity of Chileans as a just people, or Chile as a just culture. Yet, as Coombe also notes that culture can be defined as "shared meanings of experience generated in social practices," one wonders about the

[28] Steve J. Stern, *Remembering Pinochet's Chile* (Durham, NC: Duke University Press, 2004): "In recent years, influential criticism of the postdictatorship society of the 1990s has invoked the dichotomy of remembering against forgetting to characterize Chile as a culture of oblivion, marked by a tremendous compulsion to forget the past and the uncomfortable. A second influential idea [is that] amnesia occurs because the middle classes and the wealthy, as beneficiaries of economic prosperity created by the military regime, developed the habit of denial or looking the other way on matters of state violence" (Id. at xxvii.); Elizabeth Jelin, *State Repression and the Labors of Memory* (Minneapolis: University of Minnesota Press, 2003).

[29] Michael McCann, comment at Cause Lawyering Conference, Amherst Massachusetts, March 10, 2007.

[30] Rosemary J. Coombe, "Contingent Articulations: A Critical Cultural Studies of Law," in *Law in the Domains of Culture*, ed. A. Sarat and T. Kearns (Ann Arbor: University of Michigan Press, 1998).

dissonance between the series title and Chileans' experience with "social practices" under the dictatorship.

JPT's descriptions of its two main characters offer a revealing contrast in both personal and lawyering style. The show's background material states that the chief prosecutor, José Luis Orrego, abandoned a successful career with a prominent Santiago law firm to work for what the show describes as the "new justice." Although his new salary is only a quarter of what he earned in private practice, he is convinced that his work as a prosecutor will contribute to the public good. However, we are also told that he is inexperienced in the criminal area and that each case that he investigates is a new experience for him. He is described as married with one daughter, Catholic, and from a good family. He is also apparently a fastidious clean freak, orderly and refined, obsessed with suits from Italy and ties from New York.

The chief public defender, Esteban Perez, is depicted as the polar opposite to José Luiz in ways both personal and professional. The show's background material indicates that "his entire life is dedicated to resolving his cases. He brings action to the series."[31] In contrast to José Luiz's bookish tendencies, Esteban is described as learning about life from the street, rather than from books. He conducts his own investigation of crimes on-site. He has little sympathy for the Prosecutor's office, arguing that it has all of the resources and the power to make numerous accusations while obtaining few convictions. On the personal side, he lives alone in a disorderly apartment. He cannot maintain a stable amorous relationship, as he is constantly late for dates and always thinking about his cases. He dresses casually, often appearing on screen with his sports jacket off and his tie loosened.

Each of the main characters has a female junior attorney assisting him, though the character of Rocío Castañeda, the assistant prosecutor, is more fully developed than Esteban's assistant, María Ignacia Larráin. A single mother living with her 15-year old son, Rocío always wanted to be a lawyer, but needed to overcome many personal struggles, including physical abuse by her former husband, to reach that goal. Her relationship with José Luiz, the chief prosecutor, is tense because of their different work styles: "He is tied to the law, while Rocío is characterized by her belief in people, for trusting people's word, particularly vulnerable women." [32]

[31] *Justicia Para Todos* Web site (http://www.tvn.cl/programas/).
[32] Id.

I have selected descriptions of the following five episodes from *JPT* to explore whether the show's view of cause lawyering is more nuanced and perhaps less cynical than that of Dorfman.

1. Sectretos: Violencia Intrafamiliar ("Secrets: Intrafamily Violence")

In this episode, a husband is twice charged with domestic violence against his wife. The husband, prosecuted by José Luiz and represented by Esteban, escaped the first charge because he claimed – and his wife agreed – that it was all an accident. But after the second incident, none of the main characters doubt that he is guilty. However, during the ensuing trial, even though the husband's daughter implicates him, his wife is afraid to testify against him and thus fails to provide incriminating testimony. The husband is convicted of a lesser offense that prohibits him from having any access to his family. Nevertheless, overcome by jealousy because of his wife's relationship with another man, he returns to her house, murders her, and kills himself. Rocío, the assistant prosecutor, senses that something terrible will happen after the trial, but arrives too late at the wife's home to prevent the murder-suicide.

2. La Micro ("The Bus")

Two gunshots are fired in a crowded city bus. Two teenagers are injured; one of them dies. The evidence indicates that a woman fired the shots, but she claims she acted in self-defense because the teenagers were about to rape her. José Luiz and Rocío prosecute her for homicide, and Esteban defends her. Esteban's investigation reveals that she had previously been raped and frequented a firing range to learn how to operate a handgun. Rocío learns from another girl that the dead teenager had previously raped her. Troubled by this revelation, Rocío does not know whom to believe. Nevertheless, the prosecution continues and the girl on the bus is convicted of homicide.

3. Tráfico de órganos ("Organ Trafficking")

An adolescent boy is found dead in a motel room, missing a kidney. Hours later, a man dies in a traffic accident while transporting a kidney. Prosecutor

José Luiz suspects illegal trafficking in bodily organs. He eventually discovers that a family is negotiating with a trafficking ring for a kidney transplant. José Luiz requests the family's help in breaking up the ring, but the family ignores him and continues to negotiate for the transplant. José Luiz illegally taps their phone and thus learns about a clandestine clinic where transplants are performed. He arranges for the clinic to be surrounded by the police. However, at the exact time that the police storm the clinic the boy is undergoing a kidney transplant. The boy's father grabs a gun and threatens to kill José Luiz if he interrupts the operation. José Luiz relents. The father eventually gives himself up, the transplant ring is disbanded, and the boy survives after a successful transplant.

4. El tío ("The Uncle")

A young girl is run over, but not killed, by a car in the street. Hospital personnel attending to her realize that she has clear signs of having been raped. The girl blames her uncle, who is charged with rape and defended by Esteban. The uncle denies responsibility, arguing that his niece is a rebel and that her boyfriend is responsible for the crime. During the course of the investigation, Esteban – who defends the uncle – learns of the testimony of other women who were raped by him. He does not bring this out at the trial of the uncle, who is acquitted because the evidence presented by Rocío is insufficient. However, he later shares the testimonials with Rocío, who uses them to prosecute the uncle for these previous crimes.

5. La ley de la cárcel ("The Law of the Jail")

Esteban visits an inmate in a local jail to discuss the charges pending against him. At the same time, other inmates, in a different part of the prison reserved for violent criminals, obtain a gun and decide to take hostages to press their demands for improved conditions. They soon discover that there is a lawyer in the jail (Esteban), whom they consider to have "fallen from heaven" ("el abogado está caído del cielo") because he will help them get what they want from prison officials. Esteban tries to convince them to discuss their grievances with the warden without taking him hostage, but one of ringleaders tells him that "we already did that and were ignored."

José Luiz and Rocío arrive at the jail separately, once they learn what has happened, though José Luiz initially believes it is Rocío who has been taken hostage (one wonders if he would have rushed to the jail if he had known it was his chief rival in trouble). José Luiz is hesitant to take any action, deferring to the prison warden, who wants to send in storm troopers to rescue Esteban. Rocío disagrees, and wants to draw the prisoners out by negotiating with them. She reproaches José Luiz for his lack of initiative, telling him that he is an excellent prosecutor, but not the person she thought she knew. She accuses him of risking Esteban's life to save his own skin by not challenging the warden's misguided strategy.

In the meantime, the prisoners, seizing on their good fortune in kidnapping a defense lawyer, decide to hold a "trial" of a prisoner named Montecinos, who has been convicted of raping a young girl during the robbery of a home ("You know how we treat rapists," the ringleaders tell Esteban). Esteban, fearing that the other prisoners will kill Montecinos, agrees to defend him in a trial in which the prisoners serve as judges.

Esteban, in preparing Montecinos for the trial, tells him to do whatever the other prisoners tell him to do so that he can avoid being killed. During the trial, Montecinos testifies that he entered the house to steal things and left after completing the crime. He denies raping the girl. Esteban then calls Salgado, another prisoner and long-time friend of Montecinos. Salgado testifies that he was with Montecinos on the night in question, but that he stayed outside while Montecinos entered the home. However, Montecinos told him afterward that although he did not rape the girl, he did rape the maid.

Meanwhile, apparently stung by Rocío's rebuke, José Luiz becomes more assertive, telling the warden that he must accede to the prisoner's demands or risk an official investigation ("What are you afraid of – that people will learn of the bad conditions in the jail?"). The warden agrees to the prisoners' demands.

Soon thereafter, one of the ringleaders tells Esteban that the trial is over because their demands have been accepted. But Esteban wants to continue the trial, fearful of what might happen to his "client." The ringleader tells Esteban that even if Montecinos raped the maid rather than the girl, it is still a terrible thing to do. Later that night, after Esteban has been released, the prisoners murder Montecinos.

Rocío visits Esteban at home that evening to make sure he is OK. He ends up confessing that he recently broke up with his fiancé because he loves Rocío. They end the episode with a kiss.

VI. Observations

When juxtaposed with *Death and the Maiden*, the *JPT* episodes outlined above, as well as the descriptions of the main characters, suggest several observations and tentative conclusions about mass culture depictions of cause lawyering in Chile during the post-authoritarian period. For example, in both the movie and the TV episodes, the cause lawyers who believe most ardently in the importance of the rule of law (Gerardo and José Luiz) are portrayed as honorable in an idealistic sort of way, but out of touch with what is really going on in the world and thus unable (and perhaps unwilling) to alter it. Quite literally, they "stand there" at various times. Gerardo watches helplessly as Paulina conducts her trial of Miranda. José Luiz permits the prosecution of a rape victim who committed a murder in self-defense and is immobilized by the threat to his life from the family seeking the illegal kidney transplant and by the perceived threat to his career when he initially refuses to challenge the prison warden's misguided plans for resolving the hostage crisis. Even Rocío is rendered physically useless when she arrives too late to stop the murder of the freed defendant's wife.

Of course, this view of cause lawyers as rigid and out of touch is neither unique to Chile nor particularly new. As one commentator observed about Atticus Finch, the quintessential cause lawyer in *To Kill a Mockingbird*:

> Atticus cannot see beyond his law books. Indeed, he seems scared to do so, as if it would unleash the real demons in the town. He plays along with the system. Atticus is a willing participant in a ritual that he knows to be absurd. . . . Atticus Finch is as childlike as his daughter Scout. His vision of law is as unrealistic and yet as touching as her vision of childhood. Both hold views that are more eccentric than the town's identifiable eccentric, Boo Radley.
>
> In a town like this, willful, if nonviolent, disobedience to the "law" is the only possible alternative. . . . In fact [*Mockingbird*] is the first great film of the Sixties that makes a convincing case that a new kind of lawyer is needed, one who will fight to eliminate the "system" rather

> than participate in it. The film shuts the door on the Fifties, while illuminating the hypocrisy of the decade's child-like vision.[33]

Without overextending the comparison to *To Kill a Mockingbird*, *JPT* may be playing a similar role in Chilean cultural life by offering a rather nuanced view of cause lawyers in that country. For although José Luiz is obsessed with the ideal of the law as an even-handed distributor of justice, Esteban knows that the legal arena is not a fair fight and that the rules of the street must sometimes be used to make up the difference. This view is perhaps most pronounced in "La ley de la cárcel," although in that episode it is the prisoners, rather than *any* of the lawyers (with the possible exception of Rocío), who recognize that only through disorder (in literally taking the law – personified by Esteban – hostage) can any form of justice (i.e., improved prison conditions) emerge.

Esteban's disheveled appearance and disorderly apartment, in contrast to José Luiz's impeccable taste in clothes and model home life, further symbolize that some cause lawyers must reach beyond the confines of the legal system and rely on disorder to achieve social justice. José Luiz's assistant Rocío certainly recognizes the limits of the law in bringing about justice, particularly for women. Indeed, one wonders how differently Rocío would have reacted to Paulina's abduction of Miranda in *Death and the Maiden* had she been the human rights lawyer in that film. Perhaps Dorfman would have had her serve as Paulina's advocate, rather than as an ineffective and ultimately irrelevant mediator.

Thus, *JPT*, not unlike *Death*, suggests that the rule of law can bring about order, but not necessarily justice, and that sometimes disorder produces a deeper form of justice. Yet, *JPT* can also be seen as illustrating the limits of disorder and the lack of rule of law, as exemplified by the mock trial in which prisoners mete out their own version of very rough justice despite the best efforts of cause lawyer Esteban.

A second distinction between the portrayal of cause lawyers in *Death* and *JPT* is the extent of personal background revealed to the viewer. As noted earlier, *Death* suggests that the only relevant part of people's past is their role during the dictatorship. A decade later, as the nation continued to seek refuge from the memory of the dictatorship, *JPT* reveals extensive

[33] John J. Osborn, Jr. "Atticus Finch – The End of Honor: A Discussion of *To Kill a Mockingbird*," *University of San Francisco Law Review* 30 (1996):1139.

information about the personal backgrounds and histories of its cause lawyers, but nothing about their role during the dictatorship. It is as if they were born, raised, and graduated from law school within the fourteen years between the end of the dictatorship and the premiere of the show.

Thus, for example, in Rocío we see a cause lawyer whose troubled background compels her to show her boss, the privileged and traditional José Luiz, that the world (as well as the administration of justice) is far more complicated than he might think. And though the characters' amorous relations are clearly included to heighten the entertainment value of the program, *JPT* focuses far more on them than does *Death*. Indeed, in one episode alone ("La ley de la cárcel"), we witness (1) a confession of love and a kiss between an assistant prosecutor and a public defender, (2) the previously monogamous José Luiz having an affair (he and his lover are together in his car when he hears of the prison hostage crisis over the radio), and (3) Esteban's fiancée going out dancing with another man on the night of the prison crisis. One might interpret this different treatment of personal details as an evolutionary merging of the public and the private in mass culture, a moving away from the bright line division identified twenty years ago by Johnson (and reflected in Dorfman's storytelling). One might also question whether this merger reflects a diminution in the popular culture of the privileging of male-dominated public issues over more personal concerns, or simply a desire to garner higher ratings. Perhaps they are one and the same.

Third, the cultural view of cause lawyering in Chile provides an interesting contrast to the trend in American television over the past half-century to portray those lawyers who enforce the law more sympathetically than those who defend the rights of the accused.[34] According to Rapping, by the 1990s law enforcers who represented the power of the state to track down criminals became the major defenders of justice on American TV.[35] Though they may be foiled in their attempts to put the "bad guys" away because of flaws in the system or the deviousness of defense lawyers, prosecutors have assumed the "white hat" role that had been the exclusive domain of characters like Perry Mason and the attorneys on *The Defenders* in the

[34] Elayne Rapping, *Law and Justice as Seen on TV* (New York: New York University Press: 2003); Steve Greenfield, Guy Osborn and Peter Robson, *Film and the Law* (London: Cavendish Publishing Limited: 2001).

[35] Rapping, *Law and Justice as Seen on TV*.

1950s and 60s. And in shows like *Law and Order*, the legal system itself has become the hero, whereas the individual attorneys operating within it are symbolically interchangeable.[36]

One might expect a similar dynamic in a post-authoritarian society such as Chile, which is struggling to overcome a recent past marred by widespread impunity for violations of the law and basic human dignity. By the same token, one might expect a television show designed in part to educate citizens about their new, post-authoritarian legal system to assume a Polyanna-like, preachy attitude toward its subject, glossing over the troubled spots to achieve a general understanding and acceptance of the new order.

Yet this is not the case. In *JPT* the legal system, even after significant criminal law reform, is cast in anything but a heroic light; rather, it is portrayed as flawed, just as it is in *Death*. In the episodes described above, for example, an abusive husband avoids incarceration and kills his wife, a rape victim is convicted of murder despite significant evidence that she was acting in self-defense, strict enforcement of the law would have resulted in the denial of a kidney transplant (and presumably death) for a young boy, and prison inmates are portrayed both as victims of an inhumane corrections system and judges in a system of informal justice. If the new Chilean legal system is designed to punish the guilty, free the innocent, and thus bring about the kind of justice denied by the former military regime, *JPT* must surely have planted some seeds of doubt in many viewers' minds, given the acknowledged power of mass media to reshape and redistribute "the forms and positions (and consequently, of the masses) within contemporary life."[37]

Fourth, as noted earlier in this essay, one of the dominant themes in both *JPT* and *Death* is the tension between the rule of law and social justice. In *Death*, Gerardo is trying to support the rule of law because he believes (or hopes) it will bring about social justice, but Paulina tells him that he (and, by extension, the law) is blind to injustice. Similarly, in *JPT*, following the rule of law does not necessarily result in justice being done. Indeed, the series reveals that there are such severe limitations and inequalities in the social system that it is sometimes necessary to engage in lawlessness to obtain justice. Thus, the family of the boy in need of a kidney transplant

[36] Id.

[37] Lawrence Grossberg, "The Formation of Cultural Studies: An American in Birmingham," in *Relocating Cultural Studies*, ed. V. Blundell, J. Shepherd, I. Taylor. (New York: Routledge, 1993): 21–66.

breaks the law (and physically threatens its embodiment in the person of José Luiz) to achieve justice for their son; the prisoners must literally take the law (and a cause lawyer) into their own hands to press their demands for humane treatment. In addition, although Esteban follows the law in defending the uncle accused of rape, in the process he denies justice to the family of a rape victim (although, perhaps to soften the callousness of such an outcome, Esteban redeems himself somewhat by providing evidence that achieves a measure of justice for others victimized by the uncle). The tension between José Luiz and Rocío exemplifies this conflict further. He is the refined embodiment of a privileged and professional approach to cause lawyering. Having been on the receiving end of injustice several times, she (like Paulina) is intimately familiar with the limits of the rule of law and professionalism. This awareness enables Rocío to make the searing distinction between José Luiz's considerable skills as a lawyer and his lack of integrity as a human being.

This tension between law and social justice is not problematic for all cause lawyers, but it typically ensnares those at one end of what Sarat and Scheingold refer to as the cause lawyering continuum; that is, those cause lawyers whose mission is to "make the profession live up to its own avowed ideals and to somehow stretch those ideals from the representation of individual litigants to causes."[38] Gerardo and José Luiz occupy perhaps the furthest post of this continuum, because for them the rule of law *is* the cause. And because the rule of law does not always translate into justice for the accused or for the victims of crimes, these cause lawyers most vividly personify the tension between law and justice.

To be sure, there are more radical cause lawyers in Chile: those at the other end of the continuum who "challenge established conceptions of professionalism with efforts to decommodify, politicize, and socialize legal practice."[39] These lawyers often work directly with members of low-income communities, training them to act as their own advocates, rather than representing them in court proceedings.[40] However, such lawyers do not appear to be part of the popular cultural landscape in Chile.

[38] Austin Sarat and Stuart Scheingold, "Cause Lawyering and the Reproduction of Professional Authority: An Introduction," in *Cause Lawyering: Political Commitments and Professional Responsibilities*: 3–28.

[39] Id.

[40] Stephen Meili, "Legal Education in Argentina and Chile," in *Educating for Justice Around the World*, ed. L. Trubek and J. Cooper (Ashgate/Dartmouth, 1999): 138–57.

Fifth, there are important distinctions in the views of cause lawyering presented in *Death* and *JPT* that may reflect a softening of the critique of such lawyers since the period immediately after the dictatorship. These distinctions fall along both professional and personal lines. On the professional level, *JPT* introduces the public to a side of cause lawyering that Gerardo never overtly exhibits: doubts about the rule of law and professionalism that lead to a willingness to skirt those conventions when necessary to achieve some form of justice, whether social or personal. Esteban, the public defender, knows the system is rigged against his clients and will use his street smarts to overcome this inherent disadvantage. He takes the same approach to the prison trial of Montecinos, advising his client to do anything the "judges" say to save his skin. And, as noted above, his physical appearance and lawyering style suggest defiance of the kind of professionalism that is critical to José Luiz's (and Gerardo's) sense of what it means to be a lawyer.[41] Lawyers like Esteban and Rocío exercise moral judgment and act on it in ways that Gerardo never could: they trust their instincts, their intuition about the credibility of ordinary people, and their moral compass in ways that sometimes compel them to act beyond the confines of the law. Whatever instincts and passion Gerardo may have possessed previously have been repressed by his privileging of the rule of law.

Even some of the personal attributes common to cause lawyers in both *Death* and *JPT* are portrayed more sympathetically in the latter. For example, both Gerardo and Esteban are passionate about the law to such an extent that it interferes in their amorous relationships with women. But Gerardo's passion skews his moral judgment such that he cannot meaningfully assist his own wife in her quest for justice. On the other hand, Esteban's passion for the law is part of his appeal as a character: he is sympathetically depicted as a loser at love but a street-fighting defender of the accused. Perhaps it is fitting, then, that he eventually falls in love with Rocío, telling her during their embrace that bad luck always seems to come between them, but that he is persistent.

Finally, *JPT* conveys the idea that, despite its flaws, the new justice system (and the lawyers who play a role on either side of it) is important because those who are initially accused by the police are often not guilty. The

[41] Other chapters in this volume highlight the role of clothing and appearance as a way of humanizing and/or demystifying lawyers (see Chapters 7 and 13).

accused enjoyed no such protection under the military dictatorship. And while Esteban sees this phenomenon as cause to criticize the prosecutor's office because it makes many accusations with few convictions, an equally compelling implication is that, absent the recent procedural reforms in which defense lawyers play a critical role, many innocent people would go to prison, as they did during the military regime. This is a far less cynical view of the justice system and of cause lawyers than the one portrayed in *Death*, where the legal system – even after the fall of the dictatorship – is depicted as completely inadequate in bringing the guilty to justice.

VII. Conclusion

At first glance, *Death and the Maiden* and *Justicia Para Todos* provide us with two quite different examples of how popular culture defines and understands cause lawyers. In *Death*, the cause lawyer is portrayed as detached and ineffective, disengaged from the real world and blind to its truth. Although *JPT* highlights similar flaws in its cause lawyers (particularly the lead prosecutor, José Luiz), it also reveals their more human side (particularly of the assistant prosecutor, Rocío, and the public defender, Esteban). The show thus makes cause lawyers more accessible and sympathetic to the viewing public by depicting them as just like the rest of us, subject to similar temptations, weaknesses, and ambitions. In this way *JPT* humanizes a legal system that, for long stretches of Chilean history, has been neither human nor humane.

Like Gerardo in *Death*, the cause lawyers in *JPT* are portrayed as flawed, but they struggle against the limitations of the legal system and their own personal backgrounds and demons to achieve what they think to be a just result. And in contrast to the heroic legal system portrayed in U.S. television shows like *Law and Order* where the lawyers are replaceable parts, the cause lawyers in *JPT* are depicted as engaged in a heroic battle against injustices in society at large, as well as in the new legal system. Some, like Esteban and Rocío, are more conscious of this struggle. Others, like José Luiz, find themselves wrapped up in it without exactly knowing what they are up against.

The relationship between cause lawyers and their avowed causes is also depicted differently in *Death* and *JPT*. In *Death*, cause lawyer and cause are one: Gerardo is the personification of the rule of law. And Dorfman's rather obvious cynicism about the privileging of the rule of law over the truth renders his portrayal of Gerardo consistently negative. *JPT* permits more space between the cause lawyers and their causes. That space is narrowest in the case of prosecutor José Luiz, who sees himself as the guardian of the rule of law within Chile's new system of justice. The other characters are more conflicted, perhaps because they are serving more than one cause. Sworn to uphold the rule of law as an assistant prosecutor, Rocío nevertheless often finds herself at odds with its strictures as she pursues the cause of what she perceives to be justice. And Esteban is willing to bend the rules of the legal system – and perhaps the truth – to defend the rights of his clients, even when those clients are forced on him by kidnappers in a prison.

And yet despite these differences, *Death* and *JPT* both present a similarly cynical critique of the work of cause lawyers, at least to the extent that they seek to uphold the cause of the rule of law in post-authoritarian Chile. This cynicism toward cause lawyers and the rule of law they defend is perhaps best demonstrated by the mock trials depicted in both the movie and the television series. For those mock trials, which brazenly flout the rule of law, expose the truth: Paulina's ad hoc trial of Miranda reveals that he raped and tortured her, and the prisoner's ad hoc trial of Montecinos reveals that he raped a maid during a robbery.

In contrast, "real" trials conducted according to the rule of law seem more often than not to result in injustice and the skirting of the truth. In *JPT*, courtroom trials lead to the exoneration of the guilty (the abusive husband who later kills his ex-wife, and the uncle who raped his niece) and the conviction of the innocent (the woman convicted of murder who acted in self-defense to prevent her rape). And although *Death* portrays no courtroom trials, its criticism of the human rights commission predicts – which is accurate, as it turns out – that many perpetrators of state violence will go free. Indeed, Dorfman uses the lack of "real" trials against rapists to demonstrate the failure of the post-authoritarian regime to fully come to terms with the abusive past.

Another intriguing aspect of the two mock trials is the role of the cause lawyers within them. Both Gerardo and Esteban attempt to subvert the mock trial process by advising their clients to do whatever their adversaries desired (which presumably entails lying). However, their lawyerly advice proves ineffective in protecting their clients. Miranda eventually gives a convincing and compelling confession of guilt, and the inmate witness called by Esteban implicates Montecinos in the rape of the maid.

The cynicism reflected in *Death* is understandable, given that its author was a political exile and the film was released shortly after the brutal and lawless Pinochet regime. But it seems more incongruous in *JPT*, one of whose explicit purposes was to educate the public about legal reforms enacted a decade after Pinochet left power. Why would a program designed to familiarize Chileans with the new criminal law system cast that system in such a negative – or, at best, contradictory – light? The most likely reason is that television producers and promoters, like politicians, watch the public opinion polls. If they see that less than a quarter of the people have confidence in the judicial system, it would be programmatic suicide to release a series that is blind to the problems within that system and the lawyers who populate it. In this way, *Death* and *JPT* illustrate the ways in which mass media simultaneously reflect, refract, and shape public sentiment about the rule of law and the lawyers dedicated to upholding it.

Ultimately, both *Death and the Maiden* and *Justicia Para Todos* depict cause lawyers as part of, and mired in, the post-authoritarian conflict between memory and forgetting. In *Death*, Gerardo sees the law as a means to part with the past and move on; Paulina refuses to let him forget. In *JPT*, although there appears to be little explicit reference to the dictatorship (and thus, a viewer might assume, a desire to move beyond it), the very foundation of the series is the legal reform that the dictatorship's abuses made necessary. Nevertheless, despite their ambivalence about, or criticism of, the role of Chile's recent past in charting the country's future, both *Death* and *JPT* use cause lawyers to remind the viewer that human rights still matter – perhaps now more than ever. And yet, both *Death* and *JPT* can also be interpreted as suggesting that the rule of law – and the cause lawyers who attempt to uphold it – is, at best, a flawed means of guaranteeing those rights.

10

Paulina Escobar as Cause Lawyer

"Litigating" Human Rights in the Shadows of *Death and the Maiden*

Ben Fleury-Steiner and Aaron Fichtelberg

"To worry or to smile, such is the choice when we are assailed by the strange; our decision depends on how familiar we are with our own ghosts."
– Julia Kristeva, *Strangers to Ourselves*

"At first, it is something you simply don't talk about. Then it occurs to you that people whose houses are broken into or who are mugged in Central Park talk about it all the time. Rape is a much more serious crime. If it isn't my fault, why am I supposed to be ashamed? If I shouldn't be ashamed, if it wasn't "personal," why look askance when I mention it?" – Susan Estrich, *Rape*

"If he's innocent, then he's really fucked."
– Paulina Escobar, *Death and the Maiden*

I. Introduction

The world of popular cinema presents the unique possibility for reimagining the world of cause lawyering. It does so especially when the film in question is a complex, emotionally powerful morality tale, such as Roman Polanski's adaptation of the celebrated Ariel Dorfman play, *Death and the Maiden*.[1] Although the film superficially presents its central figure Paulina Escobar (played by Sigourney Weaver) as victim – indeed, there can be no doubt that her character has experienced profound victimization at the hands of a ruthless, patriarchal state (i.e., one that condones rape and torture) – viewing the film as metaphor for the long, hard struggle toward emancipation from a world once marked by fascist control and the

[1] For a provocative reading of Dorfman's play, see David Luban, "On Dorfman's Death and the Maiden," *Yale Journal of Law & the Humanities* 10 (1998): 115.

taken-for-granted rape culture that sustains it, Paulina's character takes on new dimension. The novel context that Paulina confronts and the ways that she faces her former tormentor differ from both a simple revenge narrative and a vindication tale. Rather, as it unfolds, the film invites the viewer to reimagine her as cause lawyer practicing her craft in a unique way in a very unorthodox situation.

Death and the Maiden is not a law film in the traditional sense. It is a complex and multilayered drama set in a time of momentous legal and societal upheaval. In contrast to most law films – especially the majority of American legal cinema – that represent lawyers in stark moral dichotomies (i.e., as either "good" advocates or "evil" crooks),[2] *Death and the Maiden's* characters are far more complex and thus invite a reading that attends to a world of cause lawyering animated by a series of provocative questions: How does the fall of dictatorship problematize the identity of person (i.e., gender identity), motive (i.e., cause), and role (i.e., lawyer)? How does the role of the cause lawyer in constructing a narrative of justice conflict with a professional commitment to the normative force of law? How does the lawyer as victim conflict with the lawyer as professional? Finally, is the cause lawyer a gendered figure, and is the justice that such a lawyer pursues itself gendered?

This deeply moving and often disturbing film invites, we argue, the viewer to confront these difficult questions and problematizes the roles of law and justice in times of social upheaval. By contrast to the less nuanced, more obviously formalistic, legal thriller (e.g., any number of films adapted from John Grisham's numerous novels), *Death and the Maiden* unsettles stable categories of just/unjust and thus "trial," "case," "lawyer," and "cause." However, on its deepest levels, the story of *Death and the Maiden* is one of victimization – not of the victimization of one person by another, but of the victimization of humanity by brutality as such. Torturer and tortured are both victims of the dehumanizing brutality that totalitarian regimes require, and the legal process, carried out by the cause lawyer herself, becomes a means by which society can reconstruct its lost humanity.

[2] For critical analyses of law and popular culture, see Richard K. Sherwin, *When Law Goes Pop: The Vanishing Line between Law and Popular Culture* (Chicago: University of Chicago Press, 2002); Carrie Menkel-Meadow, "Can They Do That? Legal Ethics in Popular Culture: Of Characters and Acts," *UCLA Law Review* 48: 1305; Austin Sarat, Lawrence Douglas, and Martha Merrill Umphrey, *Law on the Screen* (Stanford: Stanford University Press, 2005).

II. Synopsis of the Film

Death and the Maiden follows three characters through a dramatic series of subtle, interconnected events in the context of a post-totalitarian society, recently freed from a military regime that retains one hand on the levers of power as it negotiates its departure into the sunset with its successor. The analogy of course is to Latin American states in the shadows of their former right-wing juntas – post-Pinochet Chile, post-Videla Argentina, or post-dictatorship Brazil – but there are numerous African, Asian, and European societies, such as South Africa post-apartheid, that would see their experiences reflected in the film. Throughout the story, a series of suspenseful interactions between a female victim (Paulina), her complex "hero" husband (Gerardo Escobar, played by Stuart Wilson), and her victimizer (Dr. Roberto Miranda, played by Ben Kingsley) are eventually revealed as artifice in a complex morality tale about the long slog from authoritarian rule to a democracy characterized by equal rights and a respect for the rule of law.

Death and the Maiden in no way romanticizes such a complicated story, and the "redemptions" that are offered to the characters or to the viewer are ephemeral. Eschewing the traditional narrative and cinematographic tropes, the film is intentionally shot to pull the viewer into various fleeting zones of comfort with its characters, only to have the proverbial warm blanket of sentimentalisms suddenly stripped away. A character may seem to be an innocent victim only later to appear dangerous and vice versa. The common thread throughout the narrative is one of dehumanization: each character is dehumanized in one form or another as a result of the totalitarian regime, and each must find his or her own way to redemption.

Death and the Maiden opens with Escobar – a leading human rights lawyer and activist who, along with his wife, the human rights activist Paulina, played an integral role in bringing about the fall of the dictatorship – making his way home from a historic meeting with the country's new president. Escobar has been appointed to the Counsel to the country's human rights commission, an institution not unlike the post-apartheid South African Truth and Reconciliation Commission (TRC). As part of the Counsel, Escobar's job will be to evaluate the country's war criminals' applications for amnesty, clearly a necessary stage in the reconciliation process (assuming of course, the reconciliation is a desirable or achievable goal at all). But we soon learn that only accounts of murder and not widespread rapes will be heard by the Counsel. This policy imposes a procedural limitation of this new institution's powers that is not only obviously controversial[3] but is also deeply personal for Escobar – indeed, his wife was raped and tortured brutally by a physician beholden to the old regime who thus will never be held legally accountable for his crime.

In a seemingly inconsequential sequence, Escobar's drive home from the meeting with the president is suddenly interrupted by a flat tire. Unsurprisingly, a Good Samaritan pulls over to the side of the road offering to drive him home. Escobar accepts the ride, arrives home, and soon thereafter Paulina confronts him about the meeting with the president: Gerardo has taken the post despite the fact that Paulina will never have the chance to confront her rapist, an action that causes Gerardo further shame as we learn also that he has recently been unfaithful in his marriage to Paulina. Her anger and frustration are obvious and conflict with Escobar's earnest effort to make a difference in the new regime.

Suddenly a thundering knock at the door sends Gerardo downstairs to discover his Good Samaritan driver, Dr. Miranda. Upon learning from a radio broadcast that Escobar had been appointed to the commission, Dr. Miranda has, apparently innocently enough, returned to congratulate Gerardo. But brief pleasantries between the two characters are suddenly complicated by a somewhat awkward discussion: Gerardo and Dr. Miranda agree that the authoritarian regime should be punished, but Dr. Miranda wants the death sentence to be widely used, a policy Gerardo as a human rights attorney deeply opposes (see Chapter 9). The story draws a seemingly clear moral line between retribution and forgiveness. Indeed, if one was to

[3] Rape has historically been excluded from redress by human rights institutions: "Women and girls have habitually been sexually violated during wartime, yet even in the twenty-first century, the documents regulating armed conflict either minimally incorporate, inappropriately characterize, or wholly fail to mention these crimes. Until the 1990s, men did the drafting and enforcing of humanitarian law provisions; thus, it was primarily men who neglected to enumerate, condemn, and prosecute these crimes. While males remain the principal actors in international (and domestic) fora, in recent years, women have broken through the glass ceiling and are changing the traditional landscape by securing high-level positions in international legal institutions and on international adjudicative bodies. It is impossible to overemphasize how crucial it is to women's issues, gender crimes, and the law in general to have women in decision-making positions in international fora, particularly within the United Nations structure, and as judges, prosecutors, and peacemakers"; Kelly D. Askin, "Prosecuting Wartime Rape and Other Gender-Related Crimes Under International Law: Extraordinary Advances, Enduring Obstacles," *Berkeley Journal of International Law* 21: 296.

read this scene absent the rest of the film – as many American law films can be read – we are left with a prototypical Hollywood narrative: "cause lawyer as humane hero."

But in a masterful cinematic move, Polanski catches the viewer completely off guard: Paulina has been listening in on the conversation and is convinced that Dr. Miranda is the man who repeatedly raped and tortured her during her detention. As Gerardo and the doctor continuing talking and guzzling alcohol, Paulina plots her revenge. Now passed out on the couch, Dr. Miranda is suddenly attacked by Paulina, who proceeds to knock him unconscious and bind and gag him to a chair. After the doctor awakens, we see Paulina standing over him and learn where the title of the film comes from: a cassette of Schubert's "Death and the Maiden" is playing, the very music Dr. Miranda played as he viciously tortured and raped Paulina at the time of the dictatorship.

The ruckus awakens Escobar, who rushes to the scene but is stopped dead in his tracks by Paulina, who now stands armed with a pistol. An enraged wife-victim-activist demands justice: if the unfaithful Gerardo and his commission will turn the other cheek to the brutality she has suffered at the hands of Dr. Miranda, then she will conduct her own trial. Escobar is torn between his love for his wife (magnified by his infidelity), his desire to protect a man he believes is innocent, and his desire to preserve his political future in the new regime. The bulk of the film's dramatic impact comes from Paulina's recounting of her suffering and Dr. Miranda's denial of responsibility (as well as the viewer's doubt as to who is in the right). At Escobar's insistence, an impromptu trial unfolds, and Dr. Miranda offers dozens of pieces of evidence that purport to exonerate him, all of which strike Paulina as a little "too convenient."

In the film's climax, as he is hanging from the edge of a cliff, Gerardo admits he was wrong, and equally, if not more, importantly to Paulina Dr. Miranda admits in graphic and disturbingly personal detail to torturing and raping her. In a representation of Paulina's continued, albeit shaken, commitment to human rights, both men are spared a watery death sentence in the violent ocean waves crashing far below. In the film's denouement, the characters are placed in the most civilized of environments: a musical recital, where amid dress gowns and tuxedoes and the softly playing piece that is the source of the film's title, the stench of their dehumanization barely lingers.

III. Paulina Escobar as "Radical" Cause Lawyer

Scholarship on cause lawyering has long focused on the politicization of legal practice and provides important insights for understanding Paulina Escobar as cause lawyer. Scheingold's study of Seattle cause lawyers who identify with the National Lawyers Guild calls attention to "left-legal activist" or "radical" cause lawyers who "aspire to politicize legal practice. That is to say, they are committed both to transformative politics and to a fusion of their political lives and their legal practices." One of the most important findings of Scheingold's research is that radical cause lawyering is dependent on the historical moment and may be constrained by professional obligations. For example, his research finds important differences between the accounts of lawyers of different generations, finding that left-leaning activist lawyers in 1990s experienced much more adversity in terms of professional support than left-leaning lawyers from the 1960s.

Regarding professional obligations, Scheingold observes, "In a number of ways, the aspiration to politicize legal practice, even in a watered-down form, puts left-activists at odds with generally accepted professional understandings of representation."[4] This observation is particularly relevant for understanding the new professional obligations placed on an activist turned official of the new regime; Gerardo Escobar is forced into the difficult situation of reconciling his commitment to social justice for women and his new professional obligations that foreclose the prosecution of mass rape.[5]

Attending to the historical moment is critical for understanding Paulina Escobar as radical cause lawyer. Perhaps analogous to the upheavals of the 1960s as experienced by some of Scheingold's second-generation left-leaning cause lawyers, Paulina must negotiate a world characterized by dramatic change. Yet even though the authoritarian regime has crumbled, her cause is lost in the new regime's decision to deny justice to her, and all the women she symbolizes in the film. In this respect, Paulina Escobar represents radical cause lawyers who see themselves as taking part in "something larger," as "identifying more with their causes than with their

[4] Stuart Scheingold, "The Struggle to Politicize Legal Practice: A Case Study of Left-Activist Lawyering in Seattle," in Austin Sarat and Stuart Scheingold, ed., *Cause Lawyering: Political Commitments and Professional Responsibilities* (New York: Oxford University Press, 1998), 118–19.

[5] For a close reading of Gerado Escobar as classic cause lawyer, see Chapter 9.

professional role as lawyers."[6] At the same time, like contemporary radical cause lawyers, Paulina is a realist who must use the law to achieve goals that may be readily achievable – namely, confronting both her rapist and husband who refuse to acknowledge meaningfully her victimization.

That Paulina has been raped by a representative of the fascist regime, that she is consumed with anger and grief, and that she is capable of violence to achieve such ends – but as a committed veteran to the cause of human rights ultimately resists imposing the death sentence – invite the reader to reimagine her neither as passive victim nor as a vigilante pursuing a purely personal revenge. Rather, Paulina's behavior invites the viewer to see her as a complex sort of *advocate*. She does not resort to simple violence or to mere emotional appeals for justice: rather, she chooses the discourse and symbolism of law to achieve her desired ends. She uses the language of law to reclaim not only her own dignity but also the dignity of all who were victimized by the previous regime, particularly the women who were rendered voiceless by her husband's human rights commission. With eyes wide open to the messy business of transitional justice, Paulina, not unlike indigenous cause lawyers operating in times of profound social upheaval,[7] is anything but a naïve victim. She is relentless in her mission to break the silence of the rape culture of the old order and, as we have learned, the threat of the perpetuation of rape culture in the new democracy facilitated by a silence about the past.

It is *Death and the Maiden's* complex, unresolved, but ultimately tragic narrative of "a perilous and uncertain future" for Paulina and the struggle for equal rights she represents that make the film especially relevant for considering what popular culture may teach us about the often daunting challenges that confront lawyering for change after protracted lawlessness and systematic oppression. But such idealistic aspirations, as *Death and the Maiden* makes abundantly clear, are far from easily accomplished, and it would be simplistic to see the film as triumphalist. The fascist law's

[6] Corey S. Shdaimah, "Intersecting Idenitities: Cause Lawyers as Legal Professionals and Social Movement Actors," in *Cause Lawyers and Social Movements*, ed. Austin Sarat and Stuart Scheingold (Stanford: Stanford University Press, 2006), 242.

[7] The representation of her struggle as unflinchingly painful, conflicted, and therefore open for the viewer to confront more directly presents a microcosm of an emotional economy of trauma, fear, and rage that characterizes much of fascist rule and its aftermath – namely, the dehumanization of women and the subsequent denial of such dehumanizing actions.

violence and the challenges implicit in confronting its oppressive legacy that are imbued in the new due process of law[8] take real emotional tolls on human beings, even the most heroic of cause lawyers.[9] Paulina must employ the law's violence to confront the fascist regime, as evidenced in her capture and subsequent trial of Dr. Miranda.[10]

Such a cinematic spectacle forces the viewer to reimagine cause lawyering in a moment of profound social upheaval; a moment in which "authority," "law," and "justice" are concepts that are contested by the outgoing regime as the nascent political order. Not in the obvious sentimentalities that may be read from the film – the *Thelma and Louise*-like female avenger and her emotionally unstable, "Dirty Harry-like" tactics to get justice at any cost – but in her willingness to confront her victimization and to articulate her anger in terms of law and justice. Paulina's litigation reveals that these crimes are not simply against her physical body – although that is certainly evident in her actions – but are also violations of the new body politic and the rule of law as such. Paulina's trial is a metaphor for the struggling feminist cause lawyer fighting within and against the entrenched rape culture that threatens to be reproduced in the new democracy.

8 For decades feminist social and legal scholars have catalogued the pernicious gendered violence that is perpetuated by the legal process in the United States. See Susan Estrich, "Rape," *Yale Law Journal* 95: 1087.

9 The kind of approach to law and film in this essay necessitates the use of ideal types. Thus, when we use the phrase "the most heroic of cause lawyers" we are not implying some idealized, one-dimensional vision of cause lawyering. As the literature on cause lawyering makes clear, cause lawyers are complex and thus have many different motivations for advocacy See Stuart Scheingold and Austin Sarat, *Something to Believe In: Politics, Professionalism and Cause Lawyers* (Stanford: Stanford University Press, 2004). As Scheingold most recently states, "For each cause lawyer, the search for 'something to believe in' is a personal quest. In some cases, the objective is pragmatic and particular; causes are chosen without much reflection and with no ideological or programmatic strings attached. In other instances, commitment to a cause reflects serious dedication to a particular objective or to some broader ideal. Cause lawyers gravitate to practice sites that are most consonant with their own priorities, and each site offers distinctive combinations of risk and reward." See Stuart Scheingold, "On the Myth of Moral Justice," *Cardozo Public Law, Policy, and Ethics Journal* 4.

10 See Robert Cover, "Violence and the Word," *Yale Law Journal* 95 (1986): 1601, for a classic account of how the state's own violence creates normative worlds with legal consequences, even for those who are actively opposed to state-sanctioned violence. But unlike the way the formal law in Cover's accounts buries its violence in legalistic language, Paulina's predicament is made completely visible in the film. Some would argue that judgment for Paulina's actions is integral for reading *Death and the Maiden* as a morality and punishment narrative. Although this may be the case, when imagining Paulina as cause lawyer our ability to see her struggle forces a more complex reading that we offer in this essay.

Even in some of its most brutal imagery, Paulina's behavior is not mere violence or vengeance, but a powerful statement about law and justice after totalitarianism. In one particularly powerful scene, Paulina stuffs her panties down the restrained Miranda's throat and grabs his penis as he urinates while trying to maintain some measure of dignity. These acts represent far more than spectacles of gendered vengeance: they stand for what a society was and may still continue to be, even after the fall of a fascist government – they embody the psychological toll of totalitarianism. Envisioning Paulina as a cause lawyer forces us to confront in far more global and visceral terms the taken-for-granted sexualized objects of a woman's panties (now stuffed down the throat of the patriarchal order) and the penis as the ultimate weapon of rape culture (now imprisoned by the hand of the oppressed). Like a rape victim recounting her violation before a jury, the terms that were used to subordinate the victim, the descriptions of her body and dress are now used to empower the disempowered. The tokens of the sexuality of the rape survivor are turned against the rapist and the order he represents.

Paulina's fearless crusade is a thoroughly deromanticized historicization of lawyering for gender equality.[11] Confronting a deeply entrenched patriarchal order has, to understate the matter dramatically, *consequences* for all involved in such a movement.[12] Paulina is psychologically scarred, and the new democratic regime (as represented by Escobar), by preventing her from confronting her rapist, gives her little support. Despite her adulterous-lawyer husband's reluctance to support her in the face of the old regime they both struggled to overthrow and his willingness to defend the accused rapist against her charges, she steadfastly presses on with her litigation. As cause lawyer, the very breaking of this silence *constitutes* Paulina's law.[13]

[11] For a fascinating early history of feminist lawyers in the United States, see Virginia G. Drachman, *Sisters in Law: Women Lawyers in Modern American History* (Cambridge, MA: Harvard University Press).

[12] One of the extreme consequences of participation in the women's movement has been to suffer the pains of long-term imprisonment. For a harrowing personal account, see Angela Y. Davis, *Angela Davis: An Autobiography* (New York: International Publishers, 1974.).

[13] Our reading of "law" here takes it cues from Santos's legal pluralism: "The impact of legal plurality on the legal experiences, perception and consciousness of the individuals and social groups living under conditions of legal plurality, above all the fact that their everyday life crosses or is interpenetrated by different and often contrasting legal orders and legal cultures" and experiences of individuals with law must not be marginalized as something other than "law."

It should not be surprising that Paulina's law receives little support from the patriarchal legal order, be it in the old or the new regime. As Orit Kamir observes in her fascinating reading of the film, Paulina's situation, and her willingness to allow her husband to "defend" Dr. Miranda, risks secondary forms of victimization:

> *Death and the Maiden* suggests that, just as husbands and rapists, abusers and jurists, often share world-views and interests, so old and new regimes, dictators and liberal legal systems have more in common than is immediately apparent. Victims of tyrannical regimes are likely to suffer a "second rape" perpetrated by new legal systems – much like rape victims.... As *Death and the Maiden* demonstrates, bystanders and legal systems – such as Gerardo – have much in common with rapists, feel much sympathy for them, and have much to gain from their brutal aggression.[14]

Paulina as cause lawyer is litigating simultaneously the old and new regime – both are on trial in Paulina's case. Hers is a trial that confronts gendered acts of violence once explicitly condoned and now implicitly reproduced by a new democratic order that she, in a cruel twist of irony, was part of creating. But once the old and new orders lies are exposed, Paulina as cause lawyer puts representatives of both on trial.

Not only are both regimes, personified by Gerardo Escobar and Dr. Miranda on trial, but also the form of justice that they both prescribe are placed in jeopardy by Paulina's refusal to play along. What matters is that her story is told and that her abuser acknowledge and describe his misdeeds, even more than that he be punished for them (once he confesses, she allows him to go free). She is not concerned, as her husband is, with the niceties of due process for Dr. Miranda, protections that her husband insists on providing. She does not use the law to demand justice in an abstract sense: she wants a narrative that legitimates her experiences and her victimization.

See Boaventura de Sousa Santos, *Toward a New Legal Commonsense* (London: Butterworths): 229–31.

[14] See Orit Kamir, "Cinematic Judgment and Jurisprudence: A Woman's Memory, Recovery and Justice in a Post-Traumatic Society (A Study of Polanski's *Death and the Maiden*)," in *Law on the Screen*, Austin Sarat, Lawrence Douglas, and Martha Merrill Umphrey, ed. (Stanford: Stanford University Press, 2005): 21.

IV. The Challenge of Paulina's Law

Paulina's cause is more than just reforming the new human rights commission to include rape as a crime to be prosecuted by the new democratic regime. By exposing the pervasive link between the dictatorship and new democratic legal institutions such as the human rights commission, she forces the viewer to reconsider an alternate legality – a world of law characterized by confronting atrocity on terms dictated by the oppressed; a legality in which historical memory is fundamental to any possibility of achieving social change and thus a democratic rule of law.[15] Such legality is not just a law of substance by which violations are met with the force of the state, but it is a law in which human dramas of transgression, victimization, and confession are central to the realization of democratic justice. Justice requires not only the creation of new institutions but also a reckoning with the old ones, a recognition that the previous regime's totalitarianism has dehumanized the populace. Thus Paulina's cause is not only democracy as an institution that had previously ignored it but it is also a restorative and therapeutic cause.

Paulina's trial has resulted in a profoundly sobering verdict: the persistence of an oppressive rape culture in the new democracy. The human rights commission now attended to by her emotionally abusive and therefore complicit husband excludes rape as a crime because of fears of a vigilante backlash. But Paulina's *refusal* to participate in lethal vigilantism, as depicted in the climactic verdict from the cliff, unmasks such claims as tacit defenses of the patriarchal order. Indeed, hers is a legality that demands public attention as opposed to a law constituted by private acts of vengeance. The objective of Paulina's law goes far beyond the symbolic healing of national human rights commissions. For Paulina as cause lawyer genuine reforms are only possible if every single "Paulina" in the country is able to confront his or her oppressor in an open, uncensored hearing.

By contrast to the overly sentimentalist, linear journey to "genuine reform" heard so often in the mainstream politics of international human

[15] This is not to suggest that the victim's perspective should be the only perspective considered. *Death and the Maiden*, we contend, provides a far more nuanced and problematic account of transitional justice that is closer to the findings detailed in Priscilla Hayner's compelling study. Hayner's exhaustive research reveals that the truth of giving voice to victimization must also be recognized as crucial to societal change. See Priscilla Hayner, *Unspeakable Truths: Confronting State Terror and Atrocity* (New York: Routledge, 2001).

rights,[16] the film's refusal to provide simple answers makes abundantly clear that societal change does not develop in a clean, evolutionary process. It is a world fraught with potentially violent confrontations, a struggle against a toxic past that has already seeped into the so-called democratic present.

Paulina's law and Paulina's justice can be contrasted to the image of the cause lawyer expressed by her husband. As an intellectual elite trained to use legal tools for the advancement of a particular social issue that he believes in, Gerardo Escobar clearly represents the classical cause lawyer. He has accepted that the ideals he wishes to achieve (human rights, democracy) require political compromise and at times silence on important parts of his goals. Moreover, in his willingness to defend Dr. Miranda, he is willing to give the accused rapist and torturer the full protection of law (even offering to serve as his defense counsel).

Unlike the cool, calm, and detached lawyer of the hegemonic law, Paulina as cause lawyer refuses to hide behind her victimization and settle for merely symbolic acts. As Richard Wilson in *The Politics of Truth and Reconciliation* persuasively demonstrates in his analysis of post-apartheid South Africa from below, the desire for retribution in a new democratic regime is real, and the demand for a full hearing at the local levels is robust and must go beyond symbolic rhetoric.[17] Although one could make the case that Paulina's law is a recipe for vigilante justice, reading Paulina as cause lawyer reveals a different interpretation. Perhaps more analogous to the local tribunals that constitute something like Rwandan *Gacaca* or "Justice in

[16] "When a period of authoritarian rule or civil war ends, a state and its people stand at a crossroads. What should be done with a recent history full of victims, perpetrators, secretly buried bodies, pervasive fear, and official denial? . . . While individual survivors struggle to rebuild shattered lives, to ease the burning memory of torture suffered or massacres witnessed, society as a whole must find a way to move on, to recreate a livable space of national peace, build some form of reconciliation between former enemies, and secure these events in the past. Some argue that the best way to move forward is to bury the past, that digging up such horrific details and pointing out the guilty will only bring more pain and further divide a country. Yet can a society build a democratic future on a foundation of blind, denied, or forgotten history? In recent years, virtually every country emerging from a dark history has directly confronted this question." Hayner, 3–4.

[17] For Wilson this was a primary shortcoming of the top-down approach to human rights talk in post-apartheid South Africa. "Human rights talk became the language not of principle but of pragmatic compromise, seemingly able to incorporate any moral or ideological position. The ideological promiscuity of human rights talk means that it was ill-suited to fulfill the role of an immovable bulwark against ethnicity and identity politics." See Richard A. Wilson, *The Politics of Truth and Reconciliation in South Africa* (New York: Cambridge University Press, 2005), 5.

the Grass,"[18] Paulina's law is all about confronting the highly personal (her resultant infertility) details and aftermath (her inability to enjoy her beloved Schubert) of one's victimization at the same time that it represents through its very imagery the need to confront the broader societal order. Paulina's law is more than a private, victim-centric jurisprudence; it is a legality inextricably bound to wide-ranging public concerns.

For Paulina the cause and the law become meaningless without the visceral, often disturbing private details of oppression confronted in full view of the community. Although Gerardo's multiple betrayals of Paulina may be read as a challenge to the efficacy of "global human rights" for transforming local cultures, the film nevertheless is generative of such an inquiry, especially in the context of gender violence.[19]

The story of Paulina Escobar as cause lawyer may also be read as a tale not dissimilar from the complex narratives that animate the women's rights movement in the United States. Breaking hundreds of years of silence about discrimination and victimization, members of the women's rights movement fought for more than a century to force sweeping changes in, to name some noteworthy examples, the law of voting, the workplace, and educational opportunities. These changes began with angered – indeed, often disobedient – women activists who refused to be silent and powerless. From this perspective, *Death and the Maiden* can be read not simply as a story about a human rights law animated by questions of the morality of punishment – although, it certainly can be read as such – but as a story constituted by a field of endless struggle for equal justice under law. Although Escobar and Miranda come clean in the face of an impending

[18] "The explicit purposes of the gacaca courts are threefold: (1) the reconstruction of that which was destroyed during the genocide; (2) the acceleration of processing defendants from a large number of jurisdictions; and (3) the reconciliation of Rwandans and the re-enforcement of their unity. The gacaca courts also have important ancillary goals: (1) establishing a record of what occurred and settling the past through truth-telling; (2) eradicating the culture of impunity; (3) redressing wrongs committed; (4) encouraging broad participation of all affected by the genocide; and (5) reestablishing trust and solidarity" See Brenda V. Smith, "Battering, Forgiveness, and Redemption," *American University Journal of Gender, Social Policy, and Law* 11 (2003): 955.

[19] Sally Merry presents a fascinating investigation of the tensions between global law and local justice. Through observational analysis at the UN and through rigorous fieldwork with grass-roots feminist organizations in several countries, Merry provides a sobering account of gender violence as rooted in deep cultural and religious beliefs. See Sally E. Merry, *Human Rights and Gender Violence: Translating Law into Local Justice* (Chicago: University of Chicago Press, 2005).

death drop to the sea, Paulina Escobar as cause lawyer is far too dynamic to see their confessions as constitutive of "closure."

Death and the Maiden's final scene reinforces an interpretation of Paulina's law as one constituted by a relentless struggle for equality at every level of society. While attending a performance of the title work, Paulina, now willing and able to hear her beloved Schubert again, spots Dr. Miranda and his family in the audience. When Paulina as empowered cause lawyer makes eye contact with Dr. Miranda, her gaze is expressionless, perhaps even pained. But underneath is a determination to go on living and supporting the new democracy – indeed, she is accompanied by the equally expressionless Gerardo. The story of Paulina Escobar as cause lawyer resonates: victimization is not something one gets over; indeed, the struggle for democracy entails an endless interrogation of an idealistic present woven inextricably to its brutal past. Nonetheless, it is clear that she is no longer personally destroyed by her experience.

It is not clear that the same can be said of Dr. Miranda.

V. Conclusion: Paulina's Law as Her Own, Now Ours

> I know how one says "Jew" and how one says "political"; and I soon realized that the translation of my account, although sympathetic, was not faithful to it. The lawyer described me to the public not as an Italian Jew, but as an Italian political prisoner.
>
> – Primo Levi, *The Reawakening*

Our reading of *Death and the Maiden* reimagines Paulina Escobar as a dynamic cause lawyer in a time of social upheaval and violent struggle. As a reminder of past crimes that the defenders of the old and new orders would just as soon forget, she is neither pure victim nor is she a woman seeking mere vengeance: she is a radical cause lawyer. Not a formally trained attorney, she is rather an advocate for her own and the nation's cause of confronting gender oppression, which makes her voice unique and *Death and the Maiden* such a powerful film. She gives voice to countless voiceless women who will not have their story told in the courtrooms of the new regime and thus remain lost to hegemonic (male) law. Like Primo Levi's rejection of a formalistic legal voice to narrate his own damaging victimization at Auschwitz – Levi takes ownership of this through the vehicle of short stories, novels, and essays – *Death and the Maiden* brings us into Paulina's private world, a world that cannot be translated into a straightforward reality by lawyers or anyone else.

Thus, for Paulina to tell her story she must create her own legality – a trial in which her torture and rape are given full account. It is not simply the details of the crime that Paulina wants, but equally importantly, her oppressor must testify to his own lust for power: "I could hurt you or fuck you. And you couldn't tell me not to." These words are anything but sentimental redress. They speak to a kind of law only through which Paulina can discover justice at the same time as Miranda's confession reveals Paulina as cause lawyer: beyond the admission of wrongdoing, we are confronted by the psychology of an insidious rape culture that made Paulina's torture and rape legal in the first place.

In this film, sexual violence and rape are confronted by the one who has lived it, and the voice of law must pay heed. Although the new democracy will not officially condone such barbarism it refuses to confront it; Paulina as cause lawyer rejects this evasion and forces us the viewers to reimagine a law that attends to the messy work of confronting atrocity. The trial in their remote cabin is not simply the trial of a man or of a dead military regime. It is a trial of a conception of law and order that refuses to acknowledge the unique nature of rape and the unique demands of rape victims. It is not an exaggeration to suggest that patriarchal political and legal theory are in the dock and subject to Paulina's law.

The phenomenology of atrocity that animates the work of Primo Levi is helpful for understanding Paulina's dilemma.[20] Many have written of Levi's complex and wholly compelling writings as variously embodying "memoir," "autobiography," "personal narrative," etc. But as both Levi's writings and *Death and the Maiden* demonstrate, the reader/audience can also interpret these tales not simply as works of gripping, historical literature or cinema. They may be constituted as their own respective jurisprudences of atrocity: Levi and Paulina Escobar vis-à-vis their respective mediums (the written word and film) can be reimagined as cause lawyers whose respective objectives are not simply to believe in a specific cause, as if such a cause were easily attainable.

Theirs is a law focused on achieving something that is more difficult but ultimately far reaching. It is a conception of law that forces the viewer/reader

[20] See Primo Levi, *The Reawakening* (New York: Touchstone Books, [1945] 1995).

to break free of law's impersonal formalisms and to reimagine it as a complex living, breathing, historically situated legality that must be confronted on the terms of those who govern, have lived, and will continue to live it. If we are to consider seriously the lessons of Paulina Escobar as cause lawyer beyond the historical and temporal confines of *Death and the Maiden* read as conventional legal narrative, we must necessarily reimagine cause legality in far more pluralistic terms. That is, we must realize that

> [t]o keep in our minds an understanding of the past that does not hinge on unwarranted associations and conclusions is a first step, but it also is an objective that will need to be renewed with each look backwards. The struggle that lies ahead . . . is to oversee ongoing developments and structurings of law's theories, practices and meanings as we progress into the future in legal cultures that cannot stand still, and that inevitably, often imperceptibly, will be besieged from within and from without in ways that challenge each generation's capacities of discernment and understanding, and that require each generation to reformulate law for ever-changing contexts.[21]

[21] See Vivian Grosswald-Curran, "Fear of Formalism: Indications from the Fascist Period in France and Germany of Judicial Methodology's Impact on Substantive Law," *Cornell International Law Journal* 35: 186.

THE CULTURAL RECEPTION OF LAWYERS AND THEIR CAUSES

11

Cause Lawyering 'English Style'

Reading *Rumpole of the Bailey*

Leslie J. Moran

I. Introduction

Rumpole of the Bailey, a character that comes from the pen of English author and barrister Sir John Mortimer QC, is in the first instance a rather unexpected choice of subject for a study of the cultural life of cause lawyering. Rumpole is a barrister who plies his trade in the criminal courts. In his first appearance on TV, in December 1975 in a drama screened as part of the British Broadcasting Corporation's (BBC) prestigious series, *Play for Today*,[1] Rumpole's redoubtable wife Hilda chastises him by calling him an "Old Bailey hack." "Old Bailey" describes not only the location of his lawyering, London's central criminal court, but it also has a more withering tone that suggests Rumpole has failed to rise above the lowliest form of practice: criminal trial advocacy. This tone is amplified by the term "hack," which emphasizes the everyday, the commonplace, and the mundane quality of the criminal work that is his stock in trade. His clients tend to be an assortment of ordinary and everyday underdogs; a black working-class teenager, a child in the care of the State, a hippie, a family of minor misfits, and so on. "Hack" also suggests that he is more a "hired gun" (doing whatever work he can to scratch out a living) than a "moral activist"[2] whose legal practice is politically engaged and dedicated to the service of social justice. As a down-at-the-heel aging but forever "junior"

[1] Irene Shubik, *Play for Today: The Evolution of Television Drama* (Manchester: Manchester University Press 2000).

[2] David Luban, *Lawyers and Justice: An Ethical Study* (Princeton NJ: Princeton University Press 1988): xxii.

barrister, Rumpole is decidedly at the bottom end, the unglamorous end, of the legal professional pecking order. His very name, Rumpole, is a play on his lowly status: Rump-ole, "ass-hole."[3] As John Denvir[4] notes in his comparison of Rumpole and Atticus Finch, the fictional lawyer commonly held up in the United States as the model of the "good lawyer" with high ideals, Rumpole, at first sight, is hardly the stuff of which forensic champions of social justice are made. His credentials as a political animal and a moral activist, however, cannot be quickly dismissed.

In the remainder of this essay I explore the character of Rumpole as a morally committed politically engaged lawyer in more detail. My analysis concentrates on the Rumpole found in the television drama and *Rumpole of the Bailey* TV series.[5] This is the Rumpole known by the mass audience. The TV programs also incorporate some of the materials found in the Rumpole novels. It is also through the television series that Rumpole became an international popular cultural phenomenon. At its peak in the mid-1980s the program was attracting a UK audience of more than ten million viewers.[6] The series was broadcast by more than 300 public television stations in the United States (representing 95 percent of PBS stations) as part of the *Mystery* series.[7] It also had a long run in Australia, on the Australian Broadcasting Corporation's network. VHS and DVD editions of the shows have enabled the series to have an even wider audience by breaking out of the institutional and temporal confines of television broadcasting. Victoria MacCallum[8] has described the Rumpole TV series as not only one of the first British legal drama series[9] but also one of its most popular. She also suggests that it has had an enduring cultural impact as a template for future British legal dramas.

[3] Graham Lord, *John Mortimer: The Devil's Advocate, The Unauthorised Biography* (London: Orion Books Ltd 2005): 207.

[4] John Denvir, "Rumpole of the Bailey," in *Prime Time Law: Fictional Television and Legal Narrative*, ed. Robert M. Jarvis and Paul R. Joseph (Durham, NC: Carolina Academic Press, 1998): 145.

[5] Rumpole also appears in a series of novels and radio plays. Both draw heavily on the TV programs.

[6] "Untitled," *Media Week* (January 9, 1987): 10

[7] Lynn Lovdahl, "Rumpole of the Bailey: British Legal/Mystery Comedy," Museum of Broadcast Communications, http://www.museum.tv/archives (last accessed May 22, 2007).

[8] Victoria MacCallum, "Law on Television," *Law Society Gazette* (2002).

[9] This is far from the case. Her comment I would suggest is indicative of the lack of knowledge and scholarship on the history of British legal drama. See further below.

For all of these reasons it is surprising that there is almost no scholarship that examines Rumpole. It is a particular surprise that he has not been the subject of British law and popular culture scholarship. A consideration of this state of affairs provides my point of departure. Thereafter I explore the social, political, cultural, and jurisdictional context out of which the TV character Rumpole emerges. The objective here is not to fix the meaning of Rumpole's character in an original moment, text, or context but rather to explore the factors that shaped and informed the character's many dimensions. I then examine a range of materials drawn from a variety of sources: scholarly articles and reviews[10] from law journals, Web sites, newspaper articles, obituaries, and short stories.[11] My objective is to examine how the character Rumpole has been read and used, particularly by people associated with the legal communities.[12] I want to read this data not for the image that it offers to the public as a resource for making sense of law and lawyers but as examples of lawyers using popular cultural resources to craft their own image and, in many instances, doing that with an audience of lawyers in mind.[13]

When using this data, one always needs to take into account the context of the use of Rumpole. For example, the comments made by lawyers reported in the obituaries for Leo McKern, who played the part of Rumpole to universal acclaim, are likely to have a very particular inflection. The form and function of the obituary tend toward its being a celebration of a person's life. Expressions of hostility, or comments that are more critical of the character, which for many was inseparable from the actor, are unlikely in this setting. But this need not lead to this data being dismissed. These

[10] The reviews drawn from legal publications all focus on the novels. This is despite the fact that Rumpole is probably best known via the TV series, which also provide the basis for the novels. Perhaps there is an assumption (or a need to assume) that members of the legal community do not watch TV.

[11] These are short stories written by lawyers and legal scholars in which the character of Rumpole appears. See Douglas S. Miller, "Rumpole and the Equal Opportunity Harasser (or Judge Bork's Revenge)," *Journal of the Legal Profession* 20 (1995): 165 and Jennifer James, "The Clementi Code," *New Law Journal* 156 (2006): 802.

[12] I concentrate here on responses by lawyers. For examples of uses of Rumpole by members of the judiciary, see Justice Michael Kirby, "The Judiciary in Federation Centenary Year – Good News, Bad News and No News," *Australian Institute of Judicial Administration* (2001), http://www.aija.org.au (last accessed June 7, 2007) and George F. Archer. "The Ancient and Hard-Won Rights: A Chat with John Mortimer QC," *Litigation* 13 (1986): 34.

[13] Pierre Bourdieu, "The Force of Law: Toward a Sociology of the Juridical Field," *Hastings Law Journal* 38 (1987): 805.

comments still provide an insight into the process of using the character as a cultural resource.

The database I use is a sample of existing data rather than an exhaustive archive. With that in mind I use it to offer a range of examples of uses of Rumpole rather than a final and exhaustive statement of the uses of this particular cultural resource. Finally, I offer some conclusions drawn from my reading of this legal figure.

II. Rumpole and the Legal Scholars

Very little has been written about this important fictional English lawyer. In part this is a reflection of the fact that scholarship on law and popular culture in general and on popular representations of lawyers in particular is dominated by work that focuses on U.S. culture. His absence from the pages of British scholarship on lawyers in popular visual culture is hardly surprising as that scholarship has also tended to be preoccupied with Hollywood and U.S. commercial TV rather than indigenous popular culture.[14] This U.S. cultural focus in British legal scholarship can be understood in several ways. First, it reflects the global reach and impact of U.S. (Hollywood) film and commercial TV. Second, it offers clear evidence of the need to be skeptical about the idea of an indigenous or national culture that is or can be hermetically sealed from the global reach of U.S. culture.[15]

But the enduring British scholarly preoccupation with U.S. popular culture does not support a conclusion that British popular representations of law and lawyers are nothing more than U.S. popular cultural forms rebranded for the British market. Such a position merely tends to ignore indigenous popular culture.[16] It also tends to put out of the frame of analysis

[14] For example, see the essays on film and television in the edited collection of British scholarship on law and popular culture: Steve Greenfield and Guy Osborn, *Readings in Law and Popular Culture* (London: Routledge 2006).

[15] Bill Grantham has explored some of these issues in the context of the question of national cinema and film finance. See Bill Grantham, "Cultural 'Patronage' Versus Cultural 'Defence': Alternatives to National Film Policies," in Leslie Moran, Emma Sandon, Elena Loizidou and Ian Christie, eds., *Law's Moving Image* (London: Glasshouse Press 2004): 187.

[16] Jason Bainbridge, "'Rafferty's Rules': Australian Legal Dramas and the Representation of Law," *Media International Australia Incorporating Culture and Policy* 118 (2006): 136; Steve

the particular, juridical, social, political, institutional, cultural, and aesthetic factors that inform representations of law and lawyers in general and indigenous representations in particular.

Studies undertaken by Miller[17] and Bainbridge[18] of Canadian and Australian legal dramas, respectively, suggest that in both these national/jurisdictional contexts local social, cultural, and political factors have an impact on legal dramas, on their plot lines, characters, mise-en-scène, and aesthetics that make indigenous legal dramas distinctive. For example, both authors suggest that the respective indigenous legal dramas reflect the local characteristics of courtroom practice, its manners, and its choreography (in particular, prohibitions that circumscribe the movement of advocates), which differ significantly from those found in the United States. Both note the way the more static courtroom performance reduces the dramatic potential of this forensic space in Canadian and Australian legal drama. Miller suggests that in Canadian legal fictions courtroom battles frequently fail to result in a just outcome. Bainbridge notes that in Australian dramas the courtroom encounter has a reduced potential for gladiatorial spectacle[19] and more limited opportunities for cathartic moments during which good order is reestablished. The courtroom is used more as a place that offers opportunities for a critique of archaic and alienating ritual than a venue for the realization of social justice.[20] Bainbridge suggests that Australian legal dramas focus more on the minutiae of everyday life and the private rather than the public lives of the lawyers represented.[21] The strong Canadian television tradition of news reporting and analytical documentary, Miller argues, feeds into the aesthetic sensibility of Canadian drama in general and of legal drama in particular, which shows a strong preference for realism and docudrama.[22]

Greenfield, "Hero or Villain? Cinematic Lawyers and the Delivery of Justice," in *Law and Film*, ed. Stefan Machura and Peter Robson (Oxford: Blackwell 2001): 25; Mary Jane Miller, "Mirrors in the Robing Room: Reflection of Lawyers and Law in Canadian Television Drama," *Canadian Journal of Law and Society* 10 (1995): 55.

[17] Miller, "Mirrors in the Robing Room."

[18] Jason Bainbridge, "'Rafferty's Rules.'"

[19] Ross Levi, *The Celluloid Courtroom: A History of Legal Cinema* (Westport, CT: Praeger, 2005): 39.

[20] Jason Bainbridge, "'Rafferty's Rules'": 147.

[21] Ibid., 145.

[22] Miller, "Mirrors in the Robing Room": 58.

To date there has been little or no attempt to undertake this type of analysis of British legal drama.[23] A pioneering study by Robson[24] is the first to attempt to document the long and continuing tradition of home-produced British TV programs about lawyers. Although Robson notes the national and international importance of Rumpole, it is perhaps hardly surprising that he devotes little more than a page to the series in his survey of more than forty home-grown legal dramas. He does make some useful preliminary points about the distinctive features of British legal TV shows in general. For example he suggests that drama is the preferred format of the legal show. In substance, British legal TV evidences a preoccupation with character and with the private life of the legal characters, a focus, he suggests, that precedes the emergence of similar themes in U.S. legal TV. He also argues that British TV portraits of law and lawyers tend to be more skeptical and critical of law as a vehicle for social justice.[25] Social class, gender, and race are common themes. How if at all does Rumpole fit into this scheme of things? Before answering that question I want to introduce another effect of a preoccupation with U.S. legal drama.

Most of the existing scholarship on Rumpole is from the pens of scholars in the United States. This draws attention to the global impact of British legal drama in general and of Rumpole in particular. Rumpole is a rare phenomenon: a fictional English lawyer who has become something of an international popular cultural phenomenon, particularly in the United States and in Australia. His appearance on U.S. television is of particular note. Miller comments that the American TV networks are "unique" in their "obsessive chauvinism regarding foreign television."[26] The appearance and success of the Rumpole series on American TV networks provide some evidence that this particular character has overcome this chauvinism. But before considering these American and other readings of Rumpole

[23] The nearest attempt is scholarship on British cinema that has included work on British crime cinema. See Steve Chibnall and Robert Murphy, eds, *British Crime Cinema* (London: Routledge 1999). Steve Chibnall and I. Q. Hunter are commissioning editors of a book series on British popular cinema. There is no book on British legal cinema in the series.

[24] Peter Robson, "Lawyers and the Legal System on TV: The British Experience," *International Journal of Law in Context* 2 (2007): 333.

[25] Robson, "Lawyers": 340.

[26] Miller, "Mirrors in the Robing Room": 61. This is manifest not only in the limited numbers of non-U.S. shows but also in the tendency to buy formats and then remake the programs for U.S. consumption. Examples include *The Office* and *Queer as Folk*. There seem to be no law TV examples.

in more detail, let me explore the various indigenous institutional, organizational, cultural, and jurisdictional factors that generated the fictional character Rumpole.

III. Rumpole and British TV Drama

Rumpole has his origins in Britain's public service television channel, the BBC. He was created as the central character in a TV drama broadcast as part of that channel's prime-time *Play for Today*, a pioneering anthology drama series. "Rumpole of the Bailey" was a one-time hour-long drama.[27] The *Play for Today* series, scholars of British TV have noted, is associated with the golden age of British TV drama.[28] This golden age, beginning in the 1960s and continuing until the end of the 1970s, is closely associated with the public service channel, the BBC. Funded by a national tax, the television license, the BBC was something of a haven from the more commercial populist (and conservative) media environment associated with Britain's first commercial TV stations.

Cooke[29] suggests the drama produced during this golden age had several key characteristics. They tended to be by writers known for their left-of-center politics, such as David Hare, Mike Leigh, Dennis Potter, Alan Bennett, Beryl Bainbridge, Carol Churchill, and Ian McEwan. Such writers generated high-quality, politically engaged, challenging drama focusing on contemporary social issues. A preoccupation of much of this work was everyday lives and the impact of contemporary social and political changes on those lives. The stories were character driven rather than plot driven. Their dominant aesthetic was social realism with a strong dose of documentary drama. They had a reputation for edgy radical political content. The single play, one-hour format, David Hare has argued, became "the most important new indigenous art form of the 20th century"; this format allowed writers, directors, and producers great freedom both substantively

[27] Rumpole was not Mortimer's first fictional lawyer (see Kidwell, "The Dock Brief"), but is perhaps his most developed.

[28] Dave Rolinson points to one of the dangers of the phrase "golden age." Not all the dramas that made up *Play for Today* fall within the category of high-quality radical television. However, this does not diminish the political and televisual importance of many plays that make up this anthology. See Dave Rolinson, "Introductory Essay," *Play for Today*, http://www.hull.ac.uk/filmstudies (last accessed May 25, 2007).

[29] Les Cooke, *British Television Drama: A History* (London, BFI Publishing, 2003): Chapter 3.

and aesthetically in a context that gave them access to mass audiences.[30] This is the context in which Rumpole makes his debut. How, if at all, is this context reflected in the original Rumpole drama and in the character of Rumpole as a lawyer?

In some ways the first appearance of Rumpole hardly fits the mold of cutting-edge drama. By the time Rumpole first appeared in 1975, courtroom drama was an established British TV drama format.[31] Several features of the original Rumpole drama are typical of the one-hour courtroom show. First, it deals with a single case. In a jurisdiction that at the time worked with a split profession granting almost exclusive rights of advocacy in all but minor matters to barristers, the lead courtroom character is a barrister. The drama begins by staging the incident that is the subject of the criminal charge, in this case an act of violence charged as attempted murder. It proceeds through various pretrial encounters between instructing solicitors, the barrister, and the client and the negotiations between counsel for the defense and the prosecution. It focuses particular attention on the advocate and skills of advocacy. Several courtroom sequences provide a certain climax to the drama. The forensic skills of cross-examination and lawyerly insight play a key role in the courtroom plot: Rumpole exposes police wrongdoing and brings to an end the pending miscarriage of justice. Although the program denies us the visual delight of witnessing the jury's verdict of "not guilty," we are left with no doubt that this is the outcome.[32]

The visual style of the show again shows little evidence of aesthetic innovation. If anything its look is rather conservative. With the exception of the short opening sequence of the drama that stages the violent incident that is the subject of the criminal charge, and a sequence showing Rumpole entering the Old Bailey, both of which are shot on location,[33] the rest of the production is studio based. Using a small number of sets – Rumpole's kitchen and bedroom, the lobby of the Old Bailey, the cells, the courtroom – the drama has the aesthetics of studio naturalism, rather than grainy realism or a documentary drama style.

[30] Quoted in Dave Rolinson, "Introductory Essay."

[31] Robson, "Lawyers."

[32] Carol Clover notes that the absence of some images of the jury in a filmic jury trial (the diagetic jury) is commonly associated with the representation of another jury, the extradiagetic jury: the audience as the jury. I would suggest that this is the case in the first Rumpole drama. See Carol Clover, "Movie Juries," *DePaul Law Review* 48 (1998): 389.

[33] The opening sequence also uses found footage of a cricket match to add to the realism.

So far there is little evidence of the substantive or aesthetic radicalism or innovation that others have identified with the *Play for Today* setting. But Rumpole's innovations, and its more radical political edge, I want to suggest, lie elsewhere.

As courtroom drama the first Rumpole drama shows evidence of a willingness to break some of the format's conventions. For example, the courtroom scenes are not made up of the traditional gladiatorial battle between opposing advocates.[34] In the first Rumpole drama, counsel for the prosecution never speaks in the courtroom scenes. Instead, the battle is between counsel for the defense and the judge. This is a significant departure from the overwhelming majority of courtroom dramas in which the judge is a largely silent, marginal figure.[35] In Rumpole the courtroom is a forensic space that provides a platform for dramatizing Mortimer/Rumpole's political critique of the judiciary. The courtroom climax, where guilt or innocence is determined, where justice and good order are reestablished, is formally missing. At best this cathartic moment is low key. The drama's climax and resolution lie elsewhere.

It is also perhaps something of a misnomer to call Rumpole a "courtroom drama." As the producer of the original Rumpole drama noted, the courtroom plot is "slender."[36] The audience is offered only the barest details of the alleged offense, the police interrogation, and so on. Character is center stage, and the central character is that of Rumpole.

The courtroom drama and the miscarriage of justice plot provide one setting in which character is developed. A dominant aspect of Rumpole's character that emerges in this setting is his unrelenting cynicism, which appears in the opening scenes. As he prepares to leave home for the Old Bailey he comments that his client is obviously guilty. His primary concern in dealing with his client is to ensure that the proceedings are quickly dealt with by a guilty plea so that he can have a lunch of steak and kidney pudding with his son Nick, who is leaving the same day to study in the United States. Rumpole's cynicism is also to the fore in his exchange with a fellow barrister in the court's robing room. There, he dismisses his client

[34] Levi, *The Celluloid Courtroom*.

[35] David Black, "Narrative Determination and the Figure of the Judge," in *Law and Popular Culture, Current Legal Issues* 7, ed. Michael Freeman (Oxford: Oxford University Press, 2005): 677.

[36] Shubik, *Play for Today*: 179.

as someone who uses violence just for fun. His client is another hopeless example of the malaise of contemporary Britain, a young person engaging in mindless violence. His conference with the client, a "Jamaican teenager" Oswald Gladstone, follows the same path. It is filled with Rumpole's clever and cynical reposts until, in exasperation the client asks, "Are you taking the mick?" to which Rumpole replies, "I'm sorry it's a bad habit." The cynicism subsides, only to return, producing another exasperated rebuke from Oswald, "You've got another case you want to do. You want to go and work for those rich villains. So what's wrong with my case? Too much hard work?"

Rumpole's indifference to the truth and to the threatened miscarriage of justice portrayed in this exchange provides a vehicle for Mortimer to suggest that Rumpole's main professional interest is to make money in the shortest time possible and with the least expenditure of energy. It also adds another dimension to his character. Having announced his indifference to the truth of his client's guilt or innocence, Rumpole responds to his client's professed innocence by dedicating his lawyerly skills to the service of his client's instructions. Rumpole is a consummate professional who will dedicate his skills to those who pay, in this case by way of legal aid. He leaves the prison cell to wage the gladiatorial forensic battle on his client's behalf. The first courtroom sequence shows Rumpole to be a master of his art.

Another court setting in which Rumpole's world-weary cynicism is explored is in his preliminary encounter with his instructing solicitor in the court's cafe. Although the solicitor and his clerk make repeated attempts to draw Rumpole's attention to the political aspects of the case – the impact of racism on his client's experience – their arguments and the evidence in support are repeatedly belittled and rebuffed. Rumpole dismisses the politically engaged solicitor and his equally concerned clerk as "difficult." Their commitment to social justice is, Rumpole explains to a fellow barrister, not only misguided but evidence of their incompetence; the instructing solicitor "can't tell a dodgy car salesman from a political prisoner." This sequence stages the interface between social justice, politics, and the legal profession. It is the solicitor and his clerk not Rumpole who are identified as "cause lawyers." Under Rumpole's cynical gaze the audience appears to be given a clear message that this is not the stuff of Rumpole's practice and that to take up such a position is to be either a mad or a bad lawyer.

Such is the unrelenting nature of Rumpole's cynicism that at times the character seems to be little more than an arch misanthrope.[37] But Mortimer seeks to avoid any tendency to read Rumpole's cynicism as mere misanthropy early in the courtroom plot by way of a voice-over. Through the voice-over that accompanies the location images of Rumpole entering the Old Bailey, we hear Rumpole offering an explanation of his cynicism. It is, he explains, a response to the grinding daily reality of work at the Old Bailey that "blunts the sensitivity";

> When I was young (if I can remember) I used to suffer with [the accused]. I used to cringe and suffer with them and go down to the cells full of anger. Now I hardly listen to the years pronounced and I never look at the dock. I never watch their faces when sentence is passed.

Far from being misanthropic, Rumpole's cynicism is a response to his commitment to his clients and his struggle for social justice in their encounter with the legal system and in particular the criminal justice system. It is his response to the enduring brutality of the criminal justice system in which he works day after day. It is evidence of his (now blunted?) political and moral commitment.

So Rumpole's cynicism is a pointer to the political and moral dimensions of Mortimer/Rumpole's critique/character. This gives his cynicism and his misanthropy a more satirical inflection.[38] Having offered this explanation of Rumpole's character (and "it blunts the sensitivity" is repeated, again by voice-over, later in the drama), the audience is directed to read his cynicism in a particular way, to focus on the sense of irony, and to take it as satire[39] that works with some idea of an alternative and, more specifically, a leftist critique.

Another device that turns the Rumpole drama away from courtroom drama and from plot to character is the use of a second story-line. The first one-hour drama devotes a considerable amount of screen time to Rumpole's dysfunctional family relationships.

[37] John Kidwell, "The Dock Brief," *Legal Studies Forum* 25 (2001): 287.

[38] Ibid., 287.

[39] Peter Goodrich, in his study of the uses of satire in legal scholarship, notes that it is closely connected to leftist critiques of law. See Peter Goodrich, "Satirical Legal Studies: From the Legalists to the Lizard," *Michigan Law Review* 103 (2004): 397.

This domestic story literally frames the courtroom plot. We first meet the character Rumpole not in court but at home. We see him, not performing the traditional role of the lawyer or that of the patriarch, but cooking breakfast for his wife Hilda, who lounges in bed in her pink, frilly-edged nightie demanding her boiled egg and toast. The show ends not with the legal injustice in the court but in the family kitchen with a conversation between Hilda and Rumpole.

Nor is the story of Rumpole's domestic relations a subplot. It is more a parallel story that provides an opportunity to explore character and is thereby intimately connected to the courtroom plot. Here the public and the private are more heuristic devices used by the writer than part of the divided lived reality of the character Rumpole. To understand its connection with the courtroom plot we must return to the first courtroom scene.

The scene shows Rumpole's formidable advocacy skills being put to use to expose police bad practice and secure the release of his client. Immediately prior to this scene we have been witness to Rumpole's cold indifference both to truth and to his client's guilt or innocence. Nick, Rumpole's son who is in court to meet his father for lunch, witnesses his father's forensic performance. We then cut to the scene in which Nick and Rumpole are at lunch.

The conversation turns to Rumpole's courtroom performance and Nick's anger and hostility about the apparent amorality and indifference of his father's business. This anger quickly spills over into Nick's concerns about Rumpole's relations with the rest of his family. Rumpole's courtroom persona, Nick suggests, is also his domestic persona. As Rumpole's cynicism and apparent indifference to truth make it impossible to know whether his courtroom skills are dangerously indifferent to or devoted to moral and social goods, so is it impossible to know whether his cynical asides and endless banter with his wife and son are merely evidence of his playfulness (and perhaps his indifference to familial love and devotion) or of his contempt and hatred of his wife and lack of interest in his family. Any answer to this domestic crisis and ontological confusion (Who is Rumpole?) is postponed by the arrival of instructing solicitors, who demand another conference with the accused.

The focus on Rumpole's domestic relationships returns to provide the climax of the drama. It comes immediately after the courtroom plot has been resolved in favor of Rumpole's client. We return to the family kitchen, at the stove, where the drama began.

Hilda, not Rumpole, is now cooking, not breakfast but the evening meal. The conversation turns to Nick and the lunch-time encounter. After defending Rumpole from the harsh criticisms of their son by noting that Rumpole is a member of an honorable profession, a drunken Hilda empties the final dregs of the gin bottle into her glass and we return to the 'who is Rumpole' question that is resolved in the following exchange:

> Rumpole: He [Nick] said you didn't know exactly who I am. You do know that don't you? Yes, of course you do.
> Hilda: You are Rumpole, aren't you?
> Rumpole: Of course! Horace Rumpole. What on earth was he on about? Everybody knows me, down the Old Bailey; an amiable eccentric who spills cigar ash on his waistcoat and tells the time with a gold hunter and calls everybody 'Old sweetheart' and I read Wordsworth in the loo. [Long pause] Who am I exactly?

Silence follows. It endures. Hilda, after staring blankly at him, leaves the table (and the screen) to attend to the cooking. Rumpole is alone on the screen. As the yawning silence persists, we witness the anguish and despair on his face. The release from this interminable silence only occurs as the credits finally roll. We see the obvious pain dissolve as Rumpole returns to the world of work, his next Old Bailey brief.

Before leaving this first Rumpole drama, I want to briefly turn to some of the aesthetic characteristics of that drama. The first is the use of the voice-over. It is used in a very familiar way, as a device to develop character. It works by adding information that is not to be found in the interaction between the characters in the drama. It is particularly used to add the moral and political dimensions of the Rumpole character. Of particular interest is the way it achieves this by creating a special intimacy between the audience and the character of Rumpole. The voice-over makes the audience a party to something that is overtly denied to the other characters in the scene and thereby forges a relationship, an understanding, that is unique to the audience and the character of Rumpole.[40] We are familiar with the device of the voice-over, even though in the past, and it still remains the case, its use in courtroom drama and lawyer shows is rare.[41]

[40] "Book Review: Rumpole of the Bailey," *American Bar Association Journal* 67 (1981): 1162.
[41] Wilcox suggests it is a particular rarity on American television. See Wilcox, "The Rumpole Books," 118.

The intimacy that is created by the voice-over is the context in which many of Rumpole's criticisms of the law, criminal justice, and the abuse of power by those in authority are delivered. Space dictates that I only offer one example. It comes from the first courtroom sequence of the original drama and takes the form of a commentary about the judge:

> Judges used to scare the living daylights out of me. Terrible old darlings who went back to their clubs and ordered double muffins after death sentences. Bright purple with rage, they used to be. Or white as paper, with voices like ice cracking as they put the boot in. All the same you could work on those judges. You could divert that rage onto the opposition. Or move them to tears about an old lag's army records. "Yes, my Lord he has his little foibles and faults but he did extremely well on the Somme." But this one is a civil servant. Not a tear in him. He can't seem to come to terms with himself. Humm, there he is giving me a look of vague disgust like Queen Victoria with a bad period.

Here Mortimer/Rumpole explores some of the qualities and characteristics of those who hold judicial office – their use of fear, their callous indifference, pomposity, and on occasions their malleability – by using the artful deployment of cliché that pampers to their prejudice.

This brings me to a second aspect of the aesthetics, the use of the camera.[42] The visuals that accompany this voice-over are worthy of comment. As this monologue begins, the camera and thereby the audience take up the position occupied by Rumpole. We/Rumpole look up toward the judge on the bench. As Rumpole's monologue proceeds, the camera slowly zooms in on the judge's features. This visual device creates an experience of the monologue as an ever-closer examination by the audience of this figure of authority dressed in scarlet fur-trimmed robes and an archaic wig, with a stiff body, sometimes staring at the jury with cold, bored indifference, later looking down his nose and giving Rumpole (and the audience) a withering look as the jury members are sworn in. Through this visual technique, Rumpole's critique is experienced as our own.

One final observation I want to make about the original Rumpole drama relates to the mise-en-scène. The body figures large. It works, literally,

[42] Camera work and editing are also central to creating the extradiagetic jury referred to above. See Carol Clover, "Movie Juries."

to flesh out the character of Rumpole. His rather down-at-the-heel legal practice is mirrored in his rather dishevelled physical form and sartorial style. Rumpole, played by the actor Leo McKern, is short and portly with a large bulbous nose, jowls, a glass eye, and erratic eyebrows.[43] There is something of a preoccupation with his bodily functions. We twice observe him urinating at the barristers' urinals. There are constant references to eating: endless cheese sandwiches, the occasional mashed spuds or steak and kidney pudding and down-market claret, which he calls "Chateau Fleet Street" or "Chateau Thames." He is frequently surrounded by clouds of smoke and covered in ash from his small cigars. Critics have described the character as "irredeemably gross,"[44] "shapeless,"[45] and "crumpled."[46] One actor described the sartorial style of the character Rumpole as looking like "a heap of dirty washing,"[47] "scruffy."[48] But his "grotesque" physical form and his shabby attire are not signs of his failure to make his way as an Old Bailey hack, but rather speak of his political credentials. One critic explained, "In habits and style he has more in common with his clients than with other members of the legal profession."[49] The authors of a fan-based Web site explain that his appearance as "a relatively poor man" shows he is a "common man" who can mix with "common people." His grotesque qualities, the same authors suggest, speak of his authenticity, of his "disgust for sham, and a contempt for pettiness."[50]

The original drama blends together substantive and aesthetic elements that are both traditional and innovative. One instance is in the shift from plot to character. Character provides the disturbing climax of the drama. The ontological void that Rumpole faces at the end of the drama is not the stuff of which cathartic courtroom conclusions and happy endings are

[43] Lovdahl, "Rumpole."
[44] John Haughton "Wise After the Event," *The Listener* 117 (1987): 8.
[45] "Rumpole Star McKern Dies," *BBC News* (2002a), http://news.bbc.co.uk (last accessed May 22, 2007).
[46] "Stars Pay Tribute to Rumpole Actor," *BBC News* (2002b), http://news.bbc.co.uk (last accessed May 22, 2007).
[47] Henry Szeps quoted in Jim Waley, "Leo 'Rumpole' McKern: Final Verdict" July 28, 2002, http://sunday.ninemsn.com.au (last accessed May 22, 2007).
[48] Gordon McKerrow "Rumpole Series Above Usual Standard," *Television Today* (July 5, 1979): 20.
[49] Moira Retty, "Television Review," *Television Today* (November 7, 1991): 19.
[50] Kevin Smith, and Paul Urbahans. "Editor's Prerogative: Horace Rumpole," http://www.thrillingdetective.com/eyes/rumpole.html.

made. Mortimer also resists one-dimensional characters or narratives. For example, although the drama mobilizes sympathy and empathy for the victim of the miscarriage of justice – a black teenager who was abandoned by his family at an early age – that character is also given characteristics that might tend to alienate the viewer. For example, he is shown to have a tendency to celebrate his criminalization, to play the celebrity. Rumpole himself is also a complex character, a combination of potentially alienating cynicism and a lawyer driven by the demand to make money and also a dedication to social justice. He is charming and ebullient and profoundly alienating and alienated.[51] Mortimer suggests, "[Rumpole] can say the things that I think which if I said them they sound rather trendy and left-wing and objectionable. If he says them they sound rather crusty and conservative and totally acceptable."[52] Of particular interest is Mortimer's suggestion that Rumpole's conservative characteristics (and I would add his charm) may work as a device for disseminating a more radical political agenda to a wider and otherwise more hostile audience. The drama's edginess may in part lie in this potentially subversive combination. It may also be an effect of some of the aesthetic devices that work to develop a particular intimacy between the character and the audience.

The BBC's anthology drama series, *Play for Today* provided a very particular institutional home for Rumpole's birth. It was a home protected from some of the pressures of the outside world of commercial TV. It nurtured and sustained left-leaning political drama. It fostered challenging, edgy drama. In that place Sir John Mortimer invented a legal drama and a legal character that offered a politically informed left critique of law, legal institutions, and the legal profession.

IV. Rumpole and the English Legal Tradition

Having devoted some time to the impact of the media on the generation of the character of Rumpole, I want to briefly comment on the significance of certain jurisdictional peculiarities. Some have been noted already, such as the impact of the split profession and the importance of the barrister rather than the solicitor as the advocate. The manners and conventions of

[51] Bernard Davies, "One Man's Television," Broadcast no. 959 (April 23, 1978): 8.

[52] Sir John Mortimer, "Interview with Sir John Mortimer," *The Classic Drama Series: Rumpole of the Bailey* (London: DVD/VideoAcorn Media UK undated).

English courtroom practice, which prohibit the movement of advocates in the courtroom, are clearly in evidence in the courtroom sequences of the first, and indeed every Rumpole drama. Rumpole is fixed in place. The drama works through the eloquence of the character expressed in the various verbal exchanges. If there is movement, it is achieved by the camera and editing.

Mortimer himself has drawn attention to the importance of the English legal tradition in his explanation of the character of Rumpole. Rumpole is partly based on Mortimer's father, a barrister who specialized in divorce litigation, and partly on a character study built out of snapshots of Old Bailey hacks who sold their services to anyone who would pay their fees. The character also owes much to the life and work of Mortimer himself.

Mortimer has on occasion described Rumpole as his "alter ego."[53] More specifically, Mortimer's own reputation and practice as a civil liberties and human rights barrister provide much of the perspective and substance to the character of Rumpole and the drama more generally.[54] As a barrister Mortimer is well known for his civil rights advocacy. He has a particular reputation based on his involvement in several high-profile cases concerned with obscenity and freedom of expression, including the prosecution of the publishers of D.H. Lawrence's *Lady Chatterley's Lover*. Experiences drawn from his civil liberties practice appear in episodes of Rumpole. For example, Mortimer was counsel representing the newspaper *Gay News* in a notorious blasphemy prosecution. The newspaper had published a poem by the poet James Kirkup about the reflections of a centurion stationed at the foot of the cross that holds the crucified Christ. The poem offers a meditation on the centurion's love of Christ as a fantasy of sexual relations with the body of the dead Christ.[55] During the course of the trial the judge interrupted the proceedings with the following comment to the jury: "It may come as a relief to you in the middle of this sordid little case, to know that England is 106 for 2 wickets in the Test Match in Melbourne." This comment is reproduced in one of the Rumpole episodes.[56]

[53] Archer. "The Ancient": 71.

[54] Mortimer's name and reputation as a politically committed lawyer are also forged by links to other barristers such as Geoffrey Roberston who have a reputation for involvement in high-profile litigation involving civil liberties and more recently human rights. See Geoffrey Robertson, *The Justice Game* (London: Vintage, 1999).

[55] Leslie J. Moran, "Dangerous Words and Dead Letters: Encounters with Law and 'The love that dares to speak its name,'" *Liverpool Law Review* 24 (2002): 1.

[56] Archer, "The Ancient."

Mortimer is frequently referred to by the derogatory phrase "champagne socialist," which is commonly associated with English legal characters who might fit the title of "cause lawyer."[57] The phrase "champagne socialist" links his lawyering to a more overt and specific politics. Mortimer's party political affiliations are generally left of center. He has at times been a member of the Communist Party, and in the past he has had close links with the Labor Party.[58]

Nor is it just Mortimer's legal practice and politics that have been plundered for the Rumpole plots. His family background, family relations, and educational background, respectively dysfunctional and elite (educated at Harrow and Brasenose College, Oxford) have been a rich resource that have been the subject not just of Rumpole but also of much of Mortimer's literary outpourings.[59]

These jurisdictional and biographical connections are particularly important in relation to the aesthetic sensibility of the Rumpole dramas. They inform the aesthetics of the Rumpole shows, which has been described as "studio naturalism."[60] The incorporation of these jurisdictional and biographical features suggests that the aesthetic is far from eschewing realism.[61] I am using realism here as a reference to a mode of description/depiction of a particular relation between two objects: the thing described/depicted (that which is outside and before the text) and the result of the process of description/depiction (that which is "in" the text). The jurisdictional and biographical references work to connect the thing being depicted – the world of law, lawyers, their clients, and the world of politics and justice – to the image found in the TV series.

Quoting Roman Jakobson, Paul Willemen explains realism in the following terms: as "an artistic trend which aims to reproduce reality as faithfully as possible and which aspires to achieve the maximum of verisimilitude."[62] The term "verisimilitude," Willemen explains, suggests that realism is about social conventions of representation and "rules of a genre" that work

[57] Lord, *John Mortimer*.

[58] Ibid.

[59] Mortimer and his wife Penelope have also both penned several volumes of an autobiography. See Lord, *John Mortimer*.

[60] Shubik, *Play for Today*: 180.

[61] The tendency to suggest that Rumpole is not a realistic drama misunderstands the nature of realism. For example, see Garry Slapper, "Judge John Deed," *New Law Journal* 151(2001): 1866.

[62] Paul Willemen, "On Realism in the Cinema," *Screen* 13 (1972–3): 36.

as a "set of restrictions within a particular culture."[63] The phrase "studio naturalism" suggests not so much an aesthetic that has abandoned the conventions and rules of realism but one in which they are a little more obvious than is normally the case in dramas that use more location shots and documentary styles.[64] "Studio naturalism" also draws attention to another dimension of realism: "emotional realism."[65] Writing about realism in relation to the TV show *Dallas*, Ang notes that emotional realism operates by connotation:

> ... the same things, people, relations, and situations, which are regarded at the denotative level as unrealistic, and unreal, are at [the] connotative level apparently not seen at all as unreal, but in fact as "recognizable."[66]

This suggests that although the "studio naturalism" of Rumpole may give rise to characters, plots, and the mise-en-scène that seem rather unrealistic to some, it does not necessarily mean that it does not produce realistic, "recognizable" characters, etc. The realism comes through the viewer's engagement with the fiction.

V. Rumpole and the TV Serial

All of these qualities and characteristics were first generated in the context of a single one-hour drama. They also feature large as some of the building blocks for the seven TV series that followed (43 sixty-minute episodes produced between 1978 and 1992).[67] It is through these episodes that Rumpole is best known. What impact did the movement from the single drama to the TV series have on Rumpole?

[63] Ibid., 38.

[64] Peter Robson suggests that the rather "dated" look of studio naturalism is or at least becomes an aesthetics of choice rather than an aesthetics of economic and technological necessity as it gives the drama a "heritage" look and generates feelings of nostalgia. See Robson, "Lawyers": 340.

[65] Christopher Williams, "After the Classic, the Classical and Ideology: The Difference of Realism," *Screen* 35 (1994): 275, 277.

[66] Ien Ang, *Watching* Dallas: *Soap Opera and the Melodramatic Imagination* (London: Methuen 1982): 42.

[67] There were significant gaps between the series. For example a three-year gap separated the second (1979) and third series (1983). A similar gap separated series 5 (1988) and 6 (1991). A two-hour special, *Rumpole's Return*, was broadcast in 1980 between series 2 and 3.

The serialization of Rumpole coincided with a move to one of Britain's commercial TV stations, Thames Television. This institutional shift and the change in format are indicative of changes that were going on in British television in the late 1970s.[68] The golden age of drama at the BBC and the single-play anthology format were in a state of decline. Structural changes, bureaucratic challenges, and financial pressures on the BBC created by the declining value of public funds in contrast to the growing revenue generated by commercial operations were all factors contributing to this decline.[69] All informed the move of Rumpole to the commercial channel.

The move also reflects changes that were taking place in the values associated with public broadcasting and commercial television. These values were not only shifting but also converging. This convergence has been described in both positive and negative terms. On the one hand, the high standards and political edge of public broadcasting were being reduced to the lower quality and more conservative values associated with commercial TV. Yet, at the same time standards associated with commercial television were being improved as the commercial channels drew on writers, narratives, and technological and aesthetic developments taking place in public service TV. How did all of these factors affect Rumpole?

The Rumpole series that is reborn on commercial TV does draw on the original drama. For example, it uses the same one-case-per-episode format. The courtroom plots tend to be rather schematic and character dominates. Rumpole's cynicism provides a vehicle for political commentary. His family life and, in particular, his relations with his wife Hilda remain a part of the drama. Rumpole's body, played throughout the forty-three episodes by Leo McKern, is an abiding central aspect of the mise-en-scène. Studio naturalism remains a key element of the visual style. But there were also changes.

Many of these changes are responses to the new opportunities and challenges associated with the serial format. For example the serial format allows a wider range of cases with the potential for a wider range of miscarriages of justice plot lines. In the seven TV series that follow, Rumpole fights against potential miscarriages of justice in many different settings: a prosecution for the supply and use of illegal drugs[70] and proceedings involving

[68] See Shubik, *Play for Today* and Cooke, *British Television Drama*.
[69] Shubik, *Play for Today*: 181.
[70] "Rumpole and the Alternative Society" (Series 1).

allegations of a breach of state security,[71] rape,[72] fraud,[73] and terrorism,[74] to name but a few. Several episodes explore miscarriages of justice in the context of a charge of murder.[75] Other cases involve freedom of speech,[76] police corruption,[77] and gender discrimination.[78]

Winning the case, a feature of the original drama, does not carry over into the series. From the very first series Rumpole's skills do not always succeed in securing social justice and in the release of the accused. Rumpole's explanation for his failure is that the character of the accused tends to get in the way. Although Mortimer may not have wanted to suggest by this explanation that our hero Rumpole can always defeat social injustice through the law, another factor may also be at work here: the demands of serialization. To retain an audience from episode to episode and from series to series, a degree of variety is needed. Defeats as well as victories may be, in part, a device to retain an audience.

The series format provides more time for character development. Having multiple episodes enabled the character of Rumpole to be expanded. For example in the first series, all of the plot lines are located in the past, from 1967 to 1977. This gives Rumpole a history. We have the experience of learning about Rumpole's family history and his earlier career as a barrister. We learn more about the factors that have informed his enduring position as a "junior" barrister, his indifference to career "progression," and his skepticism about those who have and aspire to positions of authority. In the second episode of the first series, "Rumpole and the Alternative Society," we also learn more about his romanticism (signified by his use of the poetry of Wordsworth in particular), and of his amorous past.

The move from a single drama to serial format makes character development not so much a luxury but a necessity. Character development is needed to keep the audience engaged and the revenue from advertising flowing into the TV company not only over the duration of each series

[71] "Rumpole and the Official Secret" (Series 4).
[72] "Rumpole and the Honorable Member" (Series 1).
[73] "Rumpole and the Barrow Boy" (Series 5).
[74] "Rumpole and Portia" (Series 5).
[75] "Rumpole and the Heavy Brigade" (Series 1); "Rumpole and the Sporting Life" (Series 3); "Rumpole and the Miscarriage of Justice" (Series 7).
[76] "Rumpole and the Fascist Beast" (Series 2); "Rumpole and the Bubble Reputation" (Series 5).
[77] "Rumpole and the Learned Friends" (Series 1).
[78] "Rumpole and Portia" (Series 5).

but also from one series to the next. But the popularity of the series in part feeds on stability of the character that breeds familiarity, which may impose limits on character development. Character development then becomes a problem and a challenge for a series. Already by mid-1979 commentators[79] in media trade papers were commenting that the character of Rumpole had become fully developed. Thereafter media commentators begin to complain about the limitations of the character and its potential to undermine audience interest and the earnings potential of the show. Although these criticisms persisted,[80] they did not curtail the production of several subsequent series.

The serial format affects character development in other ways as well, so that it develops in ways more associated with soap operas than single drama. Although each new episode's story-line brings new contexts and new characters through which character can be elaborated, character is also developed by way of the introduction of "running characters," who appear in each episode. A particular function of these characters is to sustain interest across episodes. The Rumpole series has several running characters who did not appear in the original drama. For example, in the first episode Rumpole's character is developed by way of the introduction of other members of his chambers, fellow barristers such as Claude Erskine-Brown and George Frobisher. Then from episode to episode these characters also begin to develop. For example, in the first episode we are introduced to Guthrie Featherstone QC MP. He appears first as a member of chambers who by the end of the first episode has been elevated to be head of chambers. As the series progresses we witness his elevation to the bench and then his performance as a judge. Over time we also learn of his amorous pursuits and of his wife. The objective is to use this wider stable of rolling characters to both widen the audience and to get the audience "addicted."[81]

Another related issue is changes in the nature of the narrative. A feature of serial drama found in almost all of the Rumpole series is flexi narrative.[82] In

[79] Laura Swaffield, "Success Is a Danger," *Television Today* (July 12, 1979).

[80] Stephen Day-Lewis, "Courtroom Drama Loses Its Edge," *Broadcast* (December 6, 1991): 21.

[81] Shubik, *Play for Today*: 190.

[82] Cooke, *British Television Drama*: 176. There is a need for some caution here as the use of multiple plot lines is not consistent across the whole of the seven series or within each series. Flexi-narratives are a more dominant feature of the later series, maybe echoing developments elsewhere in narrative styles of contemporary drama.

flexi narrative, another serial format characteristic that has its origins in soap opera, several narrative strands are woven together. Cooke describes this format as a hybrid of traditional drama and drama serial.[83] Some narratives develop from week to week, and some, involving guest characters, are resolved in a single episode. Other narratives and running characters appear in multiple episodes, allowing characters to develop week by week. In Rumpole most of these characters are to be found in Rumpole's chambers. Chambers joins together with the two plot lines (courtroom/miscarriage of justice and Rumpole's domestic life) found in the original drama. It provides an enduring opportunity for Mortimer to explore the politics of the legal profession and to offer a more detailed and sustained critique.

Rather than a main plot and subplots, in many episodes of Rumpole plot hierarchy is less clear, and the different plots are "inseparable"[84] and tend to mirror each other. For example, in "Rumpole and the Married Lady," the third episode from the first series, the courtroom plot line – a tale of marital strife that has led to divorce proceedings – connects with a plot line about Rumpole's own strained relations and non/mis-communication with his wife. A third plot line, focusing on Rumpole's working environment – his chambers – uses the arrival of the first woman in chambers, Ms. Phillida Trant, and the domestic ennui of a fellow barrister, George Frobisher, to reflect on the gender politics of heterosexual colleagues' intimate marital relations.

Another change is in the use of the voice-over. As noted earlier, it is used in the single drama not only to extend the character of Rumpole but also to prepare the audience to read Rumpole's cynicism as satire. In contrast, at least in the early episodes, the voice-over is not used as the mechanism for delivering the political critique. Humor is provided more by way of puns, laconic remarks, absurdity, and repartee.

In the absence of a voice-over highlighting the satire rather than the misanthropy, which on a weekly basis might bore an audience, different devices are used to announce and frame the humor and the politics: the style (the artwork and the music) of the opening and closing credits and the commercial break singers that accompany each episode. These all portray Rumpole through a cartoon image, which uses a style similar to that of

[83] Cooke, *British Television Drama*: 176.

[84] Richard North. "Pure and Impure," *Listener* (April 13, 1978): 18.

the nineteenth-century satirical cartoonist, George Cruikshank.[85] Humor is foregrounded by the aesthetics. The sequencing of the visual images always leaves us with an image of Rumpole as a figure committed to Justice. He stands atop the Old Bailey in an embrace with the statue of Justice. His rather dishevelled physical form and sartorial style are now the mirror image of Justice. His body is almost literally integrated into that of Justice; he provides the sword (now an umbrella) to her scales. The deep sonority of the music, produced by a bassoon, contra-bassoon and a cello, was chosen, the producer explains, to emphasize the humor of the drama to follow by making a link between the deep sounds of Rumpole/McKern's deep voice and the particular sonority of these instruments.[86]

How, if at all, do serialization and the move to a commercial channel affect the political dimensions of Rumpole? Through the seven television series, Rumpole is shown to be a dogged champion of social justice. No matter what temptations he may face, Rumpole is in the final instance integrity personified. A highly skilled and inspiring advocate, Rumpole is shown in many of the episodes dedicating his formidable forensic skills to the fight for social justice through the courts. His two basic commandments – never appear for the prosecution and always plead not guilty – firmly align him to the cause of the accused. His dedication to social justice is wide ranging, as is his critique of social injustice. Prisons and the practice of imprisonment are subject to withering criticism. He exploits opportunities to expose the cruelties of the criminal justice process and the injustices of a pedantic commitment to the letter of the law. He attacks the incompetence, prejudices, and mercenary objectives of his fellow legal professionals, exposing the vanity, insularity, peevishness, and prejudice of a judiciary that is drawn exclusively from the social elite. Rumpole is a character who constantly challenges and exposes the values of those with power and those who occupy positions of authority, including his wife Hilda, who gives voice to a rather different set of rules and sense of good order, that of bourgeois respectability.[87]

Various media commentators have described the moral and political agenda of the character of Rumpole that emerges from this series. One

[85] Shubik, *Play for Today*: 186.
[86] Ibid., 187.
[87] Richard North, "Pure and Impure": 475.

television reviewer described the character as something of an "old fashioned liberal."[88] This characterization perhaps echoes one of the working titles of Mortimer's first sketch of Rumpole written for the BBC's *Play for Today* slot, "Jolly Old Jean Jacques Rousseau."[89] The same reviewer also noted Rumpole's anarchic tendencies, which he suggests have their origins in Mortimer's father (one of the sources of the character).[90] The reference to anarchism, in particular the Russian anarchist, Peter Kropotkin, is also echoed in a second working title for the original Rumpole TV play, "My Darling Prince Peter Kropotkin."[91]

Rumpole's lowly status is not so much a reflection of a failed career or a career in tatters but a testament to his resistance to the forces of greed and corruption he invariably associates with power, authority, and social elevation. It also speaks of his commitment to the pursuit of social justice at the level of the everyday encounters people have with the law in general and with criminal justice in particular. Rumpole's credentials as a cause lawyer of the popular imagination are at this point beginning to improve. As Denvir concludes, Rumpole is much more the good lawyer and lawyer as hero than one might at first suspect.[92]

But there is also a difference between the single drama and the series. The delivery of the political critique seems more muted in the latter. Although Rumpole's cynicism is still a key part of his character, I suggest that its presence and its political edge have been changed and softened. A comparison between the single drama and the very first episode of the Rumpole series can be used to highlight this change.

In key respects the plot line in both is the same. Both courtroom plots involve a confession, questionable police behavior, and mistaken identity, all leading to a potential miscarriage of justice. Nick, Rumpole's son, witnesses his father's courtroom performance in both. As noted above in the single drama Nick's outrage at his father's courtroom performance provides an opportunity to examine the nature of Rumpole's cynicism both in relation to his legal practice and his family relationships.

[88] Ibid.

[89] Shubik, *Play for Today*: 177 and Simon Farquhar, "Rumpole of the Bailey," *Film and Drama BBC Four* (2003), http://www.bbc.co.uk/bbcfour (last accessed May 22, 2007).

[90] North "Pure and Impure."

[91] Lord, *John Mortimer*: 207.

[92] Denvir, "Rumpole of the Bailey."

In sharp contrast, in the first episode of the new series Nick shows no signs of outrage. Nick, now a naïve and impish schoolboy, rather than a more mature, challenging university graduate who is embarking on an academic career as a sociologist, finds Rumpole's advocacy skills rather entertaining. The lunch-time conversation between father and son has changed its focus. It is now about Nick's minor (but potentially criminal) transgressions at private school. Nick's transgressions provide the link joining his (and thereby Rumpole's) life to the criminal career of the young boy who is in the dock. The critique of Rumpole's cynicism and of his lawyerly behavior in court and its relationship to his domestic relationships has disappeared.

There is also a very different approach to the miscarriage of justice storyline. In sharp contrast to the single drama, the cause of the "false confession," the dubious police practices, and the miscarriage of justice in the first episode is not so much corrupt authority or the social structures that generate and perpetuate social injustice but domestic social relations. It is in the final instance a result of an ongoing family feud between two warring families of petty criminals.

Although it is dangerous to reduce the whole of the seven series to this one episode, I suggest that this episode is indicative of some key differences between the character of Rumpole in the single drama and in the subsequent series. His character in the series has a softer edge. The bleak ontological void that threatens to consume Rumpole at the end of the very first drama is no longer a feature. Although he remains a complex character, the different dimensions of his character are not drawn so extremely. The critique of the injustices arising from social divisions of class, race, and gender, although still present, is sometimes deflected, individualized, and domesticated. But the moral and political edge is not completely lost. One of the challenges of the format is that the political critique has to be made durable and seductive over a period of time, avoiding audience boredom and disinterest. At the same time there is in the serial format more time to develop and broaden the show's political and critical aspects.

VI. Rumpole and His Readers

There is ample evidence of the character of Rumpole being used as a cultural resource for lawyers in various parts of the common law world. For example English commentators have eulogized the character of Rumpole as "England's finest."[93] A comment by Philip Dunn QC, senior counsel from Melbourne, Australia, is typical of another common use. Rumpole, he explained was "a role model for a generation of barristers."[94] In both of these examples there appears to be little attempt to single out or identify particular characteristics, qualities, or attributes of the character. But does this necessarily suggest that all Rumpole's diverse qualities (both good and bad, professional and domestic) and his left-leaning political critique have been appropriated?

Much of the data suggest that in many instances the reading and use of Rumpole involve a process of selection and editing. Parts of the character may stand for the whole. His advocacy skills are identified most frequently as *the* character of Rumpole as a positive fictional lawyer. For example, in one of the newspaper reports recording the death of the actor who played Rumpole, Leo McKern, we find Lord Irvine, the then-Labor government minister (Lord Chancellor) with responsibility for the legal system, singling out Rumpole's qualities as an advocate: "his refusal . . . to give up in the face of adversity, no matter how open and shut the prosecution appeared. He exposed the weaknesses. . . . served the truth and won round the jury."[95] An American scholar Jamieson Wilcox suggests that the U.S. legal audience engaged in a similar process of selection. Rumpole is a character with exemplary "lawyerly virtues," which he identified as a "love of language . . . ready wit . . . imaginativeness that lets him solve his mysteries . . . capacity for detachment . . . independence of mind . . . "[96]

Rumpole has also been used as a resource to exemplify lawyerly skills that are perhaps less obvious. For example Milford uses examples of Rumpole's nonverbal behavior in court to illustrate the power of those skills in the courtroom.[97]

Wilcox's catalogue of "lawyerly virtues" that make up this particular reading of Rumpole is not limited to advocacy skills. Rumpole also is a

[93] Wendy Graham, "England's Finest: Rumpole and His Real Life Role Models," *Picturing Justice: The Online Journal of Law and Popular Culture*, http://www.usfca.edu (last accessed May 11, 2007).

[94] Fergus Shiel, "A Toast to Warty Old Rumpole," *The Age* (July 25, 2002), http://www.theagre.com.au (last accessed May 22, 2007).

[95] Waley, "Leo."

[96] Jamieson Wilcox, "The Rumpole Books by John Mortimer: Literature on a Life in the Law," *University of Cincinnati Law Review* 55 (1986–7): 117, 124.

[97] Lee Stapleton Milford, "Non-Verbal Communication," *Litigation* 27 (2000): 32.

character who exemplifies standing up for justice, no matter how unpopular or odious the client or cause.[98] This suggests a use of Rumpole to draw attention to the importance of the commitment of lawyers to moral and social justice. It is a use of Rumpole highlighted and analyzed by John Denvir.[99] Rumpole, he notes perhaps somewhat surprisingly, has many of the qualities of the American fictional character, Atticus Finch, who is the embodiment of the ideal good lawyer/lawyer as hero, the "patron saint"[100] of American lawyers. To reach this conclusion Denvir emphasizes not only Rumpole's lawyerly skills but also gives particular prominence to the moral and political aspects of the character.

An English legal commentator writing in 1999 about the barrister, Bill Clegg QC, who at the time was defending the accused in Britain's first war crime trial, draws on a different but related aspect of Rumpole's character. It is the mise-en-scène and more specifically the untidy, rather down-at-the-heel qualities of Rumpole that are put to work on this occasion to craft an image of lawyerly virtues, the lawyer as hero. In this instance Rumpole personifies the advocate as a "down to earth" character, one who has the "common touch." The writer explains, "Clegg, you perceive, is a kind of down-market Rumpole."[101] In this comparison, these qualities are valorized and attributed to Clegg as a very particular image of the lawyer as a champion of social justice. Through this use of Rumpole, Clegg is portrayed as hero as common man, in contrast to counsel for the prosecution who is elite privilege personified, "... old Eatonian, son of a baronet and a high Tory MP."[102]

Again it is a use of Rumpole that Denvir explores in a U.S. context. His project is to understand the popularity of Rumpole among lawyers in the United States. The answer he offers suggests that those who resort to Rumpole may appropriate more than merely his legal skills and his commitments to the moral and social good. The character of Rumpole, Denvir suggests, does not have many of the attributes associated with the quintessential lawyer as hero; he has neither the elegance, calm, poise, nor domestic harmony associated with the character of Atticus Finch.

[98] Wilcox, "The Rumpole Books": 124.
[99] Denvir, "Rumpole of the Bailey."
[100] Michael Asimow, "When Lawyers Were Heroes," *University of San Francisco Law Review* 30 (1995): 1131, 1138.
[101] "News Analysis," *The Lawyer* (April 5, 1999): 10.
[102] Ibid.

However, other aspects of his character, particularly those I have identified in the mise-en-scène, can be mobilized to generate an alternative lawyer-hero. The mise-en-scène that is Rumpole's mildly grotesque body and his shabby style is brought into the frame as evidence in support of a reading of Rumpole as an alternative lawyer-hero: as an "outsider."[103] In contrast to Finch who is, Denvir suggests, a rather melancholic and a tragic hero, Rumpole is a legal character as hero who is "anything but tragic."[104] Denvir suggests that Rumpole's laughter and his iconoclasm, attributes that are missing from fictional U.S. lawyers in general and the traditional U.S. patron saint Atticus Finch, in particular, are used by U.S. lawyers who battle against injustice and bureaucracy and to make sense of their daily battles. Rumpole offers a legal persona that is (or at least at the height of his popularity was) hard to find in U.S. popular culture. Resort to Rumpole in this manner shows us something of a cultural gap in the United States and provides a means of filling that gap.

Denvir's analysis also involves a process of selection and editing. He is wary of Rumpole's anarchic tendencies and dismisses them as "petit bourgeois" and "unlikely" aspects of a legal character, never mind a legal hero.[105] Rumpole's unrelenting determination to challenge all those in authority and his refusal to reduce any of his characters to the either/or of good guy/bad guy are taken by Denvir as troubling evidence of a missing political agenda and have to be explained away. Denvir also is bothered by the political edge that informs the unrelenting satire and irony. He now wants to read Rumpole's cynicism as evidence of a lack of politics, more a refuge from politics rather than a form of political engagement.

This, I want to suggest is a very particular reading of Rumpole. More specifically it is a reading of Rumpole informed by the lingering influence of the *American* hero, Atticus Finch. In *To Kill a Mockingbird*, good order and justice do not come through positive law or through the activities of the lawyer Atticus Finch. They come in the end through violence done by an outsider, Boo Radley, whose outsider status is symbolized in his characterization as mentally retarded. Locked away from the world but constantly experiencing the injustice of the world (in but not of the world) he is the figure who brings good order to the small town through an act

[103] Denvir, "Rumpole of the Bailey": 148.
[104] Ibid., 150.
[105] Ibid., 153.

of violence. I disagree with Osborn's reading of the film that suggests an alignment between the character Atticus Finch and Natural Law.[106] If there is a connection between this character and Natural Law then it is merely in Finch's final willingness to condone Boo Radley's violence. It is a connivance that also involves the sheriff, another figure of the legal establishment. But the character that has a direct link with Natural Law is the mysterious outsider, Boo Radley. He, I suggest, is the figure of Natural Justice who brings the social justice and good order into being.

But how does this help us make sense of Denvir's response to Rumpole? The relationship between Natural Law and the lawyer, the turn to a higher Natural Law that gives a firm political ground, and the moral and political legitimacy of violence performed by a mysterious outsider Boo Radley are missing from the Rumpole story. They are missing, I suggest, for a very good reason. Rumpole is from a different political, jurisprudential tradition and tells a very different story. For Rumpole, there is no higher law for him or anyone else to embody or to mobilize. There is only political struggle. In part this might be a reflection of the importance of positivism in England or in Mortimer's legal training. It might also be a reflection of English constitutional jurisprudence, which has until very recently eschewed any idea of a higher law, no matter what its source, secular or divine. It might also be a reflection of his left-of-center politics.

Archer offers an interesting twist to the use of Rumpole in the United States that does not blunt the character's political message. Archer suggests that, for American viewers, the Rumpole series might have provided the first "accurate" television depiction of "the struggle for the ancient and hard won rights."[107] This reading of Rumpole as an American resource is politically somewhat different from that offered by Denvir. It seems to suggest that Rumpole might help demythologize a commonly held position about the relation between law (Natural Law) and politics and more specifically help reveal the political struggle that is an inevitable feature of law. Those in the United States who view and use Rumpole may find this different jurisprudential and political message a useful resource.

Before leaving the United States, I want to consider a rather different use of Rumpole found in the U.S. literature. This is the way the character

[106] John Jay Osborn Jr. "Atticus Finch – The End of Honor: A Discussion of *To Kill a Mockingbird*," *University of San Francisco Law Review* 30 (1995): 1139.

[107] Archer, "The Ancient": 71.

is used to make sense of the peculiarities of the English legal system and perhaps more importantly to thereby differentiate and distance the United States from other common law systems and the English legal system in particular. Landsman suggests that Rumpole has come to "personify for many Americans the archetypical English barrister."[108] An article by American legal commentator Paul Cline demonstrates the point.[109] His examination of the idiosyncrasies of the English split profession is accompanied by one of the cartoon-like images of Rumpole used in the TV series. Here the injustices, the idiosyncrasies, the prejudices, and the problems represented in the characters and plots of the several Rumpole series might be put to work to suggest that law, justice, and lawyers in the United States are a very different kettle of fish.

I want to finish this section by turning my attention to the role played by aesthetics in the lawyers' use of Rumpole, particularly the use of the voice-over and of realism.[110] In part my attention was drawn to the importance of aesthetics by the users of Rumpole who highlighted the significance of the voice-over and of Rumpole's tendency to mutter comments that are audible only to the audience and not to the characters who share the screen with him.[111] As noted above the voice-over and, I would add, the muttered asides create a special, intimate, relationship between the audience and Rumpole. One Australian source, a Web site devoted to plain English legal information, also explained the importance of this production technique because of the way it is used to impart the political critique and commentary that, it suggests, show "the truth" of the legal system.[112]

[108] Stephen Landsman, "The Servants," *Michigan Law Review* 83 (1984): 1105. ff1. This use of Rumpole by American lawyers can be seen in the work of other American legal commentators. For example, a picture of Rumpole is the sole image accompanying a short article by Paul Cline (1988) that sets out the idiosyncrasies of the split legal profession in England.

[109] Paul C. Cline, "Barristers and Solicitors in the United Kingdom," *Judicature* 71 (1988): 352.

[110] This does not exhaust the question of aesthetics. Another issue relates to the use of humor. One use of humor is to create a strong link with the character. For a useful introduction to humor, see Simon Critchley, *On Humour* (London: Routledge 2002). Several factors might be of importance here. Both Jarvis (Robert M. Jarvis, "Situation Comedies," in *Prime Time Law*: 167) and Robson (2006) note that comedy and humor have rarely been successfully used in legal TV shows. Wilcox suggests that Rumpole's use of humor, and irony in particular may have been a factor in his popularity (particularly in the United States). See Wilcox, "The Rumpole Books": 124.

[111] "Book Review."

[112] "Rumpole of the Bailey," in *Law for You, Plain English Legal Information*, http://www.law4u.com.au (last accessed May 22, 2007).

The second aesthetic theme is concerned with realism. Many examples of the use of Rumpole hinge on the "accuracy" of the character. For Simon Wilson, an Australian senior counsel based in Melbourne, Rumpole is "pretty close to the mark"; he continues that it is "for that reason most Australian barristers enjoy it."[113] Accuracy has many dimensions offering a variety of points of connection. These include a "meticulous attention to detail, well written scripts and top-notch actors,"[114] or "it is impossible to think of 'Rumpole of the Bailey' without Leo McKern and vice versa."[115] Another commentator explained that McKern brought Rumpole "to life."[116] Accuracy is also represented by invoking Rumpole's creator, Sir John Mortimer. As noted above it is common to note that "Mortimer is inseparable from his alter-ego, barrister Horace Rumpole."[117] The suggestion that the character of Rumpole is "more human"[118] than other fictional lawyers is another mode of reference to accuracy. In part this may be a reflection of Mortimer's refusal to write one-dimensional characters. Rumpole is self-reflective; he is prone to the odd existential crisis. Wilcox suggests that it is this complexity and self-reflection that inform the use of Rumpole by U.S. lawyers who use the character to reflect on their own virtues and vices.[119] It may also be a pointer to another dimension of the realist aesthetics, but this time to the emotional realism[120] of Rumpole.

Last but not least, some uses of Rumpole read him to produce negative attributes of the legal profession. For example Rumpole has been cited as the figure of a lawyer who is out of touch with modern legal reality, condemned as the embodiment of forensic skills that are outdated and no longer suitable for modern (criminal) litgation.[121] Peter Robson, quoting the well-known British legal journalist and author Marcel Berlins, gives an example of how the character of Rumpole is indicative of misunderstandings about the nature of English law and English lawyers,

[113] Shiel, "A Toast to Warty."
[114] Lovdahl, "Rumpole."
[115] "Rumpole."
[116] Waley, "Leo."
[117] Archer, "The Ancient" and Farquhar, "Rumpole."
[118] Marcus D. Williams, "Books for Lawyers: Rumpole for the Defense," *American Bar Association Journal* 70 (1984): 120.
[119] Wilcox, "The Rumpole Books": 126.
[120] Christopher Williams, "After the Classic" and Ang, *Watching* Dallas.
[121] See Andrew Mimmack, "Editorial," *Magistrates' Court Practice* 6 (2002): 1 and Naomi Rovnick, "The Revolution in Litigation Starts from the Bottom," *The Lawyer* (September 29, 2003).

who are neither "cosy"' nor "comic," both of which are qualities attributed to Rumpole.[122]

VII. Conclusion

Any study of the cultural life of cause lawyering in England has to address a problem and meet a particular challenge. Existing scholarship on popular cultural representations of morally and politically engaged English lawyers might suggest that if there are legal heroes to be had in that context then they are copies of American heroes and, more specifically, reproductions of that famous U.S. patron saint of lawyers, Atticus Finch.[123] This is a problem. But to go no further than this would be to miss the challenge arising out of the limits of scholarship on images of law in British popular culture. This essay is an attempt to meet that challenge through the study of one very important English fictional legal character. Focusing on the cultural, political, social, and economic factors that inform his emergence and dissemination allows for a detailed consideration of the particularities and characteristics of this fictional figure. It does not limit the uses and meanings that might be generated by those who go on to make use of the character, but it does offer an insight into the richness and the peculiarities of this particular cultural resource.

The character that emerges from publicly funded TV during one of its most creative and politically challenging moments is morally engaged and politically committed, but not in an easy or straightforward way. He is far from the shining hero. He is a character more mired in the grinding routine of social injustice using cynicism and irony to keep up his struggle. But his is not a fixed character. In part this evolution is demanded by the dictates of his move to the different cultural and economic environment of the world of commercial TV. In part it is a movement that takes place in various uses of Rumpole. The figure of Rumpole gives rise to a number of different Rumpolean personas, each shifting the meanings of Rumpole, editing and

[122] Robson, "Lawyers": 346.

[123] I would suggest that this is in good part the character of the English cause lawyer Gareth Puddingrce. One of her cases was fictionalized in the firm, *In the Name of the Father*. Blum raises good points about the way her legal practice is embedded in politics. Less attention is paid to the very familiar tropes of lawyer as hero that inform this fictional representation of Puddingrce. See Carolyn Patty Blum "Images of Lawyering and Political Activism in *In the Name of the Father*," *University of San Francisco Law Review* 30 (1995): 1065.

selecting, valorizing and revalorizing the character. The U.S. literature draws attention to the way in which a fictional character that has its origins in another jurisdiction and a different politics may provide a resourse that is difficult to find in that other place, the United States. Based on the limited data, any conclusions are necessarily tentative, but they do suggest that this particular legal fiction has been a rich resource. In the UK Rumpole DVDs have been deleted from the manufacturer's catalogue, which may suggest that his ability to generate profits has diminished. However, it would be premature to suggest that Rumpole as a cultural resource has been exhausted.[124]

Acknowledgments

Particular thanks are due to my colleague Professor Linda Mulcahy for giving me access to her Rumpole archive and to Peter Robson for his meticulous reading and incisive comments on an earlier draft.

[124] Rumpole recently reemerged in a novel to offer a critique of the British government's attack on civil liberties and human rights in response to the war on terror. See John Mortimer, *Rumpole and the Reign of Terror* (London: Viking, 2006).

12

Now You See It, Now You Don't

Cause Lawyering, Popular Culture, and *A Civil Action*

Stuart A. Scheingold

I. Introduction

Jonathan Harr's *A Civil Action* is a subtle, complex, and compelling book that nonetheless can be briefly summarized. Two corporations have engaged in dumping toxic waste that has leeched into the wells that supply water to Woburn, Massachusetts. The pollutants included a known carcinogen, TCE,[1] and the pollution has been connected by scientific research at Harvard University to a number of health problems – although not *directly* to the chronic myelogenous leukemia clusters that are at issue in the Woburn civil litigation. The book recounts the ultimately futile efforts of a small-time, distinctly lower hemisphere lawyer, Jan Schlichtmann, to represent the families of the leukemia victims in a class action lawsuit against the W. R. Grace and Beatrice Foods corporations, which are represented by attorneys who are members in good standing of the lawyering elite of Massachusetts.

Harr's account of the ephemeral triumphs and inexorable collapse of Jan Schlichtmann's legal populism provides a convincing portrait of the intrinsic contingencies of cause lawyering *by personal injury attorneys*. The objective of this essay is to determine the extent to which the window Harr opens onto this segment of the cause lawyering bar and its class action tactics stays open as his modestly marketable and utterly convincing nonfiction book is repackaged as a popular film, starring John Travolta as Jan Schlichtmann, and then remarketed as a paperback best seller. Accordingly I trace the journey of *A Civil Action* from the relatively high-culture

[1] Jonathan Harr, *A Civil Action* (New York: Random House, 1995): 135 and 208.

world of serious nonfiction into popular culture – based on my reading of the book and the film along with the reviews of critics who transmit their respective versions of *A Civil Action* to the public.

As it turns out, the film and the reviewers have not so much represented as misrepresented the book – with each, in effect, colonizing Harr's complex and multifaceted narrative for their own purposes. In the end, Harr's shrewd and fine-grained portrait of a personal injury lawyer's efforts to mobilize the law to empower victims of corporate misbehavior is transformed into a validation of the campaign of the so-called tort reform movement to discredit personal injury lawyers and regulatory interventions into corporate practices more generally.[2] Because Harr's research and reporting so clearly identify the source of the leukemia clusters as corporate wrongdoing and their efforts to conceal it, the media end up obscuring his findings and inverting their meaning.[3]

I begin immediately below with my own reading of the book, which I next compare and contrast to the book reviews. I then move on to the film and film reviews and deal with them in the same manner. The essay concludes with a brief summary of its main themes and a consideration of what might be learned from this one case study about the cultural status of personal injury cause lawyering.

II. The Cause Lawyering Narrative

Drawing the boundary between cause and conventional lawyering is an intrinsically contingent enterprise that becomes particularly problematic when it comes to personal injury attorneys. Perhaps no branch of legal practice has been so subject to professional and public opprobrium as have plaintiffs' attorneys in personal injury practice. They have been considered prototypically opportunistic. According to the widely accepted lore, these ambulance chasers are determined to transform any accident, however

[2] See Chapter 8 and its extensive analysis of the perverse impact of the tort reform movement on public discourse in the United States. *Distorting the Law* (Chicago: University of Chicago Press, 2004).

[3] It could be argued with substantial justification that I, much like the media, have appropriated Harr for my own purposes. There is absolutely no reason to believe that he knows of, or cares about, cause lawyering, as such. And given, for example, the dramatic impact and the success of the film, he might well see the journey of *A Civil Action* into popular culture as more in keeping with his purposes than my academic reading of his efforts to reach the general public.

minor and however accidental, into a strategic game of naming, blaming, and claiming – that is finding someone, preferably with deep pockets, who can be made financially responsible for the plaintiff's injury.

However, Auerbach[4] among others has argued that this characterization of personal injury lawyers as deeply flawed human beings is a figment of the exclusionary sentiments of elite white Anglo-Saxon Protestant lawyers trying to maintain the homogeneity of the bar and control of the market for legal services.[5] Through *this* lens personal injury lawyers can readily be seen as serving the purposes of cause lawyering. The contingency fee opportunities available to personal injury practitioners have provided representation to impecunious clients who have been victimized by the dangerous practices of callous and impregnable institutions – both private and public.

Accordingly, I begin by indicating briefly what, according to the increasingly extensive cause lawyering literature, distinguishes cause lawyers from conventional lawyers. I then go on to examine Harr's portrait of Jan Schlichtmann for what it adds to our understanding of cause lawyering. I argue, as I have already suggested, that Harr provides an authentic account of personal injury cause lawyering – its vagaries and its virtues. This does not mean that Jan Schlichtmann emerges as the model cause lawyer – or even the model personal injury cause lawyer. On the contrary, the virtue of Harr's portrait is that it reveals Schlichtmann's flaws as well as his strengths, both his feats and his failures. Most fundamentally we learn what he is up against as well as what he is up to. Many of his wounds are self-inflicted, but others are a function of the structural forces arrayed against him.

More specifically, Harr weaves together the following three elements that shed light on cause lawyering in personal injury practice:

1. The resource imbalance between the corporate defendants and the plaintiff law firm, combined with the legal opportunities to delay, to obfuscate, and to manipulate legality – thus, enabling the defendants to bleed the plaintiffs dry
2. A judge predisposed to side with the defendants' attorneys who are members of a legal elite that includes the judge but not the plaintiffs'

[4] Jerold Auerbach, *Unequal Justice: Lawyers and Social Change in Modern America* (New York: Oxford University Press, 1976).

[5] Richard L. Abel, *American Lawyers* (New York: Oxford University Press, 1989).

attorney, Schlichtmann, who is a parvenu practitioner from the lower hemisphere of a sharply stratified bar

3. Schlichtmann's grandiose expectations that lead him to reject big settlement offers in a vain attempt to win even larger sums for his firm and his clients while at the same time striking a blow for social and political justice

Much of the magic of Harr's account of Jan Schlichtmann as a kind of cause lawyer manqué is the way in which he brings these personal and structural forces so vividly to life while evoking for the reader a sense that victory is possible and personal injury cause lawyering can and might, even in this star-crossed litigation, succeed in providing some measure of social justice.

1. Cause Lawyering in Brief

To understand why I deem Harr's cause lawyering narrative to be authentic and revealing, it is necessary to clarify the operative meaning of cause lawyering as drawn from the cause lawyering literature.

> Definitionally, cause lawyering is associated with both intent and behavior. Serving a cause by accident does not . . . qualify as cause lawyering . . . political or moral commitment [is] an essential and distinguishing feature of cause lawyering. Lawyers are drawn to causes by a search for something in which to believe or as an outlet to express their already formed beliefs.[6]

In short, whether or not the activities of an attorney may be fairly characterized as cause lawyering depends on his or her motivations. For this reason, Jonathan Harr's focus on the forces driving and sustaining Jan Schlichtmann's decision to represent the families of Woburn leukemia victims is especially suitable for sorting out the boundaries between cause and conventional lawyering.

The mutability of cause lawyering is another of its aspects that is relevant and is woven into the fabric of Harr's narrative. Although one cannot

[6] Stuart Scheingold and Austin Sarat, *Something to Believe In: Politics, Professionalism, and Cause Lawyering* (Stanford: Stanford University Press, 2004):

according to the literature be a cause lawyer by accident, research reveals that "the accidental can be transformed into the intentional when a lawyer's ideals are awakened by service undertaken for other reasons."[7] Moreover, the literature also reveals that cause lawyers regularly cross and recross the boundaries between cause and conventional lawyering. Jan Schlichtmann's mixed and fluid motivations percolate throughout Harr's account of the Woburn litigation.

Finally, along with the work of personal injury firms, cause lawyering can be found in many sites of legal practice – corporate pro-bono work, small-firm fee-for-service lawyering, salaried practice, and so forth. Each of these sites provides its own distinctive combination of risks and rewards – for the attorneys as well as for clients and causes. In taking us so deeply into the Schlichtmann's firm of personal injury lawyers, Harr adds much to what we know about this particular site of cause lawyering, especially about the patterns of risk and reward that are peculiar to it.

In sum, Harr's project probes the nature of, and the interaction among, Jan Schlichtmann's inclination to do good, his narcissistic personality, and the structural opportunities and obstacles that he must negotiate.

2. Something to Believe In

We learn that even before he went to law school, Jan Schlichtmann wanted, in Harr's words, "to do something useful, something to benefit society."[8] This led him to the ACLU and ultimately to law school after working with an ACLU lawyer on a case involving the suppression of a protest by a "group of nuns and welfare mothers."[9] According to Harr,

> Working on this case, Schlichtmann experienced a profound revelation. The concept of a system of justice – laws and courts that permitted *welfare mothers* to challenge *governors!* – seemed to unfold gloriously before him. He suddenly discovered that lawyering wasn't just wills, divorces, and sordid criminal matters. The law, he decided, was perhaps the highest calling a man could aspire to.[10]

[7] Scheingold and Sarat, *Something to Believe In*, 5.
[8] Harr, *Civil Action*, 57.
[9] Harr, *Civil Action*, 57.
[10] Harr, *Civil Action*, 57.

After law school his continued commitment to pursuit of something to believe in made him persona non grata during a job interview at the prominent firm of Skadden, Arps, Slate, Meagher, & Flom and at another firm representing clients before the FCC.[11]

In solo practice he stumbled into personal injury litigation and quickly discovered that he could marshal expertise and gamble successfully on behalf of a victim whom other lawyers were unwilling to represent. As Harr tells it, Schlichtmann immediately "realized that he had found his calling. 'This,' he said to himself, 'is what I want to do with my life.'"[12] Note, however, that Harr leaves no doubt about the mixed motives that drive Schlichtmann and that led him to take on the Woburn case, despite realizing that it was potentially a "black hole."[13]

> If he were to win it, he would set new legal precedents and gain a national reputation among his fellow plaintiffs' lawyers. He would no doubt make a lot of money. And he would have helped the families of east Woburn. Fame, fortune, and doing good – those were, in combination, goals worth striving for, he thought.[14]

In other words, the plight of the families was a very big part of the story for Jan Schlichtmann but he was also acutely aware of the notoriety and prestige that would accrue to him if he could successfully illuminate the victimization at the bottom of this black hole.

From a somewhat different but complementary perspective, Harr also introduces us to the grandiosity that is so prominent in Schlichtmann's narcissistic personality and the attraction of cause lawyering. Recall that he saw law, according to Harr, as "perhaps the highest calling a man could aspire to."[15] And he chose to represent the Woburn victims because he could "set new legal precedents and gain a national reputation."[16] We also learn that Schlichtmann was buoyed by his appearance on television in connection with the Woburn case.[17]

[11] Harr, *Civil Action*, 48–49.
[12] Harr, *Civil Action*, 61.
[13] Harr, *Civil Action*, 75.
[14] Harr, *Civil Action*, 75.
[15] Harr, *Civil Action*, 57.
[16] Harr, *Civil Action*, 75.
[17] Harr, *Civil Action*, 59.

3. The Mixed Blessing of Narcissism

Although Harr tips us off to Schlichtmann's narcissism early on, it becomes a continuing theme that is woven, in almost a clinical fashion, into the book from beginning to end.[18] Along the way, Harr does not simply identify the elements of Schlichtmann's narcissism and demonstrate how they fuel his motivation, his tactics, and his staying power. In addition, he helps us understand just how and why a narcissistic personality may be intrinsic to high-stakes personal injury practice in general and to politically meaningful cause lawyering in particular. Finally, Harr reveals that narcissism is a two-edged sword that can also betray a cause lawyer, the cause, and his or her clients.

Well before the Woburn litigation, we view Schlichtmann's narcissistic grandiosity through the eyes of Teresa, a would-be girl friend. Although he denies he is an "ambulance chaser.... I represent victims,"[19] he also quickly and proudly proclaims on first meeting her that he had just settled a hotel fire case for $2.5 million – "the biggest wrongful death settlement in Massachusetts history"[20] (p. 54) – and goes on to tell her about his picture appearing in the paper and about his Porsche.[21] Moreover, as soon as his fledgling firm, Schlichtmann, Conway & Crowley, made some money, it was spent on a splashy new office that included a grand piano. Schlichtmann is convinced that "the appearance of success often begets success."[22] He also believes, and Harr seems to agree, that the TV appearances that are so personally gratifying are also useful to the Woburn litigation.[23]

It is, however, Schlichtmann's penchant for risk-taking that is both essential and threatening to his practice. As an impecunious solo practitioner in his very first case, he had gone $15,000 into debt, rejected a low-ball settlement offer of $5,000 and then an enhanced offer of $75,000, went to trial, and was awarded $250,000. Harr concludes that "Schlichtmann's gamble had paid off, but it had been foolhardy, dignified only by his inexperience

[18] I do not mean to suggest that Harr writes as a clinician – far from it. On the other hand, what he tells about Schlichtmann provides sufficient raw material for constructing at least the broad outlines of a clinical diagnosis.

[19] Harr, *Civil Action*, 55.

[20] Harr, *Civil Action*, 54.

[21] Harr, *Civil Action*, 55.

[22] Harr, *Civil Action*, 124.

[23] Harr, *Civil Action*, 82.

and the fact that he'd won. It was not necessarily the best sort of lesson for a fledgling lawyer."[24] His gambles continued to pay off – he won five cases in a row, including one on which he spent $200,000 of his firm's money, rejected a $1 million settlement despite the judge's advice that the lawyers try harder to settle,[25] and ended up with a jury verdict of $4.7 million.[26] Whereas most personal injury lawyers tend to take on many small sure-winners to maintain financial stability ["plaintiffs can be expected to lose two times out of three"[27]], Schlichtmann "had grander visions. He wanted his firm to deal only in those cases that promised big rewards and required big investments."[28]

This same penchant for risk-taking that paid off so handsomely ultimately led to disaster in the Woburn case. At one point near the end of the litigation, we learn that the firm had invested $2.5 million in the Woburn case[29] and that by end of the litigation Schlichtmann himself "owed his creditors $1,231,542" and that the piano and his Porsche were long gone. Nonetheless, he had turned down a $20 million settlement offer[30] – precisely the amount that he originally figured that the case was worth. Why? He had been persuaded by Charles Nesson, Harvard Law Professor and his advisor, that the case was actually worth $175 million (or more) and was also just the kind of political case with broad social justice implications that Schlichtmann longed to win. All this, Nesson argued, would be sacrificed by not getting a landmark settlement.[31] In the end, however, Schlichtmann was forced to settle for $8 million – leaving him with a profound sense of failure. "This was a case I thought would have some real importance.... It never happened."[32]

With all of that said, however, Harr makes it abundantly clear that the energy, the inspiration, and the relentless optimism generated by

[24] Harr, *Civil Action*, 63.
[25] Harr, *Civil Action*, 130.
[26] Harr, *Civil Action*, 131.
[27] Harr, *Civil Action*, 125.
[28] Harr, *Civil Action*, 125–26.
[29] Harr, *Civil Action*, 429.
[30] Harr, *Civil Action*, 231.
[31] Harr, *Civil Action*, 250–51.Nesson's influence was probably enhanced by his Harvard credentials, which took on exaggerated importance for the prestige-conscious and déclassé Schlichtmann.
[32] Harr, *Civil Action*, 453.

Schlichtmann's narcissism made him a formidable opponent in this high-stakes litigation. At the very end when all was essentially lost, Schlichtmann's optimism flagged and even turned into despair. He felt personally wounded and betrayed by the jury, the judge, and even by representatives of W. R. Grace with whom he was negotiating. Yet he was still sufficiently resilient to finish what he had started: facing up to his disappointed clients and salvaging what he could from an extremely desperate situation.[33]

4. Structural Opportunities and Obstacles

For Harr, however, the crux of the story was not simply Schlichtmann's personal strengths and weaknesses but the structural parameters of the civil litigation system. The system provided Schlichtmann and his clients with a mechanism for exposing wrongdoing, mobilizing evidence for determining liability, and bringing that evidence before a judge and jury with the authority to assess responsibility and impose penalties – very substantial penalties indeed. Yet, the evidence marshaled by Harr is clearly meant to make us understand that, in balance, Schlichtmann faced very long odds and was constantly swimming upstream against a fast flowing, *almost* irresistible current.

The opportunities afforded in litigation stem from the contingency fee system, the openness of the courtroom to legitimate scientific evidence, and sympathetic juries.[34] The Woburn litigation was jump-started by a Harvard School of Public Health study that demonstrated that the wells in question were associated with a variety of health problems. Moreover, during the discovery process, additional data were added to the mix. Although not specifically focused on leukemia, these data could in the worst-case scenario put the defendants' lawyers on the defensive,[35] and in the best-case scenario they could be linked circumstantially to leukemia by way of damage to the immune system.[36] The substantial awards earned by Schlichtmann's firm in earlier litigation provided the capital that allowed them to go forward

[33] Harr, *Civil Action*, 394–401. Although Schlichtmann's personalized sense of injury and betrayal are consistent with an underlying narcissism, his resilience may not be.

[34] Harr, *Civil Action*, 96, 155.

[35] Harr, *Civil Action*, 132–36.

[36] Harr, *Civil Action*, 136–41. See also 198–208.

with the Woburn litigation – meaning, in essence, that the contingency fee system benefited both the firm and the impecunious clients who would not otherwise have been represented.[37]

However, this silver lining was tarnished by the clouds that hovered over each of the structural opportunities. Far and away the most imposing of those clouds was the resource differential between Schlichtmann and his partners and the defendant corporations. The same deep pockets that made Grace and Beatrice such attractive targets also insulated them. As Harr presents the circumstances of the case, the corporations had ostensibly unlimited funds to mobilize scientific expertise and to stretch out the litigation – with a realistic expectation that Schlichtmann's funds would sooner or later run dry. For example, in pretrial maneuvers the defendant attorneys raised Rule 11 and barratry as grounds for dismissing the plaintiffs' complaint. Rule 11 prohibits frivolous lawsuits; the defendants claimed that because there was no medical evidence about the causes of leukemia, this was by definition a frivolous lawsuit. Barratry is the crime of stirring up litigation by soliciting clients; the defendants argued that public statements made by Schlichtmann amounted in effect to an effort to solicit clients and stir up litigation.[38]

Harr leaves little doubt that he believes that these pretrial maneuvers, not the lawsuits, were frivolous. He also leaves the reader with the distinct impression that Schlichtmann labored under another burden: he was not part of the legal elite while the lead counsel for the two corporations and the judge were. In part, this critique is about cronyism but it is also about the stratification of the bar. The shady professional standing and reputation of personal injury lawyers make them ethically suspect and their behavior intrinsically distasteful. To take just one instance, consider a point in the trial where the defense has clearly been misled by the lead counsel for Beatrice Foods, Jerome Facher. The judge cannot bring himself to believe that Facher, the partner in a prestigious corporate firm and a sometime lecturer at Harvard Law School, could do anything like that intentionally. When Schlichtmann begs to differ the judge is indignant: "[Y]ou have two

[37] Moreover, without an infusion of cash from the settlement of a companion case during the Woburn litigation, the firm might have had to quit much earlier (Harr, *Civil Action*, 146).

[38] Harr, *Civil Action*, 104.

problems, Mr. Schlichtmann – a tremendous sense of *over*entitlement and an underlying paranoia."[39]

Harr strongly suggests that this predisposition to take umbrage and to express it was bound to prejudice Schlichtmann in the eyes of the jury.[40] Then in his final report to the Court of Appeals on the Beatrice litigation, the judge brought Rule 11 crashing down on Schlichtmann. Judge Skinner claimed that Schlichtmann "knew that there was no available competent evidence tending to establish the disposal of the complaint chemicals by the defendants itself, either at the tannery site or on the 15 acres.' Accordingly, the judge found that Schlichtmann had violated Rule 11 by pursuing a frivolous claim that had no support in fact. This constituted clear misconduct."[41] This ruling is just as dumbfounding and infuriating to the reader as it was to Schlichtmann and his associates, because it is preceded by several pages that unequivocally established that the judge had turned his back on arguably valid scientific findings and on perjury by a key witness for the defendants, without even admonishing Facher for countenancing all of this chicanery.[42]

To present these opportunities and obstacles in so linear a fashion is to belie Harr's accomplishment. As my scattered citations suggests, these themes emerge bit by bit over the course of the book, and the reader is left in a state of uncertainty to the very end of the novel. In other words, the pieces of Harr's legal and medical narratives do not fit neatly together, and there is until the very bitter end of the litigation not only adversity dogging each victory but a continuing hope of triumph in the face of adversity.

III. Media Representations and the Colonization of *A Civil Action*

As I have already indicated, the media offer only very partial accounts of Harr's tour de force – accounts in which cause lawyering, as such, never appears. Recall the elements of cause lawyering in personal injury practice

[39] Harr, *Civil Action*, 345, italics added.

[40] Near the end of the book we learn that at least some of the jurors were aware of, and puzzled by, the judge's animus toward Schlichtmann. Oddly, however, it did not lead them to think that judge was biased nor did it seem to either undermine Schlichtmann as somehow suspect or elevate him as a victim (Harr, *Civil Action*, 383).

[41] Harr, *Civil Action*, 487.

[42] Harr, *Civil Action*, 469–86.

as defined in the cause lawyering literature and brought to life in the book version of *A Civil Action*:

- Cause-driven attorneys, drawn from the lower hemisphere of the bar, who are emboldened by their sense of mission and by narcissistic personality traits to take on corporate Goliaths
- Corporations represented by attorneys drawn from the upper hemisphere of the bar who have at their disposal virtually unlimited financial resources with which to exploit the procedural obstacles of civil litigation and who often can count on the sympathy of upper hemisphere judges

What dominates media representations are the arbitrary vagaries of the struggle between David and Goliath – leading inexorably to an indictment of the process of civil litigation. As for Schlichtmann, he is portrayed not as cause-driven but as money-obsessed – and any inkling of his idealism that survives can only be seen as at best incidental and perhaps accidental. Because Schlichtmann's idealism sinks without leaving a trace and is effaced and civil litigation is disparaged, cause lawyering largely disappears from media accounts of *A Civil Action*. These generalizations, however, conceal variations among the media that are attributable to distinctive patterns of incentives and disincentives.

1. Book Reviews

Book reviewers are virtually unanimous in their praise of *A Civil Action* as an exciting thriller, an instructive work of nonfiction, and an instance of a brave and resourceful author triumphing over his abstruse material and his dire financial circumstances. As I note later, there is a certain irony in the last element of reviewers' tribute to Jonathan Harr, as they find grievous fault with Jan Schlichtmann who has struggled against much the same obstacles. In any case, the book reviewers end up appropriating *A Civil Action* for media-driven purposes.

- Reviewers for mainstream news outlets are particularly prone to scapegoating Schlichtmann and in so doing to invoke and contribute to pejorative views of personal injury lawyers.

- Reviewers for opinion journals appropriate *A Civil Action* for purposes that reflect their own personal values and/or the values of their publications.

The net effect is to efface cause lawyering from *A Civil Action*.

The most prominent theme pursued by the print media is Jan Schlichtmann as reckless, publicity seeking, and money-obsessed. For example, *Time*[43] characterizes him as "the sort of lawyer who inspires anti-lawyer jokes. He was arrogant, humorless and sleekly vulpine in his $1,000 suits, $65 ties and Porsche 928." The reviewer for the *Houston Chronicle*,[44] Richard H. Hanneman, seems to agree with *Time* – noting that "Schlichtmann, just a few years out of law school, is not likely to endear himself to many readers. He spent lavishly, drove a Porsche, wore custom-made Italian suits and was as abrasive as he was arrogant. Hanneman concludes, however, that despite his profligate ways and his focus on "the potential for millions – even hundreds of millions – in judgments and fees," he becomes a "sympathetic character, due largely to Harr's skill."

Hanneman thus introduces another prominent theme among book reviewers – shining the spotlight on Harr and implying that it is a major feat to be able to present Schlichtmann with all of his warts as a character deserving of some grudging praise. Harr, in contrast to Schlichtmann, emerges from the reviews as an altogether admirable man who risked all that he could to complete this book; in effect, it became his vocation. Hanneman writes, "Harr had no idea he was embarking on an 8 1/2-year project. Random House gave him an $80,000 advance and a due date less than three years away. . . . Six extensions later, Harr says, 'I didn't have two dimes to rub together.'" The fact that in the end, he hit the jackpot when Robert Redford paid $1.25 million for the film rights is implicitly seen as a fitting reward for a job well done.

One need not begrudge Harr either the virtually unanimous praise or his monetary return to question this tendency to draw contrasts between him and Schlichtmann, rather than acknowledging their similarities.[45] Both

[43] October 2, 1995.

[44] October 1, 1996.

[45] Harr is universally and justly praised for transforming a technically complex and seemly interminable lawsuit into a "gripping true story" (*The Oregonian*, October 9, 1996) with a "finely etched cast of characters" (*Houston Chronicle*, September 22, 1996).

men, it could be said, bet heavily on something in which they believed deeply – with Schlichtmann accepting the higher stakes and the longer odds because he had much more (at least financially) to lose. Only by sweeping aside Schlichtmann's idealism, which is portrayed so prominently in *A Civil Action*, can his emergence as a sympathetic character be seen as a tour de force. Once that is done, it opens the way for further contrasts between Schlichtmann's self-aggrandizing lifestyle and Harr's self-abnegating ways. The *Time* review notes, "Jonathan Harr was a baby-faced magazine writer in old jeans, beat-up boots and a rumpled sports jacket who did his best work when blending with the furniture."[46] If we go one step further and ask why the reviewers devote so much attention to Harr, it seems fair to conclude that this is their métier. After all, these are mostly professional book reviewers who are intimately involved in the literary and publishing worlds and thus as much interested in the author as the book and as much in the process by which books are written and marketed as in the final product.[47]

Accordingly, it should come as no surprise that, when an attorney is the reviewer, lawyering and the legal process tend to be emphasized. Attorney Ross Reeves tells readers of the *Virginia Pilot*[48] community newspaper that this immensely complex and bewildering litigation validates a well-known and widely accepted legal "corollary" – namely that big cases make bad law: "Big cases overwhelm the legal system and marginalize justice." He is thus philosophical, so to speak, about the results of the litigation. In contrast, nonlawyer reviewers are inclined to see the case, rather like Dickens in *Bleak House*, as an indictment of virtually all civil litigation. Writing in *USA Today*,[49] Bob Minesheimer declares, "The story turns as

[46] Oct 2, 1995.

[47] *The Oregonian* (October 9, 1996), after the obligatory salute to Harr's "gripping true story," devotes almost its entire review to recounting how a modest selling hardback was transformed into a best seller. In so doing we learn some of the tricks of the trade. "Then there was the cover. The cliché about not judging a book by its cover may be true, but everybody does it, anyway. A cover has to sell the content of a book, not the other way around, and the original cover of "A Civil Action" didn't do that. 'The simple, plain, elegant cover didn't work,' Harr said. 'It was a flop.' When "A Civil Action" didn't win a National Book Award, Random House decided to do something. A new cover was ordered with a banging gavel and a laudatory quote from Grisham. About 50,000 more copies were sold, paving the way for the paperback, which has a solitary man walking through snowy Boston Common ..."

[48] November 19, 1995.

[49] September 14, 1995.

much on money as anything else.... In the end, truth is among the casualties of this case." Hanneman, in the *Houston Chronicle*, quotes, with evident approval, the wily and jaded attorney Facher's dispiriting declaration: "'The truth is at the bottom of a bottomless pit.' As Herr (sic) writes: 'In the enclosed ritualistic word of the courtroom... reality was often a shadowland.'"[50]

Even those who acknowledge that the litigation was not fruitless and that Schlichtmann was not a fraud end their review on a sour note. Lawyer Reeves offers a fairly balanced view of Schlichtmann as an "honest and talented, albeit mercenary and self-absorbed, trial lawyer."[51] Reeves is also agnostic about the outcome, claiming that "the reader is hard-pressed to decide where the truth lay and whether justice was done." He concludes poetically but mournfully that "Schlichtmann's intensely personalized pursuit of justice evokes Ahab – the paradigm anti-hero – and his relentless pursuit of the white whale. Like Melville's whale, justice eludes easy definition and defies capture. And, like the Pequod crew, those who surround Schlichtmann are borne by his obsession to the brink of destruction." Similarly, Mark Dowie in the *Los Angeles Times*,[52] although acknowledging that "justice is served, albeit in small ways," more or less echoes Reeves. In the end he sees Schlichtmann as a "sad and quixotic figure" and the litigation in many ways as self-defeating: "Woburn families receive some recompense, defendants are billed millions by their lawyers, and Schlichtmann's witnesses, consultants, staff and co-council (sic) are paid bonuses – by Schlichtmann, who is left penniless and wondering if he has chosen the right profession, the right life.... Little doubt remains that a crime has been committed, that the perpetrators are unpunished."[53]

Whereas newspapers and news magazines thus suggest that Harr, the scrupulous reporter, effectively conceals his own sympathies and allows attentive readers to draw their own conclusions, policy journals read *A Civil*

[50] October 1, 1996.

[51] November 19, 1995.

[52] September 24, 1995. It is perhaps worth noting that it is a reviewer for the *Los Angeles Times* who tells us, "The book becomes almost cinematic, as Harr captures detail, color and anecdote, sketching them in clear and unself-conscious prose."

[53] The USA Today Information Network (Sep 14, 1995) quotes, with apparent approval, Schlichtmann's claim that "fame, fortune and doing good – those were, in combination, goals worth striving for"; it concludes that his efforts are all for naught, because "he's pushed beyond extremes by his own zealousness and an obstinate judge."

Action as an indictment of corporate malfeasance and impunity – albeit with differing inflections on the lessons to be learned from the litigation.

Ruth Conniff, writing in *The Progressive*,[54] offers the most adamant and unequivocally Manichean reading of A *Civil Action*:

> The David and-Goliath struggle between Schlichtmann and the teams of corporate lawyers the companies hire reminded me of Ralph Nader's early crusades against the auto industry. The story is a powerful antidote to the brainless, pro-corporate complacency that has settled over our culture. If you want to persuade your Republican relatives that trial lawyers and the meddling government bureaucrats who make health and safety regulations are not the enemy, and that corporations are not benign Santa Clauses of free market prosperity, give them this book. Or take them to the movie. They won't fall asleep.

Others are slightly more circumspect as, for example, Suzanne Keen in *Commonweal*,[55] who instructs us that Harr "probes the relationship between corporate money and the judicial system. In a world governed by status, reputation, and old school ties, he suggests, victims represented by personal injury lawyers suffer the consequences of class prejudice." In all of these accounts, the judge's bias against Schlichtmann figures prominently.[56]

There is also substantial agreement, among the policy journals, on Schlichtmann as a tragic and deeply absorbing character who sustains the drama of Harr's narrative. However, there is no such agreement on Schlichtmann as a cause lawyer or indeed on the litigation as a venture in cause lawyering. Leonard Glantz's review in *Public Health Reports*[57] comes the closest to my own cause lawyering reading of A *Civil Action*:

> [Schlichtmann] is presented as the perfect plaintiff's lawyer – a bright, relentless, flashy gambler with a heart. In A *Civil Action*, Schlichtmann is portrayed as a figure of enormous complexity. A worker for civil liberties before he became a lawyer, he became a personal injury

54 December 1998.

55 November 3, 1995.

56 Leonard Glantz's review in *Public Health Reports* (January/February 1998) echoes Keen's suspicion of the judge's social class and professional bond with the defendants' lawyers, and Timothy Noah (*Washington Monthly*, September 1995) concludes that the judge is "clearly biased" – and "slow witted," to boot.

57 January/February, 1998.

> lawyer with an alacrity that made it seem almost predetermined. While most trial lawyers try to keep their strategies secret, Schlichtmann reveled in the tactic of renting an expensive hotel room, enlarging his exhibits, and displaying his evidence to his adversaries. The goal was to demonstrate that a case was so strong there was really nothing the defense could do but settle before trial. Until the Woburn case, this strategy had worked. Indeed, Schlichtmann had never lost a case. However, when he employed this tactic in the Woburn case, opposing counsel simply walked out of the room. This was a different kind of case, one in which he was going to have to convince a jury.

However, this reading of Schlichtmann is clearly ancillary to the major lesson of Glantz's policy-oriented review. He concludes,"The book is a wonderful exposition of the clumsiness and inefficiencies of the tort system in areas of great complexity." In much the same vein, Timothy Noah[58] dismisses Woburn-type litigation: "Suffice it to say that the reader leaves *A Civil Action* convinced that a courtroom is almost never a logical place to go if you want to solve society's problems, even when justice is on your side."

It would be tempting and not entirely incorrect to sum up in ideological terms the differences between newspapers and news magazines, on the one hand, and the policy and opinion journals on the other. Certainly, *The Progressive* interprets *A Civil Action* in terms entirely consistent with its grassroots-democracy political preferences. And although it is more difficult to pigeonhole the *Washington Monthly*, its reviewer, Timothy Noah, a reporter for the *Wall Street Journal*, might be expected in the spirit of the corporate campaign for tort reform to conclude that "a courtroom is almost never a logical place to go if you want to solve society's problems, even when justice is on your side" With all of that said, however, I am inclined to believe that the major distinction is between news and opinion journalism.

Reviewers writing in and for news media tend to avoid making judgments and introducing their own values into their work. Of course, in taking as given hegemonic understandings of, for example, personal injury lawyers and class action litigation, they are making tacit judgments that reflect

[58] *Washington Monthly*, September 1995.

the prevailing orthodoxy, but without going out on a journalistic limb. In contrast, those writing in opinion journals feel free, indeed encouraged, to introduce values – their own or those of the publication – into their work. Not surprisingly, this feature leads toward the idiosyncratic inflections of *A Civil Action* that emerged in the policy journal reviews. For example, insofar as *Public Health Reports* emphasizes "the clumsiness and inefficiencies of the tort system," this slant is as likely attributable to the differences between policy and legal rationalities as to support for corporate-financed tort reform. Similarly, it should come as no surprise that the review by a professor of English, Suzanne Keen, in *Commonweal*[59] reflects both the humanistic values of the publication and her literary sensibilities.

2. *A Civil Action* in Film

The filming of *A Civil Action* definitively transformed Harr's nonfiction account of the Woburn litigation into popular culture, and the movie reviews both amplified the reach of the film and imparted meanings to it.[60] This journey into popular culture reinforced the messages of the book reviews about the futility of policy activism by personal injury attorneys. Although I argue that the film critics were much more caustic in their critique of Schlichtmann than was the film itself, the film was structured in a way that invited the opprobrium heaped on Schlichtmann by the critics. In addition, however, the critics were strictly on their own in casting further doubt on the Woburn litigation by largely ignoring corporate wrongdoing and corporate impunity – two themes that were pervasive in the book and readily apparent in the film as well.

Over the course of the film a compelling and complex portrait of Schlichtmann emerges – emphasizing both his mixed motives and narcissistic

[59] November 3, 1995.

[60] Unlike book reviews, movie reviews *originate* not only in print media but on the Internet as well. Indeed, the number of Internet reviews dwarfs those originating in newspapers. The Internet, it could be persuasively argued, is the more authentic voice of popular culture. In addition, its influence is arguably more extensive and resonant than that of the print media. It would seem to follow that the Internet is the more appropriate site for this research. For two reasons, however, my analysis is largely confined to the print media. On the one hand, a cursory reading of the Internet reviews suggests that there are few, if any, intermedia differences. Second, there is really no way to cope systematically with the volume of Internet reviews without changing from interpretive inquiry to content analysis – thus changing both the character and the scope of this research.

grandiosity. More broadly the film effectively dramatizes the excruciating complexity, both legal and scientific, of the litigation; the victimization and isolation of the plaintiffs as well as the disproportionately heavy burdens borne by them and by Schlichtmann; and how his dogged determination comes excruciatingly close to forcing his will on two major corporations. The problem is that the complexity of Schlichtmann does not begin to emerge until roughly halfway through the film.

Before then the film portrays Schlichtmann as money-driven, self-absorbed, and unprincipled. We first meet him putting a paraplegic plaintiff on display before the jury – using the client's manifest distress as a bargaining chip in a successful effort to increase the defendant's settlement offer and head off a trial. Forget about the ideal of having one's day in court with a judge and jury sifting through the evidence in an effort to render a fair and carefully considered verdict. In Schlichtmann's own words,

> The whole idea of lawsuits is to settle and to compel the other side to settle, and you do that by spending more money than you should which forces the other side to spend more money that they should and whoever comes to his senses first *loses*. Trials are a corruption of the entire process and only fools who have something to prove end up ensnared in them. And when I say prove I don't mean about the case. I mean about themselves.

In any event, with the victory under his belt, the focus shifts from the victim to the ensuing celebration and to Schlichtmann's subsequent partying and shopping spree. For Schlichtmann, in short, the plaintiff's suffering is strictly a bargaining chip that when properly deployed enhances his reputation as a fearless and formidable advocate while filling the coffers of his firm. Nor does he express any qualms about all this.

Once the film moves on to the Woburn litigation, it hardly comes as a surprise that Schlichtmann and his colleagues are fixated on deep pockets and are largely unconcerned with the devastating impact of the leukemia clusters on the children of Woburn and on their families. To be sure, Schlichtmann explains to the families and hence to moviegoers how and why money *must* be central to the firm's decision to accept or reject a case. This is not, he wants them and us to understand, about greed but about survival. His explanation is, however, offered in a spirit of professional detachment that registers absolutely no empathy for the Woburn families.

Just in case we have any doubts, the film has Schlichtmann justify his detachment as a pillar of professional probity. "The lawyer who shares his client's pain," Schlichtmann tells us, "does them such a disservice that he should have his license to practice taken away." Advocacy for Schlichtmann is most decidedly not about something to believe in. It follows that when he finally changes his mind and decides, with the warm endorsement of his partners, to accept the Woburn case, it is only as a result of the chance discovery that the putative defendants will be the corporate conglomerates, Beatrice Foods and W. R. Grace.

The civil litigation system is tarred by the film with the same cynical brush. We are bombarded with messages of an arbitrary, money-driven institution that subverts justice and rewards cynical manipulation – and only cynical manipulation. Jerome Facher becomes both the voice and the personification of these perversions. He is consistently portrayed as devious, sinister, cynical, *and effective*. Among the things that work for Facher are tactical moves that delay and disrupt Schlichtmann's case. He is shown instructing his Harvard Law School class on the virtues of throwing any and every legal monkey wrench into the proceedings:

> A plaintiff's case depends on momentum. The fewer objections he gets the better his case will go. So whenever you can you should object: relevance, hearsay, objection, objection. If you should fall asleep at the counsel table, the first thing that you say when you wake up is [after a pause for the class to respond] objection!

With respect to the victims' families, he declares, "These people can never testify." Because Facher is able to prevent them from doing so, Schlichtmann loses his only edge and thus his suit is doomed. Facher ridicules Schlichtmann for thinking that the trial jury might decide in favor of the Woburn plaintiffs simply because the defendants are "as guilty as hell." Forget about the truth, Facher explains: "The court isn't a place to look for the truth. It's all about money. The truth is at the bottom of a bottomless well." And sure enough as the trial proceeds we learn that the manifest guilt of the dumpers of toxic waste is buried beneath, and obfuscated by, the stonewalling of the defendants and the legal trickery of Jerome Facher. To further discredit the trial, we discover that the presiding judge regularly sides with Facher and shares his condescending views of Schlichtmann's skills and credentials – in essence treating Facher as a colleague and Schlichtmann as an outsider. In sum, Facher is portrayed, with the help of the judge, as successfully taking the naïve Schlichtmann to school and in the process teaching him and, hence, moviegoers that obstruction and delay are the currency of civil litigation, that truth is nowhere to be found, and that virtue is a vice.[61]

By the time of Facher's opening remarks to the jury, his indictment of personal injury lawyers and by implication the suit against Beatrice and Grace rings true:

> The idea of civil court and of personal injury law by nature, though no one likes to say it out loud, least of all the personal injury lawyer himself, is money, money for suffering, money for death as if that could somehow relieve suffering, as if somehow that could bring dead children back to life.

Conversely, when we are asked to entertain the possibility that Schlichtmann has come to feel the clients' pain, how can we possibly suspend our disbelief?

The moment of his ostensible epiphany does not arrive until halfway through the film, and it is product of a moment's reflection on an event that had occurred much earlier and that he had initially treated in purely strategic terms. During a deposition the father of one of the leukemia victims breaks down as he recounts, under Facher's questioning, the death of his son in his arms on the way to the hospital. At the time of the father's heart-wrenching story, Jan is shown as simply recognizing it as the key that will unlock the jury's sympathy and, thus, make his case.[62] Yet, subsequently Jan is shown as he is reminded of the father's story, and the actual incident is portrayed in an understated but sorrowful fashion. We are cued to believe that Jan has now been transformed from ambulance chasing to fighting for a cause.

It is difficult, however, not to be dubious – this is a case of too little, too late. How can we, in effect, suspend the disbelief that has been so assiduously cultivated up to that point – especially when that disbelief is consonant

[61] As the trial proceeds, the film interposes scenes of Facher lecturing his Harvard Law School classroom on the do's and don'ts of courtroom tactics – in effect as instructions to viewers about how to understand Facher's successes and Schlichtmann's failures.

[62] Facher, of course, sees the same thing from a reverse angle, and it is at this time that he confides in his colleagues, "These people can never testify."

with the conventional wisdom about personal injury lawyers?[63] Nor did it have to be that way, because as the book makes clear Jan was not a Johnny-come-lately to lawyering for causes. He had gone to law school because he wanted to make a difference and had, after law school, turned down an opportunity for a lucrative job with a corporate firm because that firm did not share his values or his ideals about legal practices. This information was withheld by the filmmakers, whether intentionally or not. Had we known, the epiphany would have been made not more credible but *unnecessary*. We would have realized that throughout his legal career Jan had struggled with his own mixed motives and that it was in character rather than out of character for him, when the chips were down, to embrace his clients' cause.

Finally, we come to the judgment the film levies against class action litigation. When Schlichtmann's ineptitude and the biasing of the system against him are taken in combination, it would seem to follow that the Woburn litigation was doomed to fail, and this is, indeed, the film's unmistakable parting message. Schlichtmann has managed to betray both his own partners and the families of the victims. He has betrayed his own partners by not only bankrupting the firm but also by bankrupting them individually. Jan tries to explain away their losses and convince them to stay the course rather than accepting a settlement that Jan deems inadequate and that partners see as a lifeline. A bitter exchange between Jan and James Gordon played by William Macy ensues.

> Schlichtmann: "I am so tired of hearing you moan about money all of the time. This isn't about money anymore . . ."
> Gordon: "I've lost enough because of you."
> Schlichtmann: "You wouldn't have anything without me. Everything you have I got for you."
> Gordon: "I don't have anything, Jan."

Jan gives in and he and the partners take the settlement offer to the family. Although it compensates the families to the tune of $347,000 each, the settlement is contingent on a confidentiality agreement, does not include the apology the families sought, and does not require the corporations to

[63] True, the cause lawyering literature suggests that lawyers can sometimes be transformed by their causes and their clients. It also seems fair to say, based on Harr's account, that Schlichtmann was touched by the victims and their families. But why then was he touched so long after he heard their stories? Of course, Harr has prepared us by making it clear that Schlichtmann's sympathies were never in doubt and always in play – if not necessarily and consistently paramount.

clean up the polluted sites. The families make it crystal clear that a payoff is an unacceptable alternative to an acknowledgment by the corporations of their responsibility for taking the lives of their children. The lesson of the film seems to be not only that the litigation failed but also it was bound to do so – given Jan's ineptitude and the way the system was stacked against the powerless plaintiffs and their déclassé attorneys.

The book leaves us with a very different message. It tells us that Schlichtmann was a dogged and resourceful advocate who came excruciatingly close to beating the defendants at their own game. Not only did he win a judgment against Grace, he came very close to gaining a satisfying settlement from both defendant corporations – a settlement at the $20 million level that from the outset has been seen as an unqualified success. The film is so intent on condemning Schlichtmann for his hubris and naiveté that it also fails to note the nefarious role played by Harvard Law Professor Charles Nesson, who was instrumental in convincing Schlichtmann to go for broke – which is, of course, precisely what he achieved. In short, despite all of the structural obstacles, the book teaches us that the litigation provided leverage that empowered the victims and came close to securing the relief that they sought. In addition, as the movie implies, albeit in a lukewarm and half-hearted fashion, the evidence amassed by the plaintiffs during the litigation seems to have been a catalyst that brought a hitherto supine and disinterested Environmental Protection Agency to successfully prosecute both Beatrice and Grace and led to heavy fines that financed the cleanup that was so important to the families.

3. Film Reviews

Whereas the filming of *A Civil Action* transformed it into popular culture, the film critics both amplified its reach and imparted meanings to it. For the most part these meanings simply transmitted the film's largely tone-deaf version of Harr's complex portrait of Schlichtmann and of its disproportionately negative inflection of the course and outcome of the Woburn litigation. The critics found the film's portrayal of Schlichtmann as an ambulance chaser convincing, but his idealism rang hollow. Typically, Walter Addiego of the *San Francisco Examiner*[64] declares, "Few mainstream pictures have offered such a devastatingly negative portrayal of the practice of

[64] January 8, 1999.

law in modern America – and this is a movie where the morally dubious main character turns into a hero with a worthy cause." John R. McEwen, a particularly caustic critic of the film, writes in *The Republican*,[65] "There are entire websites on the Internet full of jokes . . . about those personal injury lawyers whose TV ads promise results or no fee. In writer/director Steven Zaillian's *A Civil Action*, John Travolta plays one – Boston attorney Jan Schlichtmann, a bottom-feeder who grows a conscience. But in Zaillian's outlandish story line, Jan grows a little too much conscience for his own good. And a little too much to be believed . . . "

Similarly, the reviewers tend to agree that the film depicts a deeply flawed system of civil litigation dominated by money, oblivious to truth, and driven by strategic games of one sort or another. As Roger Ebert puts it in the *Chicago Sun Times*,[66] "The real world of the law, this movie argues, has less to do with justice than with strategy and doesn't necessarily arrive at truth. The law is about who wins, not about who should win." Under the circumstances, Ebert suggests Schlichtmann's insincerity matters less than his suspect competence: "[P]erhaps the last thing you want is a lawyer who is committed heart and soul to your cause. What you want is a superb technician." And, of course, by ignoring how close Schlichtmann came to beating the corporations at their own game, the film critics imply that a fair verdict is not just hard to come by but to all intents and purposes effectively out of reach.

There is the occasional critic who imputes Harr-like complexity to the film and welcomes it. Here's how Janet Maslin puts it in the *New York Times*.[67]

> What makes this gripping, expertly acted film by Steven Zaillian so enveloping is its avoidance of anything . . . easy. The story presents both Schlichtmann and the civil court system as stubbornly complicated. And it tells a finely nuanced tale of right, wrong and the gray area in between. . . . Just as Mr. Harr did on the page, the filmmaker presents Schlichtmann as an abrasive yet affecting character and treats everything else in the story in equally lifelike terms. Schlichtmann's glaring mistakes become as compelling as his smart moves, to the point where *A Civil Action* rings more true than most films about the law.

[65] Oakland, MD, December 12, 1998.
[66] January 8, 1999.
[67] December 25, 1998.

Jack Garner, writing for the *Rochester Democrat and Chronicle*,[68] agrees: "[T]he film starring John Travolta and Robert Duvall is a beautifully played character study, well worth seeing for its insight into the lifestyles, motives and ethics of two very different lawyers."

It is not at all clear to me how to account for these dramatically different interpretations of the film – although it seems plausible that these critics were more familiar with the book, more knowledgeable about civil justice, and more tolerant of ambiguity. And even then, Maslin sees the film "as ultimately less about winning or losing than about the difficulty of playing a game in which settlement-hungry lawyers gamble against tremendous odds and risk losing their bearings in the process."[69]

Whatever may be their differences, the film critics are as one in failing to detect or to acknowledge the larger issues of injustice, inequality, and corporate wrongdoing that permeate the book, are noted by its reviewers, and are readily apparent in the film. How are we to account for the film reviewers' disregard of the deeper meanings of Woburn? There is no reason to believe that movie reviewers are apologists for corporate wrongdoing or are unmoved by the suffering of the victims – much less that they are supporters, or even aware, of the tort reform movement whose positions they echo.[70] Yet they fail to take account of the connection between the ordeal of the Woburn families and either legal or social justice.[71]

The most plausible explanation is to be found in the quintessentially cinematic standards of judgment they apply to the film. For example, in assessing the credibility of Schlichtmann's mid-movie transformation from bottom feeder to idealist, they ask whether it makes *dramatic* sense. Throughout, their focus is equally cinematic, as is clear from earlier citations – as for example the approving Janet Maslin making reference to a "gripping, expertly acted film by Steven Zaillian" and the disapproving John R. McEwen showering his attention on the "outlandish story

[68] January 8, 1999.

[69] December 25, 1998.

[70] Mick LaSalle of the *San Francisco Chronicle* (January 8, 1999) goes so far as to tell us that in Duvall's compelling portrayal, Facher "comes across as [s]mart and unconventional.... He's likable, until we come to realize... he's the face of death that Schlichtmann is instinctively turning from."

[71] It is difficult to say whether the critics endorse these views, but they do not question them. Perhaps they have simply internalized the widespread public cynicism about personal injury lawyers and embraced a skeptical view of the U.S. legal system more generally.

line."[72] Similarly, Walter Addiego in the *San Francisco Examiner*[73] complains that the film's "no risk story telling detracts from fine performances," and Russell Smith in the *Austin Chronicle*[74] concludes, "For all its craftsmanlike sheen, this film is so sketchy, obvious and idea-poor compared to Harr's book that you can't help wishing [Steven] Zallian [the director] had paid more attention to . . . warnings about biting off more than you can chew."

And although they come to varying conclusions, they all view the film through essentially the same cinematic lens.[75] The film critics are acutely aware that theirs is an entertainment medium, and thus, they also ask whether the film makers have been able to create a movie that is as dramatically compelling as the book without compromising the integrity of Harr's multifaceted, scientifically complex, and legally abstruse case study.

There is simply no escaping the conclusion that these film reviews, taken as a whole, convey a vision of cause lawyering as superfluous, unworkable, and subversive. By largely ignoring the messages of injustice that permeate the film, the reviews imply that cause lawyering is unnecessary. By discounting Schlichtmann's idealism and questioning his competence, they imply that, even if there were a need for cause lawyering, turning to someone like Schlichtmann would be a serious mistake.[76] In short the consequence of applying cinematic standards to the film is not only to replicate but actually to amplify, through their reviews, the hegemonic rendering of the film itself and to further neutralize Harr's unmistakable message of social and legal injustice.

[72] *The Republican* (Oakland, MD), December 12, 1998.

[73] January 8, 1999.

[74] January 8, 1999.

[75] Unlike book reviewers for whom it is sufficient to evaluate Harr's project in its own terms, film critics apply multiple and competing criteria. To begin with, they assess the film not only as film but also in terms of its fidelity to the book. Yet they clearly feel compelled to make allowances for the constraints imposed by film – most notably, in the case of *A Civil Action*, the need to pare down Harr's massively detailed account to a filmable and entertaining screenplay. So, whereas book reviewers marvel at Harr's ability to create compelling drama from a lengthy, technically complex, and inclusive series of anticlimactic legal maneuvers, film critics see compelling drama as less to be celebrated than as a necessity. Yet these same film critics clearly represent themselves as discerning arbiters of high culture and can most readily be seen as such by establishing and deploying a distinctively cinematic aesthetic.

[76] No doubt some of the blame can be laid at the feet of the film makers for failing to portray Schlichtmann's long-standing commitment to lawyering for causes.

IV. In Conclusion

Through the successive interventions of book critics, the John Travolta-Robert Redford film, and film critics, Jonathan Harr's critically successful study of the Woburn litigation morphed into a cultural event. These interventions pared down and reframed for media-driven purposes his exhaustively researched, meticulously reported, and artfully written study. In the process, principal elements of his Woburn narrative largely disappeared; specifically,

- Jan Schlichtmann's tortured idealism, his tenacity, and the extent to which he empowered victims and put pressure on corporations
- The social and political victimization of innocent citizens by callous and predatory corporations

The book leaves little doubt that there has been serious corporate wrongdoing – first in the sloppy practices that polluted Woburn wells and second in the corporation's concerted efforts, abetted by their lawyers, to cover up the truth of what happened. In other words, for Harr, if not for Facher, the truth is not at the bottom of a bottomless pit. Moreover, though Harr exposes the many ways in which the deck is stacked against Schlichtmann, *A Civil Action*, unlike virtually all of the media representations of it, suggests that the civil justice system can and, in this instance, *almost* did produce substantial social justice. Whether the EPA's belated but successful prosecution of the Beatrice and Grace corporations was catalyzed by the publicity and the findings generated by the litigation is not considered by Harr, but it is plausible that there was just such a link between the Woburn suit and EPA enforcement.

Accordingly, successive media interventions leave us with a deeply alienating vision of personal injury attorneys and class action litigation. This vision discredits an important segment of the cause lawyering bar and its primary legal resource.[77] There is, to be sure, no evidence that Harr, or any of the *media*tors, is aware of cause lawyering or that they wish to discredit lawyers who commit themselves and their legal skills to furthering a vision

[77] Anne Bloom, "Taking on Goliath: Why Personal Injury Litigation May Represent the Future of Transnational Cause Lawyering" in Austin Sarat and Stuart Scheingold, *Cause Lawyering and the State in a Global Era* (New York: Oxford University Press, 2002) and Stuart Scheingold and Austin Sarat, *Something to Believe In*, 119–22.

of the good society. However, by belittling Schlichtmann's motives and methods and by implying that his faults and the faults of the civil justice system are intrinsic to personal injury lawyering, the media misrepresent Harr and call into question personal injury cause lawyering more generally. What is left is the indelible impression that there is little or nothing that personal injury lawyers and litigation can do to right wrongs.

It would, however, be wrong to take the media's revisionist versions of Harr's book as politically driven. The film and some of the book reviews represent the Woburn litigation as evidence of inequality, corporate wrongdoing, and the impunity corporations enjoy. This is hardly a right-wing message. The media are simply replicating and reinforcing the widespread disillusionment with personal injury lawyers and class action law suits and perhaps rights activism more generally. It is, in short, the currently prevailing hegemony rather than any right-wing sympathies that is embedded in the successive media misrepresentations. The implicit but inexorable conclusion is that class action lawsuits by personal injury lawyers are unnecessary, ineffectual, and perhaps a threat to economic growth; that they serve the interests of unscrupulous personal injury lawyers, not their clients. In an earlier era under the then-hegemonic influence of successful and widely approved litigation-driven movements on behalf of social justice – civil rights, environmental protection, gender equality, and the like – the media would have arguably read *A Civil Action* in a diametrically different way.[78]

[78] See Chapters 7 and 8 for confirming evidence.

13

Not What They Expected

Legal Services Lawyers in the Eyes of Legal Services Clients

Corey S. Shdaimah

I. Introduction

Laypersons hold images of lawyers. These images derive from a variety of sources including prior experiences with lawyers or government bureaucracies[1] and popular media (see Chapter 8). With the high cost of legal services, most poor people and many working and middle-class individuals have limited, if any, experience working with lawyers[2] that might inform their images or counteract stereotypes of lawyers. Given the discrepancy between income and education levels of most lawyers and poor people in an increasingly class-stratified United States society,[3] most are also unlikely to encounter lawyers among their friends and neighbors.[4] So what are the images that circulate among low-income individuals who are the populations likely to be served by what Sarat and Scheingold have called "cause lawyers"?[5] Where do these images come from? What do they tell us about the people who hold them?

[1] Austin Sarat, "The Law is All Over: Power, Resistance, and the Legal Consciousness of the Welfare Poor," *Yale Journal of the Law and Humanities* 2 (1990): 343; Joe Soss, *Unwanted Claims: The Politics of Participation in the U.S. Welfare System* (Ann Arbor: University of Michigan Press, 2002).

[2] American Bar Association Reports, "Public Perceptions of Lawyers: 2002 Consumer Research Findings," posted April 2002, retrieved January 17, 2007 from http://www.abanet.org/litigation/lawyers.

[3] Jacob S. Hacker, *The Great Risk Shift: The Assault on American Families, Jobs, Health Care and Retirement and How You Can Fight Back* (Oxford: Oxford University Press, 2006).

[4] Phillip R. Lochner Jr., "The No Fee and Low Fee Legal Practice of Private Attorneys," *Law and Society Review* 9 (1975): 431.

[5] Stuart Scheingold and Austin Sarat, *Something to Believe In: Politics, Professionalism, and Cause Lawyering* (Stanford: Stanford University Press, 2004).

This essay relies on data from interviews with thirty indigent legal services clients as part of a larger study of legal services lawyers and clients.[6] It is a report of what Richard Johnson has referred to as "studies of lived cultures."[7] This means that, although one could focus on the production of texts (broadly defined to include stock myths and cultural stories) or the way in which texts circulate, this study focuses on how a group of indigent legal services clients consume, change, and produce local meanings about the lawyers with whom they work. Much of the cause lawyering literature has largely ignored client perspectives,[8] focusing instead on lawyers' visions of themselves as advocates or crusaders for a cause. This vision, in turn, has been produced or filtered through the academic conceptual category[9] of "cause lawyers." Although academics have consulted with so-called cause lawyers (at least as research subjects), they have rarely examined how clients or publics may conceive of these lawyers. The concept or text of "cause lawyer" and the meanings that lawyers and academics ascribe to it do not necessarily resonate or even register at all with many clients. This essay goes beyond previous reports by seeking the perspectives of indigent clients about their beliefs regarding lawyers, their experiences with lawyers, and the impact of these experiences on their beliefs. Speculation on the discrepancy between texts produced by and about cause lawyers and consumers' reading and production of these texts implicates conceptions of justice and lack of confidence in the legal system.

After a brief discussion of the study and its methods, I provide an account of clients' views about and expectations of lawyers. Because clients' narratives of their expectations of lawyers are interwoven with what they actually experienced in their relationships with lawyers, these findings are reported together by theme: professional competence (legal knowledge and skills, professional cachet, and connections); motivation (altruism and financial gain); and engagement with clients (professional and personal). I then discuss the sources of clients' beliefs and explanations, followed by an

[6] Corey S. Shdaimah, *Public Interest Lawyering: The Practice and Pursuit of Social Justice* (New York: New York University Press, forthcoming).

[7] Richard Johnson, "What is Cultural Studies Anyway?" *Social Text* 16 (Winter 1986–87): 38, 72.

[8] But see Sarat, "The Law is All Over."

[9] Steve Redhead, *Unpopular Cultures: The Birth of Law and Popular Culture* (Manchester: Manchester University Press, 1995); Rosemary J. Coombe, "Contingent Articulations: A Critical Cultural Studies of Law," in *Law in the Domains of Culture*, ed. Austin Sarat and Thomas R. Kearns (Ann Arbor: University of Michigan Press, 2000).

interpretation of why clients do not revise their images of lawyers to conform with their experiences when these experiences run counter to their expectations. In this discussion, I examine what clients' expectations and integration of discrepant experiences imply for the delivery of legal services to the poor and, more generally, for the legal system and conceptions of justice.

II. Lawyers and Clients in the Study

The data reported here are based on interviews conducted in 2002–03 with thirty legal services clients of a large, urban, legal services program that I call Northeast Legal Services (NELS).[10] These clients received services for a variety of legal needs, including accusations of child abuse and neglect, Social Security Disability benefits, public housing, Temporary Assistance for Needy Families, and predatory lending. All clients were referred by lawyers who had also participated in the study.[11] Interviews were conducted in person, with the exception of one telephone interview. All but three of the in-person interviews took place in clients' homes. The intensive interviews, which lasted approximately one and a half hours, focused on clients' perceptions of current and prior interactions with lawyers and government agencies. Clients were asked to reflect on their experiences and understanding of lawyers, the legal system, and of justice, which were intertwined.

Twenty-seven clients were women; three were men. Twenty-three were African American, five were white, and two identified primarily as immigrants: one from Africa and one from Southeast Asia. The majority, by definition, were poor as they met NELS' income eligibility criterion of 125 percent of the federal poverty line, which is set as a function of annual income and family size.[12] Six clients were from a unit that serves the elderly regardless of income. Most of these elderly clients, however, have similarly

[10] To protect the confidentiality of the study participants, pseudonyms are used for clients and legal institutions.

[11] For a discussion of possible bias, see Corey S. Shdaimah, "Dilemmas of 'Progressive Lawyering'": Empowerment and Hierarchy," in *The Worlds Cause Lawyers Make: Structure and Agency in Legal Practice*, eds. Austin Sarat and Stuart Scheingold (Stanford: Stanford University Press, 2005), 270.

[12] For example, for 2003 when most of my interviews took place, the federal poverty line was $18,400 for a family of four. U.S. Department of Health and Human Services, Office of the Assistant Secretary for Planning and Evaluation, http:// hhs.gov/poverty, retrieved June 4, 2007.

limited income because otherwise they would likely hire private attorneys or not be in the situations that brought them to NELS. This assumption is borne out by their circumstances. For example, two lived in public housing and one received city housing services only available to those with incomes that meet NELS' income eligibility criteria. Ages of the clients ranged from the early twenties to the late seventies. In addition to the six clients from the unit serving the elderly, another six who were clients of other units were also elderly.

Most NELS lawyers do not look like "typical" lawyers, as many dress informally in the office. None of those I interviewed in their offices on regular weekdays wore a suit; Suzanne reported, "If I could pull off the power suit thing maybe I'd be in a law firm." Jeff, who translated complicated health insurance provisions from legalese into plain English for elderly clients, distanced himself from the lawyer that he imagined wrote them, describing him or her as "some yahoo in a suit." Other lawyers had hairstyles, jewelry, or ways of dressing that were decidedly out of the mainstream. For example, Carolyn described her lawyer Suzanne as "cool," saying she was the "first lawyer I met with tattoos and piercings."

Less obvious to clients is that NELS lawyers see themselves as a special breed of lawyer.[13] Indeed, the reigning conception of legal practice at NELS and in the public interest law community of which it is a part has its roots in oppositional lawyering movements that began in the 1960s and are allied more with the clients and causes they serve than with what they view as the legal establishment.[14] This conception, to some extent, comes across in their discussions with clients and in their interactions with other lawyers. Legal services lawyers choose to distance themselves from their counterparts in the private bar or in government service.

Yet, even though their lawyers look or act contrary to mainstream notions of lawyering, clients do not refine their views of lawyers in general. Rather,

[13] Shdaimah, "Intersecting Identities: Cause Lawyers as Legal Professionals and Social Movement Actors" in *Cause Lawyers and Social Movements*, eds. Austin Sarat and Stuart Scheingold (Stanford: Stanford University Press, 2006).

[14] Martha Davis, *Brutal Need: Lawyers and the Welfare Rights Movement, 1960–1973* (New Haven: Yale University Press, 1993); Jack Katz, *Poor People's Lawyers in Transition* (New Brunswick: Rutgers University Press, 1982). The role that NELS and other public interest law organizations have come to create for themselves in relation to the organized bar has evolved over time, but here I intend to highlight the lawyers' perception of themselves and their allegiances (see also Shdaimah, "Intersecting Identities").

they continue to identify all lawyers with more traditional societal images of what lawyers do, how (well) they do it, and for whom. They do not recognize a distinct or special breed of cause lawyer,[15] but instead see their lawyers as anomalous, individual, exceptions.

III. The Need for Lawyers

Despite, or perhaps because of, the difficulty in finding legal assistance, legal services clients view having a lawyer as crucially important.[16] Clients are not always able to articulate why or how this is the case, but it is common knowledge that one should not try to tackle legal or bureaucratic problems without professional help. Like Latonya, most clients made it clear that having a lawyer was a necessary (if insufficient) means to ensure justice:

> Well, working with [Joann] . . . let me see how I could put it. I don't know, I mean I know that – I believe that lawyers are beneficial. You know, because if you go in – if you're in a situation and you go into it alone without a lawyer you have less of a chance. But if you go into it with a lawyer, you have a better chance. That's how I feel now.

In fact, one thread that runs through many interviews is the obligation that a person in trouble has to seek a lawyer. Clients tell friends and family members (and anyone else they run into just about anywhere) to go to "their" lawyer or to contact NELS.[17] People who do not act on this advice have only themselves to blame:

> I told [a] relative about what this person is doing for me. I said go to these people. If she helped me she can help you if you are in a similar situation rather than lose your house, and they lost their house! Yes they

[15] Nor do they use any of the other specialized terms so-called cause lawyers and those who study them use such as "progressive lawyer" (Nancy D. Polikoff, "Am I My Client? The Role Confusion of a Lawyer Activist," *Harvard Civil Rights-Civil Liberties Law Review* 31 (1996): 443; "rebellious lawyer" (Gerald P. López, *Rebellious Lawyering: One Chicano's Vision of Progressive Law Practice* (Boulder: Westview Press, 1992); or "client-centered lawyer" (Steven Ellman, "Client-Centeredness Multiplied: Individual Autonomy and Collective Mobilization in Public Interest Lawyers' Representation of Groups," *Virginia Law Review* 78 (1992): 1103.

[16] Reported in Shdaimah, "Dilemmas of Progressive Lawyering." See also Patricia Ewick and Susan S. Sibley, *The Common Place of Law: Stories from Everyday Life* (Chicago: University of Chicago Press, 2000), 152.

[17] As people who have already sought out legal assistance, this might be a group of individuals who are more likely to seek help than those who have not.

> did. Lost their house, all that money they put into it and everything, they lost their house. And then I was – I said don't even – I don't want to hear it because I told you what to do, told you who to go to!... I gave the information, spreaded the good news and the good word to someone else, and they just didn't act on it. And then when they, the man go and knock on the door [knocks twice] and say the truck is outside, then they want to – "What did you say the woman's name was? [imitates derisively]." Please [with disgust]. It's too late at that point. And I can't feel empathy for you because, but sympathy at that point. Because I tried.

Lawyers, in the eyes of clients, are simultaneously necessary but untrustworthy, at least as a group. Although many legal services lawyers conceive of themselves as a special breed of oppositional outsiders, they are nevertheless lawyers who must play by the rules. Some lawyers are aware of this dual role.[18] Cause lawyering scholars have questioned whether lawyers paid by the state are sufficiently transgressive to qualify as cause lawyers,[19] and at least one lawyer in this study[20] chafed at the limits of his ability to serve his clients. He viewed himself and his work as circumscribed by his professional and institutional mandates. Despite their suspicions, clients, unsurprisingly, turn to lawyers as a last or only hope in exercising what Linda Gordon, drawing on the work of James Scott, has called "powers of the weak."[21] As Gordon's analysis suggests, just as clients are not passive consumers of lawyers or the legal system, neither are they passive consumers of cultural texts about lawyers and the legal system. They draw on, interpret, and produce texts about lawyers and the legal system that are intelligible in the constellation of their experiences.[22]

In examining client narratives about why lawyers are necessary, we can learn about how clients conceive of lawyers and their professional roles. Three related but distinct themes emerged from the interviews: (1) the need for professional knowledge to solve legal problems, (2) professional status

[18] Polikoff, "Am I My Client?"

[19] Stuart Scheingold and Anne Bloom, "Transgressive Cause Lawyering: Practice Sites and the Politicization of the Professional," *International Legal Professions* 5 (1998): 209.

[20] Pete, cited in Shdaimah, "Dilemmas of 'Progressive Lawyering,' 250

[21] Linda Gordon, *Heroes of Their Own Lives: The Politics and History of Family Violence* (New York: Penguin Books, 1988).

[22] Johnson, "What is Cultural Studies," 60; Arjun Appadurai, *Modernity at Large: Cultural Dimensions of Globalization* (Minneapolis: University of Minnesota, 1996); W. Russell Neuman, Marion R. Just, and Ann N. Crigler, *Common Knowledge: News and the Construction of Political Meaning* (Chicago: University of Chicago Press, 1992), 111–12, 119–120.

as a prerequisite for being heard or listened to, and (3) lawyers as having access or connections that are important to success in the legal system.

1. Legal Knowledge and Skills

Legal systems are specialized. Clients recognize that it takes someone with knowledge of the law and the way bureaucracies and legal systems work to be able to navigate these systems; they are too complicated to navigate alone. People need to arm themselves with lawyers who will navigate it for them or will steer them through it. Most clients characterized the bureaucracies with which they interacted as, at worst, deliberately misrepresenting what clients' rights and entitlements are or, at best, apathetic and/or incompetent. Therefore, people cannot rely on bureaucracies to find out information that may be crucial for their very survival, whether it be access to housing, medical benefits, or other basic necessities. For example, Marissa, an immigrant, sought medical help for her daughter who was born in the United States and entitled to health benefits despite the fact that Marissa herself was not. Marissa is well educated and an excellent English speaker, but she was unable to ascertain her daughter's rights to health care until she began working with her legal services lawyer:

> I tell you, the law, the legal system, if you have somebody to explain to you your rights, what they can do for you, then you can do everything, make use of the legal system and get a little bit of justice. But if you have no clue you are in a terrible mess [voice rising]. Like when I didn't have any clue of my rights like that my daughter was supposed to, uh, [get for health care I] was in a terrible situation until I could get somebody to explain all these things to me. If you don't have anybody helping you, forget it [yawns]. If you don't have that... maybe the [government agency workers] I've come in contact, I've let them know they are lies, the ones that I've come in contact they are not there to tell you [that] you're supposed to get this or supposed to get that.

Leslie talks about the need for lawyers much more generally. In explaining to me why legal services for the poor are so crucial, she indicated that in our society it is not feasible to get by on one's own:

> Services like that are needed and are necessary. Because we – our society – is a legal society. You may not like [it] but you can't live without [a lawyer]. Well, some lawyers are out to make money and

> they have no sense of right and wrong. None whatsoever, they're just out to – but you can't live without them. Not in our world anyway [laughs]. Unfortunately some of them have no sense of... integrity I think would be the word [laughs].

Leslie's quote also shows how laypeople are at the mercy of lawyers. The very lack of knowledge that makes clients dependent on lawyers also makes it difficult for clients to judge whether lawyers will serve them well or poorly. This is true particularly of legal services clients, who have little leverage over lawyers and may not have recourse, if unsatisfied.[23] I asked Ellis, an elderly gentleman, what he thought NELS could do to improve their services. He told me, "Um [drawn out, thinking] I don't think I'm that smart enough to know that [laughs]." Others weave this theme into their cautionary tale, extending a client's duty to vigilance over their lawyer's performance.[24] When I asked her about justice, Martha illustrated the importance of having a good lawyer through the examples of a friend and a nephew, who had both been involved with the criminal justice system. For her, what made the difference in these two cases was the quality of the legal representation.

> The law can work for you or against you. In [my friend's case], it worked for him. I've seen the law work against a person, too. If you get an incompetent lawyer, you're in trouble. My nephew, he got picked up for, he was messing with drugs at the time. Now, they locked him up.

Martha went on to relate that it was clear to *her* that her nephew's public defender was not doing his job, and that she exhorted her sister to speak up and demand better representation for her nephew. To do otherwise, in her opinion, was to court the risk of having the law work against her nephew.

> In that instance the law worked against him. Against him in the sense that he had, there's no other way to put it, an incompetent lawyer. Or a person who just didn't care. And [my nephew] didn't speak up for hisself. It just rolled over him.

[23] See Paul R. Tremblay, "Toward a Community-Based Ethic for Legal Services Practice," *UCLA Law Review* 37 (1989–90): 1105–07 for a discussion of legal services lawyers as street level bureaucrats who provide scarce services to clients who lack any leverage.

[24] See Carl J. Hosticka, "We Don't Care About What Happened, We Only Care About What is Going to Happen: Lawyer-Client Negotiations of Reality," *Social Problems* 26 (1979): 599, reporting that although lawyers perceived persistent clients negatively, they expended more efforts on their cases.

The difficulty of assessing lawyer performance coupled with the importance of doing so likely makes clients even more suspicious of lawyers. It also gives such suspicion an important function as it serves to remind clients of the need to be vigilant in scrutinizing their lawyers' performance. It gives them the motivation to ask questions or attempt to monitor performance as best they can, either by comparing it with previous experiences or with the experiences of friends or relatives, or by going by their own sense of justice.

2. Professional Cachet

Some clients have knowledge about their legal situation and feel competent to handle legal matters on their own, but still find it necessary to use the assistance of a lawyer. Lilly told me of a long career of political activism. She directly approached her lawyer from NELS with whom she serves on a committee that works on state and local policy issues concerning the elderly. Lilly made it clear that she had a solid understanding of her legal problem, the law, and what needed to be done. So I wondered why she turned to a lawyer, and asked her what she was hoping to accomplish. The following exchange is from our interview:

> Lilly: I was hoping that she could break the Gordian knot [laughs]. I was hoping she'd go in and say, "Look: This is this, this is what she has done, this is what the thing is, and this is the law." And that's exactly it and it was taken care of very quickly.
>
> Corey: So basically to say the same kind of things that you were saying but just having it come out of her mouth?
>
> Lilly: Ahhh! When you have it come out of someone's mouth who has a background, they will listen, especially if you say that you are a lawyer working with the senior community.... But the fact that you are a lawyer and you are working with this community and this is the law.

The power of Liz's (Lilly's lawyer) professional degree coupled with her representation of a sympathetic group (seniors) made Lilly believe that Liz would be more likely to succeed than she (herself a senior!) could. When a lawyer says, "This is the law," even if he or she only echoes what the unrepresented client has been saying, it is the lawyer who will be listened to and credited as the authoritative source. This was echoed time and again by clients like Carolyn, who was represented in child abuse and neglect and school proceedings. Carolyn said that she wanted her lawyer Suzanne to accompany her to each and every meeting "because people take you more seriously. Because when you're by yourself, you're just a parent. When you're a parent with a lawyer, they listen [laughs] a little bit more, so. Definitely, that's a plus."

Nancy saw the legal system as a clear hierarchy. She referred to her lawyer as a "mediator" and explained that people do not have the authority to speak directly to judges, but rather must go through lawyers who were part of what she called the "chain of command." Her lawyer not only understands how this hierarchy works but is also the one who has the proper authority to speak with those who have the power to make decisions. Celia, too, talked about needing a lawyer to interface with the legal system and with the mortgage company: "And you need a lawyer, you know? I needed a lawyer. Somebody to represent me or to speak for me. Somebody to speak for me legally, to present whatever papers."

In many cases, clients suspect that street-level bureaucrats deliberately provide erroneous information or withhold information, assuming that clients do not know and have no way of finding out what their rights are. Mary said,

> But if I didn't know that right, like people that don't know that right, is totally screwed because they're like – "you can't appeal that, and you have to do this." I mean and they totally tried to tell me this, and I'm like "crrrhhh [noise] no fucking way, you know, let me call Pete – I need to call my lawyer." You know, so I think their legal system is just [trails off].

Indicative of Mary's experience is her use of the phrase, "their legal system." This is not a legal system designed for all; it only helps those who are in the know and have access. Clients need lawyers for both knowledge and access. Sometimes it is sufficient to merely mention that one has a lawyer. Marissa, cited earlier on how important it is to have a lawyer to provide information, also found that invoking representation led her to be treated differently (that is, better) by otherwise unresponsive bureaucracies: "The last the time I went I said, 'The best thing for me is to go to my attorney' . . . 'Oh you have an attorney?!' ... I said, 'Yes, I have an attorney' ... She then knew I knew my rights and then that was that."

3. Connections

Clients believe that lawyers are listened to not only because of their qualifications and their professional role but also because they are part of the "system." Other cause lawyering scholars have documented the ties that lawyers have with government institutions in different countries.[25] Although most clients are unaware of the details and have little empirical evidence to back up the perceived connections between lawyers and various arms of the state, they have a sense that all arms of the government, including legal services lawyers, have connections and work together. Clients in my interviews saw the "system" as government generally, rather than limited to the courts or the particular administrative tribunals or officers before whom they appear.[26] When Arlene discussed how she started working with Marcia, she told me that Marcia already had all of the necessary documents connected to her son's Social Security Disability Insurance claim so that she did not have to go about procuring the many school and medical papers necessary for the appeal. In telling me how Marcia obtained the records, she informed me matter-of-factly, "Well you know lawyers always have connections. They got connections."

Clients are often suspicious of lawyers because they fear that they may be in cahoots with the other legal players whose very actions they are challenging. This can be in the form of an active conspiracy, but may also take the less active form of having more loyalty to the system or to other lawyers than to clients. Dara explained why clients must monitor their lawyers to ensure good service and loyalty:

> Right, like because you could sit back and not say anything and let them do whatever they want to do and they will, and you know, they

[25] Michael McCann and William Haltom, "ATLA Shrugged: Why Personal Injury Lawyers are not Public Defenders of Their Own Causes," in *The Worlds Cause Lawyers Make: Structure and Agency in Legal Practice*, eds. Austin Sarat and Stuart Scheingold (Stanford: Stanford University Press, 2005). See also Patricia J. Woods, "Cause Lawyers and the Judicial Community in Israel: Legal Challenge in a Diffuse, Normative Community" in *The Worlds Cause Lawyers Make*, 307.

[26] See also Joe Soss, "Lessons of Welfare: Policy Administration, Political Learning and Political Action," *American Political Science Review* 93(1999): 363.

> gonna get paid. And sometimes somebody work with the same side, so you know you got to be real careful. You got to be real careful as far as they're concerned.

Such connections not only raise clients' suspicions of lawyers but also, for the very same reasons, reinforce their sense that they are a necessary evil. If a client can find a lawyer who is willing to put his or her connections to the client's benefit, then there is an opportunity to achieve (the client's vision of) justice. Valerie, a former union activist, learned how to challenge people in power from a union business agent whom she greatly admired:

> And there was a lot of things that Joe taught me that stuck. . . . [He said], 'Let me tell you something: It's not *what* you know, it's who you know.' And I have never forgotten that. And it doesn't make no difference how educated you are, if you don't know the right person you're going to get no help. And I found that to be a fact. You got to know the right people to talk to who can really help you. And that is why I'm glad I met [my lawyer].

When I asked Valerie whether this was true of the legal system, she replied,

> Well these guys are pretty heavy. And they work with each other. Like if one doesn't know, the other one is there to help. And these guys are – they're heavy. They're really heavy, educated guys. And they know exactly what they're doing.

In addition to shoring up the importance of knowing the right people to have a shot at justice, Valerie's quote reveals another important benefit that clients can extract from working with well-connected lawyers, which was affirmed by the stories that many clients told. Once a client has the ear of a lawyer, that lawyer often serves as a bridge to additional legal and other forms of assistance. The overwhelming majority of clients reported being connected to other services by their NELS lawyers. These services ranged from legal assistance with domestic violence (not handled by NELS but by other legal service providers), assistance in opening dedicated bank accounts for children receiving SSDI, and securing food stamps, medical assistance, and housing. In most cases, these were services that clients did not know about before working with their lawyers or from which they had been turned away in their initial attempts to access them.

IV. For Love or Money?

1. Financial Gain and Service to the Poor

That organizations such as NELS do not reflect the communities they serve is a product of mutual forces. Lawyers who themselves come from poor and underserved neighborhoods where it is a rarity that people know or are related to lawyers have a hard time finding public interest jobs. These jobs are hard for anyone to attain.[27] Lawyers from poor communities with troubled schools might be less likely to be able to attend more expensive, elite law schools, making them less competitive and making it harder for funding-strapped public interest law organizations to hire them via grants and fellowships.[28]

Even if hiring practices were not a barrier, my study indicates that most of the clients who thought about careers in the law did so as a vehicle up and out of poverty: as a way to make money. When I asked LaTonya whether she had any images of lawyers before working with one, she replied,

> No, the only image I had is that they make *a lot* of money [laughs]. Well when I was a kid they always used to tell me that I should be – "You should be a lawyer." . . . But the only thing that attracted me to them is money. The money aspect of it, that's all.

Since clients who thought about becoming a lawyer clearly were interested in this profession as a route to high earnings and out of poverty, they assumed that most lawyers chose their profession for the same reason. Clients were baffled as to why any competent lawyer would choose to work for legal services and assumed instead that it was a job for those who were less skilled, less motivated, or less well connected. Many were incredulous to learn that their NELS lawyers did not charge a fee for their services. Joseph related, "I said, 'Well how much do I have to pay?' She said, 'You don't have to pay anything, it's legal aid, it's free.' And I says 'free'?! [laughs]."

[27] Lynn C. Jones, "Exploring the Sources of Cause and Career Correspondence Among Cause Lawyers" in *The Worlds Cause Lawyers Make*. See also Douglas Thomson, "Negotiating Cause Lawyering Potential in the Early Years of Corporate Practice" in *The Worlds Cause Lawyers Make*.

[28] Shdaimah, "Dilemmas of "Progressive" Lawyering," 235–37.

Clients' notions of free lawyers are linked to their understanding of the legal system as a place for differentiated experience: those who have money might be able to get justice; those without are usually out of luck, even if their cases have merit. Elinor, a client of the consumer advocacy unit who had worked with lawyers through her union in the past, explained that those attorneys were not legal services lawyers because "when I was working and not on disability and I could pay the lawyers. But I was really out of it this time..." Laid up with lupus and serious complications from the disease, Elinor was now bedridden and sought legal assistance due to financial problems as well as difficulties with an abusive husband. She called NELS out of a lack of alternatives, not expecting much. As she told me, she thought, "Oh they're not going to help because they're not getting paid. It's a free thing. You know I don't have no money to give them. People – the system doesn't work like that."

Elinor worries that if her NELS lawyer Ben were offered a better position, he might leave legal services:

> I don't want to see him get another j[ob] – a better position and not be Ben. But I guess if he gets a higher position, he would still be the same. I don't think he would just drop his clients, you know and say I can't answer this question for you or anything.

This is indicative of an understanding that many legal services lawyers have their jobs because they cannot find other, "better" ones.[29] Ben, in practice for nearly 30 years, was the head of his department at NELS and one of the foremost authorities in his field in the country. Highly respected, his advice and input are sought on the local and national level, which makes it all the more interesting that Elinor thinks that he might be tempted to leave legal services if he got a better offer. Her perception is particularly telling as it shows that, although Ben is well respected in the legal community at large (including the private bar) and has been honored publicly and profiled in the media, Elinor remains completely unaware of his prestige and, despite her satisfaction with his services, has no way of integrating his competence and the respect that he commands into her model of legal aid lawyers.

[29] Lisa McIntyre, *The Public Defenders: The Practice of Law in the Shadow of Repute* (Chicago: University of Chicago Press, 1987).

Some clients were aware that law school is expensive and that legal services lawyers likely reap fewer financial rewards and have more difficulty repaying student loans than lawyers in private practice. Some, like Mary, offered me advice, thinking that my research was to prepare me for a career in the law:

> Private practice is I think much better, because you have to go to school and it's so many years of school and it's a lot of money, it's like a doctor. And uh, in order to recoup that or pay your loan back, whatever you did, um, it takes a lot longer if you're with a community legal service or legal aid.

Clients who excoriate the system for its lack of justice do not usually seek to become lawyers or change their lives to rectify it; rather, if anything, they expressed a desire to move to the other side and to be one of those people who knows the right people, is able to get justice through having a lawyer at their elbow, and can make lots of money. Their bafflement with lawyers who are both competent and serve the poor, in part, is connected to this desire.

The correlation between money and perceived competence, however, is somewhat more complicated. Although some clients could only comprehend that their lawyers chose legal services work because of a lack of options and assumed that legal services lawyers *must* be less competent, many clients (sometimes the very same ones) did not see a correlation between money and competence. In fact, most clients assumed that lawyers pursuing their careers for pecuniary gain probably did not care much about their clients personally and, whether competent or not, would not necessarily put in effort for their clients or provide satisfactory services. Eloise described her frustration when she hired an attorney for her granddaughter. She felt that the lawyer was only interested in the money and did not care about her granddaughter nor did she provide her any services for the money:

> There is a question I would like to ask these lawyers. When you give them the fee, their money, which happened to me – my granddaughter got into some trouble. And we gave this lady $850. Well so far she never did anything. . . . These lawyers do that. Take people's money and they don't do anything

In contrast, when they believed that their legal services lawyers were good, clients saw foregoing money or prestigious jobs as an indication of altruism. Such lawyers in the eyes of clients are better people, and therefore would work harder for clients and provide better service. When I asked what was different about her experience at NELS, Eloise said,

> Well one thing it wasn't any money involved in these two. You know there was no money involved. This was just based on Amir's income. But these other lawyers you got to pay them! And you don't get the service that you deserve sometime.

Clients' ambivalence toward legal services and the relationship of monetary compensation to the provision of services parallel some of the debates within the cause lawyering literature that asks whether fee-based work can be considered cause lawyering.[30] Cause lawyering literature has looked largely from the outside in assessing this question, whereas these findings suggest that clients of putative cause lawyers have clear opinions that can add to the debate by pointing out in what way legal services might be cause lawyers and under what conditions. If commitment to the cause (including the cause of service to the poor) over and above a commitment to the law and/or to financial gain or prestige characterizes cause lawyering,[31] then surely from the perspective of legal services clients, legal services lawyers (or at least the competent ones who care) are cause lawyers, whatever the source of their pay.[32] Further, in the eyes of clients, salaried cause lawyers who forego higher financial compensation might in fact provide better services than those who provide solely fee-based or market rate services for causes because they are more likely to be altruistic to their causes (as well as empathic to individuals, see below). This may even hold true in comparison to

[30] Austin Sarat and Stuart Scheingold, "Cause Lawyering and the Reproduction of Professional Authority: An Introduction," in *Cause Lawyering: Political Commitments and Professional Responsibilities* (New York: Oxford University Press, 1998). See also Ronen Shamir and Sara Chinski, "Destruction of Houses and Construction of a Cause: Lawyers and Bedouins in the Israeli Courts," in *Cause Lawyering: Political Commitments and Professional Responsibilities*; Scott Barclay and Anna-Maria Marshall, "Supporting a Cause, Developing a Movement, and Consolidating a Practice: Cause Lawyers and Sexual Orientation Litigation in Vermont," in *The Worlds Cause Lawyers Make*.

[31] Sarat and Scheingold, "Cause Lawyering and the Reproduction of Professional Authority: An Introduction."

[32] This raises an interesting question for the problematic hinging of cause lawyering on motivation (discussed in Laura Hatcher, "Economic Libertarians, Property, and Institutions: Linking Activism, Idea, and Identities Among Property Rights Advocates," in *The Worlds Cause Lawyers Make* 2005). Although this definition also rests on motivation, it is on the motivation of lawyers imputed by clients served by these lawyers, based on what clients deduce from their own assumptions about lawyers and their career options.

attorneys at the private bar who provide pro bono services to causes or individual clients because the high level of altruism that clients impute to those who have dedicated their careers to causes proves a commitment to the cause and indicates a willingness to expend more effort in service thereof.

2. Crossing Bridges?

One of the most significant differences between my findings and those of legal services clients interviewed by Sarat[33] revolves around connections that are formed between lawyers and clients. Sarat found that clients, exemplified by his respondent Spencer, believe that it is impossible for anyone who has not experienced the poverty and stigma related to welfare use to understand those who have experienced this firsthand. This finding is strikingly similar to the portrayal of lawyers in popular media as emotionless and out of touch with the needs and realities of ordinary people (see Chapters 8 and 9).

Although clients in this study did not expect lawyers, for the most part, to understand their plight, there was the possibility that they could and indeed sometimes did so. Clients do not have a romantic notion that lawyers can fully understand what it is like to live like their clients and experience their troubles, but this does not preclude the possibility of a mediated or partial understanding. Where Spencer seems to see only a chasm, clients in this study frequently talked of connecting with their lawyers in a variety of ways; gaps in understanding that stem from different experiences can be bridged.

Crucial to their view of NELS' lawyers as different from the distant, incompetent, apathetic, or money-driven individuals that they expected was clients' sense that something transpires in the relationship that goes beyond the professional (without becoming unprofessional). As reported in Shdaimah,[34] clients are leery of lawyers who go too far and become friendly in a way that interferes with their professional abilities and roles. Even clients who said that their lawyers were like "friends" (and many used this term) said that they knew that it was not really friendship in the

[33] Sarat, "The Law is All Over": Power, Resistance, and the Legal Consciousness of the Welfare Poor," 343.

[34] Shdaimah, "Dilemmas of "Progressive" Lawyering."

conventional sense but more a feeling that the lawyer cared, that they were not just another case.

Clients indicate that lawyers who create the opportunity for a connection do so by being empathic, down to earth, and "hanging in there." Clients, for their part, engender or foster this connection in lawyers; connections are forged through mutual desire and hard work.

3. Empathy

Lawyer empathy was a recurrent theme in client interviews. It was an important feature of clients' satisfaction and ran counter to client expectations.[35] Dara at first thought that her lawyer was uncaring and would not be able to comprehend her life and her choices:

> Dara: I thought, I felt like she was kind of professional but distant 'cause I felt like she really couldn't understand what it was like. . . . I had two children [and then] in 1991 one of my best girlfriends had got took in a car accident so I added two, her two kids to my family and it made my family larger.
>
> Corey: So you had four children?
>
> Dara: Right. It didn't give me any more money because she hadn't worked so it wasn't like you got no Social Security and none of that stuff. It was like, they give you a welfare check. No food stamps, just you know, and that kind of like, make a tough situation a little bit more stressful so by the time we got to that point, at that time it was like, [whispers] "oh God, the stress." I really was overwhelmed. And I figured that she could not understand what it was like and where I was at that point.

Dara turned to NELS because she had no choice, even though she was not hopeful that a lawyer would understand or help. Interestingly, it was when she saw that Sheryl made consistent efforts for her and continued to work

[35] There is some indication that this was the case even when cases had not been resolved or had been resolved against the client. Although this research was somewhat skewed in that only clients who held relatively positive views of their lawyers agreed to be interviewed, there is indication that the process and treatment of clients are crucial components in their construction of their own satisfaction. This corresponds with literature on the importance of process even when outcomes are unfavorable; see, e.g.,Tom R. Tyler and Robert Folger, "Distributional and Procedural Satisfaction with Citizen-Police Encounters," *Basic and Applied Social Psychology* 1 (1980): 281.

with her that she changed her mind: "Because she really, really, I think maybe some of that she kind of, at some point understood because she really, really, really worked hard on my case, she did. She really did work hard on my case. She really worked hard on it." This to her was "proof" that Sheryl must understand; why otherwise would she go to bat for her?

The same was true of Ruth, who had a history of social service agencies betraying her trust and was currently battling child protective services for the return of her children, whom she had voluntarily placed in care when she became homeless. Her lawyer Joann "understood." Ruth, like Dara, felt that her lawyer went to work for her in a way that showed a connection and a commitment to her as a person:

> [Joann] generally acted like she cared. You know some of them don't. A lot of them just had a attitude like, "[in a bored voice] okay, well you know, I have to do this for you, that's all." But she, it was more like a personal thing like we was almost friends, like? I could tell her anything, as hard as it was, 'cause so much stuff had happened and she just made me feel like she was going to actually try to do anything she could. I guess that's what made the difference.

Latonya spoke of her relationship with her lawyer, noting that it was comfortable and that she has a sense that Sheryl knows how to read her in a way that is helpful when they are dealing with child welfare authorities:

> Like for instance, being as though she has been dealing with me for three years almost, she knows me a little bit, you know? And when we were in the meeting, the man was getting ready to say something that was getting ready to have me like really perturbed [she smiles, I laugh] and she was like "'LaTonya, don't act like you know what he's going to say." And it was good that she was there to be able to say that because . . . I was getting ready to get really nasty and everything! . . . And I started laughing, 'cause I said, "How about she know me [laughs]?!"

Getting to know one another allows lawyers and clients to learn not only good things about each other but also bad things. Again, Ruth talked about Joann and said that eventually she came to trust her because Joann stuck with her, even when she became angry:

> I didn't have to like put on no façade. Like for those social workers, I had to pretend. Well I was angry anyway – screw them. But, I'm saying, I didn't have to pretend like everything was all right when it

> wasn't with Joann. You know, if I was angry, she didn't care. You know, she would try to come out and talk to me if I walked out or whatever, and I couldn't do that with nobody else.

When lawyers stand by their clients in spite of the tensions between them, the clients can stay with the legal process rather than give up or act in a way that might jeopardize their cases.

4. "Common People"

A number of clients noted that their lawyers put them at ease by talking to them in a manner that was straightforward while not patronizing. Lorna described her experience with Steve as contrary to what she imagined:

> I felt like he was common people and not a lawyer. He didn't make me feel like he was all uptight and you know and "this is the law" [laughing, imitates a deep, authoritative voice]. He was just down to earth. Very.

Clients appreciated when their lawyers explained things in ways that they could understand or took pains to clarify their legal situation when information provided by government agencies was lacking or incomprehensible. They were also surprised and pleased to be treated with courtesy. In describing why she was more satisfied with and felt more comfortable with her lawyer than one with whom she had worked before, one client told me that the NELS lawyer responded to her phone calls. He kept her abreast of what was going on. "He would call me on the phone and say, 'Ms. Carter, so and so and so.'" When she came into the office "Mr. Brown would come down and he would greet me and 'come on in Mrs. Carter' and we would go upstairs."

Being treated as a social equal can be particularly important for clients who have experienced stigma. This was true of Janet, who felt that she was often stigmatized and treated poorly because she was recovering from a drug addiction. Based on prior experience, she expected to have a bad encounter at NELS "because of the stigma with drug addicts." She said this was generally the case in her contacts with professionals, and she compared her experiences with her lawyer Steve, who was "very sympathetic," to her treatment at the hands of emergency room doctors, who treated her with such disgust and disrespect that she tried to avoid them at all costs, even when her health was jeopardized. "But you know it changed a little bit for the better I think this time with Steve. Like I said he didn't treat me disrespectfully or anything like that." When asked if there was something in particular that Steve did to make her feel comfortable, she said, "Yeah, well he just treated me like everybody else. He didn't look down his nose at me or anything."

Clients in this study interpreted lawyers' openness as genuine. It was not what they expected, but they were not so cynical as to reject expressions of empathy and caring. They might not think that lawyers fully understood them, but they did feel that a connection was made that created an experience different from the one they expected. They did not, however, expect this experience to be replicated in encounters with other lawyers, viewing it instead as a rarity. Carolyn spoke of her lawyer, Suzanne, as follows:

> That was really helpful that she was that open and that kind. So I felt that she was a genuine person. It's not just that she was a lawyer but she was genuine. And not many lawyers will show you that kind of, uh, generosity or really treat you as a human being.

Lest it be misunderstood, clients do not only want empathy or to be treated well. They also want an honest assessment of their situation. Janet appreciated that Steve "just was real up front with me about everything. You know, he, like I said he didn't pull any punches, he was real up front and uh, he was very straightforward." They also want to be served by competent lawyers, as outlined in detail above. It is the combination of professional and competent representation put to the service of poor people with caring and empathy for them as individuals that clients find most surprising, and are most likely to praise and view as anomalous. As Lilly, speaking about Liz, put it: "It's a different kind of law, lawyerism – not law, the law itself – lawyerism than that."

When asked to explain how she would characterize that kind of lawyerism, Lilly replied,

> It's the fact that she's empathetic. She listens. She's caring. And she's productive. I think there is something very special – and I'm sure there are others in the group that are of the same caliber or they wouldn't want to work there. I think it takes special people who would work, I'm sure that they could make more out in the field, much more money. But I think it is a special thing and I think she has a special gift. As I

> told you, I worked with another lawyer, a head of a legal group and she was very efficient once she got done but you don't get the same feeling from her as you got from Liz.

V. The Source of Lawyer Images

Although some clients in this study had worked with lawyers before, their previous interactions were episodic and vaguely remembered. Most of them involved personal injury cases or divorces that were resolved without intensive or ongoing legal assistance. Therefore, most clients did not have any relationships with lawyers, nor did they know lawyers personally.[36] The two who revealed personal connections intimated that this was rare and expected that I would be surprised that they had one. Celia, who was worried about a foreclosure notice and desperate to find a lawyer who would help her save her home, told me: "I had a family lawyer – we got a lawyer in the family too, believe it or not [laughs]. Believe it or not."

Knowing a lawyer, however, does not translate into unfettered access to legal assistance. When I asked Celia if she had called her relative for help or advice, she responded that she needed to use this precious family resource selectively and was not even sure if he would come to her aid: "Um, no. Because I was trying to have him help me with another situation but everybody's so busy. Everybody's so busy so I never even um, he's hard to get in touch with."

Conversely, many clients assumed that wealthier people had ongoing, retainer-style relationships with lawyers that were professional as well as personal. Clients who experienced such a relationship with their NELS lawyers expressed incredulity at their own good fortune, and only imagined that this is what it might be like to be like wealthy people with legal services at their command. Most of them said that they would contact, and in fact had contacted, their lawyer for advice (legal and otherwise) not connected to the problem that brought them to NELS. For the most part they found lawyers responsive and helpful, whether in providing guidance, representation, or referrals.

Mary had no personal experience to relate her NELS experience to; when asking her to describe her relationship with her lawyer Pete, she could only come up with an image of a TV lawyer "like if you're watching

[36] Lochner, "The No Fee and Low Fee Legal Practice of Private Attorneys," 431.

some kind of legal show or something, and this family had . . . their own lawyer." Asking if she would feel comfortable going to her lawyer again, Mary replied, "Yeah, he's my lawyer, it's like my lawyer. He's mine [laughs]!" The idea of "my lawyer" is one echoed by many clients; all say it with pride and a sense of challenge: don't mess with me. For clients whose lives are often otherwise chaotic and are characterized by poor treatment at the hands of what Lipsky[37] famously termed "street-level bureaucrats," this relationship allows them to have one street-level bureaucrat on their side in battles with other street-level bureaucrats.

Because most clients do not have much personal or professional experience with lawyers, their images and expectations do not derive from these sources. Mary, who gave the example of a television show, was the only client out of thirty who mentioned popular media as the source of her understanding of what lawyers do and how they act. Even Mary could not initially think of a show from which she derived her "TV lawyer" image. When she searched her memory she recalled the series *Dallas*: this interview took place in 2002, two decades after the show's airing in the 1980s (and Mary was in her mid-twenties at the time of the interview).

Mary's identification of television as the source of her knowledge about lawyers, without a clear sense of where exactly her ideas came from, raises the importance of distinguishing between the source of the images and clients' perception of that source.[38] In other words, although clients do not identify popular media as an influence, this does not mean that they are immune to it. Every home that I entered had a television in a central location; in a number of cases the TV was on in the background. This might be an indication that clients passively consume popular culture, absorbing pervasive images in ways that they are not conscious of.[39] Passive consumption is reinforced by the fact that the opinions of clients in this study here mirror, to a large extent, attitudes of the general public toward lawyers as necessary but untrustworthy.[40] They also match opinions reportedly held

[37] Michael Lipsky, *Street-Level Bureaucracy: Dilemmas of the Individual in Public Services* (New York: Russell Sage Foundation, 1980), xi.

[38] Johnson, "What is Cultural Studies, Anyway?"

[39] For a review of theories of how news media enter people's consciousness, see W. Russell Neuman, Marion R. Just, and Ann N. Crigler, *Common Knowledge: News and the Construction of Political Meaning*, 8–12.

[40] Michael C. Dorf, "FindLaw Forum: Americans Believe Lawyers to be Necessary but Dishonest, Survey Finds"; posted April 17, 2002, retrieved on January 17, 2007 from http://archives.cnn.com; ABA, 2002.

about legal services lawyers and public defenders.[41] That client images may be informed by more broadly circulated public narratives does not negate the active role that they have as consumers and producers of local images that are consistent with their own experiences and social context. I argue that the persistence of these images in the face of discrepant experiences with individual lawyers attests to the consistency of these popular or stock images and their resonance with indigent clients' (overwhelmingly negative) experiences with bureaucracies and their view of the legal system.

As the expectations and images of lawyers described here reveal, most clients in this study indicated that their ideas about lawyers were drawn from a remarkably consistent stock of ostensibly real-life cautionary tales. These tales that circulated among the people I interviewed originated in the experience of others, usually friends and relatives, with court-appointed attorneys in the criminal justice system. When such images were not available, clients talked about what they imagined they would be like if they were lawyers, and projected the attitudes and choices that they might make onto their expectations of lawyers.

Finally, clients appeared to make assumptions about lawyers based on their own experiences with government bureaucracies. They viewed free legal services as connected with or similar to the social service agencies with which they interact and then extrapolated their expectations from their treatment at the hands of these agencies. Soss,[42] whose study of clients of Aid for Families with Dependent Children (AFDC) and Social Security Disability Insurance (SSDI) found "striking similarities"[43] to Sarat's[44] findings in his study of the welfare poor seeking legal services, suggests that clients learn political lessons in their encounters with one bureaucracy that carry over and inform their perception of all bureaucracies. This makes sense given client beliefs that government actors are connected, as I describe above. It may also be reinforced when even seemingly adversarial government actors negotiate with or act collegially toward opposing

[41] McIntyre, *The Public Defenders: The Practice of Law in the Shadow of Repute*.

[42] Soss, *Unwanted Claims: The Politics of Participation in the U.S. Welfare* System (Ann Arbor: University of Michigan Press, 2002).

[43] Ibid., 166.

[44] Sarat, "The Law is All Over: Power, Resistance, and the Legal Consciousness of the Welfare Poor", 343.

lawyers and when they appear to have more in common (in terms of education, class, and ethnicity) with opposing counsel than with the clients they represent.

VI. Enduring Negative Images

Legal services clients in this study experience their encounters with NELS lawyers as anomalous rather than revise their expectations and beliefs about lawyers. Although this behavior might be understandable in one or two cases, when we aggregate the data from interviews with thirty clients talking about ten different lawyers practicing in six different substantive practice areas, it begins to seem odd that their overwhelmingly positive experiences do not result in a revision of client narratives about lawyers. Not only do clients remain dubious about the value of lawyers even as they acknowledge the need for them but they also retain skepticism about legal services lawyers. This indicates that they do not see NELS lawyers as a special breed (cause lawyer or otherwise), but still interpret their positive experience as attributable to that one special lawyer with whom they had the good fortune to work. Although I do not have data that specifically answer why clients fail to revise their ideas of lawyers when confronted with discrepant experiences, the data collected in this study, viewed through the lens of cultural studies, offer us some theories for further exploration.

One explanation is suggested by the study design.[45] Lawyers who participated might be particularly attuned to their clients and attentive to lawyer-client relationships. They may not be representative of cause lawyers, or legal services lawyers more specifically, in that respect. In only four interviews did clients mention poor service or unempathic lawyers that they experienced at NELS or other legal services providers. Lawyers in this study may in fact be anomalous even in the landscape of cause lawyers whom legal services clients meet; maybe there really is no critical mass or group of "cause lawyers," despite the large body of literature claiming the contrary (some of it produced by cause lawyers). However, this is not sufficiently explanatory, even if it is the case, as clients were equally likely to mention good services at the hands of lawyers (other than the ones who referred them) from these same organizations.

[45] This idea was developed based on insights by Judie McCoyd.

Another explanation is that clients continue to have adversarial experiences with government bureaucracies and lawyers representing them even while being represented by their NELS lawyer. This reinforces rather than mitigates clients' beliefs about lawyers. NELS clients are by definition involved in an adversarial relationship with the government or their landlord or lending company, so for every lawyer who is working with them there is at least one and, for example in child welfare cases, two or more, lawyers who are against them. Clients have good reason not to trust opposing counsel. Clients may be predisposed to view opposing lawyers as, at best, callous and, at worst, out to get them. These lawyers contest the claims raised by them, most of which are tied to clients' most fundamental needs like housing, benefits to ensure survival, and their ability to reunite with or keep their children. Further, those in opposition generally represent more powerful and institutionalized interests, lending credence to conspiracy concerns. Although they see their NELS lawyers as a genuine anomaly, they continue to be faced with examples that reinforce their beliefs and expectations about lawyers more generally.

Clients' framing of the behavior and actions of opposing counsel is also reinforced by NELS lawyers. I have written of the importance of solidarity with poor and marginalized people and groups and the way that lawyers can, in collaboration with clients, create shared narratives of responsibility and shared visions of social justice.[46] Clients told me that their NELS lawyers voiced agreement with their perceptions that the "system" is unfair, punitive, and dehumanizing. Lawyers interviewed agreed that clients are treated poorly, that their rights are trampled, and that the legal system and government bureaucracies care little for the poor; most openly share these opinions with clients. Thus, NELS lawyers reinforce (often explicitly) client notions that the system is not for justice and that the other side, whoever that is and whoever it is represented by, is "out to get them" as part of the shared narrative that lawyers and clients create in collaboration.

The durability of negative images of lawyers may also be influenced by perceptions of lawyers that permeate broader society. My findings are strikingly similar to those of the American Bar Association report on the lay perception of lawyers, which did not target low-income individuals.[47]

[46] Shdaimah, "Dilemmas of "Progressive" Lawyering: Empowerment and Hierarchy," 253.

[47] American Bar Association, "Public Perceptions of Lawyers: 2002 Consumer Research Findings."

Although those who had worked with lawyers had more positive than negative experiences, the overall perceptions of lawyers remained generally negative. Those surveyed acknowledged lawyers as necessary, but many also said that they would avoid using them, if at all possible, and feared that if they needed to rely on a lawyer they would have little understanding of how to pick a good one. What was different in this study is that the opinions reported here were more pervasive and more consistently negative.

Such images of lawyers likely reinforce and are reinforced by popular culture, as reported in McCann and Haltom in Chapter 8. Further, in contrast to McCann and Haltom's analysis of popular films, which show that incompetent and callous lawyers can be saved by the plucky and smart layperson, clients here show no faith that this is the case. This likely represents the differential experience that poor clients have with government bureaucracies and their limited socioeconomic, educational, and other resources that in turn limit their agency as discussed above. Encounters with one caring and competent lawyer are not strong enough to counter clients' life experiences that are reinforced by pervasive negative images. For consumers to "read" texts that are produced or circulate in the way that some may intend, these texts need to be consistent with their own experiences and be part of their continuous and contextualized life experiences.[48] NELS lawyers may think of themselves as a special breed, and cause lawyering scholars may recognize them as such in the academy. Marginalized consumers, however, may see these lawyers as so far afield from their contextual reality as to "read" them as un-lawyerly lawyers: so unlike other lawyers that they really can barely be categorized as lawyers.

VII. Conclusion

Legal services clients in this study held consistently negative images of lawyers as well-paid "hired guns" who hold sway within the legal system and thus are able (when they so desire) to work the system in their clients' favor. Any connection to justice is coincidental: lawyers serve those with power and money and make the legal system work for them, regardless of guilt or innocence. Even clients who expressed a desire to be an attorney or admired lawyers saw the law as a bridge to status and income rather than as a means to right societal wrongs or vindicate justice.

[48] Johnson, "What is Cultural Studies, Anyway?," 68.

Lawyers working for the state are seen as allied with the government agencies that intervene in clients' lives to evict them from public housing, take their children away, or challenge their status as beneficiaries of public assistance. Those lawyers paid by the state to serve and defend indigent clients are viewed as either incompetent, uncaring, or in cahoots with opposing counsel (and often with the judge). Clients believe that "you get what you pay for": if you pay little or nothing, your lawyer will be of no assistance. Competent services are anomalous, and such experiences rarely challenge them to revise their images of lawyers more generally. This may be a reflection of their experiences that such lawyers are few and far between and that the legal system is an "iffy" place to seek justice.

Clients expect that legal services lawyers have to serve them, but are likely to provide begrudging and substandard representation. Extrapolating from prior experiences and their own aspirations, many clients assume that few lawyers would want to work for lower pay than they could get elsewhere if they were in fact competent and well connected enough to do so. Even if lawyers would have the ability to serve them well, clients assume that lawyers work through connections and wield power and, as such, would act toward clients in ways that are hierarchical, uncaring, or disrespectful. Although almost all NELS clients with whom I spoke were satisfied with their experience, all still viewed it as anomalous, unlawyerly, "lawyerism." Their experiences were not powerful enough to transform their understanding of the law, lawyers, or the legal system.

Such persistent negative images are likely to affect clients' willingness to seek legal services. More importantly, they serve as a proverbial "canary in a coal mine," warning us that faith in the legal system is low. Those who do not feel that they are likely to be treated fairly and justly have little stake in maintaining such a system. Poor clients and their lawyers experience themselves as particularly disadvantaged, reinforcing divisions among those who they feel have access to justice and those who do not. This research provides a window onto the perception of low-income individuals, often shared and reinforced by their lawyers, of the state of justice in the United States. Clients' narratives indict the legal system and government agencies generally, which clients do not see as distinct from those who operate officially within them, including the lawyers who purportedly provide service to the poor. This distrust is predicated on their experiences with government agencies and actors and on their perception of the connections among them. The mistrust reported here reflects a similar lack of faith reported across socioeconomic strata within the United States. The lack of faith in the legal system is indicative of a broader crisis in that it reflects people's respect for the law more generally and faith in our system of government to fairly regulate and protect those under its authority. The depth and breadth of this mistrust among poor clients, and the pervasive belief that they are treated differently, provide a sense of how deep the marginalization and isolation run even in those institutions that strive to be "blind."

Acknowledgments

The author thanks participants in the Cultures of Cause Lawyering conference held in Amherst, Massachusetts, for their thoughtful feedback and good company; Judie McCoyd, Patricia Woods, and Rick Abel for insights and encouragement; and Ingrid Löfgren and Vickie Souther for research assistance.

Index